Why Taiwan?

Studies in Asian Security

A SERIES SPONSORED BY THE EAST-WEST CENTER

Muthiah Alagappa, Chief Editor
Distinguished Senior Fellow, East-West Center

The aim of the Asian Security series is to promote analysis, understanding, and explanation of the dynamics of domestic, transnational, and international security challenges in Asia. Books in the series will analyze contemporary security issues and problems to clarify debates in the scholarly and policy communities, provide new insights and perspectives, and identify new research and policy directions related to conflict management and security in Asia. Security is defined broadly to include the traditional political and military dimensions as well as the nontraditional dimensions that affect the survival and well-being of political communities. Asia, too, is defined broadly, to include Northeast, Southeast, South, and Central Asia.

Designed to encourage original and rigorous scholarship, books in the Asian Security series seek to engage scholars, educators, and practitioners. Wide-ranging in scope and method, the series welcomes an extensive array of paradigms, programs, traditions, and methodologies now employed in the social sciences.

★ ★ ★

The East-West Center is an education and research organization established by the U.S. Congress in 1960 to strengthen relations and understanding among the peoples and nations of Asia, the Pacific, and the United States. The Center contributes to a peaceful, prosperous, and just Asia Pacific community by serving as a vigorous hub for cooperative research, education, and dialogue on critical issues of common concern to the Asia Pacific region and the United States. Funding for the Center comes from the U.S. government, with additional support provided by private agencies, individuals, foundations, and corporations and the governments of the region.

Why Taiwan?

GEOSTRATEGIC RATIONALES FOR
CHINA'S TERRITORIAL INTEGRITY

Alan M. Wachman

SPONSORED BY THE EAST–WEST CENTER
Stanford University Press • Stanford, California 2007

Published with the partial support of the
Sasakawa Peace Foundation (USA)

Stanford University Press
Stanford, California

Printed in the United States of America on acid-free, archival-quality paper

Library of Congress Cataloging-in-Publication Data
Wachman, Alan.
    Why Taiwan : geostrategic rationales for China's territorial integrity /
Alan M. Wachman
        p. cm.—(Studies in Asian security)
    Includes bibliographical references and index.
    ISBN 978-0-8047-5553-5 (cloth : alk. paper)—ISBN 978-0-8047-5554-2
(pbk. : alk. paper)
    1. China—Relations—Taiwan. 2. Taiwan—Relations—China. 3. National
security—China. 4. Geopolitics—China. I. Title.
DS740.5.T28W33 2007
327.5105124'9—dc22

                                                        2007007762

Typeset by Thompson Type in 10.5/13.5 Bembo

Passages in Chapters 1 and 3 appeared in "Stamped Out!: Carto-Philatelic
Evidence of the PRC's Constructed Notion of China's Territorial Integrity,"
East Asia: An International Quarterly 22, no. 2 (Summer 2005): 31-55, © by
Transaction Publishers. Reprinted by permission of the publisher.

Dedicato, come lo sono io, a mia moglie

Contents

Acknowledgments

Readers who have not authored a book may find tedious and, perhaps, disingenuous or maudlin the refrain that this endeavor would never have reached fruition were it not for the support and involvement of others. Readers who are, themselves, authors will readily appreciate why I rehearse this verity.

To thrive, marriage, parenthood, and teaching all demand time, a precious resource that a book project saps with unslakable thirst. There is no denying the wicked dimension of creativity: the selfish expenditure of time justified as a burden imposed by the enterprise. So, foremost among all to whom I am beholden for making it possible for me to write is my wife. She—with inexhaustible support from my parents and occasional assistance from "Big Rachael" Corrigan—selflessly and wordlessly shifted from my shoulders to her own the responsibility for the care of our two young children. Our youngest was born just as I embarked on this project and turned three shortly before I sent the final draft to Stanford University Press. With the travails of the book now past, I relish reassuming my full share of the obligations and fulfillment associated with fatherhood and matrimony.

There are many others who contributed to the production of this volume. I was the beneficiary of Muthiah Alagappa's prodigious goodwill and academic entrepreneurship. He encouraged me to submit a book proposal to the Editorial Committee of the *Studies in Asian Security* series. I am immensely grateful to Muthiah and the other members of the Editorial Committee for seeing merit in my proposal and for helping to shape the first version of this work. Alastair Iain Johnston, a member of the Committee, distinguished himself by unstintingly extending beyond his assigned role to offer a steady flow of dependable advice, wisdom, and encouragement. I am also thankful for the research funding provided by the East-West Center Washington.

I am grateful to The Fletcher School of Law and Diplomacy at Tufts University for summer research grants that facilitated my engagement in this project and to my students there who, perhaps unknowingly, enabled me to work out ideas central to this book in classroom interchanges they have, by now, long forgotten. I received assistance in my research from Han Wei, Hiroaki Ichiba, Cornelia Jesse, and Yu Zheng, whom I met while they were students at The Fletcher School, and Lige Shao at Stanford University.

I was privileged to receive support from the Chiang Ching-kuo Foundation for a year's sabbatical leave and, during that year, pleased to be appointed as a Starr Research Fellow by the Asia Programs division of the Center for Business and Government in the John F. Kennedy School of Government at Harvard University. Anthony Saich, Director of the Asia Programs, Julian Chang, the Executive Director, and Alene Tchourumoff were charitably tolerant of my immersion in research and greatly enhanced my productivity by demanding little of me while offering friendship, to boot.

My research was advanced by the help and hospitality I received from archivists and librarians at the Harvard University Map Collection, the Harvard Yenching Library, the Geography and Map Division at the Library of Congress, from Madeleine Barnoud at Le département des Cartes et Plans de la Bibliothèque nationale de France, and from Mark Tam at the Hoover Institution Archives.

Along the way, generous encouragement, guidance, and conscientious responses to research-related questions were magnanimously provided by Julian Baum, Allen Carlson, Tim Cheek, Edward I-te Chen, Bernard Cole, Michael Davis, Bruce Elleman, Andrew Erickson, David Finkelstein, Ge Jianxiong, Lyle Goldstein, Alan Henrikson, Michael Hunt, Macabe Keliher, Lin Chongpin, Michael McDevitt, Andrew Nathan, Niu Jun, Michael Pillsbury, Jonathan Pollack, Marcus Powers, Sergey Radchenko, Tony Saich, Fabio Schiantarelli, Annamarie Seleney, Su Ge, Lis Tarlow, Nancy Bernkopf Tucker, Christopher Twomey, Andrew Watson, Xu Shiquan, and Toshi Yoshihara.

I was fortunate to have opportunities to present preliminary findings and musings based on my research to seminars hosted by the Fairbank Center for East Asian Research and the Center for Business and Government at Harvard University, the Starr Forum on the Rise of China at the Center for International Studies at Massachusetts Institute of Technology, the Center for

Asian Studies at the University of South Carolina, the Asia-Pacific Studies Group at the U.S. Naval War College, and the Council on East Asian Studies at Yale University.

I am especially thankful to the following colleagues and friends, as well as several anonymous reviewers, for laboring through earlier versions of this text and pointing out with exquisite delicacy deficiencies demanding my attention. They valiantly provided analytical life-preservers intended to drag me back from the riptides of ignorance and muddled thinking. If the present reader concludes that my work is adrift nonetheless, it is not for want of collegial efforts by these intellectual Good Samaritans: George Capen, Thomas Christensen, Mark Elliott, Taylor Fravel, Edward Friedman, James Klein, James Lilley, Peter Perdue, Robert Ross, Emma Teng, and Yu Maochun. I am also beholden to Nancy Hearst for reviewing the text with peerless fastidiousness.

Reflecting on the past three years, this book was most influenced by two unrelated Goldsteins: Avery (of the University of Pennsylvania) and Steven (of Smith College). Each provided incisive and, ultimately, indispensable guidance about how to salvage from two successive and substantially distinct drafts—both choked in tangential and tendentious overgrowth—an argument worth cultivating.

Questions about Taiwan's status, the Sino-U.S. relationship, and the intentions of the People's Republic of China leave few professional observers impassive. Those colleagues who read earlier drafts of this work reacted differently to the text they encountered, providing several—but sharply conflicting—streams of advice about the implications of the evidence and the merits of my analysis. My acknowledgment of their assistance is not meant to imply that any of them endorses the interpretation I articulate in the pages that follow. It is meant to signal my recognition that I, and this text, have benefited greatly from their efforts.

Abbreviations

AIT	American Institute on Taiwan
ARATS	Association for Relations Across the Taiwan Strait
ASCM	anti-ship cruise missile
ASW	antisubmarine warfare
CCP	Chinese Communist Party
CGS	Central Geological Survey
CMC	Central Military Commission
COSTIND	Commission of Science, Technology and Industry for National Defense
DDG	guided missile destroyer
DF	Dongfeng
DPP	Democratic Progressive Party
ECCI	Executive Committee of the Communist International
EEZ	Exclusive Economic Zone
ICBM	intercontinental-range ballistic missile
JCP	Japanese Communist Party
JCS	Joint Chiefs of Staff
MOEA	Ministry of Economic Affairs
NPC	National People's Congress
NSC	National Security Council
NUC	National Unification Council
PLA	People's Liberation Army

PLA(AF)	PLA Air Force
PLA(N)	PLA Navy
PRC	People's Republic of China
RMA	Revolution in Military Affairs
ROC	Republic of China
SEF	Straits Exchange Foundation
SLBM	submarine launched ballistic missile
SLOC	sea-lanes of communication
SRBM	short-range ballistic missile
SSBN	nuclear ballistic missile submarine
TCP	Taiwan Communist Party
TRA	Taiwan Revolutionary Alliance

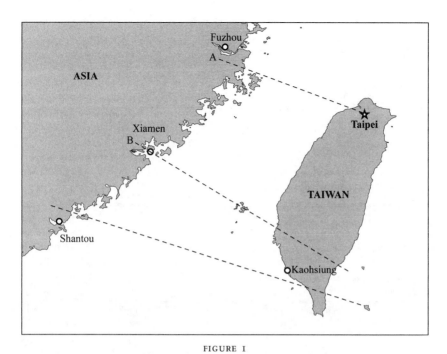

FIGURE I

Taiwan in relation to the Chinese coast and surrounding seas

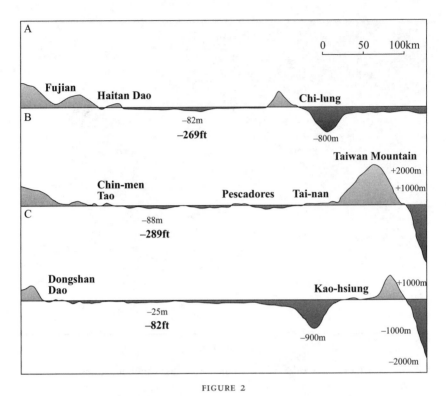

FIGURE 2

The PRC's maritime considerations in Asia

Introduction

The Question: Why Taiwan?

The enduring rivalry between the People's Republic of China (PRC) and the Republic of China (ROC) has hinged on the question: what polity exercises sovereignty over Taiwan?[1] It is a dispute about legitimate control over territory. While the PRC has negotiated—without resort to violence—a resolution to other territorial disputes, the contest about Taiwan's status has been fraught from the start by threats of, and use of, military force.[2]

After several decades of emphasizing peaceful means to resolve the cross-Strait dispute, the PRC began in the early 1990s to threaten more forcefully a willingness to use military means. Since then, the PRC has been enhancing its capacity to influence the controversy about Taiwan by force, a development that some observers conclude is a "response to central leadership demands to develop military options."[3] Whether and to what extent the leadership will decide to use military means are questions about which reasonable analysts differ.[4] None can know with certainty because, contingency planning notwithstanding, the PRC leadership is unlikely to make an unambiguous and irrevocable decision to use force too long before it is unleashed.

That the PRC is engaged in a program to accelerate development of greater military means should also not be understood to imply that from the 1990s onward the PRC has been implacably bellicose in its dealings with Taiwan. In fact, Beijing's diplomatic mien has varied, apparently in response to assessments of the long-term implications of what are identified as recent significant turning points or newly emerging trends associated with Taiwan's status. At some moments, Beijing has appeared to glower in pique across the Taiwan Strait, while at other moments it seems intent to discipline its emotions and project a semblance of patience, self-assurance, and magnanimity. Its demeanor apparently reflects a collective, even if not unanimous, prognosis among the political leadership about whether trend lines extending from the present bode well or ill for Beijing's objectives in relation to Taiwan.

Although Beijing's diplomatic posture toward Taiwan varies, since the mid-1990s some observers have identified evidence of what appears as a fixed strategy "to field a force that can succeed in a short-duration conflict with Taiwan and act as an anti-access force to deter U.S. intervention or delay the arrival of U.S. forces" sent to assist in the defense of Taiwan.[5] To be sure, the expansion of PRC military power in an era of intensified and, in some dimensions, revolutionary transformation is intended to address a multitude of security concerns.[6] It is not driven exclusively by the expectation that there will be violent conflict over Taiwan.[7] Nevertheless, it appears that the prospect of a near-term battle for Taiwan has dominated the People's Liberation Army's (PLA) "reform, modernization, procurement and training," exercising an overriding influence on choices made by the PLA.[8]

Although a fragile calm has generally prevailed in relations across the Taiwan Strait, the condition is often depicted as if it could easily give way to sudden and, perhaps, consuming violence.[9] Even more worrisome is the widespread belief that the cross-Strait controversy is "the only issue in the world today that could realistically lead to war between two major powers," the PRC and the United States.[10]

That contingency, should it come to pass, could very well implicate Japan and would likely inflict severe consequences on the population of Taiwan.[11] Even assuming that the PRC might employ force for limited objectives, it is easy to imagine that "the fallout of a war would be region-wide."[12] That fallout would have to be measured not only in terms of destruction resulting from violence, but in terms of political and economic repercussions flowing from a change in Taiwan's status or a loss by the PRC in its efforts to bring about such a change.[13] "So, this is serious stuff, and those making policy had better know what they are doing."[14]

In contrast to its handling of the Taiwan issue, in almost every other respect the foreign policy of the PRC since the 1990s has been self-consciously crafted to project abroad an impression of Beijing as peace preserving, not war prone, judicious, not reckless, measured, not rash, and equitable, not iniquitous.[15] Even as it has appreciably increased expenditures for defense, Beijing has accentuated its peaceful intentions in hopes of countering anxieties about a "China threat."[16] In the context of the diplomatic demeanor the PRC has so purposefully fashioned, Beijing's juggernaut to ready the means of affecting or resolving the dispute about Taiwan by force is apparently anomalous. Indeed, even by comparison to its approach to most other territorial disputes, the intensity of Beijing's fixation on the status of Taiwan is exceptional, in that it "increasingly shapes China's entire approach to the big questions of international relations."[17]

This study is animated by a deceptively difficult question: why? Why has the PRC acted as if Taiwan is of such paramount importance? Why has the PRC articulated with such fervor its determination that Taiwan be encompassed by China's sovereignty when the same regime has relinquished sovereignty over large tracts of what was China's territory, settled for less than it claimed in negotiations over other tracts, and ignored land that was once a part of China, about which nary an irredentist word has been uttered? Why, at a juncture when the PRC is objectively more secure from foreign aggression than at any moment since early in the nineteenth century, is the PLA surging with such resolve to prepare for the possibility of combat to prevail in a contest about the status of Taiwan? Why is Taiwan worth fighting for? What does Beijing feel is at stake?

From Hard to Soft: Beijing Shifts Strategy Toward Taiwan

The political leadership of the PRC has, at least since 1949, unwaveringly expressed its view that Taiwan is part of China and China must be unified. That has been the bedrock of its policy. However, twice since 1949 its long-term strategy for dealing with the division it seeks to repair has shifted significantly—once at about the time that the PRC and the United States normalized diplomatic relations in 1979 and a second time in the early 1990s.

For the first thirty years of this dispute, the PRC used the rhetoric of liberation, implying that its strategy for achieving unification was to free Taiwan—by force—from domination by the United States and its ally, the rump ROC regime headed by Chiang Kai-shek [Jiang Jieshi]. A *Xinhua* editorial of March 15, 1949, titled "*Zhongguo renmin yiding yao jiefang Taiwan*" [the Chinese people certainly will liberate Taiwan] set the tone as the first official use of a slogan that was to be the rallying cry for the following three decades.[18]

Use of force was the PRC's dominant paradigm in the period following the establishment of the PRC.[19] A military campaign to take control of Taiwan planned for the summer of 1950 was derailed first by anxiety about insufficient training of troops and preparations and then by the outbreak of the Korean War. However, two "offshore island" crises in the 1950s, when the PRC attacked islands under the control of the ROC, underscored Beijing's willingness to initiate military conflict in furtherance of its ambition to unify China. The second of these crises began when the PRC initiated a bombardment of the Jinmen islands on August 23, 1958, and ended with Mao Zedong's "Second Message to Compatriots in Taiwan," issued on October 25, 1958, in the name of Defense Minister Peng Dehuai.[20] With impudent pugnacity, the message announced a suspension in the shelling of the ROC-held island of Jinmen—but only on even-numbered days of the month.[21]

Thus, it remained until January 1, 1979. The PRC's strategy was to recover Taiwan by force, even though its tactics varied. Use of military force was actively contemplated and repeatedly employed in the period from 1949 to 1958. For the twenty years that followed, Beijing's political and diplomatic posture conveyed a sense of militancy even though Mao was content to sustain "an atmosphere of war, not war."[22] However, Mao pointedly reserved the right to use force against Taiwan, explaining to Nikita Khrushchev:

> Our relations with Jiang Jieshi [Chiang Kai-shek] and with the Americans are two different things. With the United States we will seek to resolve issues by peaceful means. If the United States does not leave Taiwan, then we will negotiate with them until they go from there. The relationship with Jiang Jieshi is our internal question and we might resolve it not only by peaceful, but also other methods.[23]

By the early 1970s, though, a fundamental and palpable shift in the geopolitical balance was under way that affected Beijing's strategy for dealing with Taipei. Sino-Soviet friction led to armed conflict between the erstwhile allies in 1969 and the dissolution of relations. The PRC supplanted the ROC in the United Nations in 1971, and the number of states recognizing the PRC dramatically increased at the ROC's expense.[24] In the same period, cold war contention with the Soviet Union and pressure on the United States government to extract its troops from Southeast Asia contributed to willingness in Washington to overcome historic animosities toward Beijing. Ultimately, an agreement between the PRC and the United States to establish official diplomatic relations was finalized in December 1978. This too had a bearing on Beijing's strategic outlook in dealings with Taiwan.

On January 1, 1979, the PRC announced the end to every-other-day shelling of Jinmen and a decidedly less bellicose approach to Taiwan.[25] The "hard" strategy with which Beijing persevered since 1949 was displaced by a new "soft" strategy under the rubric of "peaceful unification" [*heping tongyi*].[26] Beijing undoubtedly concluded that after Washington severed diplomatic ties with the ROC and recognized the PRC, Taipei would feel increasingly isolated and would succumb to pressure to unify. Force would no longer be needed to induce Taiwan's compliance with the PRC's demand for unification.[27] Desperation would drive Taiwan into Beijing's arms. This marked the first discernible adjustment to the PRC's long-term strategy for achieving its aim of unification.

From 1979 to 1993, the PRC's stance toward and rhetoric about Taiwan was noticeably less confrontational than it had been. In a sequence of overtures from 1979 to 1983, Beijing signaled its willingness to define unification in terms that would enable Taiwan to enjoy a "high degree of autonomy" [*gaodu de zizhiquan*] within the framework of "one country, two systems" [*yiguo, liangzhi*], which Deng Xiaoping promulgated as the principle that would guide interaction between the two sides of the Taiwan Strait following "peaceful unification."[28] When they reversed course and embarked on a strategy devised to bring about peaceful unification, the PRC leaders may have anticipated that efforts to be more yielding would lead to a satisfactory resolution of the dispute about Taiwan before the end of the decade.

The realization of this ambition was greatly complicated by the liberalization of politics in Taiwan during the 1980s, a process that utterly transformed the political dynamics of the ROC. Chinese nationalists in the ruling Guomindang [the Nationalist Party of China] lost the monopoly on political power they had had as Taiwanese nationalists increasingly asserted their views and influenced the policies of the government. In that domestic transition, and in cross-Strait relations, the ascension of Lee Teng-hui [Li Denghui] from vice president to president of the ROC after the death of Chiang Ching-kuo [Jiang Jingguo] on January 13, 1988, was a defining moment.

Lee's Guomindang bona fides were solid.[29] However, his identity as the ROC's first Taiwan-born president aroused the suspicions of Chinese nationalists. In time, Lee did reveal a greater determination than did the Chiangs to consolidate and expand international acceptance of Taiwan's autonomy as a sovereign actor. With apparently limitless moxie, he challenged Beijing's reflexive sense of entitlement to establish unilaterally the parameters of the cross-Strait relationship.

The PRC has operated from the premise that China's sovereignty is indivisible and that it resides in the government of the PRC, headed by the Chinese Communist Party (CCP). Even on the basis of the "one country, two systems" framework that Beijing proffered, unification necessitates a renunciation by Taipei of any claim to sovereignty. In contrast, Lee Teng-hui accepted that Taiwan is part of China, but viewed China as a divided state. He asserted that the sovereignty of the ROC over territory it controls is no less legitimate than is the sovereignty of the PRC over territory it controls. Lee apparently believed it was possible to consider ways to unify the two portions of China, but only if the sovereignty of both governments was regarded as equal.

This was quite a departure from the longstanding view of the Guomindang leadership that the CCP—derided as "communist bandits" [*gongfei*]—was illegitimate and that only the ROC government had any justifiable claim to sovereignty over China. Taking account of what territory each side genuinely controlled, Lee Teng-hui adopted the stance that Beijing and Taipei should acknowledge that the other governed legitimately a portion of China and was sovereign in that portion, but in that portion only. Ultimately, when Lee's view became apparent, Beijing denounced him as a "separatist" [*fenlie fenzi*] seeking to divide the nation and despoil China's territorial integrity. At first, though, it appears that the PRC leadership was not certain how to regard Lee and the developments he ushered in.

Even before Chiang Ching-kuo died and Lee became president, there were indications that Taipei was entertaining thoughts of how to adjust its posture toward the PRC to accord with pressure from within Taiwan and enticements by Beijing to undertake measures that would encourage trade across the Strait, build confidence, and advance the aim of unification.[30] After clinging since 1979 to a policy of "no contact, no compromise, and no negotiation" with the PRC—a policy known as the "three noes"—Chiang relaxed restrictions on cross-Strait trade and travel in October 1987. In July 1988, seven months after Lee assumed the role of president, the Guomindang's Thirteenth Party Congress endorsed a policy of lifting additional restrictions on travel across the Strait. On October 7, 1990, Lee established the National Unification Council [*Guojia tongyi weiyuanhui*] that devised a three-stage program embodied in the National Unification Guidelines [*Guojia tongyi gangling*] by which the ROC would work toward unification. The preamble states

> The unification of China is meant to bring about a strong and prosperous nation with a long-lasting, bright future for its people; it is the common wish of Chinese people at home and abroad. After an appropriate period of forthright exchange, cooperation, and consultation conducted under the principles of reason, peace, parity, and reciprocity, the two sides of the Taiwan Straits should foster a consensus of democracy, freedom and equal prosperity, and together build a new and unified China.[31]

On May 1, 1991, Lee terminated the "Period of National Mobilization for the Suppression of the Communist Rebellion," by which the Guomindang had, since 1947, justified a sustained war footing against the CCP, with "Temporary Provisions" [*Dongyuan kanluan shiqi lingshi*] adopted in 1948, that established a state of national emergency warranting suspension of certain constitutional provisions.[32] In other words, Lee removed the stanchion that had supported institutionalized hostility toward Beijing and dictatorial control in Taiwan.[33] At a symbolic level, this meant that the ROC no longer sought to "suppress the Communist Rebellion." It formally accepted the reality of CCP control over the mainland. At a practical level, it eliminated the most imposing barrier to democratization.[34]

These adjustments in Taiwan unfolded alongside efforts by the PRC to ease tensions across the Strait. After Lee Teng-hui became president in 1988, the PRC president, Yang Shangkun, quietly initiated contact with Lee through confidential channels. Between December 1990 and August 1992, emissaries of the PRC and ROC presidents met secretly to talk nine times in Hong Kong, Beijing, and Taipei.[35]

In addition to the confidential channel, the cross-Strait relationship was advanced during the same years by a sequence of meetings between representatives of two formally unofficial organizations. On November 21, 1990, the ROC government established the Straits Exchange Foundation [*Hai xia jiaoliu jijinhui,* hereinafter SEF] to facilitate interactions between Taiwan and the mainland, limited though they then were, and on December 16, 1991, the PRC founded the Association for Relations Across the Taiwan Strait [*Hai xia liang'an guanxi banhui,* hereinafter ARATS] as a counterpart agency. Beginning in November 1991, representatives of the two agencies met in Beijing and the following year in Hong Kong. In November 1992, after an arduous year of negotiation, they reached what both sides then accepted as a spare, but vital, modus vivendi.

Even in the absence of a formal written agreement, awareness that there was a coincidence of views was nontrivial. First, each side stated an intention to adhere to the "one China principle" [*yige Zhongguo yuanze*] and committed itself to work toward unification. This, the PRC represented as its sine qua non. For Beijing to trust that the intentions of the ROC government were at least minimally compatible with its own on the matter of eventual unification, Taipei had to invoke the "one China principle" explicitly in a manner evaluated as genuine by the PRC.[36] Second, each side understood that a common definition of the "one China principle" would not be specified and each was prepared to tolerate that. Indeed, for months, they had wrangled in vain to establish a definition on which they could concur.[37] Third, negotiators from both sides understood that each side would express orally its own interpretation of the "one China principle," rather than issue a jointly authored, culminating document. In the end, this meant that Beijing and Taipei would characterize differently the conclusion of the negotiations—not just the substance to which both sides presumably were in accord.[38]

Ambiguities notwithstanding, what was subsequently dubbed the "1992 Consensus" provided sufficient cover to both sides that it was possible to hold a high-level and much publicized meeting in Singapore between SEF Chairman Gu Zhenfu (Koo Chen-fu) and ARATS Chairman Wang Daohan, from April 27 to April 29, 1993.[39] These were among the hopeful signs of an emerging constructive relationship between the PRC and the ROC.[40]

However, the PRC may have underestimated the implications of transformations on Taiwan. Lee aimed to reform the political system by which Taiwan was governed and rationalize its external relations. This entailed breaking the throttlehold that mainland-born Guomindang loyalists had had on politics and, in the name of democracy, enfranchising the Taiwanese majority who was not then inclined to see the island as a part of China or to favor unification. The Democratic Progressive Party (DPP), then in opposition, comprised people with more radical objectives, including one faction eager to declare Taiwan—not the Republic of China—an independent and sovereign state. The liberalization of Taiwan politics and the liberalization of cross-Strait relations were utterly intertwined.[41]

From the start, Lee and his administration pledged allegiance to the notion of unification. However, to ensure that an end to hostilities across the Taiwan Strait and eventual unification progressed in a manner that accorded with Taiwan's interests, Lee pressed the PRC to view the ROC as retaining a share of sovereignty over a portion of China's territory. He challenged the diplomatic cordon that Beijing had sought to impose on Taiwan and engaged in a multifarious campaign—known as "flexible diplomacy" or, literally, "elastic diplomacy" [*tanxing waijiao*] and "pragmatic diplomacy" [*wushi waijiao*]—to assert the ROC's international personality and, to the degree possible, expand its "international living space" [*guoji shengcun kongjian*].

"Pragmatic diplomacy" flowed from Lee's notion of China as a divided state. If one viewed the state as divided, then neither Beijing nor Taipei could justly claim the exclusive right to represent all China in the international arena, only that portion of China it actually governed. Hence, Lee sought to reframe the way in which the ROC was regarded abroad. Among the hallmarks of this approach was a challenge to the prevailing practice that the ROC was necessarily to be excluded from international organizations in which the PRC was a member. Consequently, the ROC began to apply for representation in international organizations and, starting in 1993, at the United Nations.

Lee also sought to undermine the taboo associated with foreign travel by ROC leaders. Under the guise of taking private vacations, Lee Teng-hui and other key leaders of the ROC visited states that did not have diplomatic relations with the ROC, as well as some that did, to make the point that Beijing's effort to blackball Taipei was only as effective as other states permitted it to be.[42] From these actions, as well as statements made in Taipei about the ROC's sovereign status, Beijing saw what it took to be signals that Lee Teng-hui was deviating "more and more brazenly from the 'one China' principle."[43]

Meanwhile, in the PRC, Jiang Zemin assumed the post of CCP general secretary in June 1989, following the lethally maladroit reactions of the PRC leadership to the massive political demonstrations that spring. For the next several years, Jiang's role and influence gradually expanded. He became chairman of the powerful party Central Military Commission (CMC) in November 1989 and was elected president of the PRC in March 1993. Thereafter, the imprint of Jiang Zemin was perceived in Taipei as discernibly unyielding on the matter of divided sovereignty.

The transition by Jiang from partial to full power within the apparatus of both the CCP and the state mirrored a comparable transition that Lee Teng-hui made. After he assumed the presidency, Lee confronted a challenge from within the Guomindang by party stalwarts who had come to Taiwan from the mainland.[44] Ultimately, Lee won out and was only thereafter able to consolidate control over policy toward the PRC. So, during the period 1989–93, Jiang Zemin and Lee Teng-hui were both in the process of consolidating their power at home while striving to shape a path for cross-Taiwan Strait relations in response to divergent views within their own political systems. Though they may not have understood it at the time, the two men were on course for a collision.

Between April 1994 and March 1995, eighteen then-secret interactions between representatives of Lee Teng-hui and Jiang Zemin were held in Zhuhai and Macao. At what was to be the final meeting in this sequence of confidential consultations, Lee Teng-hui's representative—Su Chi-cheng—told his counterpart—Zeng Qinghong—that Lee was planning to visit both the United States and Japan.[45] Thereafter, the PRC closed down this channel.

Lee's notion that China is a divided state was anathema to the CCP leadership and Jiang Zemin, whose idée fixe it was that Beijing's "one China principle" was incompatible with any form of shared sovereignty of the sort Lee articulated. While Beijing later charged that Lee was intent on separation all along, the reality may have been that while he was president, Lee reacted to what he perceived as Beijing's intransigence by ever-more aggressive challenges to what the PRC understood as the "one China principle."[46] As Richard Bush writes, this does not support the conclusion that Lee was opposed to unification, only that he was opposed to unification on the terms Beijing struggled to enforce.[47]

Both Soft and Hard: Beijing Shifts Strategy Toward Taiwan Again

A second fundamental shift in PRC strategy occurred in the early 1990s. Having persuaded itself in the late 1970s and early 1980s that it would gain through Sino-U.S. normalization the capacity to isolate Taipei and prevail in its effort to unify the mainland and Taiwan, the PRC leadership in the early 1990s must have been exceptionally disappointed by and agitated about the way relations with Taiwan were evolving. Despite oaths of fealty to eventual unification, Taipei's words and actions increasingly left the impression in the PRC that Taiwan was seeking to consolidate an identity in the international arena that was separate and enduring.

On January 8, 1993, the ROC Foreign Minister Qian Fu [Frederick Chien] made explicit the ROC's objective to extend "our hands to seek for wider diplomatic space."[48] On January 21, 1993, the ROC Ministry of Foreign Affairs released its first *Foreign Affairs Report*, in which it explained, among other things, its view that

> "one China" is based on the common notion of all Chinese people, and this refers to the sovereign and independent Republic of China (ROC). The ROC government opposes "two Chinas," "one China one Taiwan," and "an independent Taiwan." In (the) future, the focus of our nation's diplomacy is to strengthen ties with countries maintaining diplomatic relations, elevate ties with countries having no diplomatic relations, and actively participate in the activities of international bodies, particularly, rejoining the United Nations as soon as possible.[49]

The leadership in Beijing could not abide Taipei's efforts to insinuate a view of the ROC as equivalent in sovereignty to the PRC. Where Taipei saw—and wanted other international actors to see—parity between the ROC and PRC, Beijing saw hierarchy. Where Taipei saw shared sovereignty in a divided state, Beijing saw indivisible sovereignty despoiled by an arrogant and shameless squatter regime. The PRC leadership was prepared to tolerate unification under the rubric of "one country, two systems" for the sake of achieving its objective peacefully, but it acted and spoke as if it expected Taiwan to accommodate itself to a condition Beijing had never considered as anything other than settled: the PRC is China.[50]

Jiang Zemin had given voice to this sentiment all along. Apparently striking back at the National Unification Guidelines issued in August 1992, Jiang said in his report to the CCP's Fourteenth Party Congress of October 1992,

> we are resolutely opposed to, in any form, the notion of "two Chinas," "one China, one Taiwan" or "one country, two governments" and *any acts aimed at bringing about the independence of Taiwan* [emphasis added] . . . on the premise that there is only one China, we are prepared to talk with the Taiwan authorities about any matter, including the form that official negotiations should take, a form that would be acceptable to both sides.[51]

The problem was that the ROC leadership *had* committed itself to the premise that there is only one China, but not in a manner that Beijing found acceptable. To Beijing, it seemed Lee Teng-hui was being duplicitous. He and his administration were saying "one China," when they acted as if they really meant something rather different—at least different from the way that the PRC understood the construct of "one China."

Even though the ARATS-SEF meeting between Gu Zhenfu and Wang Daohan of April 1993 seemed a high point of détente, Beijing was anxious. In August, the PRC issued "The Taiwan Question and the Reunification of China," a "white paper" in which it methodically laid out its view of Taiwan's status as part of China, how the "Taiwan Question" [*Taiwan wenti*] materialized, how the PRC proposed to unify the state, why relations across the Strait remained unsettled, and how other international actors should deal with Taiwan.

Talks using both the official and secret channels continued, but Beijing was disheartened by what it took as evidence of Lee Teng-hui's determination to create a permanent division. The distemper the PRC leadership felt was aggravated by publication in March 1994 of an interview Lee gave with a Japanese writer, Ryotaro Shiba. In the interview—reportedly conducted in Japanese—Lee spoke of "the grief of being Taiwanese." He said that the word China [*Zhongguo*] is confusing. He spoke disparagingly of the Guomindang regime, stating "Taiwan has always been ruled by power that came from abroad. Today I say this kind of thing without hesitation. Even the Nationalists are a foreign power. They are nothing more than a political party that came to rule the Taiwanese. We must make this a Taiwanese Nationalist Party. . . . I aspire to build a nation state and a society for 'the public.'" In the course of the interview, Lee suggested that his role in Taiwan was analogous to the role of Moses, leading the children of Israel out of bondage.[52] This, the PRC heard as a renunciation of Lee's commitment to unification and a signal of his plan—now revealed—to work for Taiwan's independence.

Jiang Zemin fired back on January 30, 1995, with a speech titled "Continue to Promote the Reunification of the Motherland." Much of the speech seemed to address the people of Taiwan directly, as opposed to the white paper of 1993, which seemed aimed at an international readership. Jiang summarized the logic of Beijing's posture toward Taiwan. However, there were new wrinkles. Jiang said:

> There are only two ways to settle the Taiwan question: One is by peaceful means and the other is by non-peaceful means. . . . We consistently stand for achieving reunification by peaceful means and through negotiations. But we shall not undertake not to use force. Such commitment would only make it impossible to achieve peaceful reunification and could not but lead to the eventual settlement of the question by the use of force.

The speech became known as "Jiang's eight points" [*Jiang badian*], a reference to eight assertions concerning Beijing's strategy to counterbalance inducements to Taiwan with the threat of military consequences for straying from the goal of unification. Hence, the PRC strategy had emerged as one entailing both "hard" and "soft" elements.[53]

Lee Teng-hui appeared to respond to Jiang Zemin in an address to the National Unification Council on April 8, 1995. In it, Lee made six major points, reaffirming his belief that China is a divided state and, nevertheless, that it can be unified under appropriate conditions. In the fifth point of a speech that came to be known as "Lee's Six Points," Lee objected to the PRC's invocation of military force. He explained that he had renounced the use of force in 1991 but that Beijing had refused to follow suit. Lee stated:

> We hold that the mainland authorities should show their goodwill by renouncing the use of force against Taiwan, Penghu, and Jinmen and Mazu, and that they should refrain from any military actions that could cause suspicions, thereby laying the foundation for ending the situation of hostile confrontation through formal cross-Strait talks. I must emphasize that using the so-called "Taiwan independence forces" or "foreign interference" as a pretext for refusing to make the commitment to not use force against Taiwan is disregarding and distorting the founding spirit and policy of the ROC, which will only deepen suspicions between the two sides and hinder mutual trust.[54]

By then, during the last of the confidential meetings between representatives of Taipei and Beijing, the PRC had learned of Lee's plan to visit the United States and Japan. The view that Lee was promoting independence had been brewing in Beijing but became an article of faith for the PRC when he succeeded in engineering a visit to the United States in 1995. The visit to Cornell University was, for Beijing, the final straw. Whatever hope the PRC leadership had had of fostering through private and unofficial channels a foundation for unification became unrecoverable as the PRC officials and commentators turned in fury on Lee. Détente was dead.[55]

Holding Lee Teng-hui personally responsible for taking advantage of the "soft" policies to promote independence while stringing the PRC along with talk of unification, Beijing vented with torrents of vilification in the press. A litany of Lee's presumed misdeeds and what PRC commentators took as duplicitous statements were strung together to make the case that Lee Teng-hui was an inveterate separatist.[56]

In the same period, no longer burdened by doubts or distracted by hopes, Beijing intensified its use of coercive measures and redoubled its commitment to a military buildup that would enhance its capacity to succeed in the use of force to attain its political objectives in relation to Taiwan. The missile exercises in which it engaged in 1995 and 1996, dramatic though they may have been, were acts of public political theater. The more unsettling and, perhaps, insidious development is the PRC's escalating effort to prepare military

options to settle the Taiwan issue. This process, described in the following section, began before Lee went to Cornell and has become ever-more apparent
with the passage of time.

However, despite Beijing's display of military prowess, Lee Teng-hui was
reelected to the presidency of the ROC in 1996 and was perceived as no less
provocative in his second term than he was in his first. Moreover, U.S. reactions to the missile "crisis"—dispatching two aircraft carrier battle groups to
the region—may have chastened those in Beijing who might have preferred a
continued tightening of the screws on Taiwan through military means only.[57]
As a result, Beijing has maintained a two-handed approach since then, bran-
dishing both "hard" and "soft" measures.

Interactions between ARATS and SEF continued, and a second meeting
between Gu Zhenfu and Wang Daohan occurred in October 1998, implying a
willingness to find a modus vivendi with Taipei. Yet, Beijing was deeply suspicious of Lee Teng-hui, and its mistrust plummeted to a new nadir in 1999.

First, on May 19 an autobiography of Lee was published in Japanese as
Taiwan no shucho [Taiwan Viewpoints]. In it Lee makes the point that Taiwan
exists as an international actor and Beijing's hegemonic efforts to will Taiwan
into nonexistence is a threat to the stability of Asia. In one passage, the focus
of subsequent PRC denunciations, Lee considers the merits for stability of
dividing China into regions based on identity. He writes that Taiwan—like
Tibet, Xinjiang, Inner Mongolia, and the northeastern provinces that were
once a part of Manchuria—all have a distinct identity. "Ideally," Lee writes,
"If each one were allowed to affirm its own existence, we would see Asia's
regional stability enhanced. For purposes of effective management alone,
'Greater China' would be better off divided into perhaps seven autonomous
regions which could then compete among themselves and with the world for
progress."[58]

Provocative though that comment may appear when taken out of context,
Lee's book affirms his commitment to unification. It reiterates points Lee
made in a speech before the NUC on July 22, 1998, in which he said, "We
must take this opportunity to once again state clearly and solemnly: China
must be reunified."[59] Lee further asserts, "although there will be only one
China in the future, at present there is one divided China. . . . That the two
sides are ruled by two separate political entities is an objective fact that cannot be denied." Finally, Lee elaborates a view he had expressed before, that
"Taiwan faces mainland China in a relationship that transcends the 'internal
affairs of China' thesis, placing the two political entities on a *de facto* equal
footing."[60] The PRC response at the time was comparatively tepid.

Then, an interview *Deutsche Welle* [Voice of Germany] conducted with Lee Teng-hui on July 9 was broadcast. Expanding on the notion that China is a divided state and that the ROC, like the PRC, retains sovereignty in one portion of China, Lee explained, "The 1991 constitutional amendments have designated cross-strait relations as a state-to-state relationship or at least a special state-to-state relationship, rather than an internal relationship between a legitimate government and a renegade group, or between a central government and a local government. Thus, the Beijing authorities' characterization of Taiwan as a 'renegade province' is historically and legally untrue."[61]

This, Beijing labeled Lee's "two state theory" [*liangguolun*], elevating a view he had long espoused in other public pronouncements to a theory and acting as if his reformulation revealed something new. The PRC press ignited with a barrage of inflamed denunciations that lasted weeks. Lee was disparaged in ad hominem assaults as a "sinner condemned by history," as "scum of the nation and an eternally condemned person!" and compared to "a pig looking at himself in the mirror, neither himself nor the image he sees is a human being."[62] A signed commentary carried by the overseas edition of *Renmin Ribao* [People's Daily] and, reportedly, by *Jiefangjun Bao* [Liberation Army Daily] deprecated Lee as a "rat running across the street with everybody shouting 'smack it.'" [*laoshu guojie, renren handa*].[63]

If Beijing was then rewarding flamboyant reproval, first prize would surely have been collected by Major General Peng Guangqian of the strategy research department of the Chinese Academy of Military Sciences. General Peng characterized Lee Teng-hui as an "abnormal 'test-tube baby' bred by international anti-China forces in their political lab."[64] Peng's outlandish slur came against the backdrop of unsettling suggestions in the PRC press that the PLA was itching for a fight.[65]

Military exercises, enraged commentaries in the *Jiefangjun Bao*, and hints in the Hong Kong press that an attack was planned on one of the ROC-held offshore islands were all cast as reactions to Lee's "theory." The tone of the military's rhetorical contribution is captured by the statement, "The mighty armed forces of the . . . PLA will absolutely not sit idly by and permit even one inch of territory from being split from China!"[66]

Conditions worsened after Chen Shui-bian was elected in 2000 as president of the ROC. Despite an avowed policy to suspend judgment while "listening to his words, watching his actions" [*ting qi yan, guan qi xing*], in hindsight it seems likely that Beijing never held out serious expectations that Chen Shui-bian would act in any way other than the way it feared: to promote de jure independence. The "chance" it offered Chen to prove himself was a cynical effort to give Chen time to demonstrate to the United States and others that he was as bent on stirring up trouble for cross-Strait relations as Beijing knew he would be. Beijing has, in the years since, made the case that it did everything it could to promote peaceful resolution but was impeded at each step by Chen Shui-bian. It reflects no self-awareness concerning the way its responses to Chen and Taiwan's political dynamics since 2000 have helped to create precisely the situation it claimed an interest in avoiding.

For most of the period since 1949, the PRC vacillated between sticks and carrots, hard and soft policies, to deal with Taiwan. It did not often present both. By 2005, with the passage by the PRC National People's Congress of the Anti-Secession Law [*fan fenlie guojia fa*], President Hu Jintao had become associated with an approach to dealing with Taiwan embodied in the dictum "*ying de geng ying, ruan de geng ruan*" [the hard harder, the soft softer].[67] With this strategy, the PRC has signaled its intention to make its sticks more menacing while offering carrots that it hopes will be more alluring.

PRC Military Buildup: Making the Hard Harder

Early in the 1990s, the PRC intensified its program to upgrade the quality and augment the capacities of the PLA. So, even before the PRC began to adopt a harder stance toward Taiwan, it embarked on a program of military reform and modernization. In part, this reflects the PRC's palpable increase in wealth, making possible concerted efforts to realize long-standing ambitions for a greater sense of security, power, and status.

This accelerated program of reformation was prompted by several developments. First, the collapse of the Soviet Union, the demise of communist regimes in Eastern Europe, the end of the cold war, and the resulting status of the United States as the "sole superpower" were part of a rapid transformation in the strategic environment—a transition that the PRC experienced, initially, as a threat to its security. This occasioned a thorough evaluation of the PRC's long-range strategic objectives and likely vulnerabilities in an era of shifting power relations and expanding economic interdependence in the world beyond its borders. What resulted was a commitment to transform the PLA from a force that was exclusively concerned about defense of the motherland to a force that could be deployed farther afield to secure access to vital resources and ensure the state's economic competitiveness and strategic influence.[68]

PRC military analysts digested data and impressions derived from observations of the performance of U.S. forces and weaponry in the Desert Storm campaign of the 1991 war in the Persian Gulf. They concluded that the PRC's own capabilities lagged perilously behind those of the United States, a gap that Beijing was determined to begin closing. They also internalized a lesson, long in coming, that to be a powerful state capable of securing its interests and exerting influence beyond its borders, the PRC needed to field a "modern" military that was structured, equipped, and trained in ways very different from those that had prevailed up to that point.

A fundamental doctrinal shift occurred early in the 1990s. Jiang Zemin endorsed the view that the PLA should be capable of doing more than fighting to defend China's territory in "local wars" only. Instead, it would have to prepare itself to fight "local wars under modern, high-tech conditions," [*gao jishu tiaojian xia jubu zhanzheng*], a shift that signaled Beijing's understanding that the PLA must be a more sophisticated and professional fighting force able to deploy not only on the PRC's boundaries, but in the region beyond.[69]

From Beijing's vantage, the end of the cold war and collapse of the Soviet Union had the salutary effect of prompting Moscow to see the sophisticated weaponry it had developed to confront the United States as marketable commodities and a ready source of much-needed capital. Unable to develop efficiently its own aircraft industry and with a willing seller in Moscow, Beijing was able to circumvent the arms embargo imposed on it in 1989 by the United States and European countries. Hence, in 1990, during the twilight of the Soviet Union, the PRC purchased seventy-two Sukoi Su-27 fighter aircraft, twenty-six of which were delivered in 1992.[70]

Thereafter, the PRC stepped up the purchase and indigenous production of weapon systems at a pace that has fueled concerns about the intentions of the PRC. The PRC's defense budget has risen precipitously, albeit from a comparatively low point of departure in 1990.[71] As Beijing bought and built better equipment and as the PLA adjusted doctrine and training to accommodate its newly assigned roles, the PRC has gradually eroded the security of Taiwan and elevated the cost to the United States of defending the island, should it come under attack.

This was not incidental. The particular choices Beijing has made as it has acquired weaponry and reconfigured its military suggest that early in the 1990s it decided to establish a credible military deterrent that would restrain Taiwan from pursing "independence" while readying the means to fight if deterrence fails. Anticipating that a battle for Taiwan will draw in the United States—and possibly Japan—Beijing has had to devise means of securing its objectives in an asymmetric competition with an adversary that enjoys unrivaled military might and benefits from extensive combat experience.

Meanwhile, the U.S. Department of Defense has warned, "China is pursuing long-term, comprehensive military modernization to improve its capabilities for power projection and access denial. Consistent with a near-term focus on preparing for Taiwan Strait contingencies, China deploys its most advanced systems to the military regions directly opposite Taiwan."[72] It concludes, "The cross-Strait military balance is shifting in the mainland's favor."[73]

In addition to inferring a shift in Beijing's intentions toward Taiwan from the weapons the PRC has added to its arsenals, from the early 1990s onward one detects in the timing and character of the PRC's military exercises, certain public statements by PRC officials and agencies of the government, and commentary by scholars and journalists a menacing belligerence that was largely absent from 1978 to 1993. Certainly, by 1994, it became clear that the PRC was determined to balance amicable diplomatic and economic overtures to Taiwan with unsubtle military threats.

Prominent among the evidence for this conclusion is the PRC's expanding arsenal of short-range ballistic missiles (SRBMs) capable of striking Taiwan from launch sites on the mainland.[74] In 1994, the PRC established the first brigade of conventionally tipped SRBMs across from Taiwan and has increased the number of missiles annually.[75] In 1995 and again in 1996, the PRC staged missile exercises interpreted as signals of the central leadership's displeasure with developments on Taiwan. Thereafter, the determination to develop and deploy missiles that threaten Taiwan from the PRC's coastal regions proceeded apace.[76]

In its *Annual Report to Congress* concerning the military power of the PRC, the U.S. Department of Defense reported in 2006 that the PRC had by then deployed 710–790 SRBMs in garrisons opposite Taiwan and was adding to those batteries at a rate of about 100 additional missiles each year.[77] Moreover, the PRC is reportedly devising means to use these missiles for "anti-access/ sea-denial missions" that would complicate naval operations by an adversary—say the United States or Japan—in a region surrounding Taiwan. In addition, the PRC is expected to deploy "a new road-mobile, solid-propellant, intercontinental-range ballistic missile (ICBM)."[78] As of 2006, it also had 400,000 troops stationed in the military regions opposite Taiwan and was steadily upgrading the equipment and capabilities of those units.[79]

The PRC has also been augmenting naval aviation and air force capabilities with purchases of sophisticated vessels, weaponry, and detection systems from Russia, and has sought systems to "detect, track, target, and attack U.S. carrier battle groups" that might be deployed by Washington in defense of Taiwan.[80] The Pentagon's report of 2006 states that the PRC then had in excess of 700 aircraft "within un-refueled operational range of Taiwan" and was purchasing from and coproducing with Russia other advanced fighter aircraft.[81]

While the exact configuration of the PLA Air Force (PLA[AF]) is subject to dispute, it is evident that Beijing is engaged in a significant transformation of both air force and naval aviation.[82] The PRC is dramatically improving its capacity to field "advanced precision strike munitions, including cruise missiles and air-to-air, air-to-surface, and anti-radiation munitions," enhancing its capabilities in the air and at sea.[83] The Defense Intelligence Agency—an arm of the Pentagon—is also concerned that the PRC may be developing "a combat air wing for a future aircraft carrier," indicating that debate within the intelligence community about the prospect of a PRC aircraft carrier persists.[84]

The PRC is vigorously expanding the PLA Navy (PLA[N]), which has based approximately two-thirds of its rapidly expanding force in the East China or South China Sea Fleets.[85] The PRC's purchase and deployment of "Russian-made Sovremennyy-II guided missile destroyers (DDGs)" to the East Sea Fleet and the expectation that the PRC will soon acquire more has drawn attention, as has the PRC's program to enlarge its fleet of nuclear and diesel electric submarines.[86] To be sure, the protection of commercial shipping, combating terrorism, or thwarting blockades aimed at disrupting passage on sea-lanes of communication (SLOC) and defending territorial claims contested by Japan and Southeast Asian states might all be seen to justify the expansion of the PRC's naval power. However, given that any battle for Taiwan will, because of geography, have a significant naval dimension, these developments must also be understood in the context of Beijing's policy to "make the hard harder."

This buildup of forces corresponds to persistent political signals that elements of the foreign policy establishment in the PRC are determined to do whatever is necessary to resolve the Taiwan matter to Beijing's satisfaction. Not everyone in the PRC who is able to inform the choices ultimately made by the leadership believes that military force ought to be a choice of absolute final resort. Some itch more for a fight than others.

For the most part, though, one has the impression that the PRC leadership has adopted the view that force should be used only after every reasonable effort has been made to effect a solution by other means. The problem, of course, is that there are different evaluations in the PRC of what is reasonable and what constitutes the exhaustion of other options. These views are now aired more publicly than they had been, and some are quite strident.[87] In days past when the military balance across the Strait unambiguously favored the ROC and rendered an initiation of hostilities by the PRC an exercise in futility, one could be less concerned about rumblings of jingoism in Beijing. However, those days are gone.

The keenest minds have contended, without reaching consensus, about the significance of a state's capabilities, versus its professed or ascribed intentions, as a measure of its likely future behavior. That is not a controversy anyone is expected to settle. Measuring capability alone is surely not a sufficient way to determine how a state will act as long as one must also account for deception, indecision, internal disagreement, unanticipated constraints, and shifting priorities. Conversely, a single-minded determination to do something cannot overcome the absence of means, even when self-deception, ingenuity, zeal, and a willingness to waste resources by inviting defeat are taken into consideration.

In the PRC, it appears that a segment of the foreign policy elites may be committed to the use of military force to resolve the Taiwan issue. Although it is difficult to discern how broadly this view is held and how influential it is, one thing is clear. The PRC leadership has adopted the view that the PRC must develop the *capacity* to use force, even if it has not reached a consensus about when and in what way to use it. With an emerging capacity to confront not just the forces of Taiwan but those of the United States, too, one must be vigilant about the possibility that restraint provided by Beijing's more prudent statesmen and analysts will, one day, fray. Those in Beijing who favor militarization only as a deterrent against untoward actions by Taiwan's leaders or as a hedge against the possibility that the PRC must be *prepared* to fight, even though it hopes not to, may some day find themselves marginalized in a policy debate dominated by those who are more determined to use newly acquired capabilities that the PRC has been developing.

Just as one would not wish to ignore Beijing's professed interest in stability and a peaceful international environment as one calculates the PRC's intentions for the foreseeable future, one should not ignore its expanding arsenal. Moreover, one must attend to the implications of what weapons, specifically, the PRC has decided to add to its arsenal. Nobody questions that the PRC's military capability is becoming more lethal. However, the degree to which that lethality is being developed with a battle for Taiwan in mind has been a source of concern and a subject of some dispute. Evidence that since the 1990s Beijing has been focused on developing the military capability to settle the question of Taiwan's status by force triggers a determination to understand why Taiwan is evaluated as having such importance to the PRC.

It is not difficult to understand why the political elites in Beijing are exasperated about the continued autonomy of Taiwan and why that exasperation has intensified since the early 1990s. Not only has the "soft" strategy put in place after 1978 done little to increase the prospect of unification, but Beijing cannot escape the conclusion that Lee Teng-hui and Chen Shui-bian have both exploited Beijing's softness to advance the cause of independence in ways that make the military confrontation more likely. Overall, Beijing's economic development and international stature have benefited from the absence of war, but in terms of deterring independence—to say nothing of promoting unification—the PRC may feel it has gained little from its restraint.

The question remains: Why is Taiwan worth a fight? Why has a leadership frustrated by the inability to rein in Taiwan by "soft" measures turned with such resolve to prepare "hard" military options? Considering that it has managed other territorial disputes without resort to force, why does the prospect of using force against Taiwan seem a rational option to Beijing? Considering all the PRC would reasonably expect to lose in a battle to assure itself that Taiwan is part of China, what is it that Beijing expects to gain? In what ways will the PRC be better off having settled to satisfaction the question of Taiwan's status than it has been with that status contested? If Taiwan were to "declare independence," what is it the PRC has had since 1949 that it would then lose?

Naturally, it would be unwise to expect that there are single, simple answers to each of these questions. There are a number of reasons why Taiwan is important to the PRC and, perhaps, Taiwan is evaluated differently by different segments of society. This book highlights one rationale—the geostrategic salience that some PRC analysts and strategists attribute to Taiwan in the context of the PRC's long-range economic, political, and security objectives.

This is not a rationale *ascribed* to what is said or written about Taiwan by PRC commentators and strategists. It is a rationale that certain PRC commentators and strategists, themselves, assert as vital. One may disagree with the reasoning that contributes to a view of Taiwan as having geostrategic importance—as, in fact, others in the PRC have—but it is already too prominent a view to be ignored. A measured analysis of the PRC's evaluation of Taiwan must take the geostrategic perspective into account.

Organization and Objectives

The PRC—and the CCP prior to 1949—has evaluated Taiwan's salience in various ways and has framed its strategy for dealing with Taiwan differently at different moments. Beyond the primary objective of explaining why the PRC views Taiwan as worth fighting for, a secondary aim of this book is to place Beijing's militarized strategy in historical context. Consequently, the book reviews the variations in attitudes toward Taiwan to demonstrate the conditional nature of PRC claims to the island.

The point of this is to offer a corrective to views of the Taiwan issue that stem from the notions that the PRC's position reflects a consistent and

straightforward interest in righting the injustices of history, satisfying popular nationalist ambitions, ensuring regime legitimacy, providing a bulwark
against the division of China's territorial integrity, or demonstrating resolve in
opposition to Taiwan's independence as a way of discouraging independence
movements in Inner Mongolia, Xinjiang, and Tibet.

A third prominent feature of this book is the idea that the contemporary
phase of the cross-Strait dispute cannot be correctly perceived without a consideration of geography and the effects of history prior to 1949. Chapter 2
considers the utility of thinking about geography, geopolitics, geostrategy,
issue salience, and the comparative dynamics of territorial disputes. It also
elaborates the difference between security, safety, and strategic advantage.

Chapter 3 looks back before the threshold of 1949 to address the question:
why does the PRC claim Taiwan is China's territory in the first place? It begins
by tracing the relationship between China and Taiwan since the seventeenth
century.[88] It explains how Taiwan became a part of the "mental map" of China
and how its status as part of China has been contingent on other factors, chief
among them the relationship between China and external powers. It is in this
context that Taiwan's territorial salience—a product of its location—mattered
to Chinese strategists well before the establishment of the PRC.

Taiwan was viewed often by Chinese strategists as a bridgehead or a buffer,
much the way some PRC strategists have described it since the 1990s.

Reviewing this history helps to expose a pattern of rivalry over territory
that is evident in the record of international relations in Asia, a pattern that
bears on the contemporary manifestations of the Taiwan issue. The relevance
of this pattern pertains to the present largely because both the ROC and the
PRC have operated from a "mental map" of China that approximates the
realm of the Qing empire. Moreover, the PRC's rationale for territorial integrity has much to do with the geopolitical lessons about security and regional
power that flow from the Qing.

Although Taiwan has been viewed repeatedly as having territorial salience,
it has not consistently been seen that way. Indeed, before 1942, neither
the Guomindang that governed the ROC nor the CCP expressed much
of an attachment to Taiwan. The island was then still firmly ensconced in
the Japanese empire, as a colony that the Chinese equated with Korea and
Vietnam. Accordingly, Chapter 4 traces the evolution of Guomindang and
ROC attitudes about Taiwan's salience—from indifference to strategic imperative—in the period prior to 1945.

Chapter 5 chronicles the attitude of the CCP and its leadership in the same
period. From 1921 until 1942, the CCP evinced little concern for Taiwan.

Then, the CCP suddenly reversed itself, thereafter depicting Taiwan as a part of China. The chapter makes the point that the CCP's volte-face about Taiwan was occasioned by the ROC's decision to demand that Japan return Taiwan to China after the war. For the CCP, it was a derived policy, not one that the communist leadership was led to by ideology or a distinctive worldview.

More importantly, neither the ROC's position nor the CCP adaptation of it was simply an outgrowth of irredentism. The ROC's wish to recover sovereignty over Taiwan had more to do with a wish to take back China's due from a defeated adversary than with Taiwan itself. Depriving Japan of ill-gotten gains and of the means to menace China again, rather than reuniting what had been perceived of as disunited, motivated the Chinese elite who pressed for a return of Taiwan to China. It was a quest justified in geopolitical terms.

Chapter 6 considers the CCP's attitude toward Taiwan in the period immediately prior to and soon after the outbreak of the Korean War. While Taiwan was then certainly viewed as a part of China's territory, it is striking the degree to which the CCP leadership expressed its determination to subordinate Taiwan in geostrategic terms. It certainly felt itself entitled to consider Taiwan as Chinese, but the communist leaders were also highly anxious about the risk of failing to take the island. This was not a risk expressed solely in terms of abstract principles such as sovereignty, territorial integrity, and nationalism. The pronouncements of the CCP leadership reflected a concern about geopolitics and national security.

Chapter 7 offers evidence that geostrategic considerations feature prominently in the expressions of contemporary PRC foreign policy elites about the salience of Taiwan. The end of the cold war has prompted a strategic realignment that has led to a reassessment of the PRC's relationship to major powers, especially the United States and Japan. The realignment of the international system has occurred in a period when the PRC's material power is increasing and when the PRC is comparatively safe in the international arena. This has inspired adjustments in the PRC's grand strategic vision and confidence that the long-term aim of developing a wealthier and more powerful state is feasible.

One index of power is military strength. Accordingly, the PRC has been engaged in the wholesale reform and modernization of the PLA, as this introductory chapter has already made clear. The naval dimension of this program is intended to expand the PRC's maritime domain, creating a wider realm in which it can exclude hostile forces and ensure safe passage of cargo—including oil and gas—that sustains international trade and economic growth.[89] The effort to expand the PRC's maritime domain, though, is an aim that is highly vulnerable to the competing expectations and ambitions of other states, notably the United States and Japan.

In view of Taiwan's location, the island is assessed by some PRC analysts to have special geostrategic significance. Taiwan in hostile hands is presumed, by some observers, to deprive Beijing of a platform that would enable it to have unfettered access to the Pacific Ocean. PRC naval strategists wish to develop the capacity to deny access by hostile forces to seas abutting the Chinese coast—the Yellow Sea, the East China Sea, the Taiwan Strait, and the South China Sea. Taiwan is situated in just such a way that the passage of PRC surface and subsurface vessels to its north or south could be jeopardized by rival forces based on the island.

While there are analysts who question the operational soundness of this evaluation, the notion of Taiwan as a gateway to the Pacific has taken hold. As long as it remains outside the PRC's sphere of influence—or, worse still, within the U.S. sphere—Taiwan is seen as the westward edge of an insular cordon that flows through Japan to the Philippines, putting the PRC's maritime ambitions at risk. As part of the PRC's domain, though, Taiwan becomes the easternmost edge of an oceanic arena in which the PRC can exercise "sea control" in coastal waters and with which it can puncture the belt of strategically located islands that the United States, as the maritime hegemon, is perceived to be using to check the expansion of PRC power. This is a theme expressed by outspoken and high-ranking military officers, defense intellectuals associated with military academies, strategic analysts at highly esteemed universities, editorialists and commentators in national journals, as well as anonymous keyboard warriors tapping their defiance and national chauvinism into online chat room screeds and blogs.[90]

Fueling the geostrategic concerns that some PRC analysts express are anxieties about the PRC's international stature. The domestic political developments on Taiwan since the early 1990s have sparked concern in the PRC that hopes of drawing the island back to the motherland peacefully may go unfulfilled. Liberalization and democratization have unleashed on Taiwan a period of compensatory nationalism, a reaction to decades of authoritarian rule and to political and cultural suppression. To Beijing, though, the inability to frame and set the terms for resolving the dispute with Taiwan exposes the PRC as impotent in a critical contest at a moment when it is, otherwise, determined to be viewed as ever-more powerful. Taiwan's defiance of Beijing's insistence that Taipei recognize the PRC's "one China principle," coupled with the prospective defense of Taiwan by the United States and possibly Japan, creates in the PRC seething indignation and frustration.

The final chapter explains how the geostrategic rationale has emerged in the PRC as the confluence of several factors. It considers the influence of the geostrategic argument on PRC policy and addresses the implications for bilateral relations across the Taiwan Strait as well as for international politics in Asia. The chapter underscores the point that the cross-Strait relationship cannot be disentangled from the Sino-U.S. and Sino-Japanese relationships because a grand rivalry for access to space is at issue in the waters off China's coast. That strategic competition is complicated by Beijing's view that Taiwan should be part of China's dominion in a period when the island remains in the orbit of the PRC's chief rivals. Hence, for some strategists in the PRC, the quest for national rejuvenation, power, and international prestige makes the subordination of Taiwan a strategic imperative.

Reframing the Cross-Strait Dispute
Geography and the Strategic Salience of Taiwan

Framing: Why Does Taiwan Matter to Beijing?

The PRC has succeeded, to a considerable extent, in propagating its preferred rhetorical and conceptual parameters to frame the matter of Taiwan's status. The dominant official narrative flows from a nationalist perspective. It emphasizes the paramountcy of the "one China principle" [*yige Zhongguo yuanze*], an expression of national and territorial unity that reflects the CCP's effort to legitimate itself as the party that unified China after divisions caused by imperialism. Consequently, it opposes Taiwan's "independence" [*duli*] as a state because no matter how much prestige and power the PRC enjoys, Taiwan's autonomous international status undermines the notion of national unity and the narrative by which the CCP legitimates its rule. The PRC has also proclaimed its determination to strive for the "reunification" [*tongyi*] of Taiwan and the motherland [*zuguo*].[1] Indeed, the preamble of the 1982 Constitution of the PRC states "Taiwan is part of the sacred territory of the People's Republic of China. It is the inviolable duty of all Chinese people, including our compatriots in Taiwan, to accomplish the great task of reunifying the motherland."[2]

Beijing has implied that all it aims to do is prevent the dissolution of China's national territory by permitting the continued existence of "one China, one Taiwan" or "one China, two governments," or "two Chinas," by which it means two separate states each of which inhabits and governs a portion of China's territory. Considering that it views China's sovereignty as indivisible, it does not recognize, and refuses—selectively—to countenance evidence that the ROC has functioned and continues to function as an independent state. Beijing has cast itself as the aggrieved party aiming to prevent a change in the status quo by "splittists" [*fenlie zhuyizhe*] on Taiwan engaged in "separatist activities" [*fenlie zhuyi de huodong*] in defiance of what it perceives as historical realities and the mandates of international law. It has insisted that the PRC government is the only legitimate government of the Chinese state, of which Taiwan has no option other than to remain a part.[3]

To some extent, this narrative has been persuasive. The prevailing scholarly view holds that the PRC is motivated to subordinate Taiwan to China's sovereignty because of some admixture of concern about Chinese national identity, the unfinished civil war project for national unification disrupted by the onset of the cold war, a commitment to defend China's territorial integrity and sovereignty that had been trammeled by imperialist powers of the past, anxiety about regime legitimacy in an era when popular nationalism has supplanted communism as a unifying and mobilizing ideology, irredentism fueled by what has been casually identified as China's "rising" nationalism,[4] and as a way to prevent Taiwan's persistent autonomy from generating a domino effect in Tibet, Xinjiang, and Inner Mongolia.[5]

To be sure, one can find ample support for these views in PRC sources. Few analysts would question that nationalism, historical grievances, and anxiety about regime legitimacy affect Beijing's calculations about how to deal with Taiwan. However, political convictions in the PRC are not monolithic. A degree of pluralism is discerned in political discourse, albeit bounded by both implicit and explicit constraints. On the matter of Taiwan's status, one can read in PRC sources a diversity of arguments justifying the prevention of Taiwan's "independence" and advocating the importance of unification. Different accounts of the problems associated with Taiwan emphasize causes and consequences of action or inaction differently. Indeed, different professional or institutional vantages appear to incline PRC analysts to highlight different dimensions of the controversy.

Although official statements by PRC government agencies about Taiwan have been dominated by a particular narrative and lexicon, PRC analysts and scholars speak and write with varying degrees of conformity to that set of ideas. Some barely stray from it while others elaborate greatly, drawing on professional expertise and intellectual insight to reach what amounts to the same fundamental conclusion that Taiwan is part of China and ought to be restrained from acting otherwise.

Analysts of the PRC's posture toward Taiwan who examine the problems from outside China come to the issue with their own national, professional, and intellectual orientations. Just as there is a diversity of voices within the PRC aiming to explain Beijing's stance toward Taiwan, so there are legions of analysts outside China who seek to do the same. Consequently, there is no consensus about why Taiwan matters to the PRC.

Indeed, given the highly sensitive nature of the Taiwan issue for the PRC leadership and the propensity for secrecy that dominates the institutional culture of the PRC's central leadership, there are very few people—Chinese or otherwise—who are able to state with authority what motivates the policies Beijing adopts toward Taiwan. Much of what passes as conclusive about the reasoning of the PRC leadership is inferred. Official statements are not accompanied by annotations offering reliable guidance about interpretation any more than actions resulting from policy are accompanied by manuals explaining unambiguously why the state did what it did. Moreover, policy is not the product of a single, internally and eternally consistent body. It results from compromise and contestation among the community empowered to generate decisions. Members of that exclusive community undoubtedly share certain goals, but may also prioritize rationales for those goals differently. Under these conditions, weighting the various factors that are assumed to influence policy may be an exercise in informed speculation. Moreover, rationales advanced by advocates in the PRC with different vantages on the issue may shift in response to perceptions of developments in both domestic and international contexts.

So, much of what one assumes is "known" about the PRC's stance concerning Taiwan is prevailing wisdom that may not correspond as closely as analysts believe to reality. Looking for reasons why the PRC has, since the mid-1990s, increased its use of coercive measures and expanded its range of military options, some analysts have cast the "hard" dimensions of Beijing's strategy as a reaction to the political transformation of Taiwan's domestic politics. One hears from foreign affairs analysts and scholars in the PRC that Beijing's determination to deter independence by threatening to use force is a response to the amplification of calls for independence by Taiwanese nationalists since the 1990s, the implicit or explicit defection of the ROC from the "one China principle," and a variety of political decisions on Taiwan that are read in Beijing as incremental efforts contributing to a permanent separation of Taiwan from China. In sum, Beijing is depicted—in the way it frequently depicts itself—as frustrated, angry, and less-inclined to compromise with Taiwan because of the various ways political leaders in Taipei have, by their own initiatives, invited the PRC's wrath. Beijing's stiffened resolve, coercive diplomacy, use of military force for signaling, and rapid development and deployment of military capabilities devised to influence Taiwan are cast as *reactions* to Taipei's actions.[6]

These interpretations have a degree of validity. As the domestic political transformations of the late 1980s and early 1990s liberated people on Taiwan to contest for political office and express convictions about policy, the *ancien*

Guomindang regime—deplored in its day by Beijing for inveterate hostility to communism—was swept aside at the very juncture when communism
itself was largely swept aside. As formal ideology effectively slipped out of the
cross-Taiwan Strait equation, the predictability that prevailed during Taiwan's
authoritarian era was supplanted by political uncertainty and the emergence of
democracy.[7] This has troubled Beijing. More to the point, the particular course
that Taiwan's democratic development has taken is the source of irritation.

The political leadership on Taiwan has been seen by the PRC as playing up
what are called "ethnic divisions" on the island for electoral gain.[8] Especially
since the DPP took the ROC presidency and control of the government
for the first time in 2000, the PRC has appeared to rue the passage of the
dependable, if detestable, old Guomindang. It, at least, could be counted on
to support the view that Taiwan is a part of China and unification, however
remote the attainment might be, is a desirable objective. Those views have lost
currency even within the Guomindang.

Moreover, Beijing has decried the DPP government for what are seen as
policies devised to "de-Sinify" [*fei Zhongguohua*] Taiwan. The PRC points
with indignation to official actions undertaken since the DPP won the presidency in 2000 that dislodge institutionalized symbolic rhetoric and behavior
that linked Taiwan to China while enhancing emblems of political identity
that are rooted to the notion of the island alone as a polity with a distinct
history and culture. De-Sinification, the PRC scolds, amounts to promoting
independence and resisting reunification.

Hence, the accelerated effort to establish military means to deal with Taiwan
is justified by the PRC as a reaction to behavior on Taiwan that appears to
threaten the vital national interest of unity. It is depicted as an utterly rational response aimed at deterring an outcome—"independence"—that Beijing
would not tolerate.

For all their persuasive power, interpretations that characterize Beijing's
policies toward Taiwan as reactions to perceptions of Taipei have limitations.
For one thing, this approach miscasts the Taiwan problematic exclusively
in terms of competition between the rulers of the PRC and the rulers of
Taiwan, discounting the role of geopolitics and China's anxiety about the
United States and Japan. A secondary shortcoming implicit in this mode of
reasoning is that it frames the conflict about Taiwan's status as one that arose in
1949, when the PRC was established, discounting the role of China's relations
with Taiwan before that moment.

Finally, if one is trying to understand why the PRC's strategy toward
Taiwan has varied and why Beijing has resorted to military threats, there is

merit in thinking comparatively. One has to wonder why the PRC views the threat or use of force as a rational response to its inability to settle the dispute about Taiwan's status when it has settled other territorial disputes in enduring rivalries without an explicit resort to force.[9]

Perhaps, as Paul Huth suggests, domestic pressure on political leaders inclines challenger states such as the PRC to respond in a confrontational manner to what is perceived as a defection from the status quo by target states.[10] If Huth is correct, one must still ask: what is it about a change in the status quo that unleashes this pressure on a challenger state's political leadership? It seems unlikely that any change in the status quo would, ipso facto, warrant a resort to coercive, military means. Some class of actions must induce a greater sense of apprehension than others, impelling the "domestic pressure" to which Huth points. If the confluence of certain conditions excites an urge to employ more coercive tools, including military force, what are those conditions?

Stated differently: In what way does Taiwan's "independence" threaten the PRC? Why is that threat perceived in the PRC as sufficiently grave that the use of military force is perceived by the central leadership as a rational option? It has not always emphasized its capacity to use military force to threaten or harm Taiwan and does not do so uniformly in other territorial disputes.

Indeed, one scarcely risks provoking objection by observing that Beijing has invested far more political capital in pursuit of its claims to Taiwan than it has in most of the territorial disputes it settled with neighbors. Likewise, one would find few to contest the proposition that the PRC has insistently injected into its relations with other states its uncompromising view of China's sovereignty over Taiwan while the PRC's outstanding contests about other territories rarely feature as prominently.

One does not regularly read or hear, for instance, that the future of China's "rise" and development depends on recovering sovereignty over Diaoyutai, the islands in the South China Sea, or the territory that India governs as part of the state of Arunachal Pradesh. Even though the territory that is in dispute on the eastern sector of the Sino-Indian border, south of the McMahon Line, is about equal in area to Taiwan, it does not excite widespread Chinese sentiments of irredentism.[11] In contrast, PRC sources are full of statements that proclaim the importance of reunification with Taiwan for China's broad developmental objectives.

For example, Luo Yuan, a Senior Colonel at the World Military Affairs Research Department of the PLA's Academy of Military Sciences, expresses the view that Taiwan is the key to China's future. He writes that for the development of the Chinese nation, reunification with the island of Taiwan is extremely important. His rationale is geographic and economic. He states:

Only the seas to the east of Taiwan allow China direct access to the great strategic passages of the Pacific. If this opening to the sea is controlled by other countries, China's maritime development strategy will be severely hampered. However, if the two sides of the Strait unify, it is just as likely that it will prompt speedy progress toward the Pacific so that China's maritime development strategy will vigorously flourish and rise and, therefore, in the course of maritime development Taiwan and the mainland will have common interests and the rejuvenation of the Chinese nation will also accelerate.[12]

Senior Colonel Luo is by no means alone in advancing this argument. For some segment of the PRC foreign policy elite, the nexus of geography and strategy—geostrategy—is a vital perspective from which the question of Taiwan's status should be considered. Indeed, Luo's view is representative of a body of literature that links Taiwan to the maritime development of the PRC, to economic prosperity, and to China's future.[13] One hyperbolic text asserts "If Taiwan is independent, China will not only lose the 36,000 square mile island, but the entire Pacific Ocean and half the new century."[14]

Even when stated in more measured terms, arguments in support of unification link the subordination of Taiwan to the future welfare and security of the state in ways that surpass the stated significance of other territorial objectives. For instance, although the PRC erected a colossal digital clock in Tiananmen Square to display a countdown to the retrocession of Hong Kong in 1997 and another to mark Macao's return in 1999, Beijing's triumphalism was not matched by a view that "resuming sovereignty" over either enclave would play much of a role in advancing China's status in the century that was to follow.[15]

That is not to say that the PRC has addressed all territorial disputes in a dispassionate and peaceful manner. The PRC has rattled, drawn, or wielded its saber on numerous occasions associated with contests involving territory. Beyond militarized incidents between the PRC and the ROC that had to do with control of territory, armed conflicts between the PRC and Tibet (1950), India (1962), the Soviet Union (1969), and Vietnam (1979, 1988) were entangled with territorial disputes.[16]

While each of these conflicts prompted inflamed declarations about the importance of sovereignty and the territory at issue, the matter of Taiwan's status has been portrayed by the PRC in an exceptional manner. When it comes to explaining why that is, one courts censure by venturing an account associating the priorities of the state with the perceived value of the territory itself, even though the geostrategic rationale for unification has been a long-standing theme in PRC academic and popular publications.

To be sure, the PRC's decision to prepare military means for dealing with Taiwan is susceptible to analysis from conceptual perspectives that are not tied to geography and territorial salience.[17] For example, Huth and others suggest that political "shocks" of the sort that resulted from Lee Teng-hui's visit to Cornell, the U.S. response to the 1996 PRC missile exercises, the unexpected election in 2000 of Chen Shui-bian, or the even more unexpected reelection of Chen in 2004, affect the strategy and tactics of the challenger state toward the target.[18]

Since the 1990s, broader strategic factors having to do with economic advances by the PRC that coincide with fundamental shifts in the architecture of the international structure of power have affected the PRC's worldview. These transitions have called into question the PRC's relationship to the strategic environment and have prompted Beijing to effectuate a renewed grand strategy. However, these are not "shocks," in the sense of being discrete and unanticipated events that occur with suddenness and are perceived as having significant import on prior calculations of risk and opportunity. They are gradual and fluid developments, the direction and implications of which are slow to materialize and difficult to assimilate with existing apprehensions of China's capabilities and objectives.

As the PRC's worldview evolves, it has aroused in the PRC, as well as beyond it, the reconsideration in new light of the PRC's relationship to existing or potential strategic competitors, notably the United States and Japan. It is striking that as the PRC prepares for the possibility of combat to secure control of Taiwan, the principal opponent that the PRC is girding its loins to fight is not even Taiwan, but the United States as aided by Japan.[19] This prompts one to wonder whether, from Beijing's vantage, a satisfactory resolution of the Taiwan issue is seen as the "ends" or the means to grander strategic ambitions. It also prompts one to see that Beijing's rationale for opposing "independence" and promoting unification has, for the most part, been framed in official documents and statements to reflect only one narrative about China's relationship to Taiwan. PRC analysts offering a geostrategic perspective frame the issue of Taiwan's status in an utterly different fashion. This suggests the need to look beyond the official narrative for clues about the shifting salience of Taiwan.

Bringing the Place Back In

It should be self-evident that control of territory is at stake in the dispute about Taiwan's status.[20] Yet, concepts explored in literature about territorial disputes and geography are underrepresented in studies of this controversy.[21]

A staggering arsenal of theoretical approaches has been deployed to discern the motives of actors in the saga of China's relationship to Taiwan and the dynamics of their interactions, but geography and Taiwan's territorial salience are generally regarded as incidental or irrelevant.[22] Taiwan is often represented as if its sole value to Beijing stems from the identity ascribed to it as an undifferentiated "part of China," rather than as a particular part embedded in a geographical context that has specific physical attributes.

Indeed, where the issue of territory does arise in scholarly considerations, the possibility that it is a driver of PRC policy is frequently assumed away or minimized relative to other factors. The struggle between Beijing and Taipei about Taiwan's metaphorical "international space"—the latitude in which Taiwan is able to function as an international political and economic actor—may attract more analytical reflection than does the battle over geographic space.[23] Yet for some PRC strategists and statesmen, the territorial salience of Taiwan is paramount.

Adopting a geostrategic perspective and bridging the accepted division between what students of international relations and policy do, on one hand, and what students of history do, on the other, it is possible to see that this contest can be examined on an entirely different plane as a battle by the PRC for space as a correlate of power. This line of reasoning flows from a conception of geostrategy as the "strategic application of new and emerging technologies within a framework of geographic, topographic, and positional knowledge."[24] That is to say, strategy is always operationalized as a sequence of tactical steps taken within—and in response to—a geographical context. Shifting attitudes about the development of the PRC and the cultivation of stature in the international arena have led PRC analysts who think in geostrategic terms to appreciate how the subordination of Taiwan serves strategic objectives beyond simply completing the historical mission associated with unification.[25]

As the power of the PRC expands, it has been impelled to influence or control more space as a way to secure its material interests and realize its expectation of greater status. In this context, Taiwan matters not only because of what it is, but because of where it is. Of course, one must be wary of equating the territorial salience of Taiwan solely in terms of certain permanent physical attributes.[26] This leads only to rigid and deterministic explanations of state behavior. Physical attributes of geography may be permanent, but the salience associated with them may not be. Territorial salience should, more properly, be seen as the outgrowth of ever-shifting evaluations of strategic priorities affected by geography's permanent features. Those priorities can

change in response to opportunities and vulnerabilities revealed by technological developments or by other forces that are also in flux. Hence, geostrategic
considerations flow from and feed into a complex evolutionary dynamic.[27]

It is worth noting that the geostrategic salience some PRC analysts attribute to Taiwan is not new. Before the onset of the Chinese civil war, before
the cold war, before the establishment of the PRC and competing claims
to represent China, and before the arousal of a distinct Taiwanese political
identity, Chinese statesmen looked at Taiwan as a natural barrier shielding the
southeastern coast of China from assault by foreign powers. This is why it is
worth considering the contemporary cross-Strait dispute with one eye cast
back on the history of China's relations to Taiwan prior to 1949.

Taiwan: Buffer or Bridgehead?

To reframe the way that the Taiwan issue is regarded, one must dislodge the
notion that the cross-Strait dispute can only be understood as an enduring
bilateral rivalry between the CCP-led government in Beijing and the ROC
government in Taipei. Well before 1949, rulers of China concerned themselves
about the status of Taiwan, ordinarily as an outgrowth of relations with rival
powers that sought to occupy or influence the island. In some measure, these
earlier phases of controversy about the island prefigure the current chapter of
the territorial dispute. Leaders of the PRC are not the first of China's rulers
to regard Taiwan in the sway of a rival power as a potential liability and, in
China's hands, as a strategic asset.

At key moments in the history of China's interaction with other hegemonic powers, Taiwan appears as either a potential bridgehead from which
foreign rivals of China may establish themselves close to China's shores and
adversely affect China's security or as a buffer in China's hands that interposes
a territorial layer of security on China's southeastern coast, a symbolic or
genuine source of defense against non-Chinese adversaries. This is an element
of the contemporary controversy that is overshadowed by a tendency to focus
on the recent past and present, a period dominated by the rhetoric of victimization, nationalism, and patriotism. The preoccupation with political person-
alities, semantic squabbles, and the implications of declaratory policies eclipses
a view of an underlying geopolitical dynamics.

For strategic analysts in the PRC, as it was for those in the Guomindang-
led government of the ROC toward the end of the war with Japan and the
Qing court confronting the onslaught of demands by European profiteers, the
island of Taiwan is perceived as integral to an effort by China to establish a

wider buffer between the southeastern coast and the threats that come by sea. The failure to control Taiwan excites anxieties about vulnerability to avaricious aims—actual or imagined—of China's rivals that might degrade China's national security or affect its access to the sea.

To be sure, in the hands of powers other than China, Taiwan has been a threat. The Dutch used naval power to challenge Ming officials in an effort to open a trading relationship with China and secure a base of operations on Chinese soil. The Ming directed Dutch mariners to Taiwan, which they took in 1624. Representatives of the Dutch East India Company controlled the island until they were overwhelmed by native traders and pirates who, under the command of the Zheng regime, displaced the "red hair barbarians" and, briefly, dominated China's coastal waters. Zheng Chenggong, who engineered the routing of the Dutch, also opposed the Manchu invaders who had established the Qing empire in 1644. He founded on Taiwan a separate kingdom allied to Ming loyalists in China's southeastern coastal provinces.

The Zheng regime survived, in part, on the basis of naval superiority. The Qing conquest was based on mounted, land-based military power. In time, though, the Qing co-opted former Ming naval authorities and cultivated a viable naval force that it turned to its advantage when it eliminated the Zheng strongholds on Taiwan and along China's southeastern coast.

The Qing claim to Taiwan went unchallenged for nearly two centuries. During that time, Britain emerged as the greatest naval power in the Pacific, but was content to establish a post of the East India Trading Company on Taiwan without exerting political control over the island.[28] After the Opium War (1839–42), Britain and other powers were motivated by commercial objectives to use naval prowess to penetrate to China's core, opening to trade riverine ports from which the Qing had tried to keep foreigners. Although Britain did not annex Taiwan, it practically monopolized trade with the island and, until late in the nineteenth century, was the only foreign power to maintain a consulate there.[29] The rapid emergence of Japan at the end of the nineteenth century and its capacity to project military power with the development of a naval fleet swiftly eroded Britain's dominance of the waters.[30]

In 1874, the Japanese launched a punitive military campaign against Taiwan in response to the murder of shipwrecked mariners from the Ryukyu islands by "aboriginal" residents of Taiwan's southern coast. Japan might have taken Taiwan at that time were it not for the intervention of the British who acted on behalf of the still prevailing view that China's territorial integrity served the mutual interest of all trading nations.[31]

A decade later, in the Sino-French War of 1884–85, France sought to supplant China as suzerain power in Indo-China, to which the Chinese put up effective resistance. Yet France demanded that China pay an indemnity, which the Qing court refused to do. This led France to take the Penghu [Pescadores] islands and to attack northern Taiwan, which was a potentially valuable source of coal needed to stoke the furnaces of its ships. At first, Qing defenses on Taiwan were able to deflect France's assault. To increase its pressure on China, France then imposed a naval blockade of Taiwan in October 1884.

Qing naval forces were inferior to France's and, so, could not break the blockade.[32] As a result, China's negotiating posture was severely weakened. However, France found that none of the European powers, and assuredly not Japan, were prepared to support its retention of Taiwan because to do so was to eviscerate the foundation of mutual exploitation of China from which they all benefited.[33] In the end, France did withdraw, reached a settlement with the Qing court, and left Taiwan alone.

The experience, though, highlighted for the Qing its strategic vulnerability and the potential of Taiwan to be employed as a bridgehead by hostile powers. It seems no coincidence that one outcome of the war with France was, on October 12, 1885, the Qing decision to elevate the status of the island from a prefecture of Fujian province and to designate it the twentieth province of China, with its own governor, Liu Mingchuan. Liu subsequently initiated programs to bolster Taiwan's defense capabilities, extend Qing administrative control to parts of the island that had been, theretofore, beyond imperial reach, and improve infrastructure. This seems to have reflected a creeping recognition that with foreign powers looking longingly at the prospect of taking Taiwan, the island had greater strategic significance than had been sufficient to motivate an earlier commitment by the Qing.[34]

Just ten years after that, in the course of negotiating a settlement of the Sino-Japanese War (1894–95) that had focused on competition for control of Korea, Japan used much the same tactic as had France. While Li Hongzhang and the delegation he led from China sat at Shimonoseki to negotiate with Japanese Prime Minister Ito Hirobumi and Foreign Minister Mutsu Munemitsu, Japanese forces attacked Taiwan to ensure that their demand for cession of the island was underscored by a credible threat. In the end, by the Treaty of Shimonoseki, the Qing ceded Taiwan to Japan.

China's twentieth-century leadership was certainly alert to the strategic consequences that flowed from the cession of Taiwan to Japan. For instance, the Japanese assault on Shanghai in 1937 was supported by aerial bombardment by planes that were based on Taiwan.[35] Even American planners, contemplating the prosecution of war against Japan in early 1942, understood the strategic value of the island, writing:

> Formosa in the hands of an unfriendly power, especially a naval power, is a standing threat to the peaceful development and security of the peoples of southeastern Asia and Oceania and to our free intercourse with those peoples so vital to our national well-being.[36]

One facet of the U.S. war against Japan was the bombardment of targets on Taiwan that were of strategic significance to Japan.[37] Indeed, China could not be secured without eradicating the Japanese threat from Taiwan. As plans were made for a division of territorial spoils after the defeat of Japan, Chiang Kai-shek sought to reassert China's sovereignty over Taiwan, an objective he justified, in part, by reference to the island's strategic value to the defense of China's southeastern coast.

After Chiang Kai-shek took refuge on Taiwan in 1949, he came to appreciate the geostrategic value of the island from another perspective, as it served him as a redoubt from which to launch punitive assaults on the mainland, some coordinated with the United States.[38] The CCP leadership, quite anxious about the possibility that the United States would take Taiwan to use as a springboard for nefarious anticommunist activities, was certainly motivated to take Taiwan for strategic reasons as much as for nationalistic ones.[39]

So even in the contemporary era, Taiwan in the hands of a power other than China has functioned as a real and potential threat to China. Indeed, each time the island has been ruled by a power other than the rulers of China, that power was perceived in China as hostile to the authorities on the continent. The rulers of China's continental reaches correctly perceived the Dutch, Zheng, Japanese, and ROC polities as competitors or opponents. The United States, which has deterred a PRC assault on Taiwan since 1950, has likewise been perceived by Beijing as a rival or adversary.

Peter Howarth concludes, "Ever since sea power became a major factor in the international politics of East Asia, the island of Taiwan has had a vital strategic significance. . . . the island has been controlled by the dominant maritime power of the day, or its ally." In that light, the PRC's focus since the 1980s on developing greater sea power—a subject addressed more fully in Chapter 7— may signify the "re-emergence at the beginning of the twenty-first century of the historical pattern of strategic competition between a dominant continental power [the PRC] and the pre-eminent sea power [the United States]."[40]

Limiting consideration of the Taiwan issue to the period after 1949, as so much analysis of this controversy does, one misses a pattern that extends longitudinally beyond the tenure of individual decision makers and across a diversity of political regime types. What a broader historical context reveals is that the impulse to view Taiwan from a geostrategic vantage has recurred, even if contemporary geostrategic concerns do not mirror the particular sensitivities of the past.[41] Contemporary strategists in the PRC appear to have learned, adapted, or rediscovered a perspective about the relationship between geography and security that was the motive for the Qing endeavor to control territory that had not previously been associated with the Chinese realm, an inclination that led to Qing claims to Taiwan.[42]

That is, the boundaries of the Qing—after they were pushed to their maximal point in the eighteenth century—were associated with geographic features that were ascribed with strategic value. Simply, China's civilizational "core," or "homeland," territory was seen by Chinese elite as more secure from foreign incursion when surrounded by lands perceived as buffers. For the most part, those buffer zones were territories populated by non-Han communities and polities into which the Qing expanded from the seventeenth to the eighteenth century. They include Taiwan, which was officially claimed by the Qing in 1684, before which the island had not been associated with the Chinese realm.

Part of the pattern one discerns in looking back before 1949 is that Taiwan is one of those tracts of earth that has existed on the territorial and sovereign margins of competing empires. In addition, Taiwan has never been so long or so firmly in the hands of any power that its status is unambiguous or unchallenged. These are issues to which the text returns in Chapter 3.

Naturally, the way in which Taiwan's place in international history is understood by the foreign policy elites in the PRC affects their attitude toward the cross-Strait dispute. Taiwan was the first piece of China's territory that Japan swallowed in what unfolded as a half-century expansionist meal at China's expense. The geopolitical context for China's dispute with Japan and other aggressive rival powers has been internalized as a "lesson" that Chinese strategists have learned from history and have quite consciously tried to apply to present circumstances. For example, a contemporary text states "For more than one hundred years from the Opium War to the establishment of the PRC, foreign aggressors repeatedly invaded Taiwan, and from there proceeded to the next step to attack the mainland."[43]

Although historians may refute the assertion that since 1839 foreign aggressors "repeatedly invaded Taiwan" and then used it as a bridgehead from which to attack the mainland, Japan was one aggressor that certainly used the island in that way. The belief that Japan's exploitation of Taiwan to violate China fits a pattern beginning in the nineteenth century is probably more relevant to a consideration of Beijing's posture toward Taiwan than is a flawless account of the past. An improved account would endorse the essence of the author's claim that Taiwan was repeatedly invaded by aggressors who used it as a springboard or stepping stone [*tiaoban*] to the mainland.

This history has led some PRC analysts to conclude that insufficient control of Taiwan by China's rulers is a liability that may invite aggression again. To some analysts, Taiwan is as it was in the past, a defensive hedge shielding seven southeastern provinces [*qisheng zhi fanli*] as well as a forward base from which to reach the sea.[44]

For the purpose of clarity, it is important to observe that this should not be read to mean that Chinese views of Taiwan were fixed in the past and transmitted reflexively ever since. Just as aggression against Taiwan was recurring, not constant, the characterization of the island by Chinese as a potential vulnerability has recurred, but is not constant. The salience of Taiwan has shifted over time.

Territorial Salience

States view territory as salient for tangible as well as intangible reasons.[45] Whether territory is seen as salient because it is a source of natural resources and intrinsic geographic features that can be exploited or because of impalpable symbolic value derived from its role in a nationalist narrative, it seems evident that territorial issues enhance the likelihood of conflicts between international actors.[46] When territory, such as Taiwan, is seen as salient for both tangible and intangible reasons, such conflict is even more likely.[47]

For the most part, Taiwan is described as if its principal salience was intangible. Attachment to it in the PRC is a reflection of what David Newman has termed "territorial socialization" as a function of nationalism, "the aim of which is to emphasize the importance of our territory as a key element in our personal and group identity."[48] In the case of Taiwan's place in China's history and Chinese group identity, this is not a rationale that stands up well to scrutiny.

The PRC has emphasized in its declaratory policies the importance of sovereignty, territorial integrity, and national unity—where the nation is "Chinese"—as reasons why it is determined to unify China and Taiwan.[49] These are abstract principles that Beijing asserts as categorical imperatives. If the PRC were as committed to them as it makes itself out to be, one would expect these imperatives to have applied across the range of territorial disputes in which the PRC has been involved. They have not.[50]

Beijing has also deployed a raft of arguments about its attachment to Taiwan that flow from a narrative of China's victimization in the past by foreign powers. Emphasizing matters of international law, morality, and China's primordial association with Taiwan, the PRC has sought to prompt foreign sympathy with its view and mobilize both domestic and international support for its claim. This same reasoning might apply to contested territories that Beijing does not attend to with the same sensitivity that it manifests where Taiwan is at issue.

Indeed, it is difficult to explain the apparent devotion of the Chinese leadership to Taiwan. Why does the blood of PRC leaders stir them to such emotional oaths of fidelity to unification?[51] After all, none of the leaders of the CCP or the PRC were born or raised in Taiwan. There is nothing of national symbolic import associated with the island itself. For Chinese, there is no Lexington or Concord or Gettysburg or Appomattox on Taiwan. There is no sacred mountain, no verdant valley, no tree, no river, nor any stone in Taiwan venerated in China's national mythology, canonical poetry, or long-recited songs and prayers.[52]

Indeed, the irredentist tone of Beijing's claim to Taiwan is not matched by any memory of attachment at all. Taiwan's soil never caked beneath the nails of any community on the mainland that was displaced from the island and has, ever since, longed to return.[53] One cannot explain the fiery commitment to sacrifice all that the PRC has gained in the past decades of material growth and international respectability in terms of the presence on Taiwan of any rich archaeological, architectural, religious, or cultural sites that trigger among the "Chinese people"—in whose name the PRC leadership claims to act—fervent sentiments of national pride or yearning. Taipei is *not* China's Jerusalem.

If sovereignty, an abstraction, is the motive, should it not motivate the PRC to see all contested territory as equally valued? If defending territorial integrity is the impetus, what explains the PRC's willingness to give up certain tracts while it defends others? Both within and outside the PRC, analysts comment often that Taiwan's "loss" during the Chinese civil war makes it essential that Beijing recover sovereignty over the island. Yet, if the ambition to defend sovereignty and territorial integrity determines the PRC's attitude toward contested territory, what difference does it make *when* the territory was put beyond China's grasp? What difference does it make who inhabits the territory?

The idea that Taiwan's "Chinese" population makes it more salient to the PRC than, say, uninhabited islands or territory inhabited largely by non-Han is not persuasive. After all, the PRC did fight to secure Tibet (1950), which was not populated by Han Chinese, and allowed Hong Kong and Macao—which are populated primarily by Han Chinese—to remain under foreign domination until the late 1990s.

More importantly, the identity of Taiwan as "Chinese" territory has precariously shallow roots. Despite the effort of the PRC to make it appear that Taiwan has been important to China since antiquity, about which more is said in the next chapter, for most of China's history Taiwan was unknown in China. In the sixteenth and seventeenth centuries, it entered the national consciousness as a frontier and was, even after being incorporated as a prefecture of Fujian province, only partially explored.

Indeed, not until the late 1870s did Chinese cartographers produce relatively accurate maps of the whole island.[54] Naturally, statesmen are not known for their fealty to conclusions about the past derived from a dispassionate consideration of evidence. So it is entirely likely that policy makers and the functionaries who serve them believe to be true what historians would tell them is not. Even so, the symbolic, inferred, intangible rationales matter, but they do not tell the whole story.

A comparative view of the PRC's territorial dispute behavior makes clear that unification is not motivated exclusively by a concern about unifying a *people* that is divided. It is, rather, a determination to resist the dispossession by others of land that China believes to be its own. The inhabitants of Taiwan do not matter so much as the land they inhabit. Having the island is not nearly as important as preventing others from having it. Ethnic geography is not nearly as relevant to this dispute as is national geography—the contours of territory that are assumed to constitute the state.

The attachment to Taiwan, though, is not simply an outgrowth of rationales based on intangible measures of salience. It may be more accurate—even if more complex—to recognize that different perspectives about the island coexist in the PRC. Some advocates of unification may emphasize intangible reasons for pursuing unification while others highlight more tangible indices of Taiwan's salience. As David Newman suggests, "concrete and symbolic manifestations of territory constitute a single system in which each feeds into, and reinforces, the other."[55]

So, for example, "groups that desire to retain control over territory for symbolic and historic reasons use some form of strategic and/or resource discourse as a means of backing up their claim" and to give it wider popular appeal.[56] More significantly, as in the Taiwan case, those who see the territory in question primarily from the vantage of security may justify their policy preferences in terms that they feel may be more widely embraced, focusing on symbolic and emotional reasons why the state ought to control the territory in question.

While Newman's notion offers a plausible interpretation of the Chinese situation, equally likely is that proponents of unification are not nearly so dichotomized or instrumental as the advocacy groups are in his framework. It is possible that Chinese political elites who favor unification entertain both tangible and intangible rationales for seeing unity as desirable. This need not be a case where there are sentimental nationalists and dispassionate realists, all of whom advance distinct but converging arguments to justify unification.

That said, the literature about the cross-Strait controversy is dominated by consideration of the intangible reasons why the PRC views Taiwan as salient. Reframing the conflict about Taiwan in terms suggested by the literature on territorial disputes highlights the utility of thinking about the perceived tangible value of the island and its salience relative to that of other territory. It encourages one to consider how the evaluation of territory with particular geographic attributes interacts with social factors, such as a perception of advantage or vulnerability, in ascriptions of salience that vary over time.

So thinking about why states perceive some territory to be highly salient, or how the views of a given tract may evolve, is an approach to understanding why some territorial disputes result in violence and others do not. Alone, theoretical insights derived from studies of territorial disputes cannot account for all the reasons why the PRC is determined to extend sovereignty to Taiwan. However, a failure to account for the territorial dimension of the dispute is to overlook an elemental motive: geography.[57]

Geography, Geopolitics, and Strategic Advantage

Geography, which examines the physical attributes of the earth as they affect and are affected by human endeavors, has much to contribute to an appreciation of territorial salience and, therefore, to conflict about territory. Yet, this approach has occupied only the margins of analytical discourse about Taiwan's significance to China. Perhaps the neglect of geographic indices of territorial salience reflects disesteem for geographic determinism resulting, as an overreaction to an irrational extreme, in a suspicion about the pertinence of geography.[58] That geography cannot explain everything about the state's motives for action is not reason to assume it explains nothing about those motives. Geography does not determine the strategic ambitions or policies of a state, but it does condition the choices made by policy makers, presenting both opportunities and constraints.[59]

For Chinese, a hierarchy has long existed in which "China proper" is differentiated from frontier or peripheral territories. "China proper" [*neidi*] is embraced as the primordial homeland of the Han Chinese. Lands accreted to China, most recently during the Qing, were seen as *bianwai* [beyond the boundary], or *bianjiang* [border area, frontier], or on the periphery [*zhoubian*]. They were encompassed into the Chinese realm as a buffer between China and hostile neighbors or because the lands were inhabited by hostile neighbors on whose pacification and subordination the Qing sense of security depended.[60]

As Tu Wei-ming writes, "Educated Chinese know reflexively what China proper refers to" and are deeply imbued with the idea that "geopolitical China evolved through a long process centering around a definable core."[61] Taiwan, though, was never part of that definable core. It was swept into the Chinese orbit only after Dutch and Spanish aggressors expressed interest in its potential as a base from which they might engage China in international commerce, gaining advantage over the Portuguese who occupied Macao.

The interest of the foreign powers in Taiwan resulted from technological developments that made globe-spanning commercial interactions both possible and profitable. Students of geography understand that technological development enhances material capabilities that can reveal new opportunities for the exploitation of territory, as well as new vulnerabilities against which defenses must be mounted.[62] The evolution of seafaring technology facilitated the exposure of European mariners to Taiwan and, in the context of commercial rivalries played out in the Pacific as extensions of political rivalries played out at home, prompted them to recognize the island's potential. European challenges to Qing notions of space and security impelled the court to adjust its own evaluation of the island.

That changes in technology necessitate a reevaluation of territorial salience is not a notion with purchase in the age of exploration only. This phenomenon is as relevant to the present as it ever was in the past. Skeptics who argue that geography and, therefore, geopolitics are no longer a concern relevant to international interactions because technology has overcome distance may be tilting at analytical straw men.[63] For one thing, the territorial salience of any given tract of earth is not fixed. For another, even "sophisticated" weaponry and "modern" military hardware must be deployed somewhere. Space, distance, and location all matter as they did in the past, even if they matter in very different ways than they once did.

Beyond that, access to and domination of geographic domains as an index of capability still contribute to power and, therefore, international status.[64]

This, at least, is the way Chinese analysts have expressed themselves on the issue. Access to and the domination of a maritime province still matter to states—such as the PRC—with oceanic ambitions and, therefore, can enhance the strategic salience of certain territory.[65] Territorial buffers are still valued, and strategic rivals still jostle for access to and control of potential bridge-heads. Such rivalries to exploit the geographic advantage of territory are matters of geopolitics, a factor that commands considerable attention in analyses offered by PRC scholars.[66]

In addition to technological change as an incentive to reevaluate the salience of territory, changes in the architecture of the international system also affect perceptions of territorial utility. Thinking about the influence of changes in the international system falls within the preserve of international history, which calls on one to apprehend evolving trends that outlive particular regimes and that exist beyond the history of any given state.

Changes in systemic architecture may be seen primarily as the waxing and waning of power held by international actors and the accommodations that this dynamic induces. More to the point, when power—the hard, measurable variety that states generate and project by military means—is depleted, developed, or deployed, it must be thought of as having geographic consequences. Power is wielded in places.[67] Changes in the international system can, to a large degree, be mapped onto territory. Just as the loss of regime power frequently involves the loss of territorial control, states seeking power grapple, as they must, with the questions, "Where do you use it? Why there?"[68]

This is the foundation of a geostrategic perspective. Competition for natural resources, advantageous avenues for transit and communication, the defense of sovereignty over national territory, and the search for advantage over present or potential rivals prompt thoughts about what territory must be controlled to satisfy those objectives. Policies devised to enhance the strategic utility of geography are geostrategic.[69] Geostrategic concerns are ordinarily linked, directly or indirectly, to perceptions of national security.

The value of Taiwan as a particular piece of territory is tied to perceptions in the PRC that geopolitical factors having to do with Beijing's competition with other powers make control of the island an essential variable affecting the security and welfare of the state. The involvement—interference—of the United States and Japan, among other states, is said to "embody a deep geostrategic objective [*baohanzhe shenkede diyuan zhanlüe mudi*]."[70] Analysts who adopt this perspective address the issue of Taiwan as a matter extending beyond the context of an intra-Chinese struggle for supremacy. The Taiwan issue is not just about nationalism and civil conflict. From a geostrategic perspective, the PRC's strategic advantage is enhanced by control of the island and its strategic vulnerability exacerbated so long as Taiwan remains beyond its grasp.

From a geostrategic perspective, the benefit to the PRC of subordinating Taiwan is not measured, as "resuming sovereignty" over Hong Kong and Macao was, exclusively in terms of a psychic salve to wounded national pride. In the case of Taiwan, unification is important because of ways the island fits into what Emma Teng identifies as an "imagined geography" of China.[71] How the island is imagined to fit into that geographical arena is the subject of the following chapters.

The People's Republic of Qing?

Historical Considerations: *Bu Lun, Bu Lei*

Taiwan is one of those tracts of earth that has a "history of ambiguity."[1] It has changed hands repeatedly and has been the focus of recurring struggles over identity, sovereignty, and control. For the most part, since the seventeenth century, it has "been defined as a small part of something else."[2] Taiwan, as Steven Phillips notes, has been administered as an overseas possession of a European power (1624–1661), an independent kingdom (1661–1683), a prefecture of a province (1684–1885), a province of an empire (1885–1895), a colony of a rival empire (1895–1945), and a province of a republic (1945–1949).

Since 1949, Taiwan has been the sole province claimed by a republic—the PRC—that does not exercise effective control over the island while simultaneously exercising effective control over every other province of China it claims. From 1949 to 1991, Taiwan was also the only province governed by a republic—the ROC—that claimed, but did not exercise effective control over, all of China's territory. In 1991, the ROC effectively backed away from its claim to be the government of all China and accepted that "the mainland area is now under the control of Chinese communists."[3] While it did not formally renounce sovereignty over Chinese territory it does not govern, the ROC government adopted statutes and constitutional amendments that flow from the premise that its legitimacy as a government is limited to Taiwan, Penghu, Jinmen, Mazu, "and any other area under the effective control of the Government."[4]

Since then, Taiwan's already complicated identity became more ambiguous. It has been governed as an autonomous state that no longer maintains any pretense of exercising sovereignty over the rest of China, even though it is still claimed by the PRC as "a small part of something else." Meanwhile, Taiwan has refrained from formally renouncing sovereignty over all China because to do so would signal Beijing that the government in Taipei disavows Taiwan's putative identity as part of China, a step Beijing asserts may warrant a military response.[5]

One reason why the rivalry over Taiwan has been so intractable is that Taiwan has not sat firmly within the territorial domain of any hegemonic power.[6] Control of Taiwan changed hands five times in the course of four centuries—six times, if one considers the transition from authoritarian rule to democracy in the late 1980s as equivalent to a change of regime. Each of those transactions imposed on the rulers of China the need to recalibrate their relationship to the island. When the island was held by the Dutch, by the Zheng regime, and by Japan, Ming and Qing officials were compelled to deal with Taiwan as an extension of their relationship to those other powers. While the ROC exercises sovereignty over Taiwan, the PRC's posture toward the island since 1949 has been affected by Beijing's relationship to the United States, which has effectively subsumed Taiwan into its own sphere of influence and effectively guaranteed the security of the island from assault by the PRC.

Considering that the PRC and the United States have been engaged in a decades-long rivalry, the geostrategic features of their animosities and competition have affected the PRC's view of Taiwan's salience. Just as one would not study the history of PRC relations to Mongolia, Xinjiang, or Tibet without taking account of the Sino-Soviet or Sino-Indian rivalries, this volume highlights the importance of seeing the cross-Strait relationship in the context of Sino-U.S. rivalry. Although rivalry is not expressed equally in all dimensions of the relationship between the United States and the PRC, nor equally at all moments of the relationship, on the matter of Taiwan's status there has been more competition between Washington and Beijing than collaboration.

Considering that the United States is only the latest power to draw Taiwan into its orbit, it is also important to set the present controversy against the backdrop of the past. Reviewing the history of Qing and Republican Chinese interactions with Taiwan reveals that the geostrategic salience of the island was evident to Manchu rulers, to Chiang Kai-shek, Mao Zedong, Deng Xiaoping, and others in their ruling cohorts.

The contemporary manifestation of the controversy about Taiwan's status should be, but ordinarily is not, considered as one phase in a long history of China's relationship to the island.[7] For most of China's recorded history, the Chinese elite was largely unaware that the island even existed. It was not on the frontier, it was beyond it.[8] It became part of a contested frontier only in the sixteenth century, when European maritime competition for commercial outposts in the Pacific encroached on the Ming realm. How Taiwan came to be part of China and why it was, nevertheless, contested territory are important elements in the historical narrative that have ramifications for one's understanding of the present controversy.

The Taiwan issue also should be, but ordinarily is not, considered in the context of Qing imperialism. The Qing motives for subordinating Taiwan are

in some manner particular to Taiwan, but also reflect patterns in Qing strategic behavior that deserve notice. Geography played a role then, as it does now,
in conditioning perceptions of strategic imperatives and options.

Obviously, leaders of states are unlikely to replicate strategic choices made
by their political antecedents precisely. A pattern, though, does not emerge
exclusively from events or behavior that repeats identically. Perceptions of
comparability may be sufficient to prompt the conclusion that a pattern exists.
Analogous thinking based on perceptions of comparability underlies lessons
that policy makers learn from history.[9]

Taiwan was accreted to the Qing empire, extracted by Japan from the
empire, returned to China after World War II, and then drawn into the orbit
of the United States in 1950. As with other rivalries for hegemonic power,
expansion and contraction were manifested territorially in a dynamic dance
of dominance and displacement. The power of one empire swelled over conquered terrain at the expense of another power that was vanquished or forced
to withdraw from the contested space. Politically interstitial places located at
the fringes of competing realms became the medium of exchange, the site of
contestation, and one measure of imperialist growth or decay. Taiwan was such
a place. For the PRC, these geopolitical considerations are not only matters of
the past, but are still relevant to the issue of Taiwan's status.

With the foregoing in mind, this chapter examines aspects of international
history that may be seen as establishing a pattern of strategic thought by rulers of China about control of Taiwan. It begins with a consideration of how
Taiwan was swept into the Qing orbit and concludes with a review of how
Taiwan was sucked out. Highlighting details of the territorial rivalry between
the Qing and other regional powers enables one to see that from the vantage of the PRC, the geopolitical dynamics of the contemporary controversy
about Taiwan have historical analogues.

Drawing the "Mental Map" of China

Prevailing wisdom holds that the PRC, like the ROC before it, claims "the
former Qing frontiers, and not the narrower boundaries of the Ming, make
up the 'natural' extent, or sacred space, of the Chinese nation."[10] Accordingly,
the Chinese state created in the twentieth century "nearly reconstituted the
empire of its ancestors of two hundred years past."[11] Chinese nationalists have
essentially "made the Qianlong emperor (reg. 1736–1795) one of the fathers
of their country" by claiming as China's most of the territories that his campaigns of conquest brought into the Qing domain.[12]

Two questions arise from these propositions equating China's territory with that of the Qing dynasty. First, what exactly is meant by "China"? Laura Hostetler notes that one version of the Kangxi Map Atlas of 1721 [*Fenfu Zhongguo quantu*] distinguished between that territory the Manchus regarded as comprising the Qing empire and the smaller portion of territory within that multinational empire that was regarded as China proper.[13] That is, China was during the Qing a portion of a larger empire. Pamela Crossley observes that the effort by Chinese nationalists of the twentieth century to inherit the boundaries of the Qing is ironic, given the "meticulousness with which Qing imperial ideology objectified China as a province of the empire."[14]

That the Manchus viewed their conquest of China, Mongolia, Turkestan [Xinjiang], and Tibet as part of a colonial enterprise is underscored by the different modes by which these territories were administered. It is telling that these four regions were not administered by the central bureaucracy as Chinese provinces were, but by the *Lifanyuan* [Court of Colonial Affairs].[15] The point is that China was depicted in some maps as a substantial portion of an empire encompassing other territories.

However, it was not consistently depicted in that manner. Hostetler writes of other versions of the Kangxi Map Atlas that "make China and other parts of the Qing empire appear as one coterminous entity—when in fact they were distinct administrative and cultural spheres."[16] The ROC and the PRC that followed have ignored the distinction between China as colonized territory and the Qing empire that colonized it, preferring to represent China as a nation state encompassing the "Chinese people" and the lands that China has occupied since "ancient times," even though some of those lands have only been associated with China since the Qing dynasty.[17] Thus, like the ROC of the past, the PRC today sees itself "as a 'multinationality' state that represents the culmination of millennia of Chinese imperial history."[18] Chinese nationalists, whether allied with the CCP or the Guomindang, "turn a particular moment of imperial expansion—the maximal borders attained by the Qing empire in the mid-eighteenth century—into ideal boundaries defining a timeless national culture."[19]

One reason that the PRC, like the ROC before, seeks to inhabit the domain carved out of Asia by the Manchu dynasty is because space is equated with power. Chinese rulers since the start of the twentieth century have been motivated by a collective revulsion at how China was brought low by foreign powers that chewed at China's territorial immensity. As S. C. M. Paine concludes, both the PRC and Soviet Union accepted the great power status of their imperial forebears as part of the new national identity they established in the twentieth century. For both the Qing and Romanov dynasties, dominating vast territories was seen as a marker of greatness and regime legitimacy. After economic and political decline in both China and Russia, restoring the territorial reach of the empires supplanted in revolution was embraced by the ROC and the Soviet Union as evidence of legitimacy and revived national stature.[20]

This leads one to a second, more pressing question: What precisely were the boundaries of the Qing empire that the PRC is now assumed to inhabit or claim a right to inhabit? Put differently, how can one assert that the ROC and then the PRC inherited the boundaries of the Qing empire when those boundaries were not, themselves, stable?

Qing territory waxed during the seventeenth and eighteenth centuries, but waned from the nineteenth to the collapse of the dynasty in the early twentieth century. To state that the PRC now inhabits the territories of the Qing is misleading. The PRC inhabits much of the territory that the Qing dominated at the zenith of empire, but not all of it. A more precise way of characterizing the rationale for the PRC's mental map of China is to consider Michael Hunt's observation that Ming and Qing rulers operated from a comparable "territorial agenda that is still extant. They controlled a core cultural area that roughly corresponds to today's, and at the same time identified and, by the middle Qing, secured those peripheral areas important to the security of the core."[21] This highlights the geostrategic rationale for Qing expansion. The Qing imperialist enterprise was not haphazard, but emerged from what Perdue describes as a project "to eliminate the ambiguous frontier zone and replace it with a clearly defined border through military control, commercial integration, and diplomatic negotiations with border states."[22] This was a reflection of a strategic culture in which the Manchu "ruling elite saw itself as engaged in a large-scale geopolitical competition" with neighboring rivals.[23]

While the Qing may be credited with transforming China through treaties and interactions with other powers from an "empire surrounded by borderlands of ambiguous status into a 'bordered land.' . . . It left China's maritime frontier largely undefined."[24] In the case of Taiwan, the dominant motive for expansion was not security, per se, but "take it or it will be taken." The Qing decision to take the island was justified by a policy of strategic denial intended to ensure that Taiwan did not fall into hostile, foreign hands and then become a threat to security.

The urge to enhance power and bolster security by expanding territorial control to buffer regions surrounding the heartland resulted in the subjugation of historically or potentially threatening populations on the original periphery.[25] Naturally, the cost of subduing those threats on the original periphery and asserting dominion over them was a greatly extended boundary across which lay new potentially threatening neighbors against which the enlarged and often overextended empire had thereafter to defend itself.[26]

Indeed, just beyond the edge of newly established boundaries, the Qing confronted avaricious rivals. The destabilizing internal challenges of the Taiping kingdom, among other political uprisings, were compounded by the predatory ambitions of the Russian, Japanese, and European states, each expansionist in its own way. These foreign powers grasped at and intruded into the Qing realm, exacerbating the empire's loss of power, options, and control. By the end of the Qing, much of the once peripheral territory that had been brought into the empire in the seventeenth and eighteenth centuries—Taiwan included—had fallen under the influence of rival powers, chiefly Russia and Japan.

By the twentieth century, Chinese viewed as "lost territory" [shi di] the lands now identified as the southern half of the Khabarovsky Krai, the entire Jewish Autonomous Region, the southern portion of the Amurskaya Oblast, the Chitinskaya Oblast—including the Aginsky Buryatsky Autonomous Region, a sliver of the Republic of Buryatia bounded by the southeastern half of Lake Baikal, and the panhandle bordering Mongolia, all of which were reluctantly ceded to Russia in 1858. In addition, Sakhalin Island, the Primorsky Krai [Maritime Province] bordering the Sea of Japan was just as unhappily ceded to Russia in 1860. Territory China viewed as lost to Japan includes the entire Korean peninsula over which China had suzerainty, the Ryukyu islands with which it had a tributary relationship, Taiwan, and the Penghu islands.

Before getting too deeply into the matter of what was lost and how this relates to the PRC's stance on territorial disputes, it is worth observing how it was that territory beyond China's putative boundaries came to be associated with China to begin with. Peter Perdue argues that this expansion by the Qing "represents a sharp break with the strategic aims and military capabilities of the Ming dynasty." However, Qing statesmen and historians "masked the radical implications of their achievements" to make it appear that the Qing was acting to fulfill a unifying enterprise mandated by heaven and consistent with Chinese beliefs about civilizational supremacy.[27]

Twentieth-century Chinese nationalists, out of zeal or ignorance, "built on the legacy left by Qing official historians to create the version of China's history that predominates today."[28] Exposing deficiencies in the PRC's stated rationale for claiming Taiwan should alert readers to the importance of reaching beyond Beijing's declaratory policies and ritualized narrative of disunity for evidence of motives that inform its strategy toward the Taiwan problematic.

From Frontier to Fujian: The Qing Conquest of Taiwan

The process of imperialist, hegemonic accretion is relevant to the status of Taiwan. It was a process that can be understood best by setting the subordination of Taiwan into the international history of Asia. The strategic calculus of the Qing was demonstrably geopolitical, in that the court was acutely conscious of the territorial dimension of power and the competition with rivals for control of space.

Taiwan had long been viewed as beyond the sphere of the known by those who recorded on maps and in documents a worldview of relevance to the politics of the Chinese state. It was distant enough from China's shores to be regarded as an uncultivated, savage frontier.[29] Until the sixteenth century, the island was home only to several tribal populations associated with speakers of Austronesian languages, but not to Han Chinese.[30] The fierce reputation earned by some of these tribes for brutalizing shipwrecked mariners, reinforced by fantastic reports of the untamed terrain in which they dwelled, helped to ensure that few Chinese sought direct exposure to what was assumed to be a harsh and uninviting place.

By the middle of the sixteenth century, though, economic opportunity, as well as "push" factors along the southeast coast of China, impelled profit seekers to flout Ming regulations restricting seagoing ventures and to enter into the vibrant oceanic trade that entangled Japanese, Southeast Asian, European, and, increasingly, Chinese merchants into the skein of commercial interactions.[31] The Ming court eased restrictions on maritime activities in the 1550s, partly because enforcement of the prohibition was so ineffective and aroused such resistance, and seagoing enterprises expanded. Still, as late as the seventeenth century, Taiwan remained "on the outer edge of Chinese consciousness and activity, with little or no permanent Chinese settlement, visited only by fishermen, smugglers, and pirates, and only dimly reflected in the discussions and records of the officials who administered and patrolled the South China coast."[32]

As the Portuguese, Spanish, Dutch, and English competed for access to commodities on the great islands and coastal territories bordering the Pacific, they plied the oceans in search of competitive advantage. By 1510, Portuguese had established themselves in Goa and, by 1511, in Malacca. They reached the Chinese coast by 1513, but were repulsed by Ming forces. Ultimately, in 1553, they prevailed on the Ming to grant them permission to establish storehouses on a spit of land that, in time, became the Portuguese possession of Macao.[33]

Traversing the waters between Macao and Japan in pursuit of commerce, Portuguese mariners are said to have recorded the location of Taiwan, which was identified at least as early as 1554 on a planisphere—a map of the world—created by the Portuguese cartographer, Lopo Homem, as *J. Fermosa*.[34] The term *fermosa* is an indication that to those who reported its location, the island appeared beautiful.[35] Taiwan was by no means the first place that Portuguese cartographers labeled *fermosa*, and not the last.[36] Yet, until late in the twentieth century, Taiwan was widely known in the Western world as Formosa.[37]

Evidence of Chinese voyages to and interaction with the people of Taiwan emerges from the late sixteenth century.[38] China's impetus to claim Taiwan as its own, though, came slowly and was not determined by the explorations of Chinese entrepreneurs and fortune hunters, but in response to incursions by foreigners.

While the first Europeans to identify the island were Portuguese, the first to reach its shores were Dutch. In 1604, Dutch Admiral Van Warwijk, bound for Macao with the intention of challenging Portugal's monopoly on trade with China, was put off course by a typhoon and took shelter in the Penghu islands, west of Taiwan, in the Taiwan Strait. There he initiated negotiations with authorities in Fujian province to establish commercial relations, but was firmly rebuffed and directed to consider trading from the coast of Taiwan.[39] After a show of force by a fleet of Chinese warships, Van Warwijk sailed to India and, after failing in a second effort to open trading relations in 1607, the Dutch were not heard from again for fifteen years.

What the Ming court did not know, though, is that they were not simply being pestered to trade by a single impetuous Dutch seaman. The Ming was up against a global juggernaut determined to establish trade as a mode of empowerment that was aimed, in part, at fending off the hegemonic domination in Europe by Spain.[40] While geopolitical inclinations certainly affected Ming strategy toward continental rivals, strategists at court evidently missed the implications of the European maritime enterprises until it was too late.

In 1622, another Dutch seaman, Cornelius Reyersz, led six ships on a campaign to force his way into Macao. His attempt to break Portuguese defenses failed, but he did succeed in irritating Chinese officials who undoubtedly were displeased by unseemly Dutch efforts to batter their way into a trading relationship. Reyersz sailed to the Penghu islands where he occupied one island to establish a small fort built by impressed Chinese laborers. From there, the Dutch sought to pressure the Ming empire to agree to trade. Negotiations were undertaken and, by the end of 1623, "an agreement was reached by which the Dutch were to remove to Formosa, the Chinese were to supply them with as much merchandise as they desired, and furthermore five junks laden with silk and other goods accompanied by a Chinese official were to be dispatched to Batavia."[41]

An incident then occurred that reinforced the mistrust that each had of the other. "Two sampans loaded with inflammables" were set on fire and destroyed two of five Dutch ships at anchor in the "Chinchoo" River. James Davidson implies this was sabotage. The three remaining Dutch ships then sailed back toward to the Penghu islands, destroying Chinese ships in their way. Shortly after their return, a Chinese armada blockaded the Dutch position and threatened war if the Dutch did not decamp and move to Taiwan.[42]

John Wills describes this as an effort by the Ming to repel the Dutch from the Penghu islands, regarded as imperial territory, and willingness to consider a trading relationship with them from Taiwan. His account implies that the Penghu islands were viewed by the Chinese as within China's territory and therefore settlements of foreigners were not welcome. Taiwan was outside of China, but near enough that the Dutch demand for trade might be accommodated, and so the Ming was prepared to assent to trade if the Dutch were operating from an "offshore" location (see Figure 1 on page xvii).[43]

Davidson writes that "A formal cession of the island was now made, which, considering that the Chinese had no right to it and never claimed any, was probably not a heart-rending task for them."[44] The Dutch did, in August 1624, sail for Taiwan where they established themselves near what is now Tainan.[45] They immediately set about building fortifications that were to serve as the base from which they would extend their authority and power to dominate the southeastern two-thirds of the island, west of the central mountain range.[46]

From the 1620s, the Dutch widened their jurisdiction until they had, in essence, colonized much of the western plains of the island.[47] Spanish settlers defied the Dutch claim to dominate the island and established fortifications and trading works in what are now the northern cities of Danshui [Tamshui] and Jilong [Keelung]. However, in 1642, they were defeated by the Dutch and rousted from Taiwan. Thereafter, the Dutch were able to enlarge the sphere of their control over the island and were, for a time, undisputed lords of Taiwan.

In 1644, Ming China was conquered by the Manchus, who absorbed Chinese territories into the expanding Qing empire. There were, though, Ming loyalists unwilling to acquiesce to a change of regimes. One such resister was Zheng Chenggong, the son of a Japanese woman and a powerful Chinese merchant whose large, private—some say pirate—fleet commanded China's southeast coast as the Ming empire was deteriorating. Zheng opposed the Qing by helping to defend territory in southeastern China held by a Ming prince who honored Zheng with the moniker, *Guoxingye*, meaning "lord who bears the imperial surname." The Dutch romanized this title as Koxinga, the name by which Zheng Chenggong has been known in the West.[48]

While Zheng was ultimately repulsed by the Qing from his base in Xiamen, along the coast of Fujian, he and his considerable forces sought to establish a new base of power on Taiwan. Zheng's father had been among those Chinese traders who made Taiwan a foundation of his empire even before the Dutch had set themselves up there. Indeed, Zheng's father was instrumental in serving the Ming to broker a deal with the Dutch.[49] So, when Zheng Chenggong arrived off the coast of Taiwan on April 30, 1661, with more than 25,000 men in hundreds of ships, he declared that his father had "lent" the Dutch the island and now he, Zheng Chenggong, had come to "reclaim it." After a vain effort to defend their holdings, the Dutch sued for peace and negotiated a settlement with Zheng that allowed them to evacuate without further penalty.[50] Thus ended the Dutch colonization of Taiwan.[51]

Although Zheng Chenggong died the next year, from 1661 to 1683 Taiwan was governed as a separate kingdom by the Zheng family. The Qing never acquiesced in this, nor did the Dutch—who assembled a fleet in 1662 intending to retake Taiwan after Zheng's death.[52] The Dutch forces were repulsed by Zheng Qing, Zheng Chenggong's son and ultimate successor, and so returned in 1663 to urge the governor of Fujian to assist in the expulsion of the Zheng regime from Taiwan. To this the governor agreed—but apparently to use the Dutch armada only to aid in his own effort to roust the Zheng forces from Fujian, which was accomplished without restoring the Dutch to Taiwan.[53]

The Qing sought to suppress the Zheng regime and eradicate its influence over Taiwan and the southern coastal waters of China. The Qing forbid contact with Taiwan, although trade continued surreptitiously. The Qing also turned to Shi Lang, who had himself defected from Zheng Chenggong's forces and "was one of the very few maritime experts in the very continental early Ch'ing [Qing]."[54]

After two aborted attempts to assault the island in 1664 and 1665, the Qing entered into negotiations with the Zheng regime to seek its subordination in some form of suzerain relationship with the Qing court. Wills writes, "But there was no precedent since the Five Dynasties for permitting tributary autonomy of a regime of Han Chinese language and culture." Among other stumbling blocks, the Zheng regime had "legitimized itself as part of the Ming loyalist resistance," it continued to refer to the passage of years in terms of the reign of Ming, not Qing, emperors, and was demanding as part of the settlement that leaders of the Zheng regime would not be required to shave their foreheads and braid a queue or be transferred to the mainland.[55] Efforts to reach a settlement were for naught.

Zheng Qing established a thriving trade with Siam, Japan, the Philippines, and invited the British East India Company to establish a presence on the island.[56] When three southern feudatories rose in 1673 to rebel against the Qing, Zheng Qing expanded his own foothold on the coast, reasserting control over coastal Fujian, and by the end of the decade dominating a wide swath of the southeastern coast.[57] The rebellion prompted the Qing to respond in force and, by 1680, it had suppressed the uprising and driven Zheng Qing from Xiamen, from whence he retreated to Taiwan on March 26 of that year.[58]

Finally, the Qing was determined to eliminate the Zheng regime and any further vulnerability to its autonomous, seaborne military. Zheng Qing died in 1682 and was succeeded by a twelve-year-old son, Zheng Chenggong's grandson.[59] Shi Lang was dispatched to force the surrender of the Zheng regime. He managed to wrest the Penghu islands from the Zheng forces in July 1683, and thereafter the will of the Taiwan-based forces was broken. Negotiations for surrender ensued. In the end, the Zheng rulers were compelled to reverse their stance of the 1660s in resistance to the queue or transfer to the mainland. The Qing coiffeur was imposed, and the last heir to Zheng Chenggong was invested in a respectable, but meaningless, dukedom on the mainland.[60]

Shi Lang and the Geostrategic Salience of Taiwan

Late in 1683, there was debate at court concerning the future of Taiwan. The emperor, evidently, was unimpressed by the island that had been taken in his name and disinclined to assert his sovereignty over the territory. The *Veritable Records of the Kangxi Emperor* document his response to news that the Zheng regime had been defeated. He dismissed the importance of it, commenting "Taiwan is a place beyond the seas; it is of no consequence to us." As to the idea of incorporating the island into his empire, Kangxi is recorded as saying that Taiwan "is no bigger than a ball of mud. We gain nothing by possessing it, and it would be no loss if we did not acquire it."[61]

Most officials were of the view that the purpose of the expedition commanded by Shi Lang—to eradicate the threat posed by the Ming loyalists serving the Zheng regime—had been accomplished with the surrender of the regime. There was little advantage in expending additional resources to maintain a garrison on the island. From the vantage of the court, and perhaps in the minds of China's literati, Taiwan was remote, uncivilized, and inconsequential. One official summarized the prevailing view, saying "if we were to take the land, it would not even be worth plowing; if we were to take the people, we could not even make officials out of them."[62]

Shi Lang, though, argued that the island would be a threat to the security of China's coast were it not acquired and that there was sufficient bounty on the island that the cost of garrisoning it would be amply met. He viewed Taiwan as advantageous for both economic and strategic reasons. His geostrategic rationale is especially telling. He had already approached the Dutch and knew that they might be interested in purchasing the option of reoccupying Taiwan. So, Shi argued that a failure by the Emperor to take the island as China's would leave open the possibility that it might be taken by potentially hostile powers and might again serve as a redoubt for disorderly pirates and criminals. To compensate for the costs associated with incorporating the island into the Qing empire, Shi reasoned that the court could reduce the garrisons along the southeast coast and transfer some of the troops there to Taiwan. That is, Shi sought to expand the outer perimeter of the empire from the southeast coast to Taiwan.[63]

This, then, might be dubbed the Shi Lang doctrine: an autonomous Taiwan that does not subordinate itself to China is a vulnerability because it might attract malcontents from the mainland and serve as the base for rebellion against China's rulers or because it will fall into the hands or under the sway of a rival, sovereign power.[64] A Taiwan that has been subordinated to the Chinese state is a strategically significant forward outpost of defense, shielding the rich southeastern belly of China's territories and offering China a capacity to project its own power beyond into vital sea routes. The geostrategic calculus casts the island of Taiwan as either a buffer or a bridgehead.

The reasoning advanced by Shi Lang in 1683 stemmed in part from a shrewd lucidity about geopolitics and economics. Taiwan was too close to China's coast to be allowed to remain autonomous when the waters were teeming with naval and commercial rivals. The strategy of maritime defense demanded that China secure the island for itself. Left unclaimed, Taiwan would only attract another hegemonic power that would, in all likelihood, be a threat to China.

It is impossible to know what, specifically, swayed the court, but in 1684 Taiwan was declared the ninth prefecture of Fujian province.[65] Perhaps it was Shi Lang's strategic argument. Whether or not geopolitics was foremost in the Kangxi Emperor's mind, though, it is now evident that Shi Lang's argument was quite prescient, as the subsequent history of China's relations to Taiwan illustrates.[66]

In any event, it seems the court hoped to prevent the island from becoming a haven for rebels and, so, imposed a partial quarantine as a way of curbing migration to the island.[67] It had already repatriated 40,000 of Zheng's troops, many of whom were presumably relieved to depart the harsh conditions on Taiwan and be bound for home on the mainland. Regulations concerning maritime activities also directed that men without wives or property on Taiwan were to return to Fujian; others were required to register with Qing authorities. These impositions dramatically reduced the Chinese population of Taiwan by the end of 1684.[68]

Emma Teng argues that the prevailing view of Taiwan inherited from the Ming was "that it was 'beyond the seas' (haiwai); and . . . that it belonged to a realm known as 'Wilderness' (huangfu)."[69] The term *beyond the seas* was not simply descriptive, but also a revealing metaphor. China was conceptualized by its literati as a domain largely bounded by natural features. Descriptions of Taiwan reinforced a notion of the island lying outside the domain of China. Moreover, one official participating in the debate about Taiwan's future is recorded to have said, erroneously, "since antiquity, no oceanic islands have ever entered the Imperial domain." In gazetteers, Taiwan was described as "faraway overseas," "hanging alone beyond the seas," "an isolated island surrounded by ocean," or "far off on the edge of the oceans."[70]

Just as the earth was imagined in Europe to be flat and the realm beyond it home to monstrous beings, so the Chinese literati conjured images of what lay beyond the security of China's civilized and heavenly designated provinces. Primordial savagery coupled with fantastic qualities were among the attributes that China's literary and mythological traditions associated with lands that were "overseas" generally and with Taiwan, specifically. The men and beasts inhabiting such places were imagined—because there was little actual contact—to be essentially uncultivated, uncivilized, and utterly unlike Chinese. As European cartographers graphically portrayed on maps the demons that lurked on the edges of the known and inspired terror in her mariners whose journeys took them close to the edge, Chinese cartographers represented on their maps the wild places located "beyond the seas."[71]

As to the notion that Taiwan was in the realm of "wilderness," Teng notes that the received wisdom of canonical texts such as the "Tribute of Yu" depict the world as comprising concentric zones centered on and radiating from the imperial capital of China, which is the apex of civilization.[72] Beyond that zone is a "domain of feudal princes and lords," and then, with increasing degrees of crudeness, zones of "pacification," "allied barbarians," and "wilderness."[73]

Teng makes the case that negligible contact with Taiwan and scant knowledge of it contributed to the view that it was an untamed frontier. Indeed, "the name 'Taiwan' did not even appear in Chinese sources until late Ming."[74]

It did not figure prominently in the histories of China and was not among the tributary states that reinforced China's sense of cosmological order.[75] However, in stating his case that Taiwan should be annexed by the Kangxi emperor, Shi Lang sought to dislodge the notion of Taiwan as beyond the cosmological sphere of civility and argued that Taiwan was situated in such a way as to offer China protection from threats beyond. He proposed that Taiwan be seen as a "hedgerow," buffering the southeastern provinces of China from the ravages of oceanic menaces.[76]

According to Teng, "Qing texts frequently employed the terms 'entering the map' [ru bantu] or 'entering the map and records' [ru tuji] to denote Taiwan's incorporation into the Qing empire."[77] In one respect, this was literal because theretofore, Taiwan was not depicted on maps of China.[78] Official Qing statements exulted in this event, as they did when Xinjiang was incorporated in 1759, as testament to the Qing's expansion beyond the limits of the Ming.[79] That the territory was to be depicted on the map had symbolic import, as the map was esteemed as a tangible representation of imperial domain.[80]

In the two centuries from 1684—when the Qing dynasty designated the island a prefecture of Fujian province—to 1874—when Japan announced its intention to attack that portion of the island that it asserted was not under Qing control, the Qing claim to Taiwan was essentially unchallenged. It would be a mistake, though, to conclude that the Qing controlled all of Taiwan or that its claim that the island was part of the empire equates with a contemporary claim of sovereignty. What Japan's contention in 1874 exposed was that the Qing exercised only nominal control over Taiwan during the preceding two centuries.[81] Even Chinese maps of the eighteenth and nineteenth centuries illustrate well the point that to the east of Taiwan's central mountain range lay a coastline that China's cartographers did not chart until after Taiwan had been ceded to Japan. That is, much of Taiwan was unknown to the Qing even after 200 years of ostensible rule because the regime had not entirely subdued or co-opted the preexisting "aboriginal" population that inhabited the mountains and eastern shores. Ultimately, it was friction arising from contact with those aboriginals that Japan used as a pretext to attack Taiwan and with that undermine the Qing claim to the entire island.

When the Qing began to establish a governing structure on Taiwan in the last decades of the seventeenth century, it encountered fierce resistance from the aboriginal population that actively contested the efforts of the Qing to impose administrative control. Consequently, throughout the eighteenth century and into the nineteenth, the Qing maintained an internal border between that portion of the island in the western plains over which it had established control and that portion in the mountainous central region and on the east coast where it could not. Thus, maps of Taiwan until 1880 showed an island with a clear and well-charted western coastline and an ambiguous and imprecise midline frontier, indicating that the territory inhabited by Han was limited to the western sector, and the central and eastern portions of the island were underexplored and virtually inaccessible to the Qing.[82]

It is not just that Taiwan was gradually assimilated into cartographic and documentary records of the late seventeenth and early eighteenth centuries, but that references to the island were consistent with Shi Lang's vision of its strategic salience. Teng finds frequent references to the notion of Taiwan as a protective barrier—"a 'hedgerow' for China, or a 'Great Wall for the ocean frontier,' as supporters of annexation had hoped it would be." She cites, as examples, *The Record of the Naval Defenses of Fujian Province* [*Fujian Haifangzhi*], in which it is written that Taiwan "extends from the northeast to the southwest like a standing screen; it is the outer boundary for China's four [coastal] provinces." A gazetteer of 1696 describes Taiwan as "the outer barricade for Fujian province. All its mountains face China proper."[83] Teng points out that in the decades immediately following annexation, Taiwan's central mountain chain was often shown on maps as providing a "natural barrier protecting the Chinese coast from outside forces." Moreover, maps of the Kangxi era represent Taiwan from the vantage of the Chinese coast. These images of the island from the west looking east toward Taiwan's central mountain range coupled with textual references to the island as hedgerow "reified the metaphor of Taiwan as a fence." So, concludes Teng, "where the sea had once served as the boundary between the Chinese domain and the realm beyond the pale, the island of Taiwan itself now served as this boundary."[84]

In this formulation, Taiwan is not "Chinese" in the sense of being territory deeply enmeshed in the national consciousness. It became China's for instrumental, geostrategic purposes long after the concept of China's territorial heartland had been established in the minds of Chinese elite. Even into the twentieth century, the prevailing image of Taiwan as something other than fully Chinese persisted.[85]

Taiwan was not the only territory that the Qing took for instrumental purposes associated with aggrandizement and security. This is why Beijing's contemporary declaratory policy about the history of China's relationship to Taiwan should be seen in the broader context of the Qing acquisition—and then loss—of once peripheral territories. The acquisitive phase, which lasted from the early seventeenth to the mid-eighteenth century and the disintegrative phase that lasted until the end of the dynasty in 1911, may be understood in terms of an international history of competition and friction between empires in Asia and the Pacific. Taiwan and other territories were taken as the Qing expanded and lost as it contracted.[86]

The proximate cause for the Qing acquisition of Taiwan was friction with the Zheng regime, a major irritant, perhaps, but a minor threat to the core interests of the Manchu empire. However, if Shi Lang's dialogue with the Kangxi emperor and his lieutenants is any indication, it was not concern about the just defeated Zheng regime that lie at the heart of the rationale to acquire the island, but the principle of strategic denial as it pertained to the Dutch or other foreign maritime powers—including pirates and rebels. So, the zero-sum calculus of imperial expansion to contested frontiers may have swayed the court. This was not a dynamic limited to the subordination of Taiwan. It was the strategic response of the Qing toward the frontier.

Japan's Territorial Encroachment on the Qing Domain

Just as Qing expansion was the territorial manifestation of competition for supremacy with rival political regimes, the Qing dominion ebbed in response to surges by other acquisitive powers. Long before Taiwan was pried from the Qing empire by Japan in 1895, it was evident that the Japanese had their eyes on the island. Toyotomi Hideyoshi tried without success to compel Taiwan to pay tribute to Japan in 1593, and the *bakufu* government attempted in vain to occupy Taiwan in 1609 and 1616.[87]

Japan's effort to take Taiwan was entwined in the complexities of Sino-Japanese rivalry for the loyalties of the small insular kingdom on the Ryukyu islands.[88] For more than four centuries, from 1429 until 1879, Ryukyu was an independent kingdom that maintained tributary relations with China. In 1609, uneasy relations between Ryukyu and Japan prompted the Tokugawa *bakufu* to authorize forces from the Satsuma clan in southern Kyushu to invade Ryukyu. Thereafter, the Satsuma *daimyo* was permitted to tax Ryukyu, while the Tokugawa shogunate granted the island kingdom a high degree of autonomy and the appearance of independence. In this way, Japan refrained from directly challenging China's tributary relationship with the islands and exploited commercial privileges that were the outgrowth of Ryukyu's tribute-bearing status.

As a small kingdom accustomed to playing—and paying—off greater powers, Ryukyu established diplomatic relations with the Qing in 1649, even though it remained loyal to the Ming until 1663.[89] Japan was eager to avoid conflict with the powerful Qing empire and just as eager to avoid sacrificing the golden Ryukyu goose through which it was able to conduct trade indirectly with China.[90] So, Japan sought to conceal from the Qing its suzerain influence over Ryukyu. Whether the Qing court was deceived or not, it did not then challenge the island kingdom regarding its relationship to Japan.[91]

In 1871, two hundred twenty-two years after Ryukyu established diplomatic relations with the Qing, a ship from one of the Ryukyu islands—Miyako—was wrecked off the coast of Taiwan.[92] Fifty-four of sixty-six surviving mariners were then reportedly killed by aborigines on Taiwan.[93] Evidently, between 1701 and 1876, there were fifty-three ships from Ryukyu wrecked off the coast of Taiwan. Many had received relief from the Chinese authorities, but the crews of other ships were killed by aborigines as was the crew of the 1871 wreck.[94] While Ryukyu officials themselves did nothing to protest the fate of their compatriots, Japanese officials saw in the incident of 1871 an opportunity to act on behalf of Ryukyu as a means to assert their sovereignty over the islands.[95]

In September, 1872, four years after the Meiji Restoration, the emperor of Japan abolished the Satsuma-dominated prefectural status of Ryukyu and formally subsumed the islands under Japan's mantle, making the king of the island kingdom a peer in the Japanese empire.[96] This was the first step in Japan's effort to vitiate the subordination of Ryukyu to China and to assert Japan's sovereignty over the archipelago.[97] The Japanese government notified the governments of the United States, France, and the Netherlands that it had transferred jurisdiction over the Ryukyu islands to the newly established Japanese Foreign Ministry. The unilateral action resulted from the expansionist policy of the foreign minister, Soejima Taneomi, who was unconcerned that China still asserted suzerainty over the islands and that the people of Ryukyu themselves were not disposed to becoming subjects of Japan.[98]

Japan assured Washington that the Compact of Friendship and Commerce that Commodore Matthew Perry had reached with the Ryukyu kingdom in 1854 would be honored.[99] With the loss of the Miyako ship fresh in mind, Japan also inquired about a punitive expedition that the United States had launched in 1867 after the American ship, Rover, was wrecked off the Taiwan coast and its mariners killed by Taiwan's aborigines.[100] The Japanese were much impressed by the U.S. action as a precedent for their own response to the killing of the Ryukyu crewmen, a strategy that was urged on them by the former American consul in Xiamen [Amoy], General Charles William LeGendre.

LeGendre had played a role in the American follow-up to the murder of the Rover's crew and fancied himself an authority on Taiwan. He marketed his services to the Japanese in anticipation of being rewarded with high office as governor of Taiwan, if the Japanese succeeded in subduing the island and asserting their sovereignty over it.[101] To that end, LeGendre persuaded his Japanese interlocutors that with a mere 2,000 men, they could take Taiwan.[102]

Japan's machinations to take control of Taiwan can probably be traced to this moment. In Soejima's effort to persuade his superiors of the viability of his plan to annex Taiwan, he wrote:

> I am entirely confident that I can get the southern portion of Taiwan by negotiation, if that is all we desire. In order to take the whole island, we may have to resort to military force, but that is difficult to determine at this point. If we take the southern part now, I think that, by means of diplomacy, I will be able to gain the whole island within four or five years.[103]

Evidently, Soejima—on advice from LeGendre—expected to put Japan's grievances before the Chinese, anticipating their response that the aboriginal population that had committed the atrocities was beyond the administrative reach of the Chinese authorities on Taiwan and, therefore, that China was not responsible. Soejima then planned to parlay that acknowledgment of China's impotence in the face of repeated misconduct by the aboriginal population to an admission that sovereignty over that portion of Taiwan was not in China's hands.[104]

In 1873, Soejima—with a new appointment to ambassadorial rank—headed a delegation to China to discuss, inter alia, the matter of Taiwan's aborigines and murder of the Ryukyu crew. While the Soejima mission had several objectives, on June 21, two of Soejima's subordinates, Yanagihara Zenko and Tei Ei-nei, were sent by Soejima to the *Zongli Yamen* [*Tsungli Yamen,* foreign affairs office of the late Qing] to deal directly with the issue of Taiwan and the murdered sailors from Ryukyu.[105]

For reasons that remain subject to dispute, the Chinese officials of the Zongli Yamen apparently neglected to maintain a written record of their discussions with the two Japanese envoys. The Japanese record, therefore, is the only one that offers an account of what was said.[106] According to that account, when Yanagihara addressed the killing of sailors from Ryukyu, he presented the event as the murder of *Japanese,* not Ryukyu, subjects. He then said of Taiwan's aborigines:

> Therefore, the Japanese government intends, in the near future, to send a punitive expedition against them. But since the aboriginal area is adjacent to territory ruled by the Chinese government, our ambassador thought it best to inform you before our government takes action, lest it might cause the slightest disturbance to your territory or cause suspicions on your part and thereby jeopardize the peaceful relations between our two empires.[107]

Presented with Japan's protest, the Chinese said that they had "heard only of a massacre of Ryukyuans, not of Japanese, and quickly noted that Ryukyu was a Chinese possession," a tributary state for hundreds of years.[108]

The Japanese envoys disputed the characterization of the Ryukyu islands, saying that all residents of the islands were Japanese subjects. Yanagihara questioned the Chinese about the court's failure to restrain Taiwan's aborigines and was told that Taiwan was home to two types of aborigines, those "cooked savages" within the Chinese jurisdiction and "those 'raw barbarians' who were beyond Chinese cultural influence."[109]

Yanagihara then insinuated a threat that encapsulates the reasons why China's rulers from the Qing to the present have seen strategic value in Taiwan. Yanagihara expressed his view that the barbarism of the Taiwan aborigines had affected shipwrecked mariners from several states for several years. If the aborigines were not brought to heel, he warned, the situation would invite foreign occupation of Taiwan, an eventuality that would not serve well the interests of either China or Japan.[110]

Whether disingenuously or not, the Japanese envoy evidently reported this exchange to Soejima as one in which the Chinese did not dispute Japan's sovereignty over the Ryukyu islands and also acknowledged China's lack of control over the aboriginal population. In a letter of June 29, Soejima wrote to Japan's prime minister that the Zongli Yamen had confirmed that "Chinese political rule did not extend to the aboriginal area of Formosa and the aborigines were beyond the pale of Chinese civilization."[111] Thus, he concluded that the Chinese did not dispute Japan's sovereignty over Ryukyu nor oppose Japan's plan for a punitive expedition to Taiwan.[112]

However, Japan did not instantly launch an invasion. It was not until after a vessel from Oda province was later shipwrecked off Taiwan and its crew brutalized by the aborigines that Japan sent an expedition to exact retribution.[113] The expedition to Taiwan sailed in April 1874, and when China learned of the invasion by Japan, it set about to register its objections.

Both China and Japan were eager to avoid a direct military confrontation and, in August, negotiations were initiated in Beijing.[114] While an agreement was reached about Taiwan in October 1874, the text did not resolve the issue of sovereignty over Ryukyu and on that matter was, perhaps, deliberately ambiguous. Japan has chosen to see the text as a renunciation by China of its suzerain relationship to Ryukyu. China, in contrast, views the text as referring exclusively to Japan's acts in response to the wreck of the ship from Oda, not the one from Ryukyu and, therefore, having nothing at all to do with China's claim of suzerainty over Ryukyu.[115]

Indeed, Li Hongzhang, who signed the treaty of 1874 on behalf of China, wrote in 1879 that the Chinese officials had made evident their view that Ryukyu was a Chinese dependency and "the maltreatment of the Ryukyuan shipwreckers [sic] was therefore China's internal affair, and that China would consider punishing the Taiwan aborigines accordingly. What has this to do with the Japanese?"[116]

By 1879, though, the Japanese government made Ryukyu its business by formally annexing the islands.[117] China protested this action and sought to internationalize it, involving former U.S. President Ulysses S. Grant who, traveling as a private citizen to Asia, was asked to serve as an intermediary between the Chinese court and the Japanese emperor. Li Hongzhang laid out for Grant the Chinese claim to the islands and explained that the Ryukyu chain had great strategic importance to China "as a screen off the coast of China and predicted that Japanese absorption of the Liuchius [Ryukyus] would mean eventual loss of Formosa."[118] Li's characterization of the Ryukyu islands flows from a spatial conception that has persisted through Qing and postimperial history.

After hearing out Japanese statesmen in Tokyo, Grant provided only neutral advice that the Chinese should "withdraw certain offensive correspondence which had been addressed officially to the Japanese government," that they and the Japanese consider appointing commissioners to resolve the dispute, and that the two parties not allow foreign interference to complicate the controversy.[119] Japan's annexation remained unchallenged, and the Ryukyu islands remained in Japan's hands until 1945, when they were occupied by the United States.

For Japan, taking the Ryukyu islands in 1879 was, as Li Hongzhang had envisaged, a prelude to taking Taiwan. In the intervening years, Taiwan was implicated in the Sino-French War of 1884–85, when France sought to assert itself in Indochina, displacing the Qing. Blockading and then attacking Taiwan was intended by France to pressure the Qing to accept French demands affecting Indochina. While the French tactic succeeded, it also aroused Qing concerns about the vulnerability and strategic necessity of defending Taiwan. Since the *Rover* incident of 1867, an inadequate naval presence and weak defense of Taiwan had cost the Qing prestige and power measured in both symbolic and territorial terms. While the interaction with France stimulated the Qing to see reason to bolster its presence on and control of Taiwan, in the end the court's response was too little, too late.

Japan's expansionist ambitions prompted conflict about control of the Korean peninsula that resulted in the Sino-Japanese War of 1894–95. The Qing was ill-prepared to defend its interests, rapidly vanquished, and compelled to negotiate utterly prostrate before a triumphant Japan. The conflict had not been about Taiwan, but as an outgrowth of imperialist inclinations, Japan saw the island as low-hanging territorial fruit.[120]

The impetus to include Taiwan on a list of demands that stemmed from a war about Korea emerged from the competition between the Japanese army, dominant in the Korean sphere, and the Japanese navy. While the army was pressing Prime Minister Ito to insist that the Qing court lease the Liaodong peninsula to Japan, high-ranking naval officers who had been involved in Japan's punitive expedition against Taiwan in 1874 had risen in influence by 1895 and were able to impress on Ito their belief that unless Japan took Taiwan, some other foreign power would. The prospect of Taiwan in the hands of a maritime competitor made the Japanese naval strategists anxious about the security of the Ryukyu islands and southwestern Japan.[121] Consequently, although the treaty concluding the war was the subject of substantial negotiations, Japan's demand that the Qing cede Taiwan was unaffected.

The Treaty of Shimonoseki was signed on April 17, 1895, by plenipotentiaries representing Japan and the Qing empire.[122] However, there was a period thereafter when it was not clear whether the Guangxu emperor would ratify it. From the vantage of the Qing court, the cession of Taiwan was odious, but was only one aspect of a treaty that in its entirety was viewed as a merciless abomination imposed by the victorious Japan on the vanquished Qing empire.[123]

Once the terms were publicized, the court received 130 memorials signed by more than 2,500 officials who petitioned the emperor to refrain from ratifying the document.[124] Kang Youwei and his disciple Liang Qichao drafted a "candidates' memorial" [gongche shangshu] that was signed by 1,300 candidates for the metropolitan degree who urged, among other things, that the emperor fight Japan to recover the lost territories. Admittedly, this effort was motivated primarily out of patriotic frustration at the humbling of China by Japan and not out of any visceral association with Taiwan, per se.[125] In the same period, Russian, French, and German envoys made known their opposition to the treaty, but they were focused on the cession of the Liaodong peninsula to Japan. Taiwan, it seems, was of less interest to them.

Li Hongzhang, deeply conscious of how he was to be lambasted for failing to extract better terms from Japan, sent John Watson Foster to Beijing on his behalf. Foster, a former U.S. secretary of state who was engaged to accompany Li to Shimonoseki and had served as a counselor to Li throughout the negotiations, was dispatched to urge the Council of Ministers at Court to see the necessity of ratifying the treaty. He argued, in fact, that a failure to ratify the treaty would erode the emperor's credibility internationally. Hence, on May 8, the Qing ratified the document. Shortly afterward, Japan succumbed to the "triple intervention" by Germany, Russia, and France urging that it give up its aim of seizing the Liaodong peninsula. Accordingly, on May 10, the Japanese emperor issued an imperial rescript, retroceding the territory to the Qing.[126] Japan's insistence on taking Taiwan was unaffected.

On Taiwan, elements of the local gentry disgusted by the weakness of the Manchu court and determined to avoid falling into the clutches of Japan took matters into their own hands, staging an insurrection. Court-appointed "authorities had been imprisoned or banished," and local officials worked, in vain, in hopes of attracting a comparable international intervention opposed to the annexation of the island by Japan.[127]

Gentry from Taiwan approached Britain about the possibility of protect-ing the island from Japan in exchange for exclusive rights to develop min-eral resources on Taiwan. A British commercial consortium led by Jardine, Matheson and Co. did, in fact, consider purchasing the island, and the Taiwan gentry advocated that it do so, permitting the Qing to retain only nomi-nal sovereignty.[128] Evaluating the merits of the island, British strategists con-cluded that with Hong Kong and Zhoushan already in hand, Taiwan provided only marginal additional value to the British Pacific commercial enterprise.[129] Although it might have acted if the island were ceded to France or Germany, Britain saw no reason to object to China's cession of Taiwan to Japan.[130]

On May 20, having been disappointed by the British, Taiwan's gentry approached France, hoping it would rise to Taiwan's defense. When France, too, turned aside the pleas from Taiwan, the gentry declared that Taiwan was an inde-pendent republic in a desperate effort to forestall the annexation by Japan.[131]

Britain's decision to refrain from intervening to protect Taiwan from ces-sion to Japan suggests that the island changed hands as naval hegemony was passing from one power to another. That British military and political strate-gists in London saw no advantage in taking Taiwan may have been one indi-cation that Britain's rule of the Pacific waves was waning. Beyond that, the mutual restraint that was the foundation of the "cooperative policy" that had kept the foreign powers in check and helped to maintain China's territorial integrity had frayed to the point of snapping.[132]

Evidently, Li Hongzhang felt his negotiating hand had been strengthened by the "triple intervention" and the uprising on Taiwan. Foster writes that "The Viceroy [Li Hongzhang], contrary to my advice, sought to make these occurrences an excuse to delay the transfer [of Taiwan], and telegraphed [Japan's Prime Minister] Ito asking that the subject be included in the negoti-ations respecting Lioutung [sic]."[133] In his diary for May 13, Foster writes that Li Hongzhang told him that China wanted to reopen the question of Taiwan's cession. Foster records, "I told Viceroy [Li Hongzhang] duty of China to go forward and execute Treaty in good faith—advice not very welcome."[134]

To drive home its displeasure with Li Hongzhang, the court assigned to Li's son, Li Jingfeng, the unhappy duty of sailing to Taiwan to effect the transfer of sovereignty to Japan. Considering the insurrection on the island and the distemper its proponents directed at Qing officals, Li feared for his son's safety and implored John Foster to accompany him. Thus, on June 2, 1895, Li Jingfeng, accompanied by Foster, dispatched the obligation of transferring sovereignty of the island to Japan.[135] Taiwan had gone from being China's strategic buffer in 1684—a natural barrier to menaces from the seas—to Japan's bridgehead in 1895, a first foothold in an expansionist venture that would decimate Chinese sovereignty in the first half of the twentieth century.

Conclusion

Chronicles of the cross-Strait dispute ordinarily begin with the ROC-CCP rivalry of the 1940s and, occasionally, peek back at the cession of Taiwan to Japan in 1895 and, more rarely, review the Qing history of interaction with the island dating to the early seventeenth century. Most analyses of the contemporary controversy focus on the cross-Strait dispute as if it were bounded by a logic and history that is separate from China's contest over other territories and over the island prior to 1950. It is not.

The expansion and contraction of Qing boundaries—not only in the Pacific, but also with respect to Manchuria, Xinjiang, and Tibet, among other spots— enable one to see the accretion and loss of territory as a geostrategic concern that became a powerful element in the nationalist narrative of twentieth-century China. That has had implications for the PRC's attitude toward Taiwan, as well as for other contested territories. This reinforces the suggestion that Taiwan is not simply an object of bilateral dispute between Beijing and Taipei that emerged from the Chinese civil war, but is perceived by some analysts in the PRC as a struggle for security and power in the context of an enduring rivalry with the United States for hegemonic influence in the Pacific.

States take space in the belief that security flows partially from distance, but also because control of contested territory is one index of comparative power, just as the loss of control is one measure of comparative weakness. States, to say nothing of empires, do not sacrifice territory gladly, and a national leadership customarily experiences the loss as a degradation of security and prestige. The Qing was strong enough to take Taiwan from the Zheng regime and hold it in the face of rivals who were described by Shi Lang as "drooling" over it.[136] However, the loss of Taiwan in 1895, during the long fragmentation of the Manchu empire, was then perceived as devastating. One surmises that the Qing would have resisted Japan's incursion had it the power to do so. As it happened, Japan's imperialist growth coincided with and exacerbated Qing imperialist contraction. Taiwan was one territorial emblem of Japanese expansionism and Qing enervation.

Shifting Salience (I)
From Nationalist Indifference to Geostrategic Imperative

Nationalist Indifference to Taiwan

The anxiety, shame, and frustration that motivated diplomatic machinations to retain Taiwan as part of the Qing empire before the ultimate satisfaction of treaty obligations on June 2, 1895, was followed after the cession of Taiwan by a puzzling phenomenon of distancing. Taiwan, it seems, was not simply "lost" to Japan, but expunged from the ruling elite's mental map of China.

In the final two weeks before the June 2, 1895, handover, the Qing court explicitly forbid the transfer of arms, supplies, and troops from Chinese territory on the mainland to Taiwan. Naturally, these steps were taken in accordance with the Qing's obligations under the Treaty of Shimonoseki. However, despite vigorous resistance to Japan's occupation that persisted on Taiwan for five months after the cession of the island, the Qing court disavowed interest in the fate of the island, turned its back on local efforts to fight Japanese occupation, and resumed diplomatic relations with Japan on June 22.[1] Whether the Qing foreign policy establishment perceived no responsibility or was simply overwhelmed by a sense of futility in the face of Japan's superior military power is hard to know.

Considering Taiwan's significance to Chinese politics since the mid-twentieth century, one might expect that Taiwan was viewed by Chinese elites as irredenta since 1895, but after the island was ceded to Japan, its identity as part of China appears to have slipped from their consciousness. Perhaps the loss of Taiwan was overshadowed in emotional and political significance by the implications of Japan's continued intrusion into the Chinese realm, the erosion and eventual extinguishing of Qing control, and the postimperial jockeying for dominance of the Chinese republic. Whatever the reasons, for nearly fifty years after 1895, Chinese elites seemed to have accepted as irrevocable the loss of Taiwan.[2] In the 1930s, by which time Japan's broader territorial ambitions were manifest, Taiwan was regarded by the ROC as a "bad precedent in

Sino-Japanese relations that must not be repeated in the case of Manchuria."[3] Nevertheless, "no Chinese government—Qing Empire, Nationalist Republic, or Communist Soviet—had a realistic chance of restoring sovereignty over the island, and no leader of these entities made Taiwan a major issue in domestic politics or relations with Japan. Simply put . . . few politicians even considered the island, much less devoted resources to its return."[4]

This condition changed only during the second Sino-Japanese War of 1937–45, known in China as the War of Resistance against Japan. Working from the premise that all nationalist narratives are constructed and contested, Phillips writes that the justification for seeing Taiwan as part of China is one that was very consciously fabricated in the last years of the war. Chiang Kai-shek and stalwarts of the ruling Nationalist Party who had theretofore appeared unconcerned about the status of Taiwan, built an argument that the island was indeed Chinese on the basis of five central points, all of which were subsequently inherited by the PRC. These are:

1. "racial solidarity" [xuetong] that asserts a coincidence of Han Chinese commonality and unitary Chinese rule;

2. original sovereignty—that Taiwan has been part of China since antiquity;

3. the illegitimacy of "unequal treaties" demanding the abandonment of Chinese territory;

4. the binding legal character of international agreements, such as the declarations at Cairo (1943) and Potsdam (1945), that endorsed the retrocession of Taiwan;[5] and

5. the self-identification of Taiwan's population with China.[6]

According to Phillips, "the One-China position of the People's Republic of China differs little from that developed by the Nationalists" in the early 1940s.[7]

The decision to claim Taiwan was made sometime in 1942, after Japan's attack on Pearl Harbor in December 1941 and the declaration of war by the United States. The entrance of the United States into the war and the prospect of a transition in the balance of power in Asia may have encouraged China's leaders to envisage for the first time that Japan would be defeated. It may have inspired them to consider how the projection of American naval power into the Pacific and the dissolution of Japan's empire would affect China's security and status after the war.[8] Before that moment, though, the public attitude of Chinese Nationalist leaders toward Taiwan can only be characterized as indifference.

Sun Yat-sen and the Neglect of Taiwan

Sun Yat-sen was the Abrahamic ideological progenitor of both the Nationalist and the Communist parties. His conceptual legacy runs through the nationalist veins of both parties, making the two civil war adversaries appear even more like the fraternal combatants that they were, both descended from the same "national father." Despite the subsequent struggle between the two parties over control of territory—especially Taiwan—and despite the searing animosity the leadership of both parties later developed toward Japan, Sun evidently was prepared to countenance collaboration with Japan to overthrow the Qing dynasty even if that meant ceding to Japan additional territory. Indeed, Sun was so intent on supplanting the Qing, that the status of Taiwan was inconsequential and not, evidently, among those matters with which he was concerned.

When in September 1900, Sun visited Taiwan, local opponents of Japanese colonialism were still locked in an armed struggle against Japan, and yet Sun apparently did not make any efforts to meet with activists on Taiwan who were fighting to alleviate colonialism.[9] After the overthrow of the Qing, one might have expected that Sun would have asserted a Chinese claim to Taiwan. However, it appears he was indifferent toward the island.

In 1917, Sun published a ten-chapter volume entitled *The Vital Problem of China* in which he vigorously argues that China should not enter World War I then raging on the side of the Allied powers, but remain neutral. In the course of his elaborate argument, Sun makes clear his contemptuous view of those powers that had despoiled China's sovereignty. He writes that "China has ceded the richest areas in the Heilongkiang [Heilongjiang] Valley to Russia; Burma and Hongkong to Britain; Indo-China to France; and Formosa [Taiwan] to Japan."[10] He recounts the extensive territorial concessions to foreign powers that were demanded of China, resulting in leased territories that further desecrated China's sense of territorial integrity. He then writes about spheres of influence extended by various foreign states:

> British influence extends over Tibet, Szechwan [Sichuan] and the Yangtze [Yangzi] Valley, representing approximately 28 per cent. of the whole of China, Russian influence extends over Outer Mongolia, Sinkiang [Xinjiang] and North Manchuria, representing approximately 42 per cent. of the whole of China; French influence extends over Yunnan and Kwangsi [Guangxi], and Japanese influence extends over South Manchuria, Eastern Outer Mongolia, Shantung [Shandong] and Fukien [Fujian]. The areas under French and Japanese influence each represent over 5 per cent. of the entire Chinese territory.[11]

Sun apparently regrets, but does not contest, the cession of those territories in the first list. There, Taiwan is equated with Burma and Vietnam, neither of which have been the subject of anything more irredentist than comparatively limited boundary disputes. Sun's second list, though, describes territories that are part of China over which other states hold sway. He even goes so far as to quantify the percentage of China's territory so influenced. It is remarkable that Taiwan is not mentioned in this list.

Yet, Sun writes with resolve that China may appear (in 1917) complacent vis-à-vis Japan "because she has at present no alternative but to wait for the day when she may obtain foreign assistance to avenge the injuries which she has suffered at the hands of Japan."[12] While one may wonder with hindsight whether Sun was thinking about the cession of Taiwan when he penned these lines, there is more contemporaneous evidence that he probably was not.

In a "Letter to a Correspondent of the Asahi (1919)" Sun seems to differentiate China, on the one hand, and Japan's colonies of Korea and Taiwan, on the other. Sun was bitterly critical of Japan's scheme to take Shandong, which had been held by Germany until its defeat in World War I, even as Japan urged China to enter the war against Germany and as it pledged that German concessions would be returned to China. He writes that "Japan would not ask Formosa [Taiwan] and Korea to be exploited by others for her own benefit, which shows that she treated China as inferior even to Formosa [Taiwan] and Korea."[13]

Sun reiterates this distinction between China and Taiwan in a 1923 interview with a *New York Times* correspondent in Canton, reportedly saying "The real trouble is that China is not an independent country. She is really in a worse off condition than Korea or Formosa [Taiwan]. They have one master; we have many. Their master dominates them, but has important responsibilities for the people under their subjection. China is equally dominated by the outside, but her masters rule without accepting any responsibility."[14] If Taiwan had then been viewed by Sun as part of China, he might not have spoken of a difference between Taiwan's master and China's. He might have specified that in Taiwan, China had one master, but on the continent it had several. He did not do this, though, because it seems he did not view Taiwan as part of China's territory.

Much about Sun's mental map of China and the place of Taiwan may be gleaned from his *San Min Chu I* [Three Principles of the People], the creed of the Nationalist Party. His lectures on nationalism open with a discourse about the difference between the nation as a people and the state. He asserts that since the start of the Qin dynasty [221 B.C.], China has been developing as a nation-state, which he defines as "a single state out of a single race."[15]

While he claims that China is a nation composed of a single race, he identifies "sub-races" differentiating "Mongolian, Malay, Japanese, Manchurian, and Chinese."[16] Taking the argument further, Sun states "the Chinese people are of the Han or Chinese race with common blood, common language, common religion, and common customs—a single, pure race."[17]

Considering China's history of the preceding century, Sun notes that China had lost an enormous amount of territory, principally along the eastern coast. He writes that "Further back in history, our territorial losses were Korea, Taiwan, the Pescadores [Penghu islands], and such places."[18] Then, he mentions the loss of Burma and Annam [Vietnam], reiterating that both were formerly Chinese territory. He then states: "Still earlier in the history of territorial losses were the Amur and Ussuri River basins and before that the areas north of the Ili, Khohand, and Amur rivers—the territory of the recent Far Eastern Republic [of the Soviet Union]—all of which China gave over with folded hands to the foreigner without so much as a question."[19] Clearly, Sun saw China's past territorial claims extended "to the north of the Amur, southward to the south of the Himalayas, eastward to the China Sea, westward to the T'sung Lin."[20] Yet, Sun apparently did not express any irredentist attachment to Taiwan. Dai Jitao, one of Sun's confidantes, wrote in March 1925, that twenty days before Sun died he spoke of three measures Japan should take to reestablish the confidence of people in China and East Asia. According to Dai, Sun advocated that Japan grant complete *autonomy* to the peoples of Taiwan and Korea.[21] Had he viewed Taiwan as Chinese territory, he might have expected that Japan return the island to China.

Chiang Kai-shek and the Neglect of Taiwan

Chiang Kai-shek, Sun's successor, seemed largely inattentive to the occupation by Japan of Taiwan. His focus instead appears to have been arresting Japan's progress on the continent, in the eighteen provinces that constituted the core of China, what had been "China proper." For instance, in two volumes of Chiang's statements from the period 1937–43 published by the ROC government, Taiwan is not mentioned once.[22] In July 1937, Chiang gave a number of speeches condemning Japan's aggression in China and urging his audience to "Drive Out the Invader," as a message he gave to the armed forces was entitled. None of Chiang's six speeches from July 1937 published in *The Collected Wartime Messages* mentions Japan's occupation of Taiwan.[23]

In February, 1938, Chiang gave a radio address on the fourth anniversary of the New Life Movement. With the fight against Japan clearly at the forefront, he said "The Japanese have been attacking China for more than half a year" and then he lists seven provincial capitals that Japan had taken. Taipei was not among those he listed nor did he seem to have the occupation of Taiwan in mind when he spoke of the war having begun a half year before.[24]

On July 7, 1938, the first anniversary of the Marco Polo Bridge Incident, Chiang spoke again to the armed forces and, in a redacted version of his comments, one reads that he "attributed China's present ordeal and calamity to the timidity and neglect of the permanent interests of the nation on the part of the late Ching [Qing] dynasty after the Sino-Japanese war of 1894-1895, and on the part of Yuan Shih-kai some twenty years afterwards."[25] Chiang appears to have accepted as settled the matter of Taiwan's cession and blames the Qing court for its timidity, not yet prepared to declare that the treaty resulting from the Manchu's supplication was null and Taiwan still China's domain. Appealing in another message to the international community, Chiang decries Japan's aggression and illegal plunder of China, but makes no mention of the colonization of Taiwan.[26]

Even more notable is Chiang's point of departure for an indignant message to the people of Japan. The redacted version of the text indicates that Chiang "reviewed Japan's acts of aggression against China, beginning with the invasion of Manchuria in 1931."[27] Indeed, the repeated focus on the Manchurian Incident, or Mukden Incident, of 1931 as the moment at which China and Japan fell more deeply into hostility seems to suggest that Chiang's passion was aroused by the violent nature of the grab for territory, not the connivances by which Japan extirpated Taiwan from China. Otherwise, Chiang might have spoken about the contest as one stretching to 1894. That Chiang neither included the cession of Taiwan nor mentioned the suffering of the people of Taiwan suggests that he did not see the island as China's or the people who lived there as more rightfully citizens of the Chinese republic.

In contrast, Chiang issued a message entitled, "To the People of Manchuria," in which he asserts that there was not one patriotic Chinese person who "has not solemnly sworn, on behalf of our race and especially our thirty million compatriots in the Northeast, to avenge this unprecedented wrong."[28] He even goes so far as to write that the people of the Northeast "must destroy Japan's illusion that she can keep Manchuria as a permanent colony." He incites them to start a revolution against their Japanese overlords. He tells them that "China today is a nation of four hundred and fifty million people fighting with one heart and mind for her existence as a free and independent country. You are the ones who have suffered the longest and the most." He offers no comparable word of encouragement to the population of Taiwan, even though the colonization by Japan started thirty-six years before the annexation of Manchuria by Japan.

After 1937, the conflict with Japan prompted the ROC to reconsider the status of territory "lost" to Japan. To the Guomindang elite, Chiang Kai-shek characterized Japan's seizure of the Ryukyu islands and of Taiwan in geostrategic terms: as elements in a scheme to encircle and subjugate China.[29] In 1938, Chiang began to advocate privately that China recover Taiwan. Perhaps because the ROC had yet to declare war on Japan, Chiang's views were not then publicized.[30]

A departure from this pattern occurred when Chiang spoke before the Provisional National Assembly in 1938. Chiang Kai-shek identified Taiwan as Chinese territory, but equated it with Korea. It is noteworthy that he said, "we must enable Korea and Taiwan to restore their independence and freedom, *and enable them to solidify the national defense of the Republic of China* (emphasis added)." That is, Taiwan and Korea—freed from Japanese occupation—were depicted as enhancing the security of China.[31]

For the most part, though, Chiang's public statements about the status of Taiwan are ambiguous. In his message "To the People of Japan" of July 7, 1939, Chiang offers additional evidence of seeing Taiwan as something other than Chinese. Broadcasting his views on Japan's militarism directly to the Japanese populace, Chiang sought to impress on them how their government had deceived them with regard to the war aims. In recounting Japan's misdeeds, Chiang decries the oppression of Korea. He states, "To sum it all up, the Koreans have been leading a life of slaves. And so have the Formosans [Taiwanese]."

In the passage that follows, Chiang depicts China and Taiwan as distinct, and he is unambiguous in casting the Marco Polo Bridge Incident, not the Treaty of Shimonoseki, as the start of Japan's occupation of China. He states, "Your militarists, after having enslaved Korea and Formosa [Taiwan], proceeded to try to enslave the whole Chinese nation. Their first step was the occupation of our Four Northeastern Provinces."[32]

Concerning Japan's militarists, Chiang states, "They believed that they could conquer China step by step just as the silkworm nibbles at the mulberry leaf. The first step was to seize the Four Northeastern Provinces; the second to invade Hopei, Chahar and other provinces." Chiang did not then mention the seizure of the Ryukyu islands or the cession of Taiwan at the end of the first Sino-Japanese War in the shadow of potential violence as the first step.

Moreover, he did not seem to view the Taiwanese people as sharing a political identity with Chinese. Chiang exhorts the Japanese to ask themselves:

Have not the twenty million Koreans and the four million Formosans [Taiwanese] whom you have mistakenly thought of as being completely enslaved, been waiting for an opportunity to rise in rebellion? Now, if you add another four hundred and fifty million Chinese, who, if they were to be conquered, will hate Japan intensely, no matter how you try to oppress them . . . your difficulties will only be increased.

One might understand that in the scope of Chiang's concerns, Taiwan would rank low. His juxtaposition of the population of Taiwan and of China is testament to the comparatively insignificant number of people affected by Japan's colonization of Taiwan. However, in the scope of a diatribe about Japan's incursions into China's territory and the resistance of the Chinese people, it is striking that Taiwan seems outside Chiang's notion of China, the Taiwanese [Formosans] distinct from the Chinese. All that would soon change.

Taiwan and the Cairo Crucible

By 1942, Chinese Nationalist leaders were spouting a narrative about the long-standing bond between Taiwan and China and the deep attachment of Taiwan's Han population to China. Taiwan was depicted as a part of China that the Nationalists resolved to recover from Japan.[33]

Ultimately, the decision to restore sovereignty over Taiwan to China was announced at the conclusion of the Cairo Conference on November 26, 1943, but had been decided by the allies at least one year before the conference. This decision is frequently depicted as the outgrowth of an intention by President Franklin Roosevelt to project China into the role of a leading power, "to bolster Chinese morale, and the position of the Chinese leader, Chiang Kai-shek, with assurances of generous treatment after the war."[34]

This ambition, itself, reflected a wishful calculation by Roosevelt that the ROC "might soon become a force for regional stability," as well as an eagerness by the United States to "steel Chiang's sometimes questionable resolve to fight against the Japanese."[35] The return of Taiwan to China is presented as part of a package of "promises to Chiang which were designed to keep the Nationalist leader in the saddle, stiffen Chinese determination to continue the fight, and ensure post-war Chinese friendship toward the United States."[36] Other pledges President Roosevelt made to Chiang as part of this effort at Cairo on the evening of November 23, 1943, were that China would (1) become a "permanent member of the 'Big Four' in the projected international organization," the United Nations; (2) recover the territories occupied by Japan in Northeast China as well as in Taiwan; (3) be engaged in postwar efforts to maintain regional stability in the Pacific "within the framework of a mutual defense alliance"; and (4) receive a continued stream of U.S. military assistance, and jointly administer a trusteeship for the Ryukyu islands along with the United States.[37]

Robert Dallek writes that all these "efforts to assure China's national aspirations and postwar status as a great Power particularly pleased the Chiangs." He then states that "Roosevelt suggested a public declaration" affirming that territories taken by Japan would be returned to China. Dallek leaves the impression that both the notion of returning territories to China as well as the plan to announce it were an outgrowth of Roosevelt's tender manipulation of Chiang Kai-shek.[38]

While it is evident that Roosevelt's vision for China in the postwar world did contribute to the decision announced at Cairo, it would be a mistake to construe the ROC government as a passive, but appreciative, bystander in the machinations that led to the decision to return Taiwan to China after the war. It is difficult to accept that "a series of decisions by outside powers and the retreat of the Guomindang transformed Taiwan from a peripheral and irrelevant region into an essential component of China's domestic sovereignty."[39] The government of the ROC was deeply engaged in securing an outcome at Cairo that suited its own ambition to strip Japan of territories that Japan had taken from China. The effort by Chiang Kai-shek and his associates to ensure this outcome was part of an evolving reconceptualization of Taiwan that was probably inspired by events far from China's shores.[40]

On August 14, 1941, President Roosevelt and Prime Minister Churchill met at a once secret conference aboard the *U.S.S. Augusta* and the British battleship *HMS Prince of Wales* near the former fishing village of Argentia in Placentia Bay, on the south coast of Newfoundland.[41] On that day, the two leaders issued a communiqué that is known as the Atlantic Charter. The Charter announced common aims for the war and articulated an international order that the two allies hoped to establish once the war was won.[42] The second and third paragraphs of the Charter may have been seen in China as applying to the recovery of Taiwan from Japan. These passages read: "Second, they desire to see no territorial changes that do not accord with the freely expressed wishes of the peoples concerned; Third, they respect the right of all peoples to choose the form of government under which they will live; and they wish to see sovereign rights and self-government restored to those who have been forcibly deprived of them."[43]

While Churchill may have intended that the principles articulated by this document apply to those territories taken in the preceding decade in Europe,

Chiang Kai-shek or political actors with Chiang's ear may have advocated that this document be seen as a reason to insist upon the return of territories that the Qing had lost to Japan since the Sino-Japanese War of 1894–95.[44] Surely, China had been forcibly deprived of the island. Certainly Chiang was, by 1938, thinking in terms of the dissolution of Japan's empire and the recovery of Taiwan.[45] That the island had been ceded by treaty, not simply grabbed by force, seemed to figure less prominently in the calculations of the ROC elite after the Atlantic Charter than before it.

If the ruling circle of the Guomindang was emboldened by the Atlantic Charter to consider a new stance toward Japan on the matter of China's "lost territories," the decision of the United States to go to war against Japan must have bolstered its determination. It also spurred Chongqing to declare war on Japan in December 1941 and nullify all the treaties with Tokyo that China had previously signed. Beginning in 1942, ROC officials spoke publicly about their intention to recover Taiwan. The island was, once again, located in the "mental map" of China.

At a March 1942 meeting of the Taiwan Revolutionary Alliance (TRA) in Chongqing, Sun Fo, son of Sun Yat-sen and the president of the Legislative Yuan, endorsed the TRA's call to have Taiwan returned to China.[46] Given his lineage and political stature, Sun's voice carried weight.[47] Sun Fo had been quoted in a *United Press* report from Chongqing of March 23 urging "President Roosevelt and Prime Minister Churchill to announce a 'Pacific Charter' which would pledge the United Nations to recognize the independence of India, French Indochina, Korea and the Philippines."[48] However, writing from the U.S. Embassy, Ambassador Clarence Gauss clarified that although the tone of the report of Sun's speech before a "local cultural association" was correct, "Dr. Sun, rather than announce the adoption of a Pacific Charter, stated that the Atlantic Charter could, and expressed confidence that it did, apply to all parts of the world."[49]

According to a *United Press* report from Chongqing published in the *New York Times* on April 6, 1942, Sun Fo had written a piece that was published in the CCP *Xinhua Ribao*. In it, Sun reportedly stated that Japan would be driven from the East Asian mainland within two years. He urged that China "assume leadership in the emancipation of the people's of Asia" and pledged that Taiwan would be returned to the "mother country." He is quoted as having said that "The emancipation of Formosa [Taiwan] is coming. . . . We insist upon the Roosevelt-Churchill declaration of freedom for all peoples."[50]

Seeking clarification of this new policy, John Stewart Service, the third secretary in the U.S. Embassy in Chongqing, spoke with Yang Yunzhu, direc-

China's political development in the past century which provides the basis for the revolutionary struggles of the Kuomintang."[56]

The book opens with an account of the "Growth and Development of the Chunghua [Zhonghua] Nation," in which Chiang notes what he sees as the historical pattern of popular resistance by China's people to the occupation of "territories which were necessary for her [China's] national existence." Aroused by the "humiliation suffered and the determination to live," China's people would "rise in arms and regain what they had lost, thereby bringing about national recovery."[57]

Defining China's territory up to the Opium War incursions, Chiang writes that there was "not a single region which was not required by the Chinese nation for its existence; nor was there a single region which had not been deeply under the influence of Chinese culture." Accordingly, following the various "impairments" of China's territory in the century following 1842, the Chinese people are urged by Chiang to "regard it as a national humiliation: they should not cease from struggle, to remove the disgrace and to save the country, until China's territorial integrity has been completely restored."[58] Surveying the scope of China's territorial claims, Chiang writes, "There is not a single piece of territory within these areas, therefore, which can be torn away or separated from China, and none of them can form an independent unit by itself."[59]

Chiang's rationale for this emphatic claim is that the territory exists as an organic, economic system in which each region is dependent on the natural resources of the others. More to the point, Chiang views China's territorial domain as providing "natural bulwarks of self-protection."[60] He specifies:

> In the valleys of the Yellow River, Huai River, Yangtze [Yangzi] River, and Han River, there is hardly a single place where strong frontier defenses can be built; and consequently, the Liuchiu [Ryukyu] Islands, Formosa [Taiwan], the Pescadores [Penghu Islands], the Northeastern Provinces, Inner and Outer Mongolia, Sinkiang [Xinjiang] and Tibet are all strategic regions for safeguarding the nation's existence; lop off any one of them from China is to destroy her national defense.[61]

Taiwan is among those territories that Chiang sees as offering a buffer, "safeguarding the nation's existence." All were accreted during the Qing dynasty. Most were separated from China or taken by foreign powers. All, in Chiang's vision, are necessary to ensure China's security.[62]

Turning to Taiwan specifically, Chiang highlights the strategic dimension of the island's position off China's southeast coast. He states, "Formosa [Taiwan] and the Pescadores [Penghu islands] were originally opened up and developed by the people of Han stock; and strategically situated in the southeast, they

tor of the East Asiatic Affairs Department in the ROC Ministry of Fc
Affairs in June 1942. Yang confirmed the impression Service had gotten
Chinese press reports that Chongqing was thinking about recovering s
eignty over Taiwan following the defeat of Japan. However, Yang told Sc
that statements—such as those reported in an editorial in the *Ta Kung I*
April 6—that China was also seeking recovery of the Ryukyu islands
inconsistent with the policies of the ROC. He said "neither the Minist
Foreign Affairs nor any other part of the Chinese Government contem;
their return to China in a peace settlement."[51]

Over the next several months, though, the message to Washington
Taiwan was reinforced by several reports and Yang's statement abou
Ryukyu islands was contradicted by subsequent decisions. On July 8
bassador Gauss reported on addresses made by Chinese officials the pro
day, the fifth anniversary of Japan's invasion of China. He wrote that D
Fo "predicted victory and restoration to China of all territory lost sin
Sino–Japanese war of 1894."[52]

Evidence of new thinking about Taiwan came from a variety of sc
Owen Lattimore, Roosevelt's adviser to Chiang Kai-shek, reported in /
1942, "If any western power wants Formosa, the Chinese will claim
otherwise they may not insist on possessing it, since they lack the sea
to hold it." Yet, the ROC's determination to recover Taiwan, and other
tories, was reiterated in a private meeting between Wendel Wilkie, Roo
personal envoy to China, and the president on October 7.[53]

The most authoritative statement of ROC policy, though, car
November 3, when the newly appointed Minister of Foreign Affair
Soong [Song Ziwen], held a press conference. Soong is reported to have
that "China will recover Manchuria and Formosa and the Ryukyu
after the war and Korea will be independent."[54] Thus, by November 19
policy of the ROC was to seek the recovery of territory that Japan had
from China—a policy that may well have been prompted by the pri
articulated in the Atlantic Charter.

Chiang Kai-shek, *China's Destiny,* and Taiwan's Strategic Salience

At about the time that T. V. Soong was announcing a new ROC polic
cerning China's expectations of recovering territories lost to Japan, (
Kai-shek was charting his own vision for China's future. In Novembe
he began to draft *China's Destiny*, a book that was first published in
The first five chapters of this book offer what Lin Yu-tang, in his int
tion to the authorized English version, describes as "an authoritative re'

were for many ages China's bulwark against foreign invasion."[63] It is hard to avoid the conclusion that Chiang's rationale for ensuring that Taiwan be returned to China's control was at least in part geostrategic.

How highly geostrategic considerations ranked among Chiang's tangible and intangible rationales for wanting Taiwan back is difficult to know. He mentions both. One is struck, though, by the emphasis in Chiang's statement on an "imagined geography" of China in which Taiwan serves as a physical barrier offering China's coast protection from assault. This imagery both recalls geostrategic arguments about the salience of Taiwan made at earlier moments in China's history and prefigures the analysis of contemporary strategists in the PRC, whose geostrategic rationales are the focus of Chapter 7.

Shifting Salience (II)

From CCP Indifference to Instrumental Indignation

CCP Indifference to Taiwan

A central contention of this work is that territorial salience is not fixed, but fluid. Even after the establishment of a claim to territory, the salience of disputed lands can change in response to other variables. As the previous chapter indicates, Chinese ruling elites have not always viewed Taiwan with the high degree of attachment that the nationalist narrative constructed in the early 1940s asserts.

Just as the ruling elite in the Guomindang was mostly indifferent to Taiwan until 1942, there is ample evidence that the leadership of the CCP categorized the Taiwanese and Han Chinese as distinct nationalities and, until 1942, evinced no interest in viewing Taiwan as part of China's territory.[1] Indeed, during the first two decades of CCP history, Taiwan appears to have been of peripheral interest to the party. When leaders of the CCP did speak or write of Taiwan, they encouraged opposition to Japanese colonialism, urged Taiwanese to exercise self-determination by establishing an independent state, and anticipated that this would advance the revolutionary struggle to topple imperialism. During the 1930s and early 1940s, the objective that China should be unified and independent was frequently asserted, but it was not associated with extending China's sovereignty to Taiwan.

At its inception in July 1921, the CCP was small—fewer than fifty members who were drawn together from various leftist study societies that were inspired to consolidate with funding from the Comintern.[2] An ideological orthodoxy did not emerge until the Second Congress of the CCP, held in July 1922.[3] A manifesto issued then offers an instructive first glimpse of the CCP's attitude toward Taiwan, a territory toward which it then paid no heed.

That document ends with a call to workers and peasants to join in a united front with the petty bourgeoisie to accomplish seven major tasks, including:

[2] Overthrow oppression by the international imperialists and win the complete independence of the Chinese nation.[4]

[3] Unify China proper (including the three provinces in the northeast) and establish a democratic republic.

[4] Establish autonomous rule in Mongolia, Tibet, and Muslim Xinjiang to turn them into democratic autonomous republics.

[5] Use the free federal system to unify China proper, Mongolia, Tibet, and Muslim Xinjiang in order to establish a Chinese Federal Republic.[5]

It is noteworthy that Taiwan was not mentioned. Perhaps the CCP elite also accepted that the Treaty of Shimonoseki was binding and Taiwan's loss permanent. Even where it writes of the importance of overthrowing the oppression of imperialists, the CCP did not mention Japan's colonization of Taiwan. It certainly appears that the CCP did not then view Taiwan as territory to which China had a legitimate claim.

By the Sixth National Congress of the CCP, held in Moscow, July 1928, the CCP distinguished Han Chinese from other "minority nationalities," a category that encompassed Taiwanese.[6] In a "Resolution on the Nationality Problem," Taiwanese living in China are listed as one of several nationalities, a list that included Mongols, Muslims, Koreans, the Miao and Li minorities of the southwest, and the peoples of Xinjiang and Tibet. Designation as a "minority nationality" meant that Taiwanese residing in China were not regarded by the CCP as simply residents of one Chinese province, Taiwan, residing in another Chinese province.[7]

When the CCP issued its "Outline of the Constitution of the Chinese Soviet Republic" of November 7, 1931, it established that all minority nationalities, including the Taiwanese, were equal under the laws of the Chinese soviet.[8] While the CCP was later to emphasize that Taiwanese are *not* a separate nationality but are Chinese, in the first decades of its existence, "the CCP never referred to the Taiwanese as 'brethren' (*dixiong*), or 'the offspring of the Yellow Emperor,' or 'compatriots' (*tongbao*)."[9] When they were not categorized by the CCP as a national minority, Taiwan's population was associated with the same category as the Koreans and the Annanese [Vietnamese], all oppressed peoples.

Later, Japan's colonization of Manchuria in 1931 animated intense anti-Japanese fury. The "Message to Compatriots on Resistance to Japan to Save the Nation" of August 1, 1935, was a fiery condemnation of Japan's imperialist incursions into Chinese territories. The document stated:

> Our territory has been occupied province after province; our people have been enslaved thousand upon thousand; our towns and villages have been destroyed one after another; our compatriots residing abroad have been driven away group by group; and our internal and foreign affairs have been interfered with continually. How can a country in these conditions be considered a sovereign state?! How can a nation like this be regarded as independent?![10]

The authors of the document seek to arouse the passions of all of China's population, regardless of their party or ethnic identity. They appeal explicitly for unity with people from all parties, to the nationalistic youths associated with the Guomindnag's blue shirt movement, to "nationals residing abroad who care for our motherland," and to "brothers of all the oppressed nationalities in China (Mongolian, Hui, Korean, Tibetan, Miao, Yao, Li and Yi)!"[11]

Although the document refers to people residing within China or Chinese residing overseas, it is noteworthy that Taiwan is referred to in a passage concerning non-Chinese peoples residing abroad who are also urged to sympathize with the plight of the Chinese nation. The document focuses on the erosion of sovereignty and describes Japan as swallowing China, "province after province." It encourages a defense of the nation, pledging to "Resist Japan and recover the lost territories." However, rather than include Taiwan in "the nation," the CCP entreats adherents to "Unite with the people who are opposed to Japanese imperialism (the laboring masses in Japan, the Koreans, the Taiwanese, etc.) as our allies, unite with all peoples and nations sympathetic toward the Chinese national liberation movement, and establish friendly relations with all peoples and nationals who opt for a well-considered neutrality in the anti-Japanese war."[12] Equating the Taiwanese with the Koreans and anti-imperialist Japanese implies that none are Chinese and none live within China. Although the CCP leadership continued to emphasize the centrality of overthrowing Japanese imperialists to "bring about China's independence and liberation," Taiwan was not then seen by the CCP as China's territory. [13]

Mao Zedong's Initial View of Taiwan

Early in his career, Mao Zedong associated Taiwan with Korea and Vietnam. For example, in comments about the 1931 Constitution of the CCP, Mao writes in 1934 about the "revolutionary comrades from Korea, Taiwan, and Annam" who are living in China, implying that they are not, themselves, Chinese. [14] In his "Report to the Second National Congress of Workers' and Peasants' Representatives" of January 23, 1934, Mao offers evidence that the Chinese Soviet Republic—unlike the Guomindang—sympathizes with the plight of minorities. He states, "The fact that any Korean, Annam and Taiwan comrades attended the 1st Soviet Congress and 2nd Soviet Congress is a concrete proof that the Soviets mean what [they] say. The common revolutionary interests will unite the toilers of China with those of the minorities in a firm alliance. The free union of nationalities will replace national oppression, an event that is possible only under the Soviets."[15]

Mao certainly understood that Taiwan had once been China's territory and had been "lost" to Japan in an unequal treaty. Yet, Mao did not conclude that China should reassert sovereignty over Taiwan. Two key statements provide evidence of Mao's disinterest in Taiwan.

One is recorded in Edgar Snow's book, *Red Star Over China*.[16] The passage is often used to demonstrate that Mao did not envision China extending sovereignty to the island of Taiwan and, moreover, that he endorsed Taiwan's independence. Indeed, Mao stated unambiguously that the CCP would help Taiwan to struggle for independence.

In the course of questioning Mao in 1936 about the prospects for a Sino-Japanese war, Snow asked, "Is it the immediate task of the Chinese people to regain all the territories lost to Japanese imperialism, or only to drive Japan from North China, and all Chinese territory beyond the Great Wall?"[17] One does not know what motivated Snow to pose the question in this way. It would be interesting to know whether, in differentiating "all the territories lost to Japanese" from those in "North China" and "beyond the Great Wall," he had Taiwan in mind or only Japanese-occupied territories on the mainland.[18] One may never know. Whatever Snow intended, Mao responded unequivocally:

> It is the immediate task of China to regain all our lost territories, not merely to defend our sovereignty south of the Great Wall. This means that Manchuria must be regained. We do not, however, include Korea, formerly a Chinese colony, but when we have re-established the independence of the lost territories of China, and if the Koreans wish to break away from the chains of Japanese imperialism, we will extend them our enthusiastic help in their struggle for independence. The same thing applies for Taiwan. As for Inner Mongolia, which is populated by both Chinese and Mongolians, we will struggle to drive Japan from there and help Inner Mongolia to establish an autonomous state.[19]

This passage deserves scrutiny. First, Mao is responding to Snow's question about the "immediate" tasks of the Chinese people. So, presumably, Mao understood the question to concern the recovery of those territories he identified as of "immediate" importance, Snow suggesting by his question the possibility that Mao might view some territorial claims against Japan to take precedence over others.

If Mao did understand the question in that way, he rejected the view that there was greater urgency for China to recover some portions of territory and less for the recovery of other parcels. He replies, "It is the immediate task of China to regain *all* our lost territories . . . [emphasis added]." He clarifies this in the next sentence, elaborating, "This means that Manchuria must be regained." Mao's response seems to exclude Taiwan from the category of "all" territory lost to Japan, which he appears to envisage as encompassing only territory on the mainland.

More importantly, he goes on to equate the struggle of Korea to "break away from the chains of Japanese imperialism" with that of Taiwan. To be sure, both were colonies of Japan. Yet, this reinforces the view that as of 1936, Mao did not view the recovery of Chinese sovereignty over Taiwan to be an objective of the war against Japan. Not only does Mao list "immediate" concerns to China without reference to Taiwan, but he even states that once "the independence of the lost territories of China" has been established, China "will extend" to Korea and Taiwan its "enthusiastic help in their struggle for independence."

Snow's work incorporates three comments on this paragraph, one that pertains to Taiwan. Snow writes in an endnote added to the 1968 edition of this work: "Since Dr. Sun Yat-sen and the Kuomintang [Guomindang] had always placed Taiwan among 'lost territories' to be brought back under China's sovereignty, it seems hardly likely that Mao intended to concede future 'independence' there. The CCP had never officially done so."[20] This, as the preceding chapter makes evident, is incorrect. The Guomindang had not *always* considered Taiwan as among those territories that should "be brought back under China's sovereignty" and the CCP had, as this chapter seeks to demonstrate, made official its view that Taiwan should be "independent" after the defeat of Japan. So, nothing Mao said suggested any interest in extending China's sovereignty to Taiwan.

The other passage in Snow's book that warrants consideration casts a confusing shadow on the foregoing analysis of the frequently cited passage from the interview of July 16, 1936. Snow writes that he had had some difficulty eliciting from Mao any insight into Mao's personal life or background. After Snow pressed him to represent himself as he wished to be represented, Mao put aside a list of questions Snow submitted in advance and offered a narration of his life and development to that stage. Speaking about formative events of his youth, Mao said:

> I began to have a certain amount of political consciousness, especially after I read a pamphlet telling of the dismemberment of China. I remember even now that this pamphlet opened with the sentence: "Alas, China will be subjugated!" It told of Japan's occupation of Korea and Taiwan, of the loss of suzerainty in Indochina, Burma, and elsewhere. After I read this I felt depressed about the future of my country and began to realize that it was the duty of all the people to help save it.[21]

This passage makes clear Mao's sense that it was Japan's incursions into Korea and Taiwan and the loss of suzerainty in southeast Asia and "elsewhere" that had aroused him to act. If, as a youth, Mao viewed Japan's occupation of

Taiwan as a motive to help save his country, why did he not express to Snow in 1936 an intention to seek restoration of China's sovereign status there after the defeat of Japan? If he viewed the loss of suzerainty—not even sovereignty—over other states as a source of concern for the future of his country, why did he not seek to restore those suzerain privileges? Evidently, Mao's outlook concerning those territories had changed by 1936, and he did not then view them as China's territory. As one knows, Mao's view of Taiwan was to change again.

The distinction between Chinese and Taiwanese was by no means a view that Mao alone held. As the other passages in this section demonstrate, the view Mao offered Snow was reflected in various substantial statements by the CCP and its leading figures over a number of years.[22] Indeed, Zhang Guotao, a founder of the CCP and a key political rival of Mao Zedong, was in 1936 a member of the Central Committee. Zhang issued a "Report on the High Tide of the National Revolution and the Party's Tactical Line" in which he outlined a political program for a united front government aimed at resisting Japanese aggression. Zhang stated ten objectives, the ninth of which was "to unite with the people of Korea and Taiwan, assist their independent liberation movements, and unite the workers and peasants inside Japan and all other forces against the Japanese invasion to enable them to form a consolidated alliance with China in its war against Japan."[23]

The apparent lack of concern for Taiwan also emerges as the "dog that did not bark" in documents that deal with matters of Japan's imperialist forays onto China's soil. On March 4, 1937, Liu Shaoqi wrote a "Letter to the Party Center Concerning Past Work in the White Areas." In it, he describes what he perceived as errors by the party. Dealing with the CCP's response to Japan's incursion into Manchuria on September 18, 1931, it is interesting that Liu writes, "The incident was an extremely important step taken by the Japanese imperialists in colonizing China. Their first bite swallowed up Manchuria as their colony."[24] How, one wonders, did Liu view the Treaty of Shimonoseki? Why does he designate the swallowing of Manchuria as Japan's *first* bite when Taiwan was bitten off in 1895?

From 1925 on, Mao and other CCP officials adopted the term "unequal treaties," already in use by the Guomindang, to characterize nineteenth-century treaties imposed on China under threat of force. After the establishment of the PRC, the Treaty of Shimonoseki was certainly cited as an unequal treaty. Moreover, PRC texts disparaged all unequal treaties as lacking legal validity and subject to abrogation. Yet, it seems, considerations other than the legal status of international agreements were governing the thoughts of the CCP elite when it came to matters of territoriality.[25]

Deng Xiaoping is also reported to have made statements that suggest he did not view Taiwan as Chinese territory and the people of Taiwan as Han Chinese. In his account of eighteen months' travel in wartime China, U.S. Marine Evans Fordyce Carlson—sent to China by President Franklin Roosevelt—records a conversation he had in the summer of 1938 with one "Tun Shao-p'in," who was, from other evidence he provides, most certainly Deng.[26] Carlson asked about the "ten anti-Japanese principles which . . . each Eighth Route Army man is sworn to carry out." Deng listed the ten principles, the fifth of which is to "join the Japanese, Korean and Formosan [Taiwanese] peasants in an anti-Fascist movement."[27]

In time, the designation of Taiwanese as distinct from Chinese was made even more explicit. The third section of the "Political Resolution Adopted by the Enlarged Sixth Plenum of the CCP" on November 6, 1938, outlined fourteen "Urgent Tasks Facing the Entire Chinese Nation." The twelfth is to "Build an anti-Japanese united front between the Chinese and the Korean, Taiwanese, and other peoples so as to fight against Japan with joint forces."[28]

In 1939, the CCP was rattled by signs that the Guomindang was contemplating acceptance of a Japanese "peace offer." Mao Zedong addressed a high-level cadres' meeting in June 1939 and delivered a speech entitled "Outline for Opposing Capitulation." In it, Mao railed against the "Japanese policy of enticing China into capitulation."[29] He urged his colleagues to see the conclusion of the war against Japan as vital for the continued existence of the Chinese state. He derided those who thought about capitulating by stating, "it is mere daydreaming to believe that the Japanese will make concessions and that the status quo prior to the Marco Polo Bridge Incident [July 7, 1937] can be restored."[30]

His point of reference seems to be Japan's behavior in the 1930s. Presenting a detailed account of Japan's diplomatic efforts to urge China's capitulation, Mao stated "prior to the Marco Polo Bridge Incident, [Japan] was determined to follow the hard line; it occupied the three provinces in the northeast."[31] It is noteworthy that in this long presentation about Japan's aggression against China, there is no mention of the forced cession of Taiwan. In view of Mao's effort to urge his audience to resist capitulation, how odd it is that he did not cite Taiwan as evidence in his case against Japan.

When the Soviet Union signed a neutrality pact with Japan, the CCP felt compelled to explain why its ideological mentor would reach accommodation with China's greatest foe, Japan. A "Statement of the CCP on the Publication of the Soviet-Japanese Neutrality Pact" of April 16, 1941, offers an elaborate apologia for the Soviet decision. In one section, the document focuses on a Soviet assurance not to invade Manchuria or Mongolia. The statement sought to mask the self-serving nature of the Soviet's agreement with Japan and to explain why the Soviets would not help China by attacking Japan's positions in Manchuria. The statement makes the point that "Recovery of the four northeastern provinces is our own business," and urges readers not to "blame the Soviet Union when they hear that it has promised not to invade Manchuria." It then states, "We must recover all our own lost territories by fighting to the banks of the Yalu River and driving the Japanese imperialists out of China."[32]

This is exceptionally revealing. For one thing, by rolling back Japanese occupation to the Yalu River and then claiming that China had driven Japanese imperialists out of China, the document's authors evince no sense that Japan's colonization of Taiwan was equivalent to the occupation of the four north-eastern provinces on the continent. It appears from this that the Japanese colonization of Taiwan was not as great an affront as the colonization of Manchuria. Even more revealing is that this statement implies that China will be whole once Japan is defeated. The vast tracts of land ceded to Russia in 1858 and 1860 do not figure in the CCP's notion of where China's boundaries ought to be.

Denunciations of unequal treaties might have, but apparently did not, prompt thoughts that the Treaty of Shimonoseki should be vacated and Taiwan returned any more than they prompted discussion of the inequality of the Treaties of Aigun and Peking. To the contrary, in an essay published in July 1941, Zhou Enlai wrote that because the CCP had "opposed aggression from the other nations" it should "sympathize with independence-liberation movements of other nation-states" including those of Korea and Taiwan.[33] This stance is utterly opposed to Zhou's later assertions that Taiwan is part of China.

It was this sentiment that seemed to manifest itself at the Eastern People's Anti-Fascist Congress in October 1941. The congress was attended by 130 delegates representing eighteen countries in East and Southeast Asia. Among them, according to a report in *Jiefang Ribao*, there was also "an advance party [vanguard] for the independence of Taiwan (*Taiwan duli xianfeng*)."[34] That the Taiwanese sought independence was not—two months before Pearl Harbor— significant to the CCP. The focus was on overthrowing Japan's colonialism, not reestablishing China's sovereignty over Taiwan.

Jiefang Ribao also carried a report of a speech by Zhu De in which he describes Taiwan as one of the "countries and nations," including Korea, that had been conquered by Japan "a long time ago." Although he depicts Taiwan as having been "snatched away" [*duoqu*, literally captured, or seized] from China by Japan, Zhu does not call for the restoration of Chinese sovereignty over the island or categorize it, as he does Manchuria, as Chinese territory occupied by Japan.

Indeed, Zhu refers to the anti-Japanese elements on Taiwan as fighting for "national liberation" and praises the "Taiwanese in China" who support "our units." From Zhu's military perspective, Taiwan's chief significance is as a base from which Japan supports its imperialist expansion southward, not as a segment of China that must be recovered.[35]

The view of Taiwan as something other than China's territory was made evident in the "CCP Declaration on the War in the Pacific," issued on December 9, 1941, following the response by the United States and Britain to the attack on Pearl Harbor. It is most interesting that in listing objectives that the CCP would seek to meet in pursuing its war against Japan, it urged party stalwarts to "carry out extensive anti-Japanese, anti-fascist propaganda and agitation among the Japanese army; the Japanese people; the peoples of Korea, Taiwan, and Vietnam; the Chinese people in the areas that have fallen to the Japanese; and those struggling for the establishment of an antifascist front inside Japan."[36]

The association of the people of Taiwan with those of Korea and Vietnam, not with those of China, is a characterization that consistently appears in the formal statements of China's communist leadership. It reveals that Taiwan's populace was not seen by the leaders of the CCP as comprising one element of the Chinese nation. Moreover, repeated references to the CCP's support for Taiwan's liberation and self-determination emerge from both personal expressions by CCP leaders and formal proclamations by the party organs they dominated. The record of these statements provides no clue that Taiwan was seen as territory that ought to be brought under China's sovereignty.

Liu Xiaoyuan asserts, "it would be an exaggeration to argue either that the CCP leadership in this period [prior to 1942] was committed to a policy of supporting an independent Taiwan, or that, although CCP leaders talked in terms of Taiwanese independence, what they really meant was Taiwan's reunion with China."[37]

It is, of course, possible that additional documentation will one day come to light that necessitates a reconsideration of the significance of the foregoing references to Taiwan. It is difficult to imagine, though, how additional documentation of some heretofore unpublicized assertion made before 1942 that Taiwan *should* be recovered by China will counterbalance the volume of statements by individuals and those made in the name of the CCP that flow in the opposite direction, distinguishing Taiwan from China. For that reason, one cannot avoid the conclusion that the CCP and its principal leaders neither viewed the island of Taiwan as China's territory nor felt that it was necessary to incorporate Taiwan into China following the defeat of Japan.

1942, A Year of Some Significance

The CCP's well-documented indifference to Taiwan appears to have changed abruptly in 1942.[38] The reasons for the CCP's volte-face are not transparent. Several possible influences on the CCP should be considered: the waning role and ultimate dissolution of the Comintern in 1943, the Rectification Campaign then underway, the activity of Taiwanese political activists on the mainland, and the interactions between the Guomindang, the United States, and Great Britain leading to the Cairo Conference of December.

Dissolution of the Comintern

One cannot ignore the compatibility of the CCP's early attitude toward Taiwan's liberation, self-determination, and independence and the policy outlook of the Comintern, as well as the nationality policies of the Soviet Union.[39] Initially, perhaps, Mao and others were dazzled by the notion of a revolution that transcended simply patriotic objectives and embraced the concerns of the world's weak and oppressed peoples.[40] That would account, in part, for the recurring association in CCP statements of the people of Korea and Annam with the people of Taiwan. Even Sun Yat-sen fell under the spell of Comintern notions of a unified movement of oppressed peoples. So long as China was struggling to rid itself of invaders and occupiers, this theme may have offered ideological succor to China's nationalists—regardless what party they spoke for—and so influenced both the Guomindang and the CCP. Indeed, as late as 1930, at the Guomindang's First National Congress, a Manifesto was issued in which the party also advocated "the right of self-determination of all races within the country."[41]

Throughout the 1920s and 1930s, Chinese of both parties followed the Soviet lead in calling for self-determination along the border areas. The CCP often qualified these assertions by expressing confidence that the minorities would only realize liberation through an association with the CCP and would, after casting off the yoke of colonialism, exercise self-determination by voluntarily joining a China federation.[42]

This approach was in keeping with that of the Soviet leadership, which was able to enforce its views through the Comintern by sending envoys to guide the nascent CCP. In that manner, the Soviets "left an imprint on virtually every aspect of the early CCP," indoctrinating party elite, drafting pivotal documents, defining policy, and funding the CCP's activities.[43] Although the

CCP was ultimately to assert some independence from the Comintern, the party's early ideological and tactical goals seemed to have been well coordinated by and tied tightly to Moscow.

So, the Comintern's attitude toward the status of Taiwan may have affected the way that the CCP first conceptualized its policy toward the island. For that matter, because Sun Yat-sen and even Chiang Kai-shek sought cooperative relations with the Soviet Union and the Comintern, it may have affected the Guomindang's inclinations toward the island, also.[44]

For its part, the Comintern did not view the restoration of China's sovereignty over Taiwan as the purpose of liberating the Taiwanese from Japanese colonialism. Indeed, to the degree that Taiwan was mentioned in Comintern documents, it seems not to have been associated with China. As far as the Comintern was concerned, the Taiwan Communist Party (TCP) was to be an affiliate of the Japanese Communist Party (JCP), not the CCP, because Taiwan was regarded as a colony of Japan, not territory of China.[45] Its revolutionary activity was probably aimed at combating Japan's colonialism, something it might do best in conjunction with other Japanese forces fighting against Japan's imperialist practices.

In this context, perhaps the notion of restoring sovereignty over Taiwan to China after fighting to liberate Taiwan from Japanese colonialism smacked of imperialism that the Comintern did not wish to endorse. It is also possible that the Soviet policy of appeasing Japan prevailed over any interest in stripping Japan of the colonial territory it had extracted from China, despite the ideological inconsistency this required. In any case, the Comintern apparently did not advocate that China should expect to govern Taiwan after the overthrow of Japanese imperialism, and there is no indication that the CCP objected. Moreover, the Comintern appears to have viewed China and Taiwan in separate categories.

As an illustration of this distinction, consider the founding program of the JCP. Nikolai Bukharin is thought to have been responsible for drafting the program in 1922. Among the objectives stated in that document was the withdrawal of Japan's troops from Sakhalin Island, China, Korea, and Taiwan. Had the document stated that Japan should withdraw its forces from Taiwan and "other parts of China," Taiwan would have been cast as part of China. As it was, the document leaves the impression that the island was not considered by the Comintern author(s) of the JCP program as part of either China or Japan.[46] It makes sense, then, that the Comintern and the CCP that danced to its lead would not advocate the return of Taiwan to China's sovereignty in the period after the liberation of Taiwan from Japan's grasp.

Indeed, shortly after the establishment of the JCP, the CCP met in Canton in June 1923, to hold its third Congress. In May, just weeks before this session, the Comintern issued instructions to the CCP, among which was an ambiguous statement concerning the degree to which the Chinese should agitate against the imposition of what the Chinese would soon thereafter come to call "unequal treaties." The Comintern document states that the CCP must extend an anti-Japanese boycott then emerging in China "into a general anti-imperialist movement of the Chinese democracy, aiming at the abrogation of treaties and obligations forced on China not only by England and America but also by other imperialist countries (extraterritoriality, the Boxer indemnity, etc.)."[47] As indicated above, the Treaty of Shimonoseki was evidently not then viewed as among those treaties forced upon China by an imperialist country other than England and America. Otherwise, it might have been among the targets of this general call to abrogate foreign-imposed obligations and privileges. Why the Comintern and the CCP did not emphasize this treaty and its consequences for China as a justification for opposition to Japan is puzzling.

There are other clues to the Comintern's disinclination to see the reassertion of Chinese sovereignty in Taiwan as an objective of the CCP. For instance, in 1927, after an internal dispute erupted among the Japanese communists about fundamental organizational principles, seven leading members of the JCP were summoned to Moscow. A special commission of the Executive Committee of the Communist International (ECCI) headed by Bukharin met to address the dispute. The result was a program of action for the party that included, among its objectives, that the party would advocate the "complete independence for the colonies" of Japan.[48] At the time, Japan's two colonies were Korea and Taiwan.[49]

That the Comintern did not see the colonization of Taiwan as an element of foreign aggression against China that the CCP should protest was made even more explicit in a document issued in May 1928, by the West European Bureau of the ECCI. The appeal issued by the Comintern bureau decries the military partition of China by Japan, but points to Japan's occupation of Shandong province in the spring of 1928 as the first step in this project. The document states, "The military partition of China has begun. Predatory Japanese imperialism has occupied Shantung [Shandong]." It describes how foreign powers were moving from "intervention to the open conquest of the country. Japan is hurrying to exploit the advantages of its strategical [sic] position to tear off the first morsels." The document goes on to depict Japan as "the first to start on the partition of China," but the offense that appears to arouse the indignation of the authors is Japan's occupation of Shandong, to which the appeal refers repeatedly.[50] By depicting Japan's actions in Shandong as the *first* efforts at partition, the forced cession of Taiwan to Japan thirty-three years earlier does not enter into consideration.

The Comintern's apparent disinterest in seeing Japan's occupation of Taiwan as an offense against China that the CCP should aim to reverse was manifest throughout the early history of China's relationship with Moscow. This does not appear to have been inadvertent. Moreover, this attitude certainly dominated the CCP's Sixth Party Congress of 1928 at which the CCP explicitly endorsed a war of liberation by the weak and oppressed people of Taiwan that was distinct from the revolution in China. If members of the CCP elite objected to the starkness of the Soviet formulation, they were unable to resist it there, even if many shared Li Dazhao's view that Taiwan was part of China.[51]

To be sure, the future status of Taiwan and its several million inhabitants paled by comparison to the global concerns of the Comintern for an orchestrated revolution against imperialism. This begs the question of why the CCP elite acquiesced to the Comintern and failed to resist a view of Taiwan that was inconsistent with the notion of it as among China's "lost territories."

It is possible, of course, that the view of Taiwan as something other than a territory of China and the notion that its people were entitled to self-determination may have been adopted by the CCP as genuine articles of doctrinal faith. Alternatively, the CCP may have adopted that view because it sensed that there was little margin in challenging the Comintern on a matter that was of rather peripheral importance to the CCP when far more vital and urgent matters were at stake. That, at least, may explain why in the 1920s and early 1930s, the CCP did not challenge the view of Taiwan that the Comintern evidently promoted.

However, the CCP's relationship to the Comintern did not evolve easily. The CCP frequently chafed under the yoke of other Comintern-imposed doctrines, most notably the effort to compel the CCP to ally with Chiang Kai-shek and the Nationalist Party in a united front.[52] In the late 1920s and early 1930s, several contests of will erupted between Stalin and advocates within the CCP over establishing policies other than those the Comintern wished to impose.[53] If it was prepared to resist the Comintern in important doctrinal matters, what is one to make of the apparent disinterest on the part of the CCP in objecting to the Comintern's classification of Taiwan as something other than China's territory?

By the time the Comintern was abolished in 1943, the CCP had changed its stance on Taiwan. It is possible that the CCP felt liberated to adjust its posture toward Taiwan only as the Comintern's influence was diminishing, but this is difficult to prove. One cannot discount the possibility that the Comintern was dissolved at a moment when other factors were affecting the CCP's vision of Taiwan as China's irredenta.

Rectification and the CCP Policy Toward Taiwan

It is noteworthy that the CCP position seemed to have changed some time in 1942. At that juncture, the CCP was undergoing a "rectification campaign," the objectives of which were to establish Mao Zedong as the central ideologue in the party and to enshrine a particular version of ideology as the party line. In the speech that officially launched the Rectification Campaign, Mao Zedong railed against what was known as "subjectivism" in the ideological sphere.[54] He blamed this, in part, on the influence of those non-Chinese who had affected the policies of the CCP, including Bukharin.[55] Mao thought the subjectivists were pursuing "false Marxists" and viewed them as adherents of the "international line."[56] Is it possible that there was a reevaluation of the CCP policy toward Taiwan at this time and recognition that the prevailing view of Taiwan as Japan's colony disembodied from its Chinese roots were contrary to the objective view of the island's relationship to China?

To reverse itself, the CCP leaders had to disassociate themselves from their earlier assertions on the matter. On its face, this would seem to open the leadership to charges of inconsistency and hypocrisy. Michael Hunt, though, notes that the CCP was not inevitably doctrinaire about foreign affairs. He writes, "When global commitments and foreign concepts inherent in that orthodoxy demonstrably impeded the CCP's domestic road, the leadership increasingly gave priority to the party's short-term survival and ultimately the political control on which its dreams of national revival and transformation depended. International commitments and foreign concepts that ill-served these goals came under critical scrutiny."[57] As a result, the CCP underwent an "ideological sea change" as the "Comintern-sponsored international-affairs orthodoxy" was jettisoned in the late 1930s and 1940s. Prominent among the ways that "Mao succeeded in challenging Stalin," was the CCP's rejection of Stalin's notions of imperialism. According to Michael Hunt, "Mao and his colleagues refused to let formal doctrine, especially one that issued from a foreign capital, constrain their approach to the formidable imperialists standing in their way."[58]

It is possible, of course, that this underlying tension concerning the appropriate view of imperialism was at the root of the CCP's about face on Taiwan. Japan was self-evidently an imperialist power that had plundered China since the 1890s. Why allow it to get away with possession of Taiwan? There were, though, other factors at work, too.

Influence of Taiwanese on the Mainland

Beyond its relations with the TCP, the CCP also dealt directly with non-communist Taiwanese activists fighting against Japan.[59] Flowing from the Comintern's emphasis on the establishment of a "united front" to advance revolutionary ambitions, the CCP sought to ally with and influence Taiwanese on the mainland. Where the TCP was devoted to the independence of Taiwan after the defeat of Japan, the noncommunist activists were urging the ROC government to restore Taiwan's status as a province of China, following the defeat of Japan.

This reflects the division among the Taiwanese on the mainland, *banshan ren* [half-mountain people], about appropriate political goals.[60] Many of the Taiwanese had fled to the mainland in the 1920s after the suppression of an unsuccessful Home Rule Movement, and by 1945 there may have been as many as 100,000, including those who lived in Japanese-occupied areas.[61]

The Taiwanese fractured into "dozens of expatriate leagues, parties, and societies" that one estimate puts at more than forty, comprising politically active anti-Japanese Taiwanese on the mainland.[62] Some were affiliated with the Guomindang, including the *Taiwan geming gongmenghui* [Taiwan Revolutionary Alliance (TRA)] and some with the CCP.

The CCP had managed to exert most influence over the Taiwan Independence and Revolutionary Party and hoped it would serve as a conduit for CCP influence on other Taiwanese.[63] This organization adopted as a strategy a phased, two-step process involving, first, a struggle for independence from Japan and then, second, involvement in a Chinese revolution aimed at overthrowing the old, feudal system by which China had been dominated. Its ultimate aim was for Taiwan to be part of the New China.[64] In March 1940, the Taiwanese Independence and Revolutionary Party joined forces with several other Taiwanese organizations in Chongqing on the basis of this staged strategy for Taiwan's independence and return to China as part of a revolutionary movement.

On February 10, 1941, the Taiwanese Independence and Revolutionary Party was one of nine organizations that overcame factionalism, "selfishness," and "individual prejudices" to amalgamate as the TRA.[65] The central objective of this newly established umbrella organization was to have the ROC government recognize Taiwan as a "lost territory" that, once liberated from Japan's colonial yoke, would once again be a province of China.[66]

Toward this end, the primary function of the TRA was propaganda aimed, among other things, at persuading "foreigners that Taiwan properly belonged to China" and convincing "Chinese authorities that postwar Taiwan should be considered a province of China and not a part of occupied Japan."[67] In the end, it may have succeeded in changing the views of both the Guomindang and the CCP.

According to Liu Xiaoyuan, the CCP's support for the Taiwanese Independence and Revolutionary Party and then for the TRA with which it associated itself was an outgrowth of a "united-front strategy that prompted Yan'an to shift the focus of its policy from Taiwan's independence to reunification with China."[68]

In the spring of 1942, the CCP's *Jiefang Ribao* [Liberation Daily News, published in Yan'an] and the *Xinhua Ribao* [New China Daily, published in Chongqing] carried reports of the campaign by Taiwanese to have Taiwan restored as a province of China. Liu observes that *Xinhua Ribao* initiated a column entitled "The Taiwanese Restoration [*guangfu*] Movement." From then on, he asserts, the CCP jettisoned the term "independence movement" concerning Taiwan and used the term "restoration movement" to support the quest of the TRA to see Taiwan restored as a province of China.[69]

Why, though, would the CCP allow the desire for policy consistency with a "united front" partner—the TRA—to determine its view of Taiwan? Why was the CCP prepared to endorse the eventual independence of Taiwan in every relevant statement before 1942 and then utterly reverse itself on the question of Taiwan's status at just that moment?

George Kerr suggests that there was something significant about 1942. In that year, the Taiwanese organizations on the mainland had hoped to win recognition at the Guomindang's "Third People's Political Council Convocation" in Chongqing. Kerr writes: "To their chagrin, it has found that laws regulating the Convocation did not provide for representation on behalf of Formosa. It was not considered a Chinese province by the Chinese. Disappointment was sharpened by the fact that all mainland provinces then occupied by Japanese troops were well represented."[70]

This, then, the CCP press played up as emblematic of Guomindang indifference. In the context of interparty rivalry, one does not know whether the turnabout in CCP policy toward Taiwan was motivated by genuine interest in the recovery of Taiwan or simply in scoring "points" against an apparently apathetic Guomindang.

The period 1939–41 was one in which the CCP's stance on the united front with the Guomindang shifted considerably. From 1940, it was clear that the "CCP's strategy became one of open competition" with the Guomindang "for power and influence within China." This prompted the CCP to conduct "a campaign throughout China to capture public opinion."[71] In that context, pandering to the TRA, regardless whether its views were representative of the spectrum of political ambitions held by Taiwanese elite on Taiwan, served the CCP's own objective to be seen, by comparison to the Guomindang, as "the force most committed to the defeat of Japan and the realization of Sun Yat-sen's revolutionary ideals."[72]

That the CCP changed its stripes on the matter of Taiwan independence strikes Michael Hunt as characteristic of a party that was focused on expedience, not consistency. He writes that sympathy expressed early in the CCP's history for the weak and oppressed peoples was discarded when it became inconvenient for the party to uphold this line. Simply, the party operated unapologetically out of political opportunism.[73]

Especially after December 1941, and the entrance into the war of the United States, the possibility of defeating Japan and recovering Taiwan became imaginable. The CCP was not to be restrained by its earlier pledges to support the self-determination of Taiwan's population, particularly considering that advocates from Taiwan were urging that the island be reincorporated into China. Of course, the revised CCP posture overlooked the wishes of Taiwanese who were pressing for another outcome, notably a trusteeship or outright independence. Yet, the CCP chose to truck with the TRA, perhaps because doing so offered an expanded base of support from among Taiwanese and a lever in the struggle to undermine Guomindang legitimacy as the more vigorous defender of China's interests.

Summary

That elites in the Guomindang and the CCP rather suddenly reintegrated Taiwan into the "mental map" of China after implying for years that they had no interest in claiming the island as Chinese is well supported by evidence. What is more difficult to determine is when, precisely, and why there was such an apparently swift reassessment of Taiwan's salience to China.

Hsiao and Sullivan argue that the Cairo Declaration of November 1943, expressing the allies' intentions that Taiwan be returned to the ROC after the defeat of Japan, "structured the political alternative on the Taiwan issue in such a manner that continued Communist support for 'national liberation' of the island was impossible."[74] It appears, though, that the transition in CCP attitudes occurred by spring 1942, as Liu Xiaoyuan suggests, more than a year earlier. Moreover, it is not self-evident that the CCP was bound to "keep up with the Nationalist Joneses" on the matter of Taiwan. It is not clear what pushed the CCP to abandon the Comintern-inspired view that national minorities were entitled to self-determination and that a reassertion of Chinese sovereignty over Taiwan would be an act of contemptible imperialism. In the absence of more conclusive evidence, one is left to speculate.

However, it is apparent that the nationalist argument about China's original and perpetual sovereignty over Taiwan and Taiwan's place in Chinese history advanced by both the Guomindang and the CCP since the early 1940s is a concoction. Some constellation of other influences—one would like to, but cannot, specify which—prompted a reassessment of Taiwan's salience. This underscores the point that territorial salience is malleable. It can change in response to external variables. It also highlights the merit of thinking more critically about why the PRC seeks to extend Chinese sovereignty to encompass Taiwan.

Shifting Salience (III)
From Civil War to Cold War

Civil War and Strategic Concerns About Taiwan

Almost from the instant that Japan surrendered and its expansionist ambitions were crushed, partisan rivalry between the Guomindang and the CCP for territorial domination flared, embroiling Chinese in a civil war. In that context, Taiwan was a sideshow, and a remote one at that. The most urgent of many pressing problems for both Guomindang and CCP officials in the period 1945–49 was which of them would control China. Taiwan was again part of China, but beyond the reach of the CCP and outside the main arena of interparty competition. The Guomindang swiftly moved to assert control over the island as it sought to "decolonize and reintegrate Taiwan by erasing Japanese influence and bringing the island under the economic, political, and cultural sway of the central government."[1] There was, at that juncture, little concern about the communists extending the battle for control of territory to Taiwan's shores.[2]

However, Guomindang policies and the officials sent to Taiwan to administer them aroused deep dissatisfaction among the island's population. The Taiwanese swallowed their discontentment until February 28, 1947, when indignation and frustration spewed forth after a shooting in Taipei by government agents. The incident itself was followed by popular demands for reform and widespread violent clashes with anyone assumed to be from the mainland or associated with the Guomindang regime. The military response to this political unrest fatefully rent the emerging relations between Taiwan's inhabitants and their new Chinese government.[3]

The aftermath of the military suppression of what was viewed by the Guomindang leadership as an islandwide uprising fueled a sense among Taiwanese elite of alienation from the Chinese government and may have contributed to their wish for autonomy. More broadly, Taiwanese notions of national identity emerged from an internalized sense of injustice at how the island's residents were treated by the Guomindang regime following the February 28 incident.

Taiwan in U.S. Strategic Calculations

The Guomindang's fumbling effort to reassert Chinese dominion over Taiwan-ese prompted concern in Washington. By 1948, the United States had con-cluded that it would be undesirable to have Taiwan fall into the hands of communists. Consequently, Washington was unsettled by the heavy-handed approach the Guomindang adopted on the island. Political instability seemed a breeding ground for communism.

Wei Daoming, a former Chinese Ambassador to the United States who had been sent by the ROC government in Nanjing to govern Taiwan, was irritated at his own inability to inject much-needed reforms in the administration of the island because of the persistent interference of Chiang Kai-shek and his lieu-tenants. Late in 1948, as Chiang's fortunes on the mainland were flagging fatally in the face of CCP advances, Wei made quiet overtures to Washington about securing support for a separate regime on Taiwan. Soon afterward, Chiang replaced Wei. However, discussions within the U.S. foreign policy commu-nity about the viability of supporting a separate state on Taiwan continued.[4] Keeping Taiwan out of communist hands was an objective the United States articulated in geostrategic terms; the question was how best to achieve it.

As Chiang Kai-shek's prospects for survival on the mainland eroded, the CCP worried that the United States intended to help him defend Taiwan as a final bastion in exchange for agreements "by which the island would virtually become an American colony."[5] Although the United States was not actually planning to colonize Taiwan, discussions continued in Washington about how to prevent Taiwan from falling into the hands of "Kremlin-directed Communists."[6] From the vantage of the United States, Taiwan did have strategic import. One can well understand why the CCP was anxious about U.S. intentions.

In the context of ongoing considerations of establishing a defensive perimeter in the Pacific, the U.S. Joint Chiefs of Staff (JCS) expressed to the Secretary of Defense on November 24, 1948, the view that if communists took the Chinese mainland, "This would enhance, from the strategic viewpoint, the potential value to the United States of Formosa [Taiwan] as a wartime base capable of use for staging of troops, strategic air operations and control of adja-cent shipping routes."[7]

If Taiwan fell into "unfriendly" hands the JCS warned that it would have deleterious implications for U.S. national security. They wrote:

> Unless Formosa [Taiwan] can be denied to Kremlin-directed exploitation, we must expect, in the event of war, an enemy capability of dominating to his advantage and our disadvantage the sea routes between Japan and the Malay areas, together with a

greatly improved enemy capability of extending his control to the Ryukyus and the Philippines, either of which could produce strategic consequences very seriously detrimental to our national security.[8]

In a January 19, 1949, report to the National Security Council (NSC), the U.S. Department of State "associated" itself with the JCS notion that "The basic aim of the U.S. should be to deny Formosa and the Pescadores [Penghu islands] to the Communists."[9] However, the NSC wished to emphasize the utility of and desirability of employing diplomatic and economic leverage, rather than military force. Accordingly, in early February, the president was advised to approve a plan to "develop and support a local non-Communist Chinese regime" on Taiwan, to "discourage the further influx of mainland Chinese," and "discreetly to maintain contact with potential native Formosan leaders with a view at some future date to being able to make use of a Formosan autonomous movement should it appear to be in the U.S. national interest to do so."[10]

The JCS, in a follow-on memorandum of February 10, 1949, advised that the U.S. station a small fleet of naval vessels at Taiwan's ports as a show of force in conjunction with diplomatic and economic measures. It concluded "every reasonable effort should be made to keep Formosa in friendly hands, and that diplomatic risks and difficulties are thus justified."[11]

However, the Department of State persisted in objecting that "the establishment of U.S. military forces on Formosa in the present situation would be not only diplomatically disadvantageous but also, and far more importantly, a heavy political liability for us." It would not, the Department asserted, prevent communist "agitation and infiltration" and "it might create an irredentist issue just at the time we may wish to exploit Soviet action in Manchuria and Sinkiang [Xinjiang]."[12]

Secretary of State Dean Acheson's aim, until the outbreak of the war in Korea early in 1950, was to "drive a wedge" between the Chinese communists and Moscow, with the hope that doing so would enable the United States to build some foundation for accommodation with a communist-led Chinese state as a counterbalance to the Soviet Union.[13] Consequently, he concluded, the United States "cannot afford to compromise an emerging new U.S. position in China by overtly showing a pronounced interest in Formosa [Taiwan]."[14] In any event, the U.S. efforts to establish a foundation on which might be built a Taiwanese state that was neither communist nor associated with the Guomindang foundered.[15]

By August, 1949, the conflict between the CCP and the Guomindang forces on the mainland was cascading toward its denouement. In Washington, the National Security Council was reviewing U.S. options in light of evolving conditions. It sought an update from the JCS about the strategic implications of Taiwan in communist hands. The JCS responded in a report of August 17, 1949, that its overall assessment of Taiwan's strategic significance to the United States had not changed since February. Indeed, "Since that date, the continuing sweep of Communist conquest in China has strengthened this view." However, in view of budgetary constraints and U.S. military commitments elsewhere the chiefs of staff "do not regard Formosa and the Pescadores as of sufficient military importance to the United States . . . to commit United States forces to their occupation under conditions short of war and on the assumption that in the absence of military measures these islands will sooner or later come under Communist control."[16] At the same time, the JCS also cautioned "future circumstances, extending to war itself, might make overt military action with respect to Formosa eventually advisable from an overall standpoint of national security." That, they advised, was a contingency that should be considered when and if there was "incipient or actual overt war" rather than to "risk undue military commitment in the Formosa area under present circumstances."[17]

Acheson's view, guided as it was by his wish to refrain from irreparable estrangement from the CCP, reflects his sensitivity to the geostrategic significance of an independent state on Taiwan supported by the United States. He understood, it seems, that from the vantage of the Chinese communists, it would be bad enough to lose Taiwan to forces of self-determination. It would be worse if those forces were supported by a foreign power identified as the bastion of imperialism. Hence, considerations about the desirability of an autonomous regime on Taiwan notwithstanding, the United States policy that resulted from these discussions ultimately reflected Acheson's logic. On January 5, 1950, President Truman announced his administration's posture toward Taiwan and specified that:

> The United States has no predatory designs on Formosa [Taiwan] or on any other Chinese territory. The United States has no desire to obtain special rights or privileges or to establish military bases on Formosa at this time. Nor does it have any intention of utilizing its armed forces to interfere in the present situation. The United States Government will not pursue a course which will lead to involvement in civil conflict in China.[18]

So, the United States certainly understood how Taiwan's location would serve its own strategic interests, but set policy on the basis of a broader view advanced by Acheson that the cost of being perceived by the PRC as taking control of Taiwan outweighed the benefits. By that time, of course, the administration had also decided that if it appeared the Soviets would get their hands on Taiwan, the United States would do what it could to deny them access to the island. This, perhaps, is why Truman's statement was worded as it was. He said that the United States "has no desire to obtain special rights or privileges or to establish military bases on Formosa *at this time*," and that it has no "intention of utilizing its armed forces to interfere *in the present situation*" [emphasis added].[19]

Truman's announcement of U.S. policy did not end the debate about what the United States ought to do to ensure Taiwan did not fall into Soviet hands. Indeed, the national security establishment was considering proposals to revise the policy through the spring and early summer of 1950. On June 25, 1950, when news of the North Korean assault on the south was received, no change had been made, but a perspective advanced by John Foster Dulles to "neutralize" Taiwan had gained currency.[20] Truman's decision to authorize the interposition of the Seventh Fleet in the Taiwan Strait had the consequence—perhaps unintended—of consolidating the alliance between the United States and the ROC and leaving Beijing the impression that Washington had designs on China's territory.

Political actors in June 1950, focused as they were on the Korean crisis, could not have understood that they had already stepped beyond the verge of a cold war that would persist for four decades. The neutralization of the Taiwan Strait may have been intended by Washington as a temporary measure—a response to uncertainty about whether Kim Il-Sung's attack on the south of Korea was the first barrage in a coordinated communist campaign to take other "free" (not communist) states.[21] Truman's decision had the effect, though, of leaving Beijing the impression that the United States had designs on Chinese territory. It was viewed by the PRC leadership as an encroachment on China's sovereignty and ensured that whatever other rationales Beijing had for "liberating" Taiwan, geostrategic considerations would thereafter be prominent.

CCP Perceptions of U.S. Strategic Calculations

The "neutralization" of the Taiwan Strait coupled to the U.S. response to the Korean conflict had the effect of consolidating PRC hostility toward the United States as a geostrategic rival. Only a few years earlier, when the war against Japan had just ended, the CCP leadership was ambivalent about the United States. It saw in the attitude of President Roosevelt much that was "favorable to the development of the forces of China's resistance and democracy," that is, to its own interests.[22] It is not that the CCP observers were ignorant of structural and institutional constraints within the United States that worked against the CCP's ambitions, but they held out the hope of luring Washington out of Chiang Kai-shek's snare and of "neutralizing" the U.S. influence on the internecine struggle between the CCP and the government of China.[23]

Following Japan's surrender in August 1945, actions by the United States eroded whatever rationale the CCP had for accommodating Washington. The continued show of support for Chiang Kai-shek by the United States caused a shift of attitude by the CCP so that by November 1945, the CCP Central Committee was deeply suspicious, even if not utterly hostile, toward the United States.[24] Some of this suspicion was mollified by the resignation of Ambassador Patrick Hurley and President Truman's announcement of determination to refrain from entering China's civil war.[25] By December, the CCP was articulating a cautious, but defensive, policy toward the United States.[26]

That caution was supplanted by irritation and defiance within a year. The failure of the Marshall mission and the continued support by the United States of the government of China, identified by the CCP as support for Chiang Kai-shek, pushed the CCP to see the United States as an impediment to its revolutionary aims. By the autumn of 1946, the CCP Central Committee was writing that "in order to break the American plot of peace initiative, our propaganda should now focus on 'forcing the American troops to withdraw from China.'"[27]

When the United States itself decided in January 1947 that it would terminate the Marshall mission by ending its participation in the "Committee of Three" (Marshall, Zhou Enlai, and Zhang Qun), the CCP Central Committee wrote that this was a victory for the Chinese people and those Americans who opposed the presence of U.S. troops in China and "the American government's interference with China's internal affairs." The Central Committee stated that "The Chinese people demand that our own problems should be solved by ourselves, and that the United States should end its interference with China's internal affairs and should stop all of its assistance to Chiang Kai-shek."[28] This phrase would subsequently gain currency as an element in the catechism of reproach opposing U.S. involvement in the cross-Strait controversy.

Acheson's aims notwithstanding, by spring 1949, the die had been cast in a way that would affect the CCP's attitude toward the United States. There was little hope that the CCP would be easily swayed from an antagonistic attitude toward the United States. A resolution announced in June 1949 to "lean" to the Soviet side only made explicit, and exacerbated, the emerging bipolar confrontation.[29]

During the period from January 1948 to June 1950, the CCP continued to elaborate a foreign policy that was pro-Soviet, anti-imperialist, and anti-American.

Analysts are divided as to whether this was an outgrowth of ideological identification with the Soviets and against the Americans only, or whether the CCP
policy emerged from a determination of how best to realize China's nationalistic
and development-related ambitions.[30]

By taking refuge on Taiwan in 1949, Chiang Kai-shek may have incited
Mao to view the island as other rulers of China had: as a bridgehead to be
exploited by an adversary. Chiang's presence on Taiwan also gave Washington
a reason to defend it. While one cannot know how Mao would have viewed
the island had Chiang fled to some place other than Taiwan, it seems likely
that he would still have viewed the assertion of PRC sovereignty over Taiwan
as an essential step in the establishment of a secure China, especially given
the presence of U.S. forces in Korea, Japan, the Ryukyu islands, and the
Philippines.

Indeed, from spring 1949 onward, it is evident that the CCP framed its
determination to take Taiwan in strategic terms. On March 15, 1949, a *Xinhua*
editorial, "*Yiding yao Jiefang Taiwan*" [We certainly must liberate Taiwan], cast
the United States as the adversary from which the communists would have to
free Taiwan. The author of a *Renmin Ribao* [People's Daily] article of the same
day rails against "U.S. imperialists and their Guomindang reactionary lackeys"
who envision "holding Taiwan, part of China's territory, as the springboard
for conducting aggressive operations against mainland China in the future."[31]
The CCP press reported that the U.S. National Security Council had already
advised President Truman to approve a plan to defend Taiwan and Hainan
from the communists and to include the islands as part of a region-wide military defense system.[32]

One knows now what Mao did not: that the Truman administration had,
by 1949, already forsaken hope that the Guomindang-led government of
China could survive without a massive intervention of economic and military assistance by the United States that the administration was unwilling to
provide.[33] Nevertheless, the misperception was one of emphasis, not substance.
The United States was indeed prepared to defend Taiwan from falling into
communist hands, all the while seeking some way of doing so that would not
involve the use of force or create the impression that the United States was
annexing the island. This was an awkward, and ultimately unsustainable, balance for Washington to maintain and one can appreciate why, from the perspective of the CCP, the nuances of U.S. policy were irrelevant. Washington's
"defensive perimeter" was, for the CCP, a "counter-revolutionary *cordon sanitaire*, with Taiwan at the center of a strategic line" of islands bristling with
American military assets.[34]

The United States was not then aiming to exploit Chiang's presence on the island as a way of "conducting aggressive operations against mainland China." However, by early 1950, "the interventionist argument, based upon fundamental anti-communism and post-war concepts of national security, gained urgency" in the United States.[35] The CCP was also correct to expect Chiang Kai-shek to use Taiwan as a base from which to stage operations against the mainland. In that respect, the CCP's expectations aligned well with the Guomindang's own narrative about its presence on Taiwan: that it was much like the regime of Zheng Chenggong [Koxinga], with the island itself again playing the role of "the last redoubt of the Chinese nation" fighting against a "foreign invader" that had usurped power from the legitimate ruler of China.[36]

Although the CCP failed to see that Washington hoped to avoid closing all doors to a modus vivendi with a communist Chinese state, what transpired after Kim Il-Sung initiated a general assault on the south of Korea in June 1950 bore out Mao's uneasiness about a failure by the CCP to "seize Taiwan." In the hands of the CCP's adversaries, Taiwan did, indeed, become a foundation for an alliance between the ROC and the United States that intensified the PRC's exposure to hostilities.[37]

From Tactical Concern to Strategic Alarm

The CCP reached the conclusion that Taiwan had geostrategic significance as a bulwark against imperialism in the midst of simultaneous campaigns to eradicate Guomindang defenses and reassert control over those buffer zones that had slipped from China's grasp after the collapse of the Qing. The CCP took Beijing in January, 1949. In a meeting with Deputy Premier Anastas Mikoyan later that month, Mao reportedly told Stalin's representative that he anticipated it would take the CCP another three years to liberate Tibet, Xinjiang, and Taiwan.[38] At that moment, the CCP did not have either an air or naval fleet capable of subordinating Taiwan, but the determination to take the island was clear.

By May 1949, the CCP had crossed the Yangzi River, taken Shanghai and the ROC capital, Nanjing, and was planning for the final phase of war. Chiang Kai-shek retreated to Taiwan early that month, leaving the CCP uncertain about his intentions, but determined that it would ultimately launch an assault to take control of the island.[39]

Liu Shaoqi wrote that following campaigns to liberate remaining territories held by Guomindang forces, which might extend through the winter of 1949–50, "only the control of Taiwan, Hainan, Xinjiang, and Xizang [Tibet] will then remain unresolved. While the problem of Tibet will perhaps be resolved through political channels, Taiwan, Hainan, and Xinjiang will most probably be liberated by military means in 1950."[40]

Mao wrote to Zhou Enlai early in July 1949 about the need to make preparations for an assault on Taiwan. He expressed the aim to be prepared to seize Taiwan by the summer of 1950.[41] Zhou, in a telegram two weeks later, indicated an intention to establish a PLA air force that would "coordinate the PLA's amphibious operations aimed at liberating Taiwan."[42]

At this stage, the battle to control territory was both a civil conflict for legitimacy and power as well as a geopolitical contest to ensure China's security from imperialist hostility. Mao considered it likely that the United States would take control of Taiwan if the PLA failed to secure the island swiftly.[43] He Di argues "the victorious completion of the Taiwan campaign would finally bring the civil war to its end." He cites a report by acting commander of the PLA's Third Field Army, Su Yu, in which the campaign is identified as "the last campaign to end China's civil war."[44] He Di adds, "Mao became emotional in the face of such a prospect; the one-hundred-year history of internal turmoil and political division would come to an end, and a new China with territorial integrity and administrative unification would be in his hands."[45] One cannot help wondering, though, whether the ascription of emotion to Mao and the references to the end of turmoil and division are a reading back into history of sentiments that came to be associated with the subordination of Taiwan only after 1950. The evidence that He Di provides leaves a stronger impression that Mao was motivated to accelerate the campaign to take the island by strategic, as much as nationalistic, concerns.

After all, earlier in the summer, Mao spelled out his worries about leaving Taiwan in enemy hands. In a telegram issued on June 14, Mao, writing on behalf of the Central Military Commission, urged that Su Yu "pay attention to the problem of seizing Taiwan immediately."[46] Then on June 21, 1949, Mao instructed Su and the CCP's Eastern Bureau to "seize Taiwan." His rationale was clear: "If Taiwan is not liberated and the GMD's [Guomindang's] naval and air bases not destroyed, Shanghai and other coastal areas will be menaced from time to time. If Taiwan is not liberated, we will not be able to seize hundreds of thousands of tons of vessels (still controlled by the GMD). Our coastal and inland water transportation will thus be controlled by foreign merchants."[47]

Indeed, on the very day that Mao laid out his rationale for taking Taiwan, the Guomindang initiated a blockade of ports held by CCP forces along China's coast. For the remainder of the year and early into 1950, Taiwan was in fact used by Chiang Kai-shek as Mao had anticipated: as a base from which to harass and menace the communists.[48] Whether the prospect of "liberating" the island evoked the emotions that He Di suggests, Taiwan in Guomindang hands was assuredly a source of unease. Indeed, it is likely that the urgency Mao expressed about the importance of taking control of the island was prompted by Chiang's own decision to use Taiwan as it had been used before, as a springboard for operations against the mainland.

In Moscow to negotiate a new treaty that would supplant the Sino-Soviet Treaty of Friendship that the ROC had been bullied into signing by Stalin in 1945, Mao asked Stalin to offer military support to the PRC's campaign to take Taiwan. Mao explained that the Guomindang had built naval and air bases on Taiwan. Therefore, he diffidently added, "some of our generals have been voicing opinions that we should request assistance from the Soviet Union, which could send volunteer pilots or secret military detachments to speed up the conquest of Formosa [Taiwan]."[49]

Stalin, though, was more concerned about the consequences of drawing the United States into war than he was about abetting Mao's wish to extend control to Taiwan. He demurred, telling Mao that while "Assistance has not been ruled out," and he could offer staff and instructors, "the rest we will have to think about."[50]

Even without all the Soviet assistance Mao had hoped for, the PRC decided to invade Guomindang-held islands off Zhejiang and Fujian, all the while preparing for an assault on Taiwan.[51] On March 28, 1950, Mao wrote about invading Dinghai, capital of the Zhoushan islands off Zhejiang province, and from there invading Jinmen, where Chiang Kai-shek's troops were concentrated opposite Taiwan.[52] A withdrawal of Guomindang troops from many of the offshore islands after a defeat on Hainan Island enabled Chiang to beef up the defense of Taiwan and those islands his forces continued to hold.[53] In spite of the need to revise continually the plan for a Taiwan campaign—and eventually to postpone it—Mao was determined that the liberation of Taiwan and Tibet be the principal objective of the PLA in 1950.[54]

Throughout 1949, the PLA faced considerable difficulties crushing the Guomindang forces in China's southern and western provinces. It was October 15, two weeks after Mao declared the establishment of the PRC, that Lin Biao's forces took Guangzhou, where the remnants of the Guomindang government on the mainland had been operating.[55] Despite the loss, the Guomindang military forces still held large portions of China's southern fringe. Indeed, Chiang Kai-shek flew with impunity from Taiwan to the mainland several times late in 1949 to confer with stalwart officials and military officers.[56] So, until June 1950, the CCP determination to take Taiwan must be considered in the context of a general inclination to mop up resistance to communist rule throughout China.

Xinjiang had been divided into a Guomindang-controlled south and an autonomous East Turkistan Republic, a client of the Soviet Union, in the north and west. Although PLA forces entered Xinjiang in the fall of 1949, the region was not fully subdued until 1954.[57] Hainan Island was not taken by the PLA until May 1950.[58] It was October 7, 1950, one week after the first anniversary of the establishment of the PRC and one week before Beijing sent troops to Korea, that the PLA invaded Tibet to "liberate" it, as it had pledged to do.[59]

In the period 1949–50, Mao was anxious about the possibility that New China would be throttled in its cradle by imperialist intervention. Odd Arne Westad contends that Mao saw domestic consolidation of power, a deterrent alliance with the Soviet Union, and a "rapid completion of the military takeover of the country" as the best ways to forestall such an eventuality. The drive to secure territory proceeded at a rapid, at times hasty, pace on China's periphery.[60]

U.S. Intervention and the Transformation of Taiwan's Salience

By June 1950, the Taiwan issue was wedged into the ideological and strategic divide that fueled competition between the PRC and the United States. National unity as an abstraction was overtaken by national security, which was tangibly threatened by U.S. actions in response to the Korean conflict. The rhetoric of the PRC emphasized the Sino-U.S. context for its objectives vis-à-vis Taiwan. On the eve of what was originally planned as an amphibious assault on Taiwan, the General Information Agency cast the conflict ahead as one that would awaken "the Chinese people and the people of the whole world" to "unite and strike firmly against the U.S. aggression."[61]

Xiao Jinguang, a member of the CCP Central Committee and vice commander of the PLA's Fourth Field Army and, after 1950, commander of the PLA(N), recalls a conversation with Zhou Enlai on June 30 in which Zhou stated to him, "The situation change increases difficulties involved in our plan to attack Taiwan because the United States is now standing there. This, however, is not necessarily a bad thing, since we have not completed our preparations. Our attitude is to denounce the U.S. imperialist invasion of Taiwan, which is an interference with China's internal affairs."[62]

By August 1950, the U.S. and United Nations' commitment to Korea, the threat perceived at the PRC's northern border, and the recognition by the PRC that a U.S. presence in the Taiwan Strait would exponentially complicate an already strained plan for liberating Taiwan caused the CCP Central Military Commission to write, "The decision is not to attack Taiwan in 1951. Whether or not [we will] attack Taiwan in 1952 will be decided according to the situation."[63]

Among the reasons why the PRC was irritated by the U.S. involvement in the Korean War and in the Taiwan Strait is because it appeared, from Beijing, to be the Japanese strategy redux. That is, in a speech concerning the Korean War, Zhou Enlai made explicit:

> The U.S. imperialists are pursuing the policy designed by [General Douglas] MacArthur in the East, using Japan as their base, inheriting the mantle of Japanese militarism and following the footsteps they have left since the Sino-Japanese War of 1894. They are following the old maxim that whoever wants to annex China must first occupy its Northeast, and that to occupy the Northeast one must first seize Korea. While the Japanese imperialists spent forty years inching their way toward that goal, the U.S. imperialists want to accomplish it in four or five years.
>
> To us, the Korean question is not merely a Korean question. It is related to the Taiwan question. Taking a position against China, the U.S. imperialists have extended their line of defense to the Taiwan strait, while professing nonaggression and noninterference. They have invaded Korea without justification. If we send our troops to intervene, we are justified by the need to defend ourselves and the entire peace camp. ... If the Korean question is settled well and if the U.S. imperialists do meet with a setback, chance may emerge for the settlement of the question of the Taiwan Strait and the East as a whole.[64]

This theme, the U.S. adaptation of the Japanese strategy against China, was made even more baldly in recommendations about the tone of propaganda that ought to be used in statements pertaining to the war. The CCP Central Committee hoped to explain:

> This kind of American plan is nothing but a copy of Japan's aggression of China in history. The first step of Japan's aggression was to invade Korea and Taiwan; the second step was to invade the Northeast; the third step was to invade all of China. Considering all this, we cannot make no response to America's aggression against Korea for the sake of our country's security.[65]

Moreover, "The United States brazenly invaded our country's Taiwan province." In directing a campaign of propaganda against the United States "an attitude characterized by hating, looking down upon, and despising U.S. imperialism will prevail." This was the blueprint for the anti-U.S. campaign in which the U.S. role in East Asia broadly, but aimed at China specifically, was built up to spur popular sentiments against the United States. The invasion of Taiwan was portrayed as one step in a long-term strategy to "invade all of China."[66]

In the minds of the PRC leadership, the strategic link between Taiwan and Korea was clear. This connection was highlighted in Ambassador Wu

Xiuquan's November 28, 1950, entreaty to the United Nations to condemn the United States for its "unlawful and criminal act of armed aggression against Chinese territory of Taiwan—including the Penghu Islands."[67] Indeed, his long statement is replete with references to geostrategic rivalry and efforts by the United States to use the Korean crisis as a pretext for taking Taiwan.

Wu cites the views of Japan's Tanaka Giichi, who served as both prime minister and foreign minister in the period 1927–29. According to Wu, Tanaka proposed that, "To conquer the world, one must first conquer Asia; to conquer Asia, one must first conquer China. To conquer China, one must first conquer Manchuria and Mongolia. To conquer Manchuria and Mongolia, one must first conquer Korea and Taiwan."[68]

Wu states that the Japanese effort failed, but by instigating the Korean War and occupying Taiwan the United States was seeking to take a page from Tanaka's strategic playbook. In Wu's words, "American imperialism has taken the place of Japanese imperialism."[69] What one notes in Ambassador Wu's argument is his effort to frame the PRC's determination to take Taiwan in terms of a fear that a failure to do so would leave the Chinese state vulnerable to foreign (read: U.S.) aggression. This was the Shi Lang paradigm—the rationale of strategic denial.

All that is to say, the immediate reaction of the PRC leaders was to interpret Truman's order to neutralize the Taiwan Strait as part of a scheme to "commit aggression against China and seize Asia by force."[70] They claimed, perhaps disingenuously, that the United States had instigated the Korean War by prompting South Korea (the Republic of Korea) to attack North Korea (the Democratic People's Republic of Korea) in a "premeditated" move "designed to create a pretext for the United States to invade Taiwan, Korea, Vietnam, and the Philippines."[71] Mao characterized this decision as an "open self-exposure by the United States of its true imperialist face."[72]

From 1950 to 1971, the PRC was consumed by the need to "liberate Taiwan." This posture was inextricably bound to the presence of U.S. forces on and U.S. defense of Taiwan. The underlying urge for national reunification and the elaborate historical, moral, legal, and cultural justifications for unity persisted, but the context for the territorial dispute was no longer limited to bilateral, domestic dynamics. What had been a tactical objective with limited territorial salience was transformed by the United States into a strategic anxiety driven by geopolitical competition. For the PRC to recover sovereignty over Taiwan, it had to cope—and still must—with U.S. strategic anxieties as they reflect Washington's assessment of China's role in Asia.

Taiwan in Sino-U.S. Rivalry

In the PRC, there is little disagreement that the United States "has played a critical role in severing the state on the two sides of the Taiwan Strait. Had the U.S.A. not intervened, there would be no severed state."[73] Moreover, since 1950 the United States did ally with the ROC and, even after the establishment of diplomatic relations with the PRC, has continued to support Taiwan despite the vehement protests of the PRC. The U.S. alliance with the ROC was more than a notional indignity. It resulted in the harassment of the PRC and menacing activity by the United States that was at least partly staged on Taiwan. The PRC was the target of covert intelligence and military operations by the ROC and the United States. Taiwan served as a base for intelligence gathering against the mainland and as a staging area for U.S. actions in Vietnam.[74] Mao's anxiety in 1949 and 1950 about Taiwan becoming a bridgehead used to threaten the mainland prefigured actions taken in the framework of a U.S.-ROC alliance, even though Mao's greatest fear of an American invasion did not materialize.[75]

In 1954, Beijing viewed the prospect of a mutual defense treaty between the United States and the ROC as having potentially grave strategic consequences. Mao was concerned that the treaty could permanently separate Taiwan from the mainland. Indeed, his worry was not unwarranted, as the following half century proved. As a signal of its resolve to "liberate Taiwan" and in hopes that it could deter Washington from signing the mutual defense treaty, Beijing bombarded Jinmen Island and triggered the first of two military conflicts over the "offshore" islands.[76]

The first conflict of 1954–55 and the second in 1958 were both efforts by the PRC to probe U.S. intentions and, if possible, dislodge U.S. support for Chiang Kai-shek's regime on Taiwan. The governing logic applied by the PRC in initiating and prosecuting both campaigns was focused on Washington and its reactions.[77] Shielded in the protective embrace of the United States, Taiwan remained beyond Beijing's reach. To get to the island, the PRC had to impel the United States to release the island from its defensive orbit.

PRC frustration about this condition is evident from comments made by the Chinese leadership in 1959. For instance, to Communist Party officials from Latin America, Mao reportedly said in March 1959:

> We have thrown out the North American imperialists from this continent but they are holding out on Taiwan. We have warned them to get out of there but they refuse. . . . The U.S.A. does not object to the island of Quemoy and Matsu being given back to us, but in return it wishes to retain Taiwan for itself. This would be an unprofit-

able deal. We had better wait; let Chiang Kai-shek stay on Quemoy and Matsu, and we shall get them back later, together with the Pescadores and Taiwan. Our territory is spacious, and for the time begin we can get along without these islands. . . . It is unimportant if they do not return Taiwan to us for another 100 years.[78]

Thus, since 1950, Beijing has not been able to view Taiwan without thinking of the United States and, during the cold war, of the Soviet Union. "Liberating" Taiwan meant confronting the United States.[79] The territorial dispute was more than a standoff by two opposed groups of power-seeking nationalists competing to unify the Chinese state in a civil war; it was enmeshed in the geostrategic friction of the Sino–U.S. relationship.[80]

By the early 1970s, transitions in the international arena led the PRC and the United States to see merits in shifting the nature of their relationship. One pivotal element in the PRC approach to normalization was to use it as a mechanism to isolate Taiwan. That the PRC saw this as a priority is manifested by the primacy of place discussions about Taiwan had in the record of interactions between the PRC leadership and both Henry Kissinger and Richard Nixon during discussions in 1971 and 1972.[81] One must recall that among the principal demands of the PRC was that the United States remove its troops from Taiwan and end its strategic relationship with the ROC. This was nothing new. Beijing had been making that demand since 1950.

Even after the normalization of relations and the adjustment to a less belligerent relationship, the issue of Taiwan remained at the core of tensions between the two states. Taiwan is at the heart of the three joint communiqués signed by both sides in 1972, 1979, and 1982.

Beijing's concern about the U.S. role in supporting Taiwan is easily identified in the PRC's white paper of 1993, "The Taiwan Question and Reunification of China." The document lays out the view that once the United States abides fully with the commitments it agreed to in the joint communiqués, "it will not be difficult to settle the Taiwan question that has been left over from history and Sino–U.S. relations will surely see steady improvement and development ahead."[82] In other words, from the PRC's vantage the resolution of the Taiwan issue is dependent on and impeded by the United States.[83]

The message is that the people of Taiwan can be compelled to unify with the PRC if only external forces "abide by the principles of mutual respect for sovereignty and territorial integrity and non-interference in each other's internal affairs." Those other forces are principally the United States and secondarily Japan. Beijing's anger about foreign interference as the principal hurdle to unification could not be stated more clearly than the white paper does in its comment that: "Certain foreign forces who do not want to see a reunified China have gone out of their way to meddle in China's internal affairs. They support the anti-Communist stance of the Taiwan authorities of rejecting peace talks and abet the secessionists on the island, thereby erecting barriers to China's peaceful reunification and seriously wounding the national feelings of the Chinese people."[84]

The PRC has frequently expressed its opposition to Washington's "interference in the internal affairs of China." However, this rhetorical framework may cause readers to blur the distinction between the *effects* of that "interference" and the *fact* that the United States is perceived to be interfering. That is to say, when PRC statements denounce Washington for "sending the wrong signal" to Taiwan by selling arms or providing other material support that enables the island to sustain its autonomy in the face of PRC military threats, Beijing is focused on the effects of U.S. interference. It is the supply of armaments and statements of determination to "do whatever it takes" that are seen in the PRC to embolden the advocates for independence, blunting PRC policies aimed at increasing pressure on Taipei to come to the table to negotiate a resolution and, there, succumb to PRC demands for reunification.

However, in addition to the putative effects of U.S. interference, the fact that the United States involves itself in a defense of Taiwan evokes bitter resentment in the PRC because of a prevailing image of the United States as a menacing hegemonic power intent on thwarting the development of China. Wang Jisi writes:

> Without any doubt, the single most important issue that arouses Chinese indignation about the "hegemonic behavior" of the United States has been its policy toward Taiwan. Few, if any, Chinese on the mainland doubt that Taiwan is a Chinese territory and that people in Taiwan belong to the same Chinese nation as mainlanders. Therefore, the U.S. rejection of China's territorial claim of Taiwan and its continued arms sales to the island as part of the plans to thwart Chinese efforts to reunify it are regarded as showing hostility to the Chinese nation.[85]

Moreover, in the eyes of PRC officialdom, "America's Taiwan policy, including arms sales, is motivated by a desire to delay or even prevent China's rise." It is aimed at using democratic Taiwan as a lever to pry up and displace the authoritarian regime of the PRC with a democratic one. Beyond that, "Some officials also suspect that the United States wants to turn Taiwan into an unsinkable U.S. aircraft carrier."[86] Indeed, a statement on the English-language Web site of the PRC Ministry of Foreign Affairs includes the passage "the United States still regards Taiwan as an 'unsinkable aircraft carrier' and considers the Taiwan question as a card in hand to hold back the development and growth in strength of China."[87]

The perception of the United States as a latent and, at times, genuine threat is deeply enmeshed in the genetic code of the CCP. At the very least, there is a widespread uneasiness in the PRC about why the United States continues to arm and express a willingness to defend Taiwan. That the United States remains ensconced in a quasi-military alliance with Taiwan fuels a searing indignation about Taiwan's autonomy and enhances a perception that China's disunity serves Washington's strategic objectives.

In the mid-1990s, despite efforts by Presidents Clinton and Jiang to establish a "constructive strategic partnership," the PRC government portrayed the United States as "a sinister hegemon trying to dominate the world and interfere in China's domestic affairs. According to China's official guideline, U.S. policy toward China aimed to Westernize [*xihua*], divide [*fenhua*], and contain [*ezhi*] the People's Republic with ulterior motives."[88]

Even if a less sinister view of the United States has prevailed in the early twenty-first century, "there is the notion among many Chinese that the revival of the Chinese nation would not be meaningful and real if the mainland failed to achieve reunification with Taiwan."[89] Left unsaid is that the United States is still perceived as an impediment to these aims. For unification to be achieved, Washington must still be persuaded to desist from supporting Taiwan's autonomy or deterred from intervening in a military conflict or compelled to withdraw from such a conflict. In any case, unification will be perceived in the PRC as prevailing not only over political forces in Taiwan, but in a competition with the United States.

Paradoxically, this view of national self-esteem emerges in an era when others in Beijing are prepared to acknowledge that their perception of the United States' attitude toward Taiwan was probably misguided. Wang Jisi observes:

> It is more apparent to the Chinese today that, despite conspicuous U.S. political support for Taiwan and its democratization, U.S. policy toward the island is not intended to encourage or endorse *de jure* independence of Taiwan. . . . The United States, therefore, would rather see the status quo of "no reunification, no separation," in the cross-Strait relations maintained. *This interpretation contrasts with the previous mainstream Chinese perception that the U.S. strategy toward Taiwan was designed to separate Taiwan permanently in order to contain China* [emphasis added].[90]

While Wang may capture well one end of the Chinese political spectrum in the early twenty-first century, what he characterizes as the "previous mainstream Chinese perception" of the U.S. strategy toward Taiwan has not vanished. Even if the PRC government has come to understand the United States as less inclined to seek the annexation of Taiwan or to use the island to "contain China," many PRC strategists apparently have not been comparably enlightened. There is a debate about the intentions of the United States toward Taiwan that persists in the PRC, a subject taken up in Chapter 7.

What this chapter aims to convey is that the salience of Taiwan as evaluated by the leadership of the CCP, and then the PRC, has shifted. The conflict between Chinese Nationalists in the Guomindang and Communists in the CCP has never been exclusively a bilateral battle of ideologies or will. It was internationalized at its inception because of the involvement of the United States and Soviet Union. Consequently, the CCP's determination to "liberate" Taiwan and unify China existed within an international context that imbued the island with salience reflecting more than the island's separateness. Although the PRC has emphasized its resolve to unify China, where Taiwan has been concerned that resolution has never been simply about fitting a missing piece into a nearly completed jigsaw puzzle depicting the map of China..

Certainly after June 1950, the dispute about Taiwan cannot be properly apprehended in dyadic terms only. The PRC's relationship to the international context generally, and the United States in particular, colored its perceptions of Taiwan's salience. As those relationships evolved, so did the PRC's notions of what was at stake in securing control of Taiwan. Hence, PRC rhetoric about Taiwan that characterizes the desire for sovereignty over the island in sentimental terms by reference to China's history and culture or its legal claims to the island cannot be taken as a comprehensive account of why that territory has salience.

Within the international setting, the cross-Strait controversy has been— and is—a correlate of Sino–U.S. rivalry. Since 1949 that broader rivalry has entailed friction about a range of issues, not just Taiwan. It is essentially a strategic rivalry having much to do with competition for influence. While the Taiwan issue may be the most tangible focus of conflict between Beijing and Washington, it is not the source of the rivalry. Indeed, one might characterize the controversy about Taiwan as the territorial proxy for geostrategic competition. The competitive dimension of the Sino-U.S. relationship may be masked, from time to time, in optimistic oratory, or intentionally suppressed to enable other dimensions of the relationship to flourish. So long as it exists, though, Beijing is likely to consider geostrategic factors as it assesses the salience of Taiwan.

Taiwan in the "Imagined Geography" of the PRC

> With Taiwan in hand, the Pacific Ocean will become China's
> open field to the East . . . . The strategic importance of Taiwan simply
> cannot be over-stated.
>
> *"China's Worries at Sea"*
> Jiefangjun Bao
> *January 2, 2004*[1]

> China wants Taiwan because it wants regional dominance, for
> which the "unsinkable aircraft carrier" is the key. There is a lot more
> at stake here than questions of Taiwanese identity.
>
> *Editorial*
> Taipei Times
> *December 20, 2004*[2]

> . . . if Taiwan cannot return to the arms of the motherland, China
> will meet great obstacles on its way [to] enter the outside world, will
> not be able to fully develop and utilize marine resources, and will
> face restrictions in its efforts to further open itself to the outside
> world. Then, China will become a sea-locked country.
>
> *General Wen Zongren*
> Ta Kung Pao
> *March 10, 2005*[3]

"Imagined Geography"

Chinese strategists have long understood territorial security to be related to
geography.[4] Mountains, passes, rivers, deserts, marshes, valleys, islands, and seas
were prized where they promised advantage and seen as impediments to be
overcome where they created vulnerability. Distance and space were seen
as related to the concentration or dispersion of resources and the ease or
difficulty with which an adversary could threaten the heartland. Evidence
of Ming, Qing, and twentieth-century Chinese considerations of Taiwan's
relationship to the mainland territories, specifically, suggest that the island's

geographic characteristics also mattered as elements in a holistic calculation of China's power and capability relative to its rivals.

Geography still matters to PRC strategists in the twenty-first century.[5] Indeed, one could argue that no sensible approach to the defense of the national interest, to say nothing of the territorial integrity of the state, could proceed without an assessment of geographical constraints and opportunities. How else does one know what must be defended and what one must deploy to defend it? Even if one balks at Colin Gray's notion that *"all politics is geopolitics,"* it is easier to embrace his assertion that *"all strategy is geostrategy"* [emphasis as published].[6]

So, it is not surprising that competition for control of or influence over advantageous territory—a hallmark of geopolitics—persists as a foundation for thinking in the PRC about international rivalry and affects the way some analysts there evaluate the salience of Taiwan.[7] Lieutenant General Liu Yazhou, the deputy commissar of the PLA Air Force, in words that are consistent with Colin Gray's, states: "Geography is destiny. From ancient times to the present, that has not changed. Ordinarily, as a powerful state begins to rise, it seeks to establish itself in an unassailable position. Geographically, an unassailable position is a region over which geopolitical control must be maintained."[8]

Indeed, references to geography, geopolitics, and geostrategic thought pepper the lexicon of military and civilian analysts in the PRC just as they do the expressions of statesmen and scholars who write about the contemporary strategic environment. Geographic allusions and imagery abound in pronouncements about the PRC's strategic ambitions and in analyses of the mainland's relationship to Taiwan. This profusion of concern about geography, geopolitics, and geostrategy tends to reflect two broad tendencies. Analyses either (1) emphasize the implications of real, measurable geographic features or (2) imbue geography with symbolic importance, ascribing to actuality a layer of meaning that is primarily imagined.

Liu Yazhou, for example, rehearses a characterization of China's topographical qualities that recalls the words of earlier Chinese strategists, including those of Chiang Kai-shek in *China's Destiny*. Liu states about China's geography, "high mountains stand in the northwest and southwest, great seas lie to the east and south, all of which constituted a natural barrier in the era of cold weaponry . . . only the north, where there were no natural barriers, served as a passage for adversaries."[9] Previous chapters indicate that China's strategists were accustomed to thinking in terms of natural features offering protection to the homeland. Where none existed, they sought to construct one.[10] The northern frontier notwithstanding, the "mental map" of China was one of a realm generally well shielded by natural bulwarks. The merit attributed to China's geographic periphery was not based on cosmological, spiritual, historical, or economic calculations of value. Instead, it reflected perceptions of security and vulnerability.

All this contributed to an "imagined geography" of China. Geographic features of China's domain came to be associated with characteristics that fed a narrative about what was Chinese and why. However, what is imagined about geography can change. For example, "although Taiwan never moved from its position at 23.5 degrees north / 120 degrees east, 96 miles from the Chinese coast, in terms of the Chinese geographic imagination, between the seventeenth and nineteenth centuries the island shifted from 'far, far beyond the seas' to a location firmly situated within the Chinese empire."[11] In other words, while the actual geography remained constant, the "imagined geography"—a conceptualization of geography—shifted over the course of two centuries. Taiwan was, at first, imagined to be too far away to be part of or relevant to China. However, as perceptions of distance and of the Chinese realm evolved, Taiwan was eventually imagined to have a place in a space understood as Chinese.

Much of this shift in attitude about Taiwan is discerned in the records of exploration and encounters written by those who visited the island. Texts revealed the island for readers in China and situated Taiwan in what was a newly emerging notion of China's "imagined geography." That is, "texts—which might include anything from travel writings and government policy documents to fictional literature and a wide array of other representational modes—assume a central role in the process of helping constitute (other) places. Texts, in other words, are a form of power by which places are made and remade."[12] The potency of words to shape people's evaluation of space and reshape it anew to serve developing political interests has attracted the attention of scholars who examine the relationship between geography and politics. For instance, like the Chinese who came to view Taiwan through the travel writing Emma Teng examines, Christopher Krebs notes "The Roman's image of the world was for the most part based on verbal descriptions in geographical texts."[13] Hence, Caeser wrote of *Gallia* and *Britannia*—territories that had been essentially unknown—in a treatise that made it "comparatively easy for his Roman readers to construe these two spaces and to integrate them within their mental geography."[14]

The issue, of course, is not just *that* Caeser wrote of them, but *how* he wrote of them. Geographic features and qualities can be written of in a way that enhances the value of the territory to a nation.[15] Indeed, "nationalizing-states have long made use of many devices and agencies to create an emotional bonding with particular histories and geographies" that inculcate a sense of "national cohesion" based on a "collective awareness and identity."[16] Those nationalizing objectives are served as much by a rendering of geography as they are by a rendition of history.

How Taiwan is portrayed in texts emanating from the PRC is of paramount importance to an understanding of the island's place in China's "imagined geography." Texts manifest what is believed to be true about geography. That is why this work focuses so intently on the words used by Chinese elites to describe Taiwan and its relationship both to Chinese spatiality and to the welfare of the Chinese people.

Texts reflect the way in which their authors seek to "frame" issues for readers. Certainly, "national cohesion" and "collective awareness and identity" feature prominently as objectives of official PRC statements about Taiwan. These concerns constitute the dominant narrative about Taiwan that so many analysts and observers outside the PRC assume to be the only reasons why Beijing is eager to reassert sovereignty over Taiwan. However, embedded in such statements one often finds references to geography, both actual and imagined. Moreover, expressions about Taiwan in quasi and unofficial texts disseminated in the press, in scholarly publications, and throughout Chinese cyberspace insistently link the salience of Taiwan with geography. As this chapter suggests, Taiwan's role in the "imagined geography" of China is very widely depicted in such texts as having strategic significance.

The illustrative citations in this chapter make clear that "imagined geography" can be projected on a program for national development or as a foundation for national self-defense. That is, geography can be imagined as offering *prospective* value. Imperatives that a nation anticipates and, indeed, the nation's very survival can be represented as dependent upon access to or control of space that is ascribed with geographic significance that is largely imagined.

The comparatively permanent features of the earth's surface can be ascribed with meaning again and again as comparatively transient political and national interests change. This is not limited to meaning conveyed in texts. Where cartography is concerned, one notes that the actuality a map purports to represent is filtered through the imagination of the mapmaker, informed by the graphic and epistemological conventions of the civilization and moment when it was made, and crafted for a specific purpose at a specific time. Just as places are mapped differently over time to reflect adjustments in perceptions and of power, imagined geographies expressed in words are susceptible to change.

Whether in textual or cartographic form, places can acquire the quality of a palimpsest, as Sallie Yea suggests, because "imaginary maps are never finally drawn, and their constitution is a process of continual etching and erasure."[17]

The place of Taiwan in the "imagined geography" of China provides a splendid illustration of this point. Since 1895, Taiwan has been imagined and reimagined repeatedly. Taiwan was quite literally displaced from the Chinese realm in 1895, disappearing thereafter from cartographic representations of the Chinese state. Maps and atlases produced in China while Taiwan was a colony of Japan fastidiously indicated the international boundary between Japan's sovereign realm that encompassed Taiwan and China's that did not. In some instances, this was done with a dotted line in the Taiwan Strait. Where China's territory was shaded or colored in one way and the territory of other states in a different way, Taiwan was manifestly represented as not part of China.

Taiwan "entered the map" again in the early 1940s, when—even before the island was retroceded to the ROC government—Taiwan was reimagined as part of China. Thereafter, Taiwan became lodged in a nationalist conception of the Chinese state. The loss and recovery of the island fit a grand narrative of "Humiliation, Salvation, and Chinese Nationalism" in which the shame of loss was bound up in a commemoration of China's erstwhile weakness, all of which served to inspire unity and resurgence.[18] National reconstruction and the determination to reestablish lost stature affected views of the island.

Expressing its commitment to liberate Taiwan in 1949, the PRC voiced its indignation at the United States for trampling China's sovereignty and violating its territorial integrity, even though the CCP had only come to see Taiwan as part of China several years earlier. As a nationalizing state, however, the PRC promoted "an emotional bonding" with a particular view of Taiwan's history and geography, ignoring the communal disinterest in Taiwan by Chinese elites earlier in the twentieth century. "The orchestration of such collective remembering—and, if necessary, collective amnesia—constitutes the crucial underpinning of national-state identities."[19] So, "liberating" Taiwan came to be associated with saving the Chinese nation from the shame of division at the hands of stronger adversaries. Liberation was associated with a defense of the communist revolution that was, itself, understood as a defense of China.

In short order, a specific geostrategic vision of Taiwan emerged to "over-write" the nebulous nationalist formulation of the island's geography as simply part of China. As communist advances during the civil war put the CCP in control of ever more territory and hastened the prospect of it governing as China's ruling party, recovering the island was no longer viewed as a straightforward matter of uniting "sacred territory" that had been divided. Taiwan was reimagined as it had once been imagined to provide a natural buffer, a shield that offers China a layer of security from menacing adversaries approaching from the sea. Reunification-cum-conquest became associated with the security of China. Conversely, disunity came to be associated with insecurity. This second phase of reimagination is evident in statements made by Mao Zedong in 1949 and Ambassador Wu Xiuquan in 1950, as noted in Chapter 6.

While the strategic dimension of Taiwan's place in China's "imagined geography" has remained as one element in a complex view of why unification is desirable, that factor appears to have become more prominent as military modernization and economic reform accelerated in the last decades of the twentieth century. Reforms undertaken by the PRC in the late 1970s resulted, by the 1980s, in a measurable expansion of foreign trade and investment that contributed to economic growth. By the 1990s, the PRC had reached a phase of development in which its long-held ambition of great power status seemed less fanciful than it once had. Both within and beyond the PRC, China's "rise" was presumed to mean that it is destined to become a "great power" or—in the more breathless forecasts—the next "superpower."[20]

From Sea Power to Superpower

One element in the perception of China's "rise" is its increasingly capable military. Political power still grows from the barrel of the gun, even if guns are only a necessary but not exclusive source of it. Consequently, in conjunction with intensive economic development, the PRC has been embarked on a comprehensive program of military reform and modernization.[21] This investment in armaments and the wholesale rethinking of military doctrine are not occasioned by a "clear and present danger," but as a correlate to great power ambitions.[22]

Military modernization has involved a significant strategic shift that is discerned in the development of new doctrine. By the 1980s, the PRC became increasingly concerned about expanding "strategic depth" [*zhanlüe zongshen*]. For decades, the PRC had operated from the premise that "a large land force was required to protect the Chinese interior and its industries against a protracted land war with invading Soviets."[23] However, the disintegration of the Soviet Union, the end of the cold war, and the relative security that the PRC has enjoyed thereafter have coincided with and encouraged a shift of industry and "the economic center of gravity from the interior to the coast." For Beijing, this has generated a "littoral and maritime defense requirement that it probably has not had since the mid-Ch'ing [Qing] Dynasty. For the PLA today (and more than likely tomorrow) *the essence of defending China will be defined by the PLA's ability to defend seaward from the coast in the surface, subsurface and aerospace battle-space dimensions"* [emphasis as published].[24]

As David Finkelstein points out, though, the PLA was decidedly ill-prepared for this mission at the time it was articulated. "Hence, the emphasis in military modernization over the past few years has been on naval forces, air forces, and missile forces—the three services whose force projection capabilities are required for and best suited to defend the new economic center of gravity."[25]

Coupled with economic considerations, the PRC seems also to have cultivated the ambition to become sufficiently strong militarily that it can thwart the designs of adversaries and—one increasingly suspects—wield influence abroad with assurance that it will not be lightly dismissed. It appears determined to enhance not only national security, but also its international status.[26] Simply, Beijing seeks respect and a degree of deference. Where Taiwan and other maritime territorial claims are concerned, the urge for greater international stature has lowered the PRC's threshold of tolerance for conditions that seem incommensurate with greatness.

While these interdependent ambitions are not utterly new, the PRC has not been positioned to realize them for most of its history. The PRC leadership well recognizes that it has a period of comparative quiescence in which to focus on economic and social reform and to build its military power. One objective especially well served by the absence of any significant threat to the PRC's land boundaries is the project to expand China's maritime domain. To do that, Beijing has been developing a greater naval capacity than any Chinese state has had for centuries. Success in this enterprise holds out the promise of establishing greater "strategic depth" that will enable it to hold adversaries at bay farther from China's coast.

Greater prosperity has led to a wider reliance on maritime transport to supply the PRC with raw materials and commodities and to convey goods manufactured for export by sea. This, in turn, has fueled a vision of PRC naval prowess that can safeguard not only the coastal territories of China, but seagoing vessels on which the PRC has become increasingly dependent, even though they sail far from China's shores.[27]

There are indications that the PRC is preparing a naval force that can exercise "sea control" [*zhihai*] in the seas bounded by the "first island chain" [*diyi daolian*].[28] To enlarge its "strategic frontier" [*zhanlüe qianyan*] to that extent, the PRC would have to encompass into its domain the Bohai Sea bounded by the Shandong and Liaodong peninsulas, the Yellow Sea bounded by the Korean peninsula, the Japan Sea bounded by Russia and Japan, the East China

Sea between the Ryukyu islands and the Chinese coast, the Taiwan Strait, the South China Sea, and even the waters extending beyond the Strait of Malacca into the Indian Ocean.[29] From writings by both military and civilian strategists, it does appear that the outer edge of that region is a notional perimeter that the PRC feels it must be able to defend to perceive itself as secure.

That would, among other goals, enable the PRC to defend better its eastern coast and foil an adversary's effort to deny PRC vessels access to sea-lanes of communication [*haishang jiaotongxian*, hereinafter SLOC], along which commercial and other valued resources, principally energy, are transported. The PRC may also be aiming to establish a capacity for "sea denial" in a realm east of the "first island chain," perhaps as far out as the "second island chain" [*dier daolian*].[30] Even if the PRC is not intent on sustaining such a capacity in those more distant waters on a permanent basis, it may view the capacity to do so in extremis as an important strategic objective (see Figure 2 on page xviii).[31]

These broad objectives have been characterized as building a "blue water" navy that has a capacity to regulate maritime traffic as far east as the "first island chain" if not farther, as far south as the Strait of Malacca, and as far west as the Persian Gulf, securing the passage of friendly vessels through strategic chokepoints as distant from China as the Straits of Hormuz.[32] While there is certainly evidence in the PRC press that such grand ambitions have been under consideration, there is by no means consensus among foreign observers of the PRC's military development about whether the PRC has established a policy to pursue any more than a bounded "blue water" ambition and, even if it has, whether it can muster the resources to attain even that limited goal.[33] Nevertheless, the PRC has recognized that sustaining—to say little of expanding—economic growth depends on the development of some measure of sea power [*haiquan*].[34]

Mahan, the State, and War?

Reflecting these aggrandized aims, the PRC's defense white paper of 2004 expresses a determination to strengthen its navy, air force, and nuclear arsenal to establish "command of the sea" [*zhihaiquan*].[35] This and other signals lead some observers of the PRC to conclude that Beijing is acting in accordance with the precepts of Alfred Thayer Mahan.[36] After all, a central premise in Mahan's classic, *The Influence of Sea Power Upon History, 1660–1783*, is that navies ensure the capacity of the state to conduct and protect peaceful commerce by sea.

James Holmes and Toshi Yoshihara contend that strategists in the PRC are taking a maximal reading of Mahan to justify the expansion of naval power aimed at achieving "command of the sea." Mahan's "writings lent themselves to a certain zero-sum thinking," to which Holmes and Yoshihara believe PRC readers subscribe.[37] They worry that "If China . . . opts to build its navy around Mahanian sea-power theory, it will soon embark on a massive naval modernization effort designed to put to sea a force able to meet the U.S. Navy on its own terms in Asian waters."[38]

In trawling publications by PRC military strategists, one can find ample references to Mahanian reasoning and advocacy of the idea that attaining "sea control" within the "first island chain" is essential to the prosperity and power of the PRC.[39] Much of this reflects the influence of Admiral Liu Huaqing who is widely credited with advancing the idea that the PRC should become a naval power and dramatically expand the maritime realm it could dominate, even though he was by no means the first to promote this goal.[40] As Commander-in-Chief of the PLA(N) from 1982–87 and Vice Chairman of the Central Military Commission from 1988–97, Liu earned the sobriquet China's Mahan.[41]

Liu argued that the PRC should develop the means of controlling seas adjacent to its shores—the Bohai, the Yellow Sea, the East China Sea, and the South China Sea—out to the "first island chain." He elaborated a doctrinal shift associated with Deng Xiaoping's military reforms that emphasized the importance of "active defense" [*jiji fangyu*], a departure from the Maoist doctrine that made a virtue of necessity and, in recognition of the PRC's technological inferiority, sought to "lure the enemy in deep" [*youdi shenru*] and defend China by fighting wars of attrition against better armed adversaries. Deng Xiaoping endorsed the view that the PLA ought to develop the technological capability to confront China's foes and "stop an invading army as far forward as possible."[42]

In line with this doctrinal development, Liu Huaqing envisaged the navy's role as greater than providing simply "coastal defense" [*yanhai fangyu*] and developing instead a capacity for "active offshore defense" [*jijide jinhai fangyu*]. This meant extending the range over which the PLA(N) could exercise "sea control" out at least 200 nautical miles from the PRC's coast, encompassing the Exclusive Economic Zone (EEZ) and China's continental shelf, as provided for in the United Nations Convention on the Law of the Sea of 1988 and pertinent laws of the PRC.[43]

For Liu Huaqing, that was only the first step. As the likelihood of a Sino-Soviet conflict receded with the thawing of relations between Moscow and Beijing in the mid-1980s, the PRC faced no imminent naval threat. It was Liu who articulated the significance of putting to sea a "blue water" navy that would be capable of "offshore defense" [*jinyang fangyu*] and dominate the seas out to the "second island chain," about 1,800 nautical miles from China's coast.[44]

Penetration of the "first island chain" and projection of naval power to the "second island chain" is a grand ambition that would enable the PRC to dominate not only SLOC vital to the economies of Northeast Asian neighbors, but also influence unresolved disputes about insular territories and maritime areas that the PRC claims as Chinese. Taiwan, the Diaoyutai/Senkaku islands, the Dongsha [Pratas], Xisha [Paracel], Zhongsha [Macclesfield], and Nansha [Spratly] islands, as well as contested regions of the East China Sea would all fall within that expanded maritime realm.[45] However, the prospect of a PLA(N) capable of exercising "command of the seas" even within the "first island chain" has prompted some anxiety in the United States, Japan, and India, among other places, about the nature of PRC ambitions.[46]

That the PRC should now turn to the sea and find concepts in Mahan with which to express its ambitions is certainly noteworthy, but Mahan should not be seen as the source of the PRC's maritime objectives. For one thing, a maximal reading of Mahan would justify, yea necessitate, an effort to reach for "command of the sea" that could only come by displacing the United States from the Pacific. While there are observers who have drawn the conclusion that this is the objective of the PRC, or well could be, that conclusion is disputed by others who consider the PRC's aims in the first decade of the twenty-first century to be far more limited.

Robert Ross, for instance, has argued that reaching for "command of the sea" would be folly for the PRC, which has attributes of a continental not maritime power.[47] He begins with the premise that since the cold war, the "post-Cold War bipolar regional structure is characterized by Chinese dominance of mainland East Asia and U.S. dominance of maritime East Asia."[48] He attributes to this geographic division an absence of the sort of fundamental competition for security between the United States and the PRC that leads to what theorists have labeled the "security dilemma," so he concludes that there is no reason for the PRC to feel its vital interests and national security are threatened by the United States.

Moreover, for the PRC to reach for Mahanian "command of the seas" China "would have to assume a long-term stable strategic status quo on its land borders to divert substantial resources to naval power. Yet even if China did so, its navy could not approach parity with the U.S. Navy."[49] While the end of the cold war may have brought with it a period when China's land boundaries are, in fact, secure, no reading of history would offer strategists and statesmen in Beijing confidence that they could depend on such security indefinitely. Eventually, Beijing's attentions will be drawn back to the need to secure borders.

Hence, Ross predicts "In the absence of compelling maritime interests, Beijing's continental interest and U.S. maritime capabilities should deter China from making naval power a priority. Even continued economic growth and greater energy demand will not lead it to develop maritime capabilities to defend its overseas interests and shipping lanes."[50]

Ross contends that the best Beijing could do is "develop a 'luxury fleet' similar to that developed by the Soviet Union in the latter stage of the Cold War." Indeed, the PRC has appeared to learn from the Soviet Union lessons about "naval operational doctrines, campaign theory and tactics."[51] Such a "second-order fleet might achieve coastal-water defense, pushing the U.S. Navy away from the Chinese mainland and interfering with unrestricted U.S. penetration of Chinese air space." The PRC might also develop the capacity to impose "sea denial" in a region farther from its coast. However, Ross states "Chinese capabilities could not provide the foundation for a great power navy that could challenge U.S. supremacy."[52]

From its behavior, though, it is not possible to say whether the PRC shares Ross's take on this matter. Many analysts outside the PRC see evidence that the PRC has been building its naval capacities with a short-term objective of resolving the dispute about Taiwan—including, if necessary, defeating a U.S. force sent to defend the island. Holmes and Yoshihara find in PRC publications support for the idea that by building a military force that can settle to satisfaction the Taiwan problem, the PRC will then have at hand "the backbone of a force able to dominate East Asian waters."[53]

Whether or not this is a strategically sensible goal for the PRC is of less importance to the matter of hegemonic competition than that a more capable PLA(N) projected deeper into the Pacific is likely to mean "the U.S. navy's freedom of action will become increasingly threatened." Indeed, according to Christopher Bullock, "the very presence of a capable PLA[N] in the region will threaten American deployments and hinder U.S. strategic and operational options by making naval actions more hazardous in East Asia."[54]

For the PRC to accomplish the aim of extending its maritime domain to the "second island chain," "the United States would have to withdraw its military presence from the region . . . [and] Japan would have to sit idly by in the face of U.S. withdrawal, and not engage in an arms race with Beijing to ensure Japanese maritime superiority."[55] Obviously, it seems unlikely that both the United States and Japan will play by those rules.

Command of the Seas

Perhaps for the purpose of quelling demands from abroad that Beijing increase military transparency, the PRC has issued a public document stating its objectives for national defense. These documents have been released once every two years since 1998, under the title *China's National Defense*. For the first time, in the 2004 version, the PRC states that while Beijing will continue to enhance the quality of the army, "the PLA gives priority to the building of the Navy, Air Force and Second Artillery Force to seek balanced development of the combat force structure, in order to strengthen the capabilities for winning both command of the sea and command of the air, and conducting strategic counter-strikes" [emphasis added].[56]

It is noteworthy that the text uses the phrase *zhihaiquan*, "command of the sea," a term of art concerning a maximal objective of naval power. Historically, "command of the sea" was associated with a state of dominance achieved by "decisive battle" in which a state might "*force* a battle on the enemy's naval forces, destroy them and decide the matter once and for all," a conceptualization that the naval strategist Sir Julian Corbett opposed as misguided.[57] Corbett's aversion to the idea that a state might focus on picking fights to eliminate naval rivals in an effort to "rule the waves" rather than on defending specific national interests at sea eventually took hold as analysts realized the infeasibility of comprehensive dominance at sea.

During the cold war, maritime strategists accepted that "command of the sea" was "too absolutist." The concept lost favor, yielding to the more moderate notion of "sea control."[58] Even this idea, though, generated disputes about whether control should be an end in itself. It prompted discussion about an alternative or complementary concept, "sea denial," which identifies a condition in which force is deployed by a state in such a way as to deny its adversaries the opportunity to inflict harm on it from the sea. A state can succeed in exercising "sea denial" even in asymmetric competition with a more powerful adversary, a situation suggestive of the PRC's posture toward the United States.[59]

Observing closely the development of the PLA(N) and the doctrinal shifts accompanying and informing those developments, some analysts see a parallel between the strategy adopted by the Soviet Union and that adopted by the PRC.[60] That is to say, just as the Soviet Union did during the cold war, the PRC may differentiate its strategic objectives in terms of a hierarchy of defense zones, trying to ensure it can exercise "sea control" in a zone bounded by the "first island chain" and "sea denial" in a zone of much greater area beyond that boundary.

You Ji suggests that in using the term *sea control* the PRC does not have in mind what Western naval strategists do when they use the term. Writing before the PRC took up the term *command of the sea*, You Ji states that Beijing is not aiming to "secure freedom of action for itself and to deny that of the opponent." Rather, the "Chinese concept is about building temporary and area tactical naval superiority through concentrated usage of combat facilities and the exploitation of geographic advantages." Moreover, considering that the PRC is preparing for the possibility of a confrontation with the U.S. Navy, "it is beyond the PLA's ability to obtain real and strategic sea control. Hence, it has to project sea control to feasible geographic limits." In essence, the PRC is working from a "narrowly defined and tactically oriented" notion of developing the capacity to inflict sufficient harm that the adversary "will retreat or withdraw."[61]

You Ji maintains that the PRC has made a conscious effort to avoid using the term *sea denial*. For one thing, it may not be able to deny access to the U.S. Navy and has little need to deny access to other regional navies, Japan's being a potential exception. Also, as You Ji notes, "sea denial" has an offensive character that conflicts with the defensive objectives that the PLA has embraced, to say nothing of the peaceful and nonhegemonic objectives of PRC foreign policy, writ large.[62]

Two years after invoking the concept of "command of the sea," the PRC restated its goals more modestly, in line with You Ji's view that Beijing wishes to avoid provocative rhetoric that excites concerns about a "China threat." *China's National Defense in 2006* is much less strident than the 2004 version.[63] Gone is the reference to command of the air and command of the sea, among other signals of extravagant ambition. Indeed, throughout the authors of the document seem to have written in exceptionally measured terms.

Where naval power is concerned, one reads, "The Navy aims at gradual extension of the strategic depth for offshore defensive operations and enhancing its capabilities in integrated maritime operations and nuclear counterattacks."[64] Moreover, in the section where the paper details planned developments for the PLA(N), the authors write that the aim of the PRC is to "strengthen its overall capabilities of operations in coastal waters, joint operations and integrated maritime support."[65]

Emphasis by the PRC on operations in "coastal waters" [*jinhai haiyu*] and the "gradual extension of strategic depth for offshore defensive operations" [*zhubu zengda jinhai fangyu de zhanlüe zongshen*] seem much tamer than does an assertion by Beijing that it seeks to win "command of the sea."[66] These reformulated objectives appear consistent with the reasoning that Robert Ross advanced to dismiss notions that the PRC will develop anything other than a "luxury" blue water navy.[67] Yet, observing how the PLA(N) has evolved, rather than highlighting how Beijing phrases its ambitions for naval development, Admiral Gary Roughead, commander of the U.S. Pacific Fleet, said in November, 2006, "Clearly the growth in the capacity and capability of the navy since I've first been exposed to it in the 90s, the ability to go into the blue water is very, very clear." By contrast, the PRC's intentions, Admiral Roughead suggested, were not self-evident.[68]

So, it is worth considering what was intended by the phrase *zhihaiquan* ["command of the sea"] in *China's National Defense in 2004.* Bearing in mind that the term did not appear in white papers concerning national defense issued by the State Council in 1998, 2000, 2002, and 2006, one may be justified in wondering whether its use in 2004 was utterly anomalous and since disavowed, or whether it represented a genuine aggrandizement of strategic objectives that was, to align the white paper on national defense with the PRC's broader message in public diplomacy, toned down in the 2006 version. In other words, does each successive white paper record an incremental adjustment to abiding, considered, and consensual views of military and political leaders about the trajectory of strategic planning and defense requirements? Or, is each susceptible to the collective mood of the moment about the state of the PRC's security, reflecting greater belligerence at moments of apprehension and less in times of national self-confidence?

The Sino–U.S. Contest as Context

Although one cannot determine with certainty the purposes for which the PRC leadership is expanding naval power, Beijing's belief that it must strengthen the navy rests on the premise that the PRC is a maritime power.[69] That national self-conceptualization alone is—from the vantage of China's history—revolutionary. It also underscores why, as the PRC takes more assertively to the sea, its strategists are especially attentive to the roles assumed and capabilities maintained by the United States, with which Beijing's enlarged ambitions could conflict.

Since 1949, the PRC and the United States have been entangled in a protracted contest for security and influence defined by the limits of tolerance each has for the role played by the other in the international system. There are many causes for this prolonged struggle, but surely the subordination of the Western Pacific to American naval hegemony after the Second World War has been and remains a central factor.

Even before the establishment of the PRC and the onset of the Korean War, an outraged editorial in *Renmin Ribao* [People's Daily] gave voice to the

CCP's strategic concerns about the U.S. relationship to the ROC govern-
ment that was then taking refuge on Taiwan.[70] The CCP was concerned that
American imperialists would work with Chiang Kai-shek to undermine the
communist regime by taking Taiwan as a bridgehead to launch hostilities against
and provoke political mayhem on the mainland. The defensive perimeter that
Dean Acheson defined in January 1950, stretching from the Aleutians through
Japan and to the Philippines, was extended even closer to China's heartland as
Washington reacted in June 1950 to conflict on the Korean peninsula.

At that juncture, both Taiwan and the south of Korea were more firmly
subsumed into the American domain. This move reinforced a preexisting suspicion in the PRC that the United States was intent on checking the emergence of a communist Chinese state. It prompted the outrage exemplified by
the statement of Ambassador Wu Xiuquan, who invoked the possibly apocry-
phal Tanaka Memorial as a way to castigate the United States for scheming to
take Taiwan and Korea as steps in a plan to conquer China, Asia, and dominate
the world.

Sitting in Beijing, it did appear to the leaders of the newly established
communist state that from the end of the nineteenth century, the United
States had been projecting its military forces and political influence farther
and farther from its own shores while moving closer and closer to China's.
Notwithstanding American efforts to justify its actions in 1950 as a pure-
minded defense of liberty and opposition to communist aggression, Chinese
statesmen in the PRC perceived the projection of U.S. power then as following on a half century of imperialist expansion. They were gravely worried
about the implications for the security of their state.

Indeed, from its inception in 1949, the PRC has been governed by men
who concerned themselves about the signal importance of Beijing's relationship to Washington. They have tended to establish foreign policy within the
framework of an *explicit* apprehension of the international system. The PRC's
foreign policy elites are inclined to perceive, characterize, label, and respond
to a structure as the first steps in determining what posture the PRC should
adopt for maximum advantage in the international arena.[71]

At first, uneasiness about the United States manifested itself in the rigid
bipolarity of the early cold war, during which Washington was seen as the
principal adversary dominating an imperialist bloc. When Mao Zedong
declared in 1949 that the PRC would "lean to one side," not only did he
mean that Beijing would ally itself with the Soviet Union, but also that it
would distance itself from the United States.[72]

Following the Sino-Soviet split in the 1960s, Beijing sought to counterbalance the threat of Soviet expansion and hostility by decoupling itself from a dependent relationship with Moscow. It sought security in the Sino-U.S. rapprochement, but as Soviet power eroded in the 1980s so did the potency of the Sino-U.S. condominium.

The late twentieth century and first years of the twenty-first century appear to be a juncture at which the PRC is relatively safe, even if it does not feel or act secure. It has enjoyed the breathing space it long sought to focus on economic and social development. In a milieu of comparative quietude on its borders, Beijing also has an opportunity to find means by which to reconsolidate and extend political stability at home in a period when the dislocations of economic and social transitions are making their effects felt in pockets of civil unrest.

Increasing wealth and domestic stability are building blocks in a grand strategic vision that emerged in the 1990s. The core of this vision is to develop power sufficient "to make China an indispensable, or at least very attractive, actor on whose interests the system's major powers are reluctant to trample," and "to establish Beijing's reputation as a responsible international actor, reducing the anxiety about China's rise," that might prompt other powers to impede it.[73]

To do that, Avery Goldstein argues, the PRC has embraced multilateralism, responsible management of its currency, and partnerships with other powers to "ensure China's interests while coping with the stark constraints of a unipolar world in which a potentially hostile United States would long remain the dominant power."[74] Nevertheless, strategists and statesmen in the PRC were among those who imagined and sought ways to abet the emergence of a multipolar system to ensure that any "unipolar moment" in which the United States would exercise unchecked influence over the international system would be as brief as possible.[75]

One element of the grand strategic vision is of a relationship with the United States that is cooperative, but not corrosive to China's stability and core values. Striking a balance between these objectives has been difficult in an environment where Washington seems frequently hostile or insensitive to what Beijing perceives as its vital interests.

Building on Deng Xiaoping's injunction that PRC foreign policy ought to proceed from the notion of *taoguang yanghui* [adopt a low profile], Jiang Zemin was determined in the 1990s that economic development would remain Beijing's primary policy objective, even if that meant swallowing a certain amount of bile in order to ensure a stable international environment and good relations with the "sole superpower."[76]

As part of a calculated diminution of external expectations, Beijing has framed its foreign policy to deflect anxieties by other states about the PRC's economic and military growth and the concomitant expansion of interests. It has foresworn hegemony and pledged, as a PRC Foreign Ministry statement of 2003 explains, to pursue "an independent foreign policy of peace."[77] "The fundamental goals of this policy are to preserve China's independence, sovereignty and territorial integrity, create a favorable international environment for China's reform and opening up and modernization construction, maintain world peace and propel common development."[78]

So, the PRC's relationship to the United States reflects an uneasy balance of competing sentiments. On one hand, while the worthies of Zhongnanhai no longer lie awake at night worrying that the United States might attack the PRC, they still worry about Washington's capacity and intentions to blunt Beijing's ambitions. The prevailing image of the United States is a hegemonic bully, recklessly and clumsily throwing its military weight around the globe and peevishly acting in bad faith and self-interest—as though that is something to which Americans are peculiarly predisposed—to defend its imperium. On the other hand, the PRC leadership well appreciates the futility of openly challenging the United States while there is still such a discrepancy of power between the two states. Moreover, as PRC statesmen are wont to declare, the PRC now needs to take advantage of peace to enhance the prospect of development. There is no stomach for conflict. While suspicion and resentment of the United States may be widely, even if not universally, embedded in the minds of China's political elite, only those who exhibit extreme paranoia worry that the United States seeks to attack the PRC, much less conquer it. What does animate discussion and analysis of the United States is the frustration and defiance associated with the belief that Washington—itself deluded by the idea of the "China threat"—is acting to retard China's progress toward greater power and glory. Washington's support for and prospective defense of Taiwan are imagined by some PRC observers to be a manifestation of this strategic intention, a view expressed in the PRC's white papers on national defense.

The 2006 white paper is explicit in stating Beijing's objections to the sale of arms to Taiwan by the United States and Washington's efforts to upgrade military-to-military relations with Taipei.[79] Moreover, in the section of *China's National Defense in 2004* that articulates the PRC's national defense policy, the very first item is "To stop separation and promote reunification, guard against and resist aggression, and defend national sovereignty, territorial integrity and maritime rights and interests."[80] Although the authors of the 2006 white paper have not located their comments about Taiwan in the opening paragraph of the comparable section, the emphasis in the document on the importance of "unity" and passages concerning Taiwan independence make evident that "separatist forces" still pose a "grave threat to China's sovereignty and territorial integrity, as well as to peace and stability across the Taiwan Straits and in the Asia-Pacific region as a whole."[81] This has caused some analysts to conclude that the issue of Taiwan is Beijing's paramount security concern.[82]

Indeed, the PRC's quest for sea power—even if the more restrained aims articulated in 2006 remain the operative objectives—has only enhanced the salience of Taiwan. Although the space perceived as constituting China's strategic frontier has contracted and expanded over time, Taiwan has been viewed as a part of that area since the founding of the PRC. Taiwan is part of a maritime boundary that, ipso facto, has been imagined as vital to China's national defense.[83]

Beyond that, Taiwan's proximity to the mainland—approximately 100 miles away—contributes to a heightened awareness of its strategic value.[84] While the distance is certainly real, the strategic ramifications of that distance are evaluated both in actual and imagined ways. Actual technological capability and limitations as well as perceptions of security and vulnerability contribute to how a given distance is envisaged. For instance, in April 2001, unnamed PLA officers were quoted as saying that "China's territory is absolutely not the 'backyard' where the armed forces of any country can come and go, China's territorial waters are absolutely not the 'swimming pool' in which ships of any country can cruise at will, and China's territorial airspace is absolutely not an 'air corridor' in which the military aircraft of any country can enter and exit."[85]

Given the indignation manifested in this vivid imagery, it is easy to understand why publications emanating from the PRC consistently express the view that Taiwan in the hands of a potentially hostile rival is too close for comfort. That is not to suggest that if Taiwan were 500 or 5,000 miles from China's coast the PRC would relinquish its claim.[86] However, proximity can contribute to perceptions of salience. Whether it imbues territory with greater or lesser value depends on the interplay of distance and other factors.[87] In the case of Taiwan, the principal contributing factor is the disposition of the United States. No issue rankles the PRC elites more about the United States than does Washington's apparently Janus-faced posture on the status of Taiwan. The Taiwan issue remains a powder keg with a long-simmering, but ever-shortening fuse. The PRC accepts that it cannot satisfactorily restore its territorial integrity where Taiwan is concerned without considering the interests and likely responses of the United States. Lieutenant General Liu Yazhou goes so far as to state "relations with Taiwan are relations with the U.S." Moreover, he is not alone in believing that the United States is using Taiwan as a "card" to affect Sino-U.S. relations and bolster its position in the Pacific.[88]

Some analysts in the PRC are convinced that the reason the United States continues to shield Taiwan from Beijing has to do with where, specifically, the island lies.[89] They think, as General Douglas MacArthur did when he referred to Taiwan as an "unsinkable aircraft carrier" [bu chen de hangkong mujian], in terms of territorial salience flowing from location.[90] Indeed, the metaphor "unsinkable aircraft carrier," when applied to Taiwan, is itself an expression of an "imagined geography" reflecting on the part of PRC commentators insecurity prompted by an evaluation of both the distance between China's coast and the island, as well as the relationship between Washington and Beijing. So, it is not the distance between Taiwan and the mainland alone that prompts insecurity, but the interplay of Taiwan's location and the rivalry between the PRC and the United States.[91]

The expression "unsinkable aircraft carrier" has evidently lodged deeply in the imaginations of the PRC policy elites. For instance, in a press conference following the Third Session of the Ninth National People's Congress (NPC) in March 2000, then Premier Zhu Rongji said about Taiwan, "there are some people in a certain country who have all along been against China and taken China as its potential enemy, and who want to use Taiwan as an unsinkable aircraft carrier against China; and that is why they want to see the Taiwan question drag on indefinitely."[92]

A year after, Jin Yinan, vice director of the strategic teaching and research section of the PRC's National Defense University, authored a piece in Jiefang Junbao [Liberation Army Daily] decrying Taiwan's purchase of arms from the United States. Jin writes, "Some people said half a century ago that Taiwan 'is a unsinkable aircraft carrier.' Undoubtedly, there are people today who want to make Taiwan a weapons platform, a confrontational platform, and a war platform."[93] Another analyst explained his view that by continuing to sell arms to Taiwan "The U.S. has always trumpeted that it is 'protecting Taiwan', but its real intention is to protect its own strategic interests in the Asia-Pacific region and to serve its strategic objective of global hegemonism."[94]

One might be tempted to discount these comments as inflamed rhetoric because they all were made in the period 2000–01 when Sino-U.S. relations were particularly frosty.[95] That was just after the U.S. bombing of the PRC Embassy in Belgrade, in the lead-up to and eventual election of Chen Shui-bian, in the year when an American EP-3 surveillance aircraft and a Chinese

F-8 fighter jet collided, as well as the year when President Bush made his remark that the United States would do "whatever it takes" to help Taiwan defend itself. It was also a period when the PRC was especially exercised about U.S. arms sales to Taiwan.

However, the rationale of viewing Washington's intentions as linked to the use of Taiwan as an "unsinkable aircraft carrier" that might impede the PRC's own ambitions for a "blue water" navy outlasted that moment. Long after the September 11, 2001, terrorist attacks in the United States and the much trumpeted improvement in Sino–U.S. relations that was said to result from the collaboration between Washington and Beijing in opposition to terrorism, one still finds in the PRC press indications that there remains a high degree of anxiety about the reasons for U.S. support of Taiwan. In 2004, one analyst wrote that in the United States the "hawks" perceive that,

> China's developmental potential is enormous, and if China's rapid development and its momentum toward becoming powerful and prosperous are not checked, then China could constitute a serious challenge to the U.S. status as the sole superpower in the upcoming 21st century. From their vantage, there are a number of reasons to defend Taiwan, including that . . . militarily, Taiwan is a potential base which the U.S. could use in the western Pacific. The use of Taiwan could enable effective control of sea lines of communication between northeast Asia and southeast Asia and the Middle East. Thus, the U.S. sees Taiwan as an "unsinkable aircraft carrier."[96]

PRC analysts who abide this view of the U.S. rationale for supporting the ROC point to the mutual defense treaties, bases, and access privileges Washington maintains throughout the region. This presents to those in the Chinese defense establishment inclined to hedge potential provocations they do not welcome and to Chinese nationalists a condition they perceive as ominous. To some PRC analysts, the network of American iron and soldiery made possible by the cooperation of states neighboring the PRC appears to sustain a U.S. encirclement of China.[97] While the presence of U.S. forces as an external balancer in Asia also assures a level of security in the region (a communal good that the PRC and others may take for granted as free riders), during moments of friction in Sino-U.S. relations, the benefits of a Pacific pax Americana are easily overlooked.

While there is only so much the PRC can do about Washington's relations with such capitals as Seoul, Tokyo, Manila, Singapore, New Delhi, Islamabad, and Ulaanbaatar and the accommodations the leaderships in those places make, Taipei is different. There, the irritation that Beijing feels at being hemmed in is exacerbated by the conviction that Taiwan is China's territory.

To be sure, the United States no longer maintains troops on Taiwan.[98] Beyond that, the forward edge of the U.S. strategic domain in the Pacific has receded slightly since the end of the cold war, and the American system of strategic alliances with Asian states has adjusted to suit the times. However, Taiwan is still viewed as in the U.S. "camp." It falls under U.S. sway and is, after all, armed and defended at Washington's caprice. Consequently, it has geostrategic significance to the PRC because it is perceived as a territorial marker of the imagined outer boundary of the sphere dominated by the United States.

More importantly, to observers in the PRC Taiwan is seen as falling within an American maritime domain that constitutes a *cordon sanitaire* with which Washington maintains the capacity to encircle China. In addition to Taiwan, this cordon is understood to encompass Korea, Japan (including the Ryukyu islands), Guam, and strategic relationships the United States has with the Philippines and Singapore, either vestiges or enhancements of the defensive perimeter established in the cold war. Hence, as PRC strategists and analysts consider how to develop the capacities needed to become a maritime power, they write in metaphoric terms of "breaking through" [*chongchu*] this barrier to gain access to the Pacific Ocean.

For example, You Ziping,[99] an authority on maritime strategy at the Chinese Ship Research and Development Academy in Beijing, writes that Taiwan "guards" [*e*] key channels of the Western Pacific. Others write that as part of the island chain Taiwan is used to "contain" [*ezhi*] China. Only with the return of Taiwan, You Ziping asserts, will it be possible for the PRC to gain direct access to the Pacific, overcome the predicament of being restrained to coastal waters, improve China's maritime strategic environment, and establish maritime strategic superiority. In that way, Taiwan is seen to have potential as the "gateway to the sea" [*tongwang dahai menhu*].[100] You Ziping, like other writers, invokes the image of the "unsinkable aircraft carrier," saying that even now, Taiwan plays a role in the global strategy of the United States. In his words, the United states "uses Taiwan to control China" [*yi Tai zhi Hua*].[101]

Another commentary in *Renmin Ribao* expresses anxiety that "Taiwan is a potential base which the U.S. could use in the Western Pacific. The use of Taiwan could enable effective control of sea lines of communication between northeast Asia and southeast Asia and the Middle East. Thus, the U.S. sees Taiwan as an 'unsinkable aircraft carrier.' "[102]

An anonymous article in the *Shanxi Keji Ribao* [Shanxi Science and Technology Daily], reprinted in *Sichuan Ribao* [Sichuan Daily], states, "After the end of the cold war, the first island chain and the second island chain did not vanish. On the contrary, the 'eastern arc' somewhat strengthened and became a device whereby the U.S. could contain China." The key to "break through this chain" [*dapo zheigen suolian*], the author asserts, is Taiwan.[103]

This view appears to be widely held. PRC strategists also view the autonomy of Taiwan as redounding to the benefit of Japan, with which the PRC has had a highly fractious and competitive relationship.[104] For example, in an essay published in the *Global Times*, Fudan University professor Wu Xinbo, a specialist in Sino-U.S. relations, writes that the intensifying U.S.-Japan framework for military cooperation is aimed at curbing the China threat and has consequences for the Taiwan issue. Specifically, he indicates that language in statements jointly issued by Washington and Tokyo in February 2005 that identify the peaceful resolution of the Taiwan issue as a "common strategic objective" is aimed at offsetting the increasing attraction of the PRC and "ensuring that Taiwan remains in the American sphere of influence in the Western Pacific, rather than drift toward the mainland."[105] The wary disapproval in the PRC of collaboration between Washington and Tokyo on the matter of Taiwan intensified after reports that the United States and Japan were, in pursuit of the principles articulated in 2005, to undertake planning for joint operations in the event of hostilities between the PRC and Taiwan.[106]

The close relationship that emerged after the cold war between the United States, Japan, and Taiwan is characterized by another scholar as one intended to use Taiwan as a "chip" [*chouma*] to contain China.[107] Indeed, there is a pervasive view that Japan supports the U.S. posture on Taiwan and contributes to the containment of China because it recognizes the consequence of "losing" Taiwan to the PRC. One commentator writes, "As soon as the mainland and Taiwan are unified, not only will we break through the strategic encirclement of China effected by the U.S.-Japan alliance, we will have Japan's strategic passage to the south firmly in our grasp and China shall easily thereafter be able to counter Japan."[108] Naturally, the Sino–U.S. and Sino–Japanese rivalries each have separate dynamics and sources of friction that are only partly related to Taiwan. For the most part, since 1979, the Sino–U.S. relationship has entailed both cooperation and dispute about a wide array of issues. On the question of Taiwan's status, though, the PRC has often made evident its view that the United States is not just providing political succor to Beijing's adversary, but using the island of Taiwan for what the PRC has cast as nefarious purposes.

The shrill accusations against the U.S. defense of Taiwan articulated in the 1950s and 1960s have been muted, but not silenced. Although friction in the Sino-U.S. relationship may not be limited to territorial matters, where Taiwan is concerned, it does have territorial—or, more precisely, geostrategic—implications.

In the hands of the PRC, Taiwan is imagined to increase "strategic depth" by extending eastward the outer limit of China's domain while pushing the range of U.S. influence back another step to Japan and the Ryukyu islands.[109] Ensuring that Taiwan is firmly in Beijing's grasp would enhance a perception of the PRC's expanding power because subordinating Taiwan could only be accomplished by persuading or compelling the United States to withdraw its support for the island.

Even if this view of Taiwan is not operationally significant to the security of the PRC, it is prominent in the way that some PRC strategists justify the aim of unification.[110] It reflects the role of geography as the "inspiration for the grand narrative" of the state, which in this case, is the CCP's legitimating story of defying imperialism–cum–hegemony to construct a new Chinese state that is too powerful to be toyed with by meddling and menacing rivals.[111]

By the early 1990s, the image of an insular barrier that the PRC must penetrate to become a great power punctuated official and unofficial statements about the importance of national reunification. This represents a third phase in the reimagination of Taiwan's geography and its concomitant salience to the PRC. Since then, Taiwan has been imagined as more than a part of China's territory that must be recovered and more than a buffer offering defense of the southeastern coast. The "return" of Taiwan to the motherland began to figure in a geostrategic trope as the PRC's gateway to the Pacific, the key to China's future as a prosperous and secure maritime power, and to national rejuvenation. For instance, General Wen Zongren, Political Commissar of the PLA's Academy of Military Sciences, described unification as having "far-reaching significance to breaking some international forces' blockade against China's maritime security. Breaking this blockade can embody China's maritime development strategy. Only when we break this blockade shall we be able to talk about China's rise."[112]

This strategic stream in the PRC's nationalist narrative about Taiwan has swelled with significance since the 1990s as Chinese elites have come to imagine their nation's future as a maritime and naval power. The association that some strategic thinkers make between Taiwan and China's "rise" is an embellishment of the nationalist and strategic arguments. Once more, the "imagined geography" is reflected in ascriptions of salience for reasons reflecting now current ambitions. As a development, this is utterly unsurprising. After all, "national identities are constantly being reconstituted according to a presentist agenda."[113]

While officials in Beijing promote the view that the PRC's "rise" will not threaten the interest of other states, there are military and civilian analysts in the PRC who have expressed the view that for Beijing to extend its maritime domain, the United States will indeed have to be persuaded to withdraw, or prevented from entering, that realm in which the PRC hopes to predominate. In their eyes, it is a zero-sum competition. This corresponds to the views of observers outside the PRC who conclude that the long-range objectives of the PRC are a challenge to the status quo in Asia. Analysts who cleave to this interpretation of the PRC's development view Taiwan as fitting in the geostrategic competition between Beijing and Washington.

Martin Lasater writes that a seizure of Taiwan by Beijing would "enable the PRC to project naval and air power far into the western Pacific in ways that would upset the regional balance of power."[114] John Mearsheimer writes, "An increasingly powerful China is also likely to try to push the United States out of Asia, much the way the United States pushed the European great powers out of the Western Hemisphere. Not incidentally, gaining regional hegemony is probably the only way that China will get back Taiwan."[115]

Analysts in the PRC, though, write of the relationship between the recovery of Taiwan and the development of regional power in the reverse sequence. A prominent view in the PRC seems to be that only by taking Taiwan back—unifying the state—can the PRC succeed in denying access to rival forces in the seas adjacent to China's coast and ensure that PRC forces can pass through Pacific waters east of Taiwan in greater security. Those PRC strategists and statesmen who envisage China becoming a sea power explain that taking Taiwan is the first step—the means—to a grander strategic end: greater maritime control and international status.[116]

Moreover, the opposite is also true. Failing to take back Taiwan dooms China to less than great-power status. A prominent advocate of this view is Zhang Wenmu, a professor associated with the Institute of International Strategy at Beijing's University of Aeronautics and Astronautics, who states, "at present, the Taiwan issue still embodies a contest for sea power between China and the U.S. If we lose Taiwan, we will one after the next lose the Nansha [Spratly] Islands and losing those two areas will signify that China shall thoroughly lose the fundamental capability of a rising great power to guarantee its political, economic, and national security 'space.'"[117]

For strategic analysts in the PRC who hold these views, the location of Taiwan is perceived as critical. They believe the PRC cannot accomplish its grand strategic objectives without assuring itself, first, that Taiwan is neither held by nor allied to a power that might seek to impede the expansion of the PRC's maritime reach. Beijing made this explicit in the 1998 version of *China's National Defense*, in which it states, "Directly or indirectly incorporating the Taiwan Straits into the security and cooperation sphere of any country or any military alliance is an infringement upon and interference in China's sovereignty."[118] In this respect, the assertion of sovereignty over Taiwan is not simply a contest of will between two Chinese disputants with competing national identities, different regime types, parallel histories, and distinct views of Taiwan's relationship to "China proper" [neidi]. It is perceived as a strategic imperative.

Considering Taipei's cooperative, even if unofficial, relationships to Washington and Tokyo, analysts in the PRC who view Taiwan's location as pivotal to the attainment of grand strategic objectives are especially sensitive to the possibility that Taiwan will abet the aims of those potentially hostile powers. The only way to ensure with some degree of permanence that Taiwan will not serve as host to Beijing's rivals is to extend sovereignty to the island in a way that offers Beijing the possibility of imposing effective control over Taiwan's foreign and security policies.[119]

To date, Beijing has expressed a preference to accomplish this on the cheap. It would prefer that Taipei succumb to blandishments or threats and accommodate Beijing's urge to sweep the island into its own orbit rather than to use military force to beat Taipei into submission. Beijing has also proposed a degree of flexibility in its thinking about a postunification relationship to Taiwan that recalls the suzerain relations imperial China had with bordering states within a Sinic sphere of influence. As with those suzerain relationships, though, one would be remiss in neglecting the possibility that for the PRC preserving a capacity to impose effective control on Taiwan is the sine qua non.[120]

PRC commentators are moved to expressions of distemper by the notion that the PRC is blocked from exploiting Taiwan's strategic location as a passageway to the Pacific because of the island's autonomy and link to the United States. There is a perception in the PRC that controlling Taiwan would be a great maritime and strategic asset, particularly at moments of friction with competitors for access to SLOC. That is, the image of Taiwan as buffer or bridgehead that was a reflection of Taiwan's location has been transformed. The island's location is still the source of powerful imagery, but the strategic environment—to say nothing of the technology employed for military, communication, and transportation purposes—has affected the way in which geography serves or hinders interests.

Taiwan: Imagined Gateway to Sea Power

Quite apart from the tensions in the Sino-U.S. and Sino-Japanese rivalries, Taiwan itself is imagined in China's geography to have geostrategic salience. The commonly accepted vision of Taiwan's strategic relationship to China entails the characterization of Taiwan as a "protective screen" [pingzhang] for

China's southeastern coast and the Taiwan Strait as the crux for defense of the entire coastal region. Taiwan is described in one article as the "strategic gateway of the southeast" [*dongnan de suoyue*]. The author writes that Taiwan and Hainan together constitute a "pair of eyes" [*shuangmu*] and, with the Zhoushan islands off the northeast coast of Zhejiang, constitute a strategic "horn" [*jijiao*] with Taiwan at the center. Taken together, these territories form naturally an advantageous battle array in the shape of the Chinese character *pin* offering coastal defense "sufficient to shield China's six southeastern coastal provinces and cities."[121]

Taiwan is seen as controlling a region denoted as the strategic "throat" [*yanhou*] of the Western Pacific island chains, is the strongpoint closest to the mainland, and the demarcation of the boundary between the East China Sea [*Donghai*] and South China Sea [*Nanhai*].[122] As such, "Taiwan (including the Taiwan Strait) is a defensive outpost protecting the Chinese state, safeguarding China's north-south maritime traffic and the communications hub for China's maritime security region, and defending China's maritime rights and interest and blue territorial base."[123]

Another text suggests that once unification is achieved "China's armed forces can again make use of Taiwan's territory, waters, and airspace as military bases in advance of activities in the Pacific oceanic and aerial battlefronts." So, Taiwan is imagined both as an asset in the hands of the PRC and a liability in the hands of an adversary. It is described as having the potential to be both a "bridge and springboard" [*qiaoliang he tiaoban*].[124]

Beyond protection of China's territory, Taiwan is imagined to be of value in protecting vital sea lanes. The authors of one book assert that once unification is achieved, the PRC's "coastal defense can be pushed out eastward 300–500 kilometers, increasing the strategic depth at sea." This would enable the PLA(N) to "widen its scope of operations to encompass the entire China Sea area, to access the East China Sea and the Yellow Sea from the south to fight, to defend against adversaries entering China's northern maritime area, from the north and to strike back directly at any enemy violating the south, and access the Philippine Sea area directly from the west to deal with any enemy." By controlling Taiwan and the Taiwan Strait, the PRC could also "thwart the efforts of enemies seeking to blockade China." The PLA(N) and airforce could "sweep through the length and breadth of the Western Pacific maritime area, cut the U.S.'s 'forward strategic chain' in the Pacific" [*qianyan zhanlüe lianhuan*], look down and control East Asia [*kanzhi dongya*], and control Japan's maritime lifeline to Southeast Asia."[125] Taiwan is also depicted as a strategic point of entry to the Pacific for maritime commerce and the development of China's sea power.[126]

Zhang Wenmu writes "The core of China's Asia-Pacific geopolitics is the question of Taiwan, which concerns not only China's sovereignty, but also China's sea power, as well as its overall modernization." Zhang's comprehensive—some would say expansionist—aims reflect a view that one hears from others in the PRC about Taiwan's centrality to Beijing's grand strategic vision for China. It is difficult to know how well informed these views are or how influential they may be on the senior leadership, but they do represent a stream of argumentation that is worth considering in full. Zhang writes:

> Taiwan represents China's forward base into the Pacific Ocean and a means of realizing its sea power interests. If Taiwan were reunified, China would completely break the island chains that America constructed to block China in the West Pacific, which has an even greater significance than America's seizure of Hawaii. If Taiwan were reunified, China could check Japan's designs on its northeast portion. In the south . . . protection of the islands in the South Sea can be formed together with Hainan Island and provide an effective guarantee to China's ships passing through the Malacca Strait. . . . In addition, China's reunification progress coincides with the progress of realizing China's sea power, for which reunification of Taiwan is particularly crucial. Without Taiwan, the Nansha islands cannot be protected. If it is said that the geopolitical key to the South China Sea is the Malacca Strait, then the islands of Nansha within China's sovereign sphere are the key for China to realize its sea power interests in the South China Sea. As a big power, China will inevitably have its own sea base. If Diaoyu Island and Taiwan come back to China, the security interests of China in northeast Asia and Southeast Asia will be guaranteed.[127]

This line of reasoning appears to have some purchase among military figures with institutional influence. For example, Major General Peng Guangqian of the PRC Academy of Military Sciences offers reasons why Taiwan is of strategic importance to the PRC. He states:

> Taiwan is a keystone for China to cross the Pacific and go out to the world. It is an important strategic space that affects national security and national rejuvenation, and affects China's external transformational links, trade links, and oil energy transportation links.
>
> Taiwan is the frontline for China to contest with international anti-Chinese forces, separatist forces, and terrorist forces. If "Taiwan independence" is allowed, there will be a domino effect, which will give excuses to other separatist forces. The consequence would be unimaginable. So China must never retreat.
>
> Opposing "Taiwan independence" and safeguarding unification also affects China's international dignity, image, influence, and authority. China's national rejuvenation must not be symbolized by the country's division.[128]

So, Taiwan's location is seen as linked to China's security and Taiwan is "on the frontline" of the PRC's battle with foreign "anti-China" forces, by which one assumes he means both the United States and Japan. Peng also offers a nod to the anxiety about providing "other separatist forces" a reason for hope. His conclusion mixes metaphors and blends all these concerns in stating: "Solving the Taiwan issue will remove the last stumbling block for China's peaceful rise, will obtain a certificate of eligibility for joining in the distribution of world interests, and will participate in global competition with the combined strength of the Greater China economic sphere, thereby fundamentally transforming China's international strategic and security situation. Taiwan is an aircraft carrier for China's peaceful rise and national rejuvenation."[129]

Peng's artful reversal of the "aircraft carrier" metaphor implies that by contrast to the island's use by hostile forces as a bridgehead for advances into China, the PRC can use the island as an outpost for its presumably innocuous advances into the Pacific. A somewhat less saccharine analysis would entail recognition that Taiwan is located adjacent to vital sea lanes that increasingly are the lifeline for the PRC's economic welfare. *Jiefangjun Bao* [Liberation Army Daily] published a commentary that featured discussion of how Taiwan's location was vital for regulation of passage through the sea lanes to the island's north: "Of the two sea lanes vital to the national destiny, going through the northern line is mainly for entering the Pacific, and the obstacle at present is Taiwan controlled by Taiwan independence; so long as Taiwan is overthrown, the problem will be readily solved. The North Sea Fleet and East Sea Fleet can naturally join forces in a Pacific fleet."[130]

It is striking how emphatic are those who see Taiwan as a strategic imperative. For example, Jiang Zhijun, Director of the Chinese Naval Research Institute of the PLA Navy, states "We face the sea to defend our national sovereignty, but at the same time our soft, weak underbelly is also exposed." He claims "As long as the Taiwan issue isn't resolved, we will always be hindered in our capacity to defend our nation's maritime regions." "To put it more exactly: China's security challenges mainly come from the seas."[131]

Jiang Zhijun emphasizes that "The strategic importance of Taiwan simply cannot be over-stated." Control of the island provides the PRC with greater "strategic depth." He states:

> Locked in by the "first island chain" blockade, China's sea defense force could hardly move beyond the boundary to carry out any meaningful defense operation. The only thing to do is to back up against the coastal lines to conduct shallow water defense. Since combat occurs right outside China's doorway, China will be fighting close at home and is left with hardly any maneuver room to take operational initiative. Taiwan ought to be China's natural gateway, but, if things went sour, it could then turn out to be other people's stepping board for attacks against China.[132]

Jiang Zhijun's conceptualization of Taiwan as a "natural gateway" and his focus on "exit points" recall the geostrategic thinking of China's earlier strategists. Indeed, Jiang himself casts his vision of Taiwan in terms of a national territorial patrimony that must be recovered. He reportedly said:

> Taiwan is China's ideal seaward exit way bequeathed to us by our ancestors. As long as Taiwan is in China's hand, then the Pacific would be an open area to China. Taiwan itself is a key link in the "first island chain." After Taiwan is reunified with mainland China, this "first island chain" blockade will be broken, enabling the Chinese troops to expand their defense lines out to the Pacific in the East in order to better protect the safety of China's coast and inland. By that time, the Taiwan Strait would become a safe and convenient route of communication for transporting troops and supplies between north and south.[133]

Jiang then offers an expansive vision, saying, "Once the (Taiwan) reunification mission is completed, Diaoyu (Senkaku) Island to the North and the waters surrounding it would fall into the range of the Chinese gunfire protection. To the south, the distance from China's coastal defense force to all the South China Sea islands and regions will be shortened by a big margin."[134]

To put the strategic salience of Taiwan into a broader maritime perspective, it is useful to consider the attitudes some authorities in Beijing have expressed toward the control of other putatively Chinese islands in the South China Sea. According to Li Nan, "since the mid-1980s, China has claimed sovereignty over three million square kilometers of maritime territory . . . which is codified in the Maritime Law passed by the National People's Congress in 1992."[135] Much of that span of ocean is dotted by islands, transected by sea lanes through which commerce and resources flow—not least of which are energy resources—and covering potentially valuable mineral deposits. The possibility, indeed necessity, of exploiting these resources has captured the imagination of Beijing (see Figure 2 on page xviii).

Consequently, the PRC makes explicit its claim to many of the islands in the South China Sea as well as much of the Sea, itself. Indeed, maps of the PRC commonly indicate these claims with a sketchy, "U-shaped" line, often comprising nine dashes—a demarcation of maritime territory first devised in 1914 during the earliest years of the Republic of China.[136] As with Taiwan, the islands embraced by this line may be seen as natural features on the periphery contributing to the security of the homeland territories. However, as with Taiwan, Beijing's claim to the islands and seas encompassed by the line is the source of dispute with other states—including the Republic of China.[137]

The PRC has been increasingly intent on laying out its claims in both the South China Sea as well as the East China Sea and means by which it can defend them. For instance, on July 1, 2003, the PRC promulgated "Administrative Regulations on Protection and Exploitation of Uninhabited Islands." While these are not specifically aimed at Taiwan, the calculus is clear:

> The islands are small, but they are related to our territorial integrity and national security as well as our economic development and our nation's revitalization. In military [terms], islands in important geographical or strategic locations are called "unsinkable carriers." . . . These basic spots are the starting points for drawing the borderline of territorial waters. The loss of these basic spots means the loss of sovereignty over their surrounding sea areas. Based on this, it may be said that even a small island has an immense value. From the perspective of economic development, islands are "bridgeheads" for advancing to the ocean as well as "island bridges" that link the inland areas.[138]

The salience of "even a small island" as an "unsinkable aircraft carrier" and of "bridgeheads" reveals a geostrategic mode of thinking about insular territory that extends well beyond Taiwan. It reinforces the view that in addition to claims based on nationalism, policy elites in the PRC are thinking very much in terms of geography, power projection, and security. As a corollary, the PRC is equally alert to the vulnerability these islands create in the hands of a rival.

Sea Lanes, Submarines, and Strategy

Gaining access to the Pacific may be thought of as having the capacity to secure transit by friendly vessels from the coast of China eastward and enhancing a capacity to regulate and defend north-south traffic on sea lanes passing through the Taiwan Strait and also east of Taiwan. This is part of a broad ambition to protect from disruption SLOC stretching from the Straits of Hormuz to the North Pacific via the Indian Ocean and the Strait of Malacca.[139] One facet of this ambition is to ensure access to chokepoints just north of Taiwan in the East China Sea and just south of the island in the Bashi Channel, a northern stretch of the Luzon Strait (see Figure 1 on page xvii). If the PRC controlled Taiwan, it could dominate these two passages, the Taiwan Strait, and the SLOC east of Taiwan. Without the ability to secure access to these chokepoints and sea lanes, commercial traffic on which the PRC is increasingly dependent is vulnerable to hostile actions—including blockades—against the PRC .

Another reason why the PRC may be interested in dominating these passages pertains to the ability to deploy a strategic nuclear force that would be a credible deterrent to the United States. To do that, the PRC needs not only a capacity to launch a nuclear strike against targets in the continental United States—a capacity it has had with land-based intercontinental ballistic missiles—but also the ability to survive a nuclear attack and launch a "second strike" against the United States. For this, analysts outside the PRC have suggested, Beijing is turning to submarines and submarine launched ballistic missiles (SLBM) armed with nuclear warheads.

In principle, the value of submarines is their stealth. It is difficult to detect and interdict a quiet submarine operating under favorable conditions. However, Peter Howarth writes "geography has dealt the PRC a weak hand when it comes to operating submarine-based systems as an effective strategic deterrent against the United States."[140] The problem for the PRC is that its submarines "cannot reach the open-ocean patrol area without passing through the choke points formed by the chain of islands . . . which enclose China's littoral seas. The control of these islands by members of the network of U.S. Asia-Pacific security partners enables the United States to establish a distant blockade of the Chinese fleet to prevent the projection of Chinese sea power beyond its continental shelf."[141]

Howarth's point is that the PRC does not yet have an SLBM with sufficient range to launch from the sea within the first island chain and reach a target in the continental United States. The range of the PRC's missiles is too short. Without a capacity to hit the United States in a second strike, the PRC cannot claim a credible nuclear deterrent and, therefore, is ultimately vulnerable to the United States. For the foreseeable future, the PRC would have to launch missiles from well east of the first island chain to hit a target in the United States. Here, geography and sovereignty conspire against the PRC.

Howarth explains that "China's ability to deploy a credible nuclear deterrent against the United States" depends on the ability of PRC's submarines to "pass undetected across the trip wires and ASW [antisubmarine warfare] barriers across their transit routes through the choke points between the islands enclosing the China seas."[142] In other words, submarines can be put at risk to a host of mines and detection devices, some of which are "linked to shore-based data processing facilities by fibre-optic cables."[143] So, submarines transiting the first island chain to reach open sea sacrifice a degree of stealth by sailing through one of several narrow channels. This alone enhances the adversary's capacity to detect or "kill" them—like shooting fish in a barrel. In addition, whatever power has access to the islands adjacent to the transit channel has the capacity to deploy ASW technology requiring a "hard wire" link to shore. For the United States, "the proximity of naval and air bases on Okinawa and in the Japanese home islands would facilitate the defence of the fixed and mobile ASW surveillance systems against attempts to neutralize them."[144]

If, on the other hand, Taiwan were in the PRC's hands, then the whole matter of transiting strategic passages through the island chain is turned on its head. Adversaries seeking to approach China's coast would have to pass from east to west through the island chain. The PRC's submarines would no longer be forced to expose themselves in those passages and could put to sea from ports on Taiwan's eastern coast.[145]

Another geographic factor affecting the operation of submarines is the depth of the seas surrounding Taiwan . The Taiwan Strait itself is quite shallow, with an average depth of 100 meters. It is part of an extensive band of shallow water stretching from the Bohai to the South China Sea. In contrast, the sea floor off the eastern coast of Taiwan drops precipitously to 4,000 meters within 50 kilometers of the coast (see Figure 1 on page xvii).[146]

If the PRC controls Taiwan, the shallow waters in the Strait and along China's coast may work to the PRC's defensive advantage while the deep water off Taiwan's east coast would buy the PRC ease of access to the open ocean. Howarth states: "control of Taiwan would immeasurably assist the PLA Navy to assert sufficient control over the transit routes of its SSBNs [nuclear ballistic missile submarines] to enable them to reach their patrol areas in the central and eastern Pacific from where they would be able to bring their strategic offensive power to bear directly on the United States homeland."[147]

Specialists undoubtedly differ about the significance of these geographic features, but as one thinks about Taiwan as either a geographic constraint or opportunity, it may also be reasonable to consider whether the height and location of Taiwan's central mountain range complicate efforts by the PRC to use land-based radar systems to track and target surface vessels plying the waters to the east of Taiwan.[148] In principle, radar installations located on Taiwan's east coast could "see" far eastward into the Pacific without concern that an adversary's vessels might be able to hide in the signal "shadow" east of the mountain peaks where the PRC's land-based detection systems would encounter a diffraction zone. This would enable the PRC to exercise greater influence over approaches to China from the east and would also give it a higher degree of leverage over SLOC on which Japan, Korea, and Russia are dependent.

If the PRC exercised sovereignty over Taiwan, these various geographic attributes would appear to enhance the PRC's ability to deter access by, interdict, or destroy surface and subsurface vessels approaching the Chinese coast from the east. Evaluating the significance these enhancements would offer Beijing or the difficulty the accommodations to them would impose on an adversary is not the point of this section. Rather, it is to identify a mode of reasoning that is consistent with the geostrategic rationales for sovereignty over Taiwan that appear in PRC journals and statements by PRC military analysts.

There is a community of analysts who apparently believe that sovereignty over Taiwan would enable the PRC to exercise "sea control" in the waters within the first island chain—ensuring that "the enemy is limited to fugitive use"—and project naval power farther east into the Pacific.[149] Moreover, if Peter Howarth's calculations about Beijing's strategic nuclear strategy are correct, access to Taiwan would enable the PRC to augment its nuclear deterrent and alter the strategic calculations of the United States.[150]

Geostrategic Dialectics and Taiwan's Salience

At present, there is disagreement among foreign observers about whether the PRC is aiming to content itself with a capacity to deny access to foreign powers within the seas that abut its coast or whether it is building the means to extend its power to and beyond the first island chain. Official statements and documents issued by the PRC government, statements and publications by military and civilian analysts in the PRC, and evidence based on the particular capabilities the PRC has developed and is developing do not lead observers to a uniform conclusion about what the PRC intends. One senses that even within the PRC, this is not yet a settled issue. There is little disagreement, though, that the PRC does intend—in the words of one PRC military authority—to make the twenty-first century a "marine century."[151]

Similarly, the link between Taiwan's geostrategic salience and China's "peaceful rise" and "national rejuvenation" is not universally accepted in the PRC. Evidently, there is some dispute about just how significant is the Taiwan issue and whether China's "rise" may be impeded by Taiwan's separate status.[152] There is also debate about whether its quest for reunification is the PRC's "ends" or a "means" to broader strategic ambitions.

Two analysts at the Chinese Academy of Social Sciences—Tang Shiping, deputy director of the Center for Regional Security Studies, and Cao Xiaoyang at the Institute of Asia-Pacific Studies—write of the different strategic perspectives advanced by analysts in the PRC, categorizing them as offensive realists, defensive realists, and neoliberals. They claim that, as in the United States, the arguments of the defensive realists are the mainstream. Evidently defensive realists themselves, Tang and Cao propose that "the reunification of China will not threaten the maritime dominance of the United States" because "China does not wish to repel the U.S. presence in the Asia-Pacific region, but opposes any malicious blockade of the United States against China."[153]

Indeed, in a sequence of essays published in the now-defunct journal *Zhanlüe yu Guanli* [Strategy and Management], Tang Shiping painted a rather different portrait of the PRC's security requirements than did Zhang Wenmu, whose articles appeared in the same journal.[154] Taken together, theirs might be seen as something of a debate about the merits of the aggressive development of the PRC's naval capacities, expansion of the PRC's maritime domain, and the centrality of Taiwan in those two ventures.

In contrast to Zhang, who might be classified as an "offensive realist," Tang Shiping does not view the reunification of Taiwan and the mainland as a fulcrum on which the PRC's security balances. He disputes Zhang Wenmu's conclusion that "If Taiwan were reunified, China would completely break the island chains that America constructed to block China in the West Pacific." Tang observes that even if the PRC succeeds in its quest for unification with Taiwan and even if the Korean peninsula is unified and independent of U.S. influence, that represents only two points where the PRC can penetrate the "first island chain." Moreover, the United States has bases or access privileges in Guam, Japan, the Philippines, and Singapore, as well as alliances with Australia and New Zealand, all of which create an insurmountable obstacle to any serious effort by the PRC to compete for naval supremacy with the United States.[155]

Looking beyond the arena of security, not all PRC analysts agree that unification with Taiwan is related much to Beijing's grand strategy of development. For example, Zhang Nianzhi of the Shanghai Institute for East Asian Relations aims to explain how the two are thought to be linked, but to advise readers to see China's future as separate from the question of Taiwan's independence.[156] He identifies reunification as a process of "gradual integration" and downplays the role that Taiwan should play in China's perception of its "peaceful rise."

In an effort, perhaps, to lower expectations and depress the nationalistic "temperature" aroused by the Taiwan issue, Zhang characterizes China's rise as comprising many tributaries, each reflecting different aspects of the program to rejuvenate and empower China. He suggests that many tributaries flow into a larger river that then becomes "a rising gigantic dragon." For that reason, he urges that the Taiwan issue be seen as only one of these many tributaries that cannot, alone, affect the overall flow of events. He concludes by advocating that the PRC "should have a comprehensive development concept," implying, perhaps, that it has allowed the Taiwan issue to be miscast as having a decisive influence on China's rise.[157] Liu Yazhou is even more blunt. He states: "The Taiwan problem is not essentially strategic. The more we care about it, the easier it is for the authorities in the U.S. and Taiwan to use it."[158]

Just as there was debate in the Kangxi Emperor's court about the value of exerting control and claiming sovereignty over Taiwan, there is evidently debate in the PRC's policy courts about the reasons why Taiwan should be seen as worth a struggle. Shi Lang's analytical heirs see the island as a strategic resource or liability depending on who dominates it. From their vantage, a fundamental justification for action is that a failure to take it leaves it as a threat to China's security and an impediment to the cultivation of the PRC's power. Controlling it, though, offers the PRC a forward base from which to "contest" with anti-Chinese forces, to cite General Peng Guangqian, and to go forth into the Pacific.

The notion that China has a manifest destiny in the Pacific is tied, one suspects, to a national self-perception of power that would come from the actualities of control over a vast maritime domain. Strategic depth may be essentially operational but there is a perceptual dimension that cannot be dismissed.[159] The determination to develop sea power may be fueled partly by a wish for greater security, but may also plump a sense of national self-esteem as the PRC strives to become what it imagines itself both entitled and destined to be: a great power. There are assuredly many PRC analysts who endorse the view that "If we don't have a strong and powerful ocean force, it is very difficult to enter the ranks of the world's powerful states."[160] The geostrategic perspective about Taiwan makes it seem that the PRC's ambitions for security and prosperity—goals that dovetail with a hunger for national rejuvenation and prestige—hinge on unifying the state. Taiwan is presented as the key.

8

Why Taiwan? The Great Confluence

This book was prompted by a simply stated question: why? Why is Taiwan worth fighting for? What does Beijing feel is at stake? It would be elegant to offer a response expressed as parsimoniously. However, elegance and parsimony are not the progenitors of accuracy. Beijing's attitude toward the Taiwan issue must be understood as the confluence of several streams of influence. Concerns about sovereignty and territorial integrity as abstract expressions of national-ism, anxieties about regime legitimacy that flow from transitions in the role of the CCP, worries about the "domino effect" that an acceptance of Taiwan's independence might provoke in Inner Mongolia, Tibet, and Xinjiang, and the changing dynamics of political and economic factors that dominate cross-Strait relations are several streams that certainly affect the PRC's stance on Taiwan. However, this book focuses on the Taiwan issue as an internationalized territo-rial dispute, not just a domestic conflict that is the legacy of civil war.

The book proceeds from the premise that the nationalistic arguments at the core of the PRC's declaratory policies about Taiwan do not explain varia-tions in the PRC's strategy for resolving the territorial dispute. More spe-cifically, arguments advanced by Beijing—many of which focus on or are a response to comments made by officials in Taipei—do not help to understand why the PRC has so feverishly worked since the 1990s to develop military options to compel Taiwan's submission to Beijing's wishes. For years after the normalization of Sino-U.S. relations in 1979, the PRC emphasized its inten-tion to reunify Taiwan and the mainland by peaceful means. Even though Beijing refused to renounce the right to use force, it showed little inclination to use it. As recently as the early 1990s, there was a flurry of secret and then public and quasi-official interactions between Beijing and Taipei culminating in the well-publicized meeting of ARATS chairman, Wang Daohan, and SEF chairman, Gu Zhenfu, in Singapore, April 27–29, 1993. Thereafter, relations across the Strait soured and the PRC's posture changed. Much of that has been attributed to the displeasure Beijing took in the public rhetoric and dip-lomatic initiatives of former ROC president, Lee Teng-hui.[1] Certainly, Lee's trip to Cornell University in 1995 was a pivotal moment.

If the Cornell visit was a turning point in cross-Strait relations—confirming Beijing's suspicions that Lee Teng-hui was intent on working toward independence, not unification—the U.S. response to missile exercises the PRC held in 1996 was a turning point in Sino-U.S. relations. By sending two aircraft carrier battle groups to the Taiwan area, the Clinton administration confirmed for Beijing that Washington was prepared to employ its preponderant military capability to impede Beijing's will even on a matter that the PRC articulated as a vital national interest. That the U.S. armada approached China's coast with impunity may also have been experienced as a public manifestation of Beijing's impotence in the face of what is perceived as American hegemonic power. This was not only a source of indignation and a bruising of Chinese national pride, it was perceived as a threat to the grand strategic vision that many in the PRC had constructed of a Chinese state that would be a regional power with a greater capacity to assert its interests abroad, including newly emerging maritime interests.

There has been a rather noticeable shift in Beijing's approach to Taiwan since that time, one that has involved a greater reliance on coercion and gratuitous displays of military force. To be sure, this coercive and belligerent demeanor is only the harder "hand" in a two-handed policy, the softer of which seeks to engage Taiwan's populace by encouraging economic interdependence with the PRC and a sense of common national destiny. Moreover, it is an open question whether the PRC intends to utilize military force in combat or whether it is devising means to prevail in a battle for Taiwan so as to deter its adversaries and avoid having actually to fight. As Paul Huth has found, the use of force as a means to impose a solution in territorial disputes is comparatively rare—as compared with militarization intended for signaling the adversary.[2] Perhaps, the PRC intends only to intimidate Taiwan and its allies in Washington from going too far.[3]

It is worth noting that if unification proceeds peacefully, the PRC may not invade, occupy, or govern Taiwan. It may only seek to ensure that it can veto or restrain Taiwan from interacting with other powers in ways that might degrade Beijing's sense of security and that the PRC is free to exploit Taiwan's location to advance its aims for force projection. This is suzerainty, which lies at the heart of the "one country, two systems" formula. Rooted in security, it is also a manifestation of power and prestige.

Still, the prospect of using force to resolve the Taiwan issue appears to be the organizing focus of the PRC's military modernization. That implies a fraying of patience in Beijing and hints at a steeling of national will to engage in battle should peaceful means of unification continue to prove elusive. It also seems evident that the PRC is not only preparing to fight the forces of Taiwan, but those of the United States and potentially Japan, as well. So, this is the nub of the problem: what has prompted this increasingly bellicose stance, and why now?

To suggest answers, this book has set the cross-Strait dispute against the backdrop of China's relations to Taiwan prior to 1949. What emerges from that history is a pattern of concern by China's rulers about the strategic salience of the island, a significance that flows from Taiwan's location. That concern has almost always been prompted by the perceptions of a foreign power that has sought to draw Taiwan into its own strategic realm and/or use Taiwan as a "bridgehead" to affect relations between it and China.

With that in mind, one can imagine how several disparate influences combined in the 1990s to impel Beijing to adopt an approach to Taiwan that is governed, at least in part, by geostrategic concerns. One of those is the perception in the PRC that Lee Teng-hui had "defected" from the decades-long Guomindang policy of promoting unification. The abandonment of that commitment was followed, in 2000, by the loss by the Guomindang of the presidency. The emergence of the Democratic Progressive Party as the ruling party with its history of promoting Taiwan independence was deeply alarming, made no less so by President Chen Shui-bian's style of domestic politicking and diplomacy, neither of which did much at all to conceal his disinterest in unification.

If the Taiwan issue were purely a bilateral matter between Beijing and Taipei, then one might easily conclude that the sequence of disappointments and alarms from the 1990s onward was sufficient to create a sense of distress in the PRC that the hope of peaceful unification was slipping from its grasp. From the mid-1990s on, Beijing undoubtedly felt that it no longer had a "partner" in Taipei prepared to work toward a nonviolent resolution of the outstanding dispute. Hence, one might conclude that the PRC's resort to more coercive and militarized measures was understandable, even if threatening violence was not the only imaginable—or sensible—reaction to the conditions Beijing confronted.

If the dispute were purely bilateral, one might expect that as Chen Shui-bian's political fortunes sagged after 2004, the PRC would slow or scale back military preparations aimed at prevailing in a battle for Taiwan. Although Chen's popularity plummeted and the opposition sought to recall—impeach—him in 2006, the PRC persisted in its development of the capacity to subordinate Taiwan by force and dominate the Taiwan Strait and its environs.

Other factors have undoubtedly affected Beijing's choices, chief among them the strategic rivalry with the United States and apprehensions about

Japan. Indeed, the superimposition of the Sino-U.S. and Sino-Japanese rivalries on the bilateral cross-Strait rivalry has ensured that the Taiwan issue is thoroughly internationalized.[4] The Taiwan issue is not simply a dyadic conflict. Taiwan has long fit in an "imagined geography" of China that emerged from Chinese perceptions of the international security environment.

Historical evidence presented in Chapters 3 and 4 makes clear that Beijing's determination to oppose the autonomy of Taiwan is not an inclination peculiar to the PRC. Since the seventeenth century, rulers of China's continental territories have viewed Taiwan as within a peripheral zone that China seeks to dominate and in which alien or hostile forces are intensely threatening because of their proximity and access to China's coast. The notion of Taiwan as instrumental to the security of China coexists with views of the island as peripheral to the Chinese heartland. It is as if the island is important to the motherland, but not fully accepted as a part of it.

Perhaps, during certain moments over the past four hundred years, China's rulers viewed the domination of the Western Pacific region in much the way that James Monroe viewed Latin America and the Caribbean. They may have concluded that if China does not control that space, control will be taken by other states—and those states almost certainly will not share China's interests.[5] The PRC's view of Taiwan seems consistent with that recurring geostrategic impulse. That may explain, in part, why the PRC sees Taiwan as worth fighting for.

As to the question "why now?" it is worth considering that when the structure of the international system is perceived by actors to be undergoing a significant shift, or at junctures when rival powers seek to reconfigure their relative capabilities, one notices an intensification of interest in, and greater politicization of, geography. This, as Chapter 2 suggests, can increase the likelihood of military conflict.[6]

It is probably not coincidental then that the geostrategic concerns of PRC strategists were aroused in the years after the end of the cold war, during a period when Americans were debating the merits of containment or engagement of China and Chinese were decrying U.S. unipolarity and hegemony.[7] These developments have coincided with a mounting interest in Japan to reconsider its strategic position in Asia, a process fueled in part by the PRC's emergence as a considerably more capable military power with expanding influence in a range of sectors affecting Japan's core interests. This is also a juncture at which Japan's constitutional commitment to refrain from using force in pursuit of foreign policy objectives is under intensified scrutiny by

Japanese who wonder whether that posture will serve the national welfare as well in the future as it has in the past.[8]

All that is to say that the deterioration in bilateral relations across the Taiwan Strait has occurred in a period when there is ongoing and fundamental realignment of the international system following the collapse of the Soviet Union and communism in Eastern Europe and Central Asia.[9] The first cataclysmic shocks associated with that transformation coincided with the aftermath of the Tiananmen incident of 1989 and the PRC's struggle to reposition itself in the wake of international outrage about the violent suppression of what had been peaceful demonstrations.

By the mid-1990s, not only was the PRC seeking to rebuild the confidence of its neighbors and other powers with which relations had been disturbed by the events of 1989, but it was working to demonstrate that it could not be bullied or bludgeoned into political reform. In this same period, the 1990s, the PRC was experiencing phenomenal economic growth that fed a sense of national self-confidence and anticipation about what the future might hold for the "rise of China." So, on one hand, Beijing was provoked by the insecurities of an international system in transition to see the world darkly, but on the other was buoyed by newfound confidence that—pending continued growth and stability—the PRC might have a brighter future.

Out of these twin forces a consensus about the PRC's grand strategy was forged. Continued economic growth and political stability were embraced as the foundations for future power as measured by prosperity, influence, security, and status. By the start of the twenty-first century, the PRC was well-embarked on policies aimed at taking the state, incrementally, from where it was to where it hoped to be.

To get there, the PRC understood it would have to develop the capacity to ensure its security and commercial welfare in an era when even the most sophisticated militaries were themselves undertaking substantial reform.[10] It would also have to use its emerging capacities to ensure that it could defend the transport of resources—especially oil and gas—and other commodities that are the requisites of continued economic growth. It began to think more purposefully in terms of the exploitation of maritime resources for the extraction of energy and minerals. All this reinforced a view that the PRC would have to extend its capacity to operate as a maritime power, not just a continental power. While the question remains how deeply into the Pacific the PRC needs to project naval power, the need to think in terms of naval power projection is apparently unquestioned.[11]

As Chapter 2 suggests, power projection is inherently geopolitical. The PRC's efforts to expand its maritime domain have already affected its relationship with the United States, Japan, and India, among other states. From the evidence presented in Chapter 7, it is clear that some PRC analysts frame their maritime objectives in terms of "breaking through" what they perceive as the encirclement of China by U.S. forces while acting, in turn, to contain Japan.

The encirclement by the United States is possible in part because Washington commands a superior military force. However, the United States is only able to project its military might across the Pacific to menace China's coast by gaining access to bases and other facilities in the Western Pacific. So the other dimension of U.S. encirclement as viewed by PRC analysts is the ring of islands and island states with which the United States has cooperative security relations. Taiwan is among them.

Hence, the deteriorating bilateral relations with Taipei, the transformation of the international system in an era of American "unilateralism," the emergence of a grand strategic vision in the PRC that entails the projection of power into the Pacific, and the underlying rivalry with the United States only partly having to do with Taiwan, have all nurtured a sense that the PRC is enmeshed in a geopolitical contest for its future security and welfare.

Naturally, as one assesses evidence of a geostrategic perspective about Taiwan's salience, one must be wary of analytical pitfalls that result from a failure to "distinguish an editorial by a junior officer from an official policy statement," and one must exercise "the good sense to distinguish tabloid journalism from credible news reports."[12] The argument underscoring Taiwan's pivotal role in China's future, however, permeates the rhetorical realm in statements by both influential and inconsequential military officers and in publications by scholars and analysts at both top tier and less prestigious institutions. Whether written by a general or a graduate student, assertions about Taiwan's geostrategic significance of the sort that are cited in the previous chapter are essentially the same. The consistency of imagery, concerns, and reasoning that is used to frame Taiwan's geostrategic salience is striking and contributes to a sense that the geostrategic rationales, even if it not the primary drivers of PRC policy, constitute a forceful undercurrent in presentations meant to justify the use of military might in pursuit of unification.

What is difficult to discern is whether these views—widespread though they appear to be—are relevant to the policy process in any material way. If they are, do they drive policy or simply validate it? Are declarations about the centrality of Taiwan to the PRC's security and the rejuvenation of the Chinese nation the ravings of hypersensitive "offensive realists" who react to deep insecurity and uncertainty by insisting on muscular and expansionist policies? Or are they the reasoned view of the moderate mainstream? Are characterizations of the Taiwan issue as central to the PRC's grand strategy—a means, not the end—motivated by the kind of "special pleading" that military institutions engage in to ensure that their branch of the armed services is valued and their budgets increased, or are they outgrowths of well-considered strategic calculations?[13] Are those who write most vociferously of the importance of Taiwan to the PRC's development of naval power and of the location of Taiwan as a critical "gateway" to the Pacific merely armchair strategists reflecting the landlubber's view of how navies operate and how sea power is established, or are they esteemed specialists whose views count?

The difficulty of determining how ideas flow through the policy process, and what the intentions of decision makers are, is great enough where a society is open and where there are expectations of accessibility and accountability. Secrecy, dissembling, and calculated obfuscation in the PRC make it hard to know precisely how an idea evolves into policy, who is the author, who is the editor, who is the censor, and who is the transmitter.

Perversely, the pluralism that results from reforms cheered by critics of PRC authoritarianism may make even more difficult a persuasive reading of the beliefs and intentions of Beijing's foreign policy elite. To the degree that the state speaks with one voice—even if it does so sparingly—one develops a capacity to hear and interpret that voice. There may be fewer discernible signals than one wishes, but there is less static, too.

The PRC has evolved beyond the time when it tolerated only one voice, so more ideas are "out there" to be heard. There is much more "noise" than there was in the past. However, the leadership and its agencies still step in to limit consideration of certain issues in public fora or to constrain the way particular matters are dealt with in public. So, because central control is still possible, one risks overinterpreting published words and utterances as signals or clues emanating from a central authority. Where apparently conflicting messages appear in the press from apparently reputable and authoritative sources, one is left to wonder whether the dissonance is meant to deceive or is simply an expression of greater tolerance of difference.

It is likely that conflicting statements about the centrality of Taiwan to the security and grand strategic vision of the PRC reflect an unresolved internal debate. For some, the geostrategic salience of Taiwan overwhelms in significance other rationales for unification. The coercive policies and escalation in militarized behavior since the 1990s are certainly consistent with the worldview and objectives of those who advance the notion that unification is a strategic imperative. That is, if one holds the view that Taiwan is of strategic significance both to security and national rejuvenation, one would be inclined to establish and support policies that highlight the urgency of unification and the need to prepare for military contingencies in which the process of wresting control of the island entails conflict with the United States.

That the geostrategic perspective on the Taiwan issue and the expansion of the PRC's naval power are consistent does not mean, though, that the former caused the latter. There may be other reasons why policy makers have endorsed the development of naval power that would be sufficient to cope with a "contingency" in the Taiwan Strait involving the United States. As one looks back on earlier moments of friction between China and other powers that dominated Taiwan, one sees that the expressions of strategic concerns about the island were also consistent with the actions taken to secure the island from rival powers. However, one cannot be certain that the strategic concerns did in fact prevail over other rationales.

One knows, for instance, that the Kangxi emperor was advised by Shi Lang to see the geostrategic merit in taking Taiwan, but one does not know whether the emperor was swayed by Shi Lang's rationale or by some other whim or reason to approve the incorporation of the island into his domain. Similarly, one can be fairly certain that the most senior leaders in the PRC are well acquainted with the geostrategic arguments that are advanced about the centrality of Taiwan and its salience as a means of puncturing the U.S. island-based cordon. One does not know, though, whether it is the logic of that argument or some other that impels them to coercive diplomatic measures and an increasingly militarized stance toward Taiwan. One cannot know whether they are moved primarily by the nationalistic arguments that have been the mainstay of the PRC's declaratory policy or whether they, too, harbor insecurities and uncertainties about the intentions of the United States and Japan that move them to see the quest for sovereignty and territorial integrity as a means to grander strategic ends.[14]

Nevertheless, even if one concludes that geostrategic rationales are not driving policy toward Taiwan, or that such views are advanced by individuals who do not "count" much in the policy process, or that they are the "personal" perspectives of influential individuals who operate in a political context dominated by less confrontational attitudes toward cross-Strait relations and the United States, one ought to take heed of the implications of the geostrategic reasoning. If the jingoism that accompanies geostrategic calculations has not been the principal motive for Beijing's policy toward Taiwan, militarization of the cross-Strait dispute, and the cultivation of sea power, that does not mean it will always be subordinate to more moderate approaches. Consider Japan in the late 1920s. Ian Nish writes:

> There were new forces at work in the Japanese army. . . . Army officers were becoming increasingly confident that their own vision of Things Chinese was the right one and that the approach of party politicians was suspect. The army's views were many-sided and were by no means "policy." But the time might come when the army's initiatives could prove popular, and the government of the day, either voluntarily or involuntarily, might be tempted to side with them.[15]

The *possibility*—as opposed to a foregone conclusion—that the PRC will slip into military expansionism as Japan did in the twentieth century is what commands attention. Moreover, geostrategic rationales for seeking territorial integrity are not the preserve of the PLA only. This perspective has broader appeal in the PRC.

While one cannot responsibly and precisely weigh the influence of the geostrategic rationales on Beijing's Taiwan policy, it is clear that more than disunity disturbs PRC nationalists and strategists when they consider Taiwan. If it were the case that the PRC were motivated exclusively or even mainly by disunity, all territory that the PRC claims as China's would be of equal value and the recovery of all contested territory would merit equal effort. Obviously, that is not the case. That Taiwan sits at the interface of two strategic domains— the continental domain of the PRC and the maritime domain of the United States—has meant that the struggle for access to and influence over the island is related in some measure to Beijing's effort to adjust the strategic balance at sea.

Implications

As Chapter 7 makes evident, Taiwan's location in the "imagined geography" of China is widely represented in PRC publications as having critical strategic salience. For that reason, reunification is portrayed as a vital national interest without which the security and welfare of the Chinese state will be in jeopardy. Indeed, because of the significance ascribed to Taiwan's location, reunification is represented by some writers as a strategic imperative on which the development of Chinese sea power depends. Considering that the enhancement of Chinese sea power is heralded as a key to the rejuvenation of the Chinese people—a fundamental aim since the end of the nineteenth century—Taiwan's importance to the PRC could not be more emphatically justified.

For the most part, these views—broadly circulated in unofficial sources— are absent from the more circumscribed rhetoric of formal, official proclamations about Taiwan. They do surface, though, in statements by senior and

influential military officers who the state has, in principal, the capacity to censure or censor. They are also reproduced in press organs, in journals published
by state-sponsored institutions, and on the Internet—media that the state has
otherwise demonstrated no diffidence about regulating to suit its political
interest. Therefore, one must infer that the PRC leadership is at least prepared
to tolerate the perception that Taiwan has strategic value. Beyond that, the foreign policy elites and even individuals in the central leadership *may* share the
conviction that Taiwan has geostrategic salience, although conclusive evidence
of that has yet to be presented.

Prudence alone should lead policy makers in Washington, Tokyo, and Taipei,
among other capitals, to remain open to the possibility that geostrategic rationales are among the key drivers of PRC policy toward Taiwan. That such
rationales for reunification may not have been the initial reason why the PRC
wanted to assert sovereignty over Taiwan does not preclude the possibility that
geostrategic reasoning has taken hold in response to changes in the political,
economic, and international contexts. In view of the foregoing evidence from
the PRC that geostrategic anxieties and ambitions punctuate analyses of the
Taiwan issue, one would be remiss in failing to think anew about why Taiwan
is now sufficiently important to the PRC that Beijing justifies to itself the
readying of military force.

Equally important is the need to avoid a blinkered view of Beijing's stance
on Taiwan as an outgrowth of a peculiar Chinese fascination with unity or an
inflamed reaction to historical grievances. It is worth wondering whether the
resurgence of interest in geostrategic reasoning is a response in the PRC to
more recent perceived provocations. If Taiwan is valued in part because of its
geostrategic salience, then every act by the United States or Japan that Beijing
interprets as encouraging or exploiting the autonomy of Taiwan is a strike
at the heart of the PRC's sense of security. Those in the PRC who embrace
the geostrategic vision of Taiwan are likely to dismiss as hokum U.S. claims
that its support of Taiwan reflects concern for the rights of Taiwan's people
to determine their own fate or that Americans are wont to defend democratic
underdogs from authoritarian bulldogs or any other effort to legitimate what
Beijing views as interference.

Likewise, those in the PRC who view Taiwan from a geostrategic perspective are likely to manifest reflexive and skittish suspicion about the slightest
quiver from Tokyo that presages an expansion of its role in support of Taiwan,
to say nothing of expanding its capacity to project military might in ways that
could blunt the PRC's own ambitions. Geostrategists in the PRC see U.S. and

Japanese actions relating to Taiwan as naked expressions of a broader ambition to contain China. Moreover, they find in the writings of Americans and
Japanese who advocate a restraint on China's military growth ample evidence
to support their interpretation of U.S. and Japanese policies that appears consistent with that aim.

This is the tragic dimension of the security dilemma. Policymakers fail to
recognize how they are perceived by their rivals. Herbert Butterfield writes:
"you know that you yourself mean him no harm, and that you want nothing from him save guarantees for your own safety; and it is never possible for
you to realise or remember properly that since he cannot see the inside of
your mind, he can never have the same assurance of your intentions that you
have."[16] Naturally, this is as true about Beijing's intentions as it is about those
of Washington and Tokyo and Taipei. It is not possible to know with certainty
why the PRC acts as if Taiwan is worth fighting for or how the PRC will
be better off having settled to its satisfaction the question of Taiwan's status
than it is while that status is in dispute. After all, policy ordinarily has multiple
authors, each of whom may contribute to the outcome on the basis of a distinctive shade of priorities and values. For analysts who offer a geostrategic
perspective about Taiwan's salience in the context of the PRC's determination
to enhance its sea power, there are two clear reasons why the island is worth a
fight: national security and national prestige.[17]

Whether motivated by a search for security, prestige, or both, the expansion of PRC naval prowess and growing interest in sea power is apprehended
abroad—as it is described by geostrategists in the PRC—in a zero–sum
framework. It is this calculus that prompts strategists and statesmen in Taipei,
Washington, and Tokyo to decry the PRC's militarization of the controversy
with Taiwan, the centerpiece of a broader military buildup, as provocative and
destabilizing.[18]

Thinking in terms of the bilateral, cross-Strait relationship: to the degree
that Beijing subscribes to, endorses, or encourages the dissemination of the
geostrategic views of Taiwan, it is playing the lyre of security and patriotism
as if it were Orpheus hoping to drown out the song of the Sirens.[19] However,
Taiwan's song—which is hardly capable of causing the PRC's demise—
expresses the utterly ordinary wish of a state to be allowed by a stronger
power to coexist without molestation.

Taiwan's people seek the dignity of sovereignty and the assurance that
so long as they do no harm to the PRC, Beijing will regard the island with
neighborly comity. However, the geostrategic perspective leaves adherents in

Beijing—like the sailors Odysseus ordered to fill their ears with wax—unable or unwilling to hear Taiwan's plea in any way other than as an insidious challenge to China's future that must, without concern for cost, be overcome.

In both the international and bilateral manifestations of the Taiwan issue, the geostrategic perspective advanced by PRC analysts might be characterized by a dispassionate observer as jingoistic and detrimental to compromise. Nevertheless, that perspective must be understood as a genuine expression of the national interest. Although geostrategic calculations of Taiwan's salience flow from an "imagined geography" of China and are reinforced by a particular rendition of history, they provide a seductive and potentially compelling rationale for China's territorial integrity.

Notes

CHAPTER 1

1. An enduring rivalry has been defined as "repeated or prolonged militarized competitions between the same pair of states." Paul F. Diehl, *The Dynamics of Enduring Rivalries*, vii; cf. Gary Goertz and Paul F. Diehl, "Enduring Rivalries: Theoretical Constructs and Empirical Patterns," 147; and Brian Job, André Laliberté, and Michael D. Wallace, "Assessing the Risks of Conflict in the PRC-ROC Enduring Rivalry," 513–535.

2. On the PRC's willingness to negotiate settlements of territorial disputes, see M. Taylor Fravel, "Regime Insecurity and International Cooperation: Explaining China's Compromises in Territorial Disputes," 46–83; and Fravel, *The Long March to Peace: Explaining China's Settlement of Territorial Disputes.*

3. United States Department of Defense, *Quadrennial Defense Review Report, 2006,* 29. See http://www.defenselink.mil/qdr/.

4. International Crisis Group, "Taiwan Strait II: The Risk of War," 3–24.

5. Ronald O'Rourke, *China Naval Modernization: Implications for U.S. Navy Capabilities—Background Issues for Congress,* executive summary, 23.

6. Regarding consideration by the PRC of its capacity to benefit from the Revolution in Military Affairs (RMA), see You Ji, "Learning and Catching Up: China's RMA Initiative," 97–124; James Mulvenon and David M. Finkelstein, *China's Revolution in Doctrinal Affairs*; and Michael Pillsbury, *Chinese Views of Future Warfare.*

7. The use of force does not necessarily mean the PRC will launch a full-scale, amphibious assault on the island. A coercive strategy employing military means short of war, as with a blockade, is a use of force. Naturally, miscalculation by Beijing or its adversaries could lead beyond whatever limited objective was intended and into war. Lyle Goldstein and Bill Murray, "China's Subs Lead the Way," 58–61; Thomas J. Christensen, "Coercive Contradictions: *Zhanyixue*, PLA Doctrine, and Taiwan Scenarios," 307–327.

8. Keith Crane, Roger Cliff, Evan Medeiros, James Mulvenon, and William Overholt, *Modernizing China's Military: Opportunities and Constraints,* 194; David Shambaugh, *Modernizing China's Military: Progress, Problems, and Prospects,* 307. John Culver identifies 1993 as the

year in which "procurement from the former-Soviet Union began to be directed to the Nanjing Military Region (opposite Taiwan) and military training activity near the Taiwan Strait increased." See John Culver and Michael Pillsbury, "Defense Policy and Posture II."

9. Richard Bernstein and Ross H. Munro, *The Coming Conflict with China*, 5–7, 161–165; Kurt M. Campbell and Derek J. Mitchell, "Crisis in the Taiwan Strait," 14–25; Richard Halloran, "Taiwan," 22; Michael E. O'Hanlon, "The Risk of War over Taiwan Is Real"; and O'Hanlon, "Why China Cannot Conquer Taiwan," 52.

10. Nancy Bernkopf Tucker, "Dangerous Strait: An Introduction," 1; Michael A. Chase, "U.S.–Taiwan Security Cooperation: Enhancing an Unofficial Relationship," 162; Alan D. Romberg, *Rein In at the Brink of the Precipice: American Policy Toward Taiwan and U.S.–PRC Relations*, 14; International Crisis Group, "Taiwan Strait II: The Risk of War," i–ii; Michael D. Swaine and James C. Mulvenon, *Taiwan's Foreign and Defense Policies: Features and Determinants*, 1.

11. Even if Japan chooses not to support actively a U.S. effort to defend Taiwan from attack, the PRC could target American assets on Japanese soil, thus drawing Japan into the fray. *The Japan Times*, "Japan, U.S. Mull Plan for Taiwan Crisis."

12. Alastair Iain Johnston, "China's International Relations: The Political and Security Dimensions," 84.

13. Hisahiko Okazaki suggests how the entire structure of Northeast and Southeast Asian alliances might be reoriented toward Beijing and away from Washington in the aftermath of a successful attempt by the PRC to use force to subordinate Taiwan. See Hisahiko Okazaki, "The Strategic Value of Taiwan"; regarding costs to the PRC, see Yong Deng, "Diplomatic Consequences"; and Jing Huang, "Economic and Political Costs."

14. Romberg, *Rein In at the Brink of the Precipice*, 14.

15. See, e.g., People's Republic of China, Ministry of Foreign Affairs, "China's Independent Foreign Policy of Peace."

16. Avery Goldstein, *Rising to the Challenge: China's Grand Strategy and International Security*, ch. 6, esp. 119; on the PRC's defense expenditures, see U. S. Department of Defense, *Annual Report to Congress: The Military Power of the People's Republic of China, 2006*; Crane et al., *Modernizing China's Military*.

17. Evan A. Feigenbaum, "China's Challenge to *Pax Americana*," 41.

18. *"Zhongguo renmin yiding yao jiefang Taiwan"* ["The Chinese people certainly will liberate Taiwan"]; Renmin Wang, *" 'Yiding yao jiefang Taiwan,' Zhonggong dangshide 80 ju kouhao"* ["We Certainly Will Liberate Taiwan," 80 Slogans from CCP Party History]. This slogan was emblazoned on mass-produced propaganda posters that vividly depicted the military implications of *jiefang Taiwan* [liberate Taiwan]. See, http://db1.maopost.com/wcat=mao&wlan=en&wreq=home and http://www.iisg.nl/~landsberger/tailib.html.

19. International Crisis Group, "Taiwan Strait I: What's Left of 'One China'?" 5.

20. Li Xiaobing, "PLA Attacks and Amphibious Operations During the Taiwan Strait Crises of 1954–5 and 1958," 158–167.

21. The statement read, in part, that bombardment was suspended "so that the compatriots, both military and civilian . . . may all get sufficient supplies, including food, vegetables, edible oils, fuels and military equipment, to facilitate your entrenchment for a long time to come. If you are short of anything, just say so and we will give it to you. It is time now to turn from foe to friend. Your ships and aircraft should not come on odd days." See Peng Dehuai, "PRC Defense Minister P'eng Teh-huai's Second Message to Compatriots in Taiwan, October 25, 1958."

22. Edward Friedman, "China's Dilemma on Using Military Force," 206; and "Discussion Between N. S. Khrushchev and Mao Zedong."

23. "Discussion Between N. S. Khrushchev and Mao Zedong."

24. UN Resolution 2758 was passed on October 25, 1971. Until 1971, the PRC was recognized by fewer states than was the ROC. As late as 1969, the PRC was recognized by only forty-nine states, while the ROC was recognized by sixty-seven. In 1971, that balance shifted. By the year's end, the PRC was recognized by sixty-nine states and the ROC by only fifty-four. Thereafter, the PRC was recognized by ever-more states, while the ROC side of the ledger declined. After 1975, the ROC was never recognized by more than thirty states and, in many years, fewer than that. Chien-min Chao, "The Republic of China's Foreign Relations Under President Lee Teng-hui: A Balance Sheet," 182, table 9.1.

25. In a message released on New Year's day, 1979, the Standing Committee of the Fifth National People's Congress, Beijing, announced "the Chinese Government has ordered the People's Liberation Army to stop the bombardment of Jinmen (Quemoy) and other islands as from today. A state of military confrontation between the two sides still exists along the Taiwan Straits. . . . We hold that first of all this military confrontation should be ended through discussion between the Government of the People's Republic of China and the Taiwan authorities so as to create the necessary prerequisites and a secure environment for the two sides to make contacts and exchanges in whatever area." See "Message to Compatriots in Taiwan, January 1, 1979"; and People's Republic of China, National People's Congress, *"Quanguo renda changwei gao Taiwan tongbao shu"* [National People's Congress Standing Committee Appeals to Taiwan Compatriots].

26. National People's Congress Chairman, Ye Jianying, articulated the PRC's overture to the populace of Taiwan on September 30, 1981, in an interview with *Xinhua General Overseas News Service.* See "Ye Jianying Explains Policy Concerning Return of Taiwan to Motherland and Peaceful Reunification." On the development of the PRC's approaches to Taiwan after 1979, see Swaine, "Chinese Decision-Making Regarding Taiwan, 1979–2000," 310–333; and International Crisis Group, "What's Left of 'One China'?" 6–9, 17–22.

27. This would be a reification of Sun Zi's notion that "subjugating the enemy's army without fighting is the true pinnacle of excellence" [*gu shan yong bing zhe qu ren zhi bing er fei zhan ye*]. See Sun Zi, *Art of War,* chapter 3:6, in, for instance, Ralph D. Sawyer, *The Seven Military Classics of Ancient China,* 161.

28. For a summary of this evolving policy, see International Crisis Group, "What's Left of 'One China'?" 6–9; Swaine, "Chinese Decision-Making Regarding Taiwan," 310–312; see also *Xinhua She, "Ye Jianying xiang Xinhuashe jizhe fabiao de tanhua"* [Ye Jianying's Talk with Xinhua News Agency Journalists], often referred to as "Ye Jianying's Nine Point Proposal"; and Deng Xiaoping, *"Zhongguo dalu he Taiwan heping tongyi shexiang"* [An Idea for the Peaceful Unification of Mainland China and Taiwan].

29. Lee Teng-hui was appointed as minister without portfolio (1972–78) in the waning years of Chiang Kai-shek's era and served as mayor of Taipei (1978–81), governor of Taiwan province (1981–84), and as Chiang Ching-kuo's vice president (1984–88).

30. Jay Taylor, *The Generalissimo's Son: Chiang Ching-kuo and the Revolutions in China and Taiwan,* 361–376.

31. The National Unification Guidelines were adopted by the National Unification Council (NUC) at its third meeting on February 23, 1991, and by the Executive Yuan of the Republic of China at its 2223rd meeting on March 14, 1991. They codify an approach that

Lee Teng-hui had articulated in his inaugural address of May 1990. See Richard C. Bush, "Lee Teng-hui and Separatism," 75. President Chen Shui-bian caused quite a stir when he announced at the conclusion of a National Security Conference on February 27, 2006, "The National Unification Council will cease to function. No budget will be earmarked for it, and its personnel must return to their original posts. The National Unification Guidelines will cease to apply. In accordance with procedures, this decision will be transmitted to the Executive Yuan for notice." See "President Chen's Concluding Remarks at National Security Conference"; Maubo Chang, "Three Parties United in Opposing Abolition of NUC"; S. C. Chang, "KMT Supports Motion to Recall President"; Peter Enav, "Taiwan Leader Halts China Unification Panel, Drawing Protest from Beijing"; Xinhua General Overseas News Service, "Hu Jintao Slashes 'Taiwan Independence' Attempt"; Zhuang Pinghui, "Net Buzzes with Calls for Beijing to Get Tough"; Keith Bradsher, "Taiwan's Leader Defies Beijing's Warnings."

32. Formally, the provisions were known as the "Temporary Provisions Effective During the Period of National Mobilization for the Suppression of the Communist Rebellion." They made possible the imposition of martial law and concentration of extraconstitutional powers in the hands of the president. In the fall of 1986, work began in the Legislative Yuan on a new National Security Law [anquanfa] passage of which in June 1987 heralded the lifting of martial law on July 15, 1987. Linda Chao and Ramon H. Myers, *The First Chinese Democracy: Political Life in the Republic of China*, 47–51, 149.

33. On the adjustment made to Taiwan's defense doctrine following this transition see Alexander Chieh-cheng Huang, "Taiwan's View of Military Balance and the Challenges It Presents," 279–300; Swaine and Mulvenon, *Taiwan's Foreign and Defense Policies*, 28–30.

34. Lee Teng-hui, *The Road to Democracy: Taiwan's Pursuit of Identity*, 91–93.

35. The last of those meetings occurred in Taipei when President Lee Teng-hui met with Xu Mingzhen, an aide to PRC President Yang Shangkun. See Su Chi, *Wei xian bian yuan: cong liang guo lun dao yi bian yi guo* [Brinksmanship: From Two State Theory to One Country on Each Side], 10–15, esp. table 1–1; John Tkacik, "Premier Wen and Vice President Zeng: The 'Two Centers' of China's 'Fourth Generation,'" 144–146.

36. On August 1, 1992, the National Unification Council convened by President Lee Teng-hui issued a statement that asserted "Both sides of the Taiwan Strait agree that there is only one China. However, the two sides of the Strait have different opinions as to the meaning of 'one China.' To Peking, 'one China' means the People's Republic of China (PRC), with Taiwan to become a 'Special Administrative Region' after unification. Taipei, on the other hand, considers 'one China' to mean the Republic of China (ROC), founded in 1911 and with *de jure* sovereignty over all of China. The ROC, however, currently has jurisdiction only over Taiwan, Penghu, Kinmen, and Matsu. Taiwan is part of China, and the Chinese mainland is part of China as well." See "Taiwan on the Meaning of 'One China,'" in Shirley A. Kan, *China/Taiwan: Evolution of the "One China" Policy—Key Statements from Washington, Beijing, and Taipei*, 23; and Su Chi, *Wei xian bian yuan*, 17–18.

37. A more precise way of rendering in English what was agreed would be that each side adheres to *a*, not the, "one China principle."

38. Su Chi, *Wei xian bian yuan*, 16–21; Xu Shiquan, "The 1992 Consensus: A Review and Assessment of Consultations Between the Association for Relations Across the Taiwan Strait and the Straits Exchange Foundation," 81–102; Ma Ying-jeou, "Cross-Strait Relations at a Crossroad: Impasse or Breakthrough?" 43–45.

39. The term *consensus* [gong shi] is one Su Chi, himself, claims to have applied after 1992, while he worked as a government official. Su was vice-chairman of the Mainland

Affairs Council (1993–96), director-general of the Government Information Office (1996–97), deputy secretary-general of the Office of the President (1997–99), and chairman of the Mainland Affairs Council (1999–2000). He writes that the PRC took up this term for the first time on August 28, 1995. That month, the then secretary-general of the Straits Exchange Foundation, Chiao Jen-ho, characterized the agreement of 1992 as "one China, different interpretations" [*yige Zhongguo, ge zi biaoshu*]. This has also been rendered as "one China, respective interpretations." Su Chi, *Wei xian yuan bian*, 19–20. When the DPP captured the presidency in 2000, it sought to distance itself from the notion of a "consensus" with the PRC and controversy erupted about how to characterize what took place in 1992. This flared in 2006, prompting Lee Teng-hui to deride his former subordinate, Su Chi, stating "Little monkey boy [is] trying to make up history." See Shih Hsiu-chuan, "Su Chi Admits the '1992 Consensus' Was Made Up"; Central News Agency, "Former MAC Head Admits Coining '1992 Consensus' Term"; and Ko Shu-ling, "Taiwan President Accuses KMT, China of Lying Over Consensus Term."

40. Suisheng Zhao, "Reunification Strategy: Beijing Versus Lee Teng-hui," 222–224.

41. Bush, "Lee Teng-hui and Separatism," 78.

42. In 1989, Lee Teng-hui visited Singapore, in 1994 he visited the Philippines, Indonesia, and Thailand, and in 1995 he visited the United Arab Emirates, Jordan, and the United States—none of which had diplomatic relations with the ROC. The pretext was that Lee was making private visits, sometimes for the purpose of playing golf, giving rise to the notion that he was engaged in "vacation diplomacy" [*dujia waijiao*]. In the same period, he also visited Nicaragua, Costa Rica, Swaziland, and South Africa—states with which the ROC did have diplomatic relations—while other high-ranking officials, including Lee's vice president, Lien Chan, visited states in both categories. See Su Chi, *Wei xian bian yuan*, 36, table 1-8.

43. Xu Shiquan, "The 1992 Consensus," 92; Bush, "Lee Teng-hui and 'Separatism,'" 78–79.

44. Having served out the term of his predecessor from 1988 to 1990, Lee Teng-hui was reelected in 1990 to serve another six-year term. One condition of his reelection by the Guomindang elite was the appointment of Hau Pei-tsun, formerly the minister of defense, to the premiership. Hau's credentials as a representative of interests prized by mainland-born figures within the party were seen to balance those that Lee Teng-hui might bring to the fore as president. Hau's prominence was emblematic of the continued relevance in policy making and political reform of the Guomindang's "old guard," who were unambiguous about the necessity of unification. Hau also resisted the nature of political reform Lee Teng-hui sought, generating friction between the two men over the question of whether Taiwan's would become a presidential system—as Lee advocated—or a parliamentary system with a president as figurehead—as Hau hoped. Naturally, this was not simply a battle of abstractions about the path to good governance. It was a mask on a deeper, more divisive issue, of what power the Taiwan-born, independence-leaning Lee would command versus what powers would be retained by the mainland-born, unification-seeking conservatives of the "old" Guomindang. It was a struggle over the pace and direction of liberalization, democratization, national identity, and relations between Taiwan and China. In February 1993, Hau resigned. Lee Teng-hui had prevailed. See Ya-li Lu, "Lee Teng-hui's Role in Taiwan's Democratization," 59; Peter R. Moody, Jr., "Some Problems in Taiwan's Democratic Consolidation," 31–33; and Shelley Rigger, *Politics in Taiwan: Voting for Democracy*, 151, 167.

45. Su Chi, *Wei xian bian yuan*, 13; Tkacik, "Premier Wen and Vice President Zeng," 145–146.

46. The complexities of Taiwan's vigorously competitive democratic system regularly prompt political leaders to satisfice, rather than cling to what they may genuinely believe

to be optimal political objectives. This dynamic is commonly overlooked in PRC analyses, leading Beijing to misperceive, demonize, and alienate Taiwan's leadership.

47. Bush, "Lee Teng-hui and 'Separatism,'" 70–92. For Lee Teng-hui, "the question was not so much whether Taiwan was a part of China but how it was a part of China." Bush, "Chinese Decisionmaking Under Stress: The Taiwan Strait, 1995–2004," 139–142.

48. *Central News Agency* (Taipei), "Taiwan and China: Taiwan Foreign Minster's End of Year Address."

49. Central Broadcasting System (Taipei), "Taiwan and China: First Foreign Policy Report Out; Recognized 'The Truth of National Separation.'"

50. In the period 2000–2001, the PRC very slightly adjusted its formulation. Vice Premier Qian Qichen made statements in several settings that could be interpreted as accepting the view of China as a divided state, with sovereignty shared by the PRC and ROC. For instance, he stated "With regard to cross-strait relations, the one China principle we stand for is that there is only one China in the world; the mainland and Taiwan all belong to one China; and China's sovereignty and territorial integrity are indivisible." By stating "the mainland and Taiwan all belong to one China" he was implicitly backing away from the view that the PRC is the China to which Taiwan must return. Kan, *China/Taiwan: Evolution of the "One China" Policy*, 46, n. 97.

51. Xinhua General Overseas Service, "Jiang Zemin on Reunification of China."

52. Lee's remarks are open to interpretation. He is quoted as saying "When I asked my wife what topic I should be talking about with Mr. Shiba, she told me to talk about 'the grief of being born a Taiwanese.' We then talked about 'the Exodus' of the Old Testament." He later said he felt a sense of grief at not being in a position to do anything to help ameliorate international situations such as the one then unfolding in Bosnia. He added "There used to be the grief of being born a Taiwanese and not being able to do anything for Taiwan." From the context of the interview, it is not evident that Lee was suggesting his "grief" was related to the prospect of unification. Rather, it seems he was expressing sorrow that Taiwanese were subjected in the past to a brutal and dictatorial Guomindang regime that permitted them very little voice in the governance of the island on which they lived and, equally, sadness that their economic and political achievements notwithstanding, they were effectively excluded from participation in international life because of Beijing's capacity to enforce its view of "one China." In the same vein, it is not evident what Lee's allusion to Moses and Exodus means with respect to unification. Concluding that he meant in 1994 that he was determined to lead his people to independence is reading more into his words than is justified by his statement. In response to the question "At the beginning of this interview, you mentioned 'the Exodus.' Were you trying to say that Taiwan has started a new era?" Lee said, "Yes, we have. From now on, Moses and the people are going to face a tough time. However, they did start a new journey. . . . when I think about the February 28 (1947) incident in which many Taiwanese became victims, 'the Exodus' is one conclusion." From those words, one has to assume a great deal to conclude that the journey to which he refers is a quest for independence. It is just as likely that by referring to the February 28 incident—the foremost emblem of how the Taiwanese were oppressed by the Guomindang—the journey he spoke of is the path from disenfranchised to enfranchised, from subject to citizen in a democratic republic.

See U. S. Congress, "The Grief of Being Born a Taiwanese: Dialogue Between President Lee Teng-hui and Writer Ryotaro Shiba."

53. Jiang Zemin, "Continue to Promote the Reunification of the Motherland."

54. BBC Summary of World Broadcasts, "Cross-Strait Relations; Taiwan President's Six Points for Cross-Strait Relations."

55. Julian J. Kuo, "Cross-Strait Relations: Buying Time Without Strategy"; and Suisheng Zhao, "Reunification Strategy."

56. The interview with Ryotaro Shiba was prominently featured as prima facie evidence of Lee's commitment to independence. See, for instance, Zhao Wei, "Two-Faced Tactics Cannot Conceal His True Intentions—A Comment on Li Teng-hui's Statements at His News Conference."

57. James R. Lilley and Chuck Downs, *Crisis in the Taiwan Strait*.

58. Lee Teng-hui, *Taiwan no shucho* [Taiwan Viewpoints; reissued in English under the title *The Road to Democracy: Taiwan's Pursuit of Identity*], Tokyo: PHP Kenkyujo, 1999, 182. Paradoxically, Mao Zedong once compared Chinese rule over non-Han peoples on the periphery to imperialism and advocated that in place of a single unified Chinese state, each of China's twenty-seven provinces, special districts, and dependencies would be better off as a separate state. Liu Xiaoyuan, *Frontier Passages: Ethnopolitics and the Rise of Chinese Communism*, 28.

59. This and subsequent excerpts from the speech are reproduced in Lee Teng-hui, *The Road to Democracy*, 121–123.

60. Ibid., 183; see Bush, "Lee Teng-hui and 'Separatism.'"

61. Lee Teng-hui, "Responses to Questions Submitted by Deutsche Welle," 27.

62. *Xinhua* News Agency, "China Calls Taiwan President 'Sinner Condemned by History'"; *Xinhua* Domestic Service, *Jiefangjun Bao* commentator's article titled: "'Dependence on Foreigners' Cannot Save Li Teng-hui—Second Commentary on the 'Four Cards' Behind the 'Two-State Theory'"; Yu Xin, "Li Denghui's Secessionist Ambition Is Not Dead Yet."

63. Xiao Yang, "Jiandingbuyide weihu yige Zhongguo de yuanze" [Resolutely Safeguard the One China Principle]; Reuters, "Taiwan President a Rat: China"; Jaime Florcruz, "The View From Beijing: Speaking Loud Enough for a Home Audience to Hear."

64. *Xinhua* News Agency, "Military Expert: Splitting of Motherland Is Invitation of Destruction."

65. One must recall that Lee's book was published only weeks after the PRC embassy in Belgrade was bombed by the U.S. on May 7, 1999, an event that provoked an eruption of Chinese patriotic indignation and frustration. By the time Lee's interview with *Deutsche Welle* was broadcast in July, the furor of May had subsided, but bitterness stemming from Beijing's apparent powerlessness to defend the PRC's dignity smoldered.

66. *Zhongguo Xinwen She*, "China: Army Paper on Taiwan President's Dream." Another article reported "vast numbers of commanders and fighters of the Chinese armed forces and officers and men of the Chinese armed police sharply denounced Li Denghui's [Lee Teng-hui] perverse act of splitting the motherland. Commanders and fighters of a marine corps unit training at a certain location in the South China Sea are braving the hot summer heat to receive tough sea-crossing combat skill training in an effort to fight back Li Denghui's perverse act with concrete action. Officers and men of a certain surface-to-air missile division who are training and demonstrating their skills are resolved to master the weapons in their hands and use their up-to-the-mark military skills to safeguard the motherland's sovereignty and defend the territorial integrity. A certain Second Artillery Corps unit . . . is stepping up preparations for military combat to ensure that the unit can go into action at any time and can win battles to make new contributions to smashing Li Denghui's plot in splitting the motherland." See *Zhongguo Xinwen She*, "Chinese Soldiers, Armed Police Condemn Taiwan 'Two-State Theory.'"

67. Hu Jintao's policy toward Taiwan was encapsulated in a "four point" summary articulated in 2003 but highlighted more widely in 2005 at about the time that the Anti-Secession Law was passed. See *Xinhua News Agency,* "Hu Jintao Cites Four Points of Opinion on Taiwan Work When Addressing Taiwan Deputies."

68. Yu Maochun, "Political and Military Factors Determining China's Use of Force," 21.

69. Bates Gill, "Chinese Military Hardware and Technology Acquisitions of Concern to Taiwan," 108, 123 n. 2.

70. Shambaugh, *Modernizing China's Military,* 262; cf. Gill, "Chinese Military Hardware and Technology Acquisitions of Concern to Taiwan," 109.

71. On the significance of the rising defense budget, see Richard A. Bitzinger, "Research Report—Just the Facts, Ma'am: The Challenge of Analyzing and Assessing Chinese Military Expenditures."

72. U. S. Department of Defense, *The Military Power of the People's Republic of China, 2006,* 3.

73. U. S. Department of Defense, *The Military Power of the People's Republic of China, 2005,* 4–6, 23–24, 28–32; *The Military Power of the People's Republic of China, 2006,* 6, 37–41, 44–50; Shambaugh, *Modernizing China's Military,* 329–330.

74. Jonathan D. Pollack, "Short-range Ballistic Missile Capabilities."

75. A brigade consists of approximately 100 missiles. Mark A. Stokes, "Chinese Ballistic Missile Forces in the Age of Global Missile Defense: Challenges and Responses," 114, 152 n. 14.

76. Pollack, "Short-range Ballistic Missile Capabilities," 61.

77. The rate at which the PRC is increasing its production and deployment of missiles aimed at Taiwan has been a constant source of dispute among analysts. Ibid.

78. These are identified as the *Dongfeng* (DF)-31, "an extended range DF-31A, and a new submarine-launched ballistic missile, the JL-2." *The Military Power of the People's Republic of China, 2006,* 3–4.

79. Ibid., 5.

80. Swaine and Mulvenon, *Taiwan's Foreign and Defense Policies,* 100.

81. *The Military Power of the People's Republic of China, 2006,* 4.

82. Kenneth W. Allen and Jeffrey M. Allen, "Controlling the Airspace over the Taiwan Strait," esp. 113–114.

83. *The Military Power of the People's Republic of China, 2005,* 4–6.

84. Ibid., 4.

85. As of 2006, the U.S. Department of Defense reported "China's naval forces now include 75 major surface combatants, some 55 attack submarines, about 50 medium and heavy amphibious lift vessels (an increase of over 14 percent from last year), and approximately 45 coastal missile patrol craft." Beyond the specific number and type of vessels, the report makes clear that expansion by purchase and indigenous construction is proceeding at a rapid pace. *The Military Power of the People's Republic of China, 2005,* 4–6; see also, Bernard D. Cole, "Command of the Sea."

86. The Pentagon report notes that these Sovremennyy's "are fitted with advanced anti-ship cruise missiles (ASCMs) and sophisticated, wide-area air defense systems, which represent a qualitative improvement over China's earlier SOVREMENNYY-class DDGs purchased from Russia." Previously, the Pentagon stated that these improvements "could significantly complicate U.S. naval operations in the region." *The Military Power of the People's Republic of China, 2006,* 4–5; *The Military Power of the People's Republic of China, 2005,* 4–6.

87. Andrew Scobell argues that by the mid-1990s, with the passage from power of those "dual role" elites who derived status from both political and military experience during the Mao and Deng eras, the influence of military figures on policy and the mode by which

those individuals exercised influence shifted. "Rather than make the concerns of the military known only at the highest echelons of power through informal discussions in smoke-filled rooms, in the Jiang era the PLA also lobbies more publicly in the media, through books, journals, and to political leaders through letters and visits." Andrew Scobell, *Chinese Army Building in the Era of Jiang Zemin*, 16.

88. The term *China*, here, is shorthand for the polities ruled by the Ming, the Qing, and the Republican governments.

89. A concise view of this aspect of the PRC's military development is provided in You Ji, "A New Era for Chinese Naval Expansion."

90. See, for instance, Zhu Chenghu, *Zhongmei guanxi de fazhan bianhua ji qi qushi* [Changing Developments and Trends in China-U.S. Relations], 194 and Zhao Yiping, "The Current Situation and Trends in Asia-Pacific Security—Interview with Dr. Cheng Guang-zhong," cited in Scobell, *Chinese Army Building in the Era of Jiang Zemin*, 21, n. 117, 118.

CHAPTER 2

1. The term *zuguo* means, literally, "ancestral state," but may be translated as motherland, fatherland, homeland, native land, or used by Chinese to refer to China.

2. People's Republic of China, Constitution of the People's Republic of China, adopted December 4, 1982, as reproduced at http://english.people.com.cn/constitution/constitution.html.

3. The objective of the PRC is to subordinate Taiwan to China's sovereignty. While the rhetoric used to describe how that subordination should be effected has changed, the expectation of subordination has not. Subordination does not need to occur by force nor does it need to result in PRC control of Taiwan's domestic affairs. From Beijing's vantage, it does need to eliminate uncertainty about (1) Taiwan's status as part of China, (2) the PRC government as the legitimate government of the Chinese state entitled to represent China in the international community, and (3) the legitimacy of any effort by that government to determine or limit relations between Taiwan and the international arena that bear on the security and welfare of the Chinese state. Beijing has opposed suggestions that the ROC should be regarded as a sovereign equal of the PRC and insists, through word and deed, that the relationship between itself and Taiwan should be viewed as hierarchal. Beijing has apparently explored and rejected the idea of establishing a Chinese commonwealth or con-federation. Given that the CCP has offered no indication that it is prepared to compete for power with an opposition party within the PRC, it is not surprising that it has evinced no willingness to share China's sovereignty with the government of Taiwan.

4. Nationalism has served the PRC as a vital mobilizing force since the establishment of the state. To imply that the current generation of leaders in the PRC is more inclined to employ nationalism as a unifying source of identity than did Mao Zedong and his cohort is to pervert a reading of the CCP's past. Moreover, the Guomindang, which one must recall is the *Nationalist* Party of China, was no less disposed to tweak nationalist heartstrings than was the Communist Party. How one gauges levels of "popular" nationalism in an authoritarian state that emerged from totalitarianism is analytically challenging.

5. Evidence of this is pervasive. See, for instance, Paul Dodge, "Circumventing Sea Power: Chinese Strategies to Deter U.S. Intervention in Taiwan," 392; Andrew J. Nathan and Robert S. Ross, *The Great Wall and the Empty Fortress: China's Search for Security*, 206; Robert S. Ross, "China II: Beijing as a Conservative Power"; Swaine and Mulvenon, *Taiwan's Foreign and Defense Policies*, 4–5; John Wilson Lewis and Xue Litai, "China's Search for a Modern Air Force," 103.

6. This view is consistent with the argument advanced by John Vasquez that in the post-cold war era, nationalism and the concomitant attendance to self-determination are elements of a new international norm that affects the resolution of territorial disputes. Vasquez contends that this increases the risk of war focused on territory. John A. Vasquez, "Why Do Neighbors Fight? Proximity, Interaction, or Territoriality," 290.

7. The distinction between formal and informal ideology is spelled out in Steven I. Levine, "Perception and Ideology in Chinese Foreign Policy."

8. The term *ethnic* is commonly used to differentiate "mainlanders" and "Taiwanese." Contestable though the terms may be, *mainlanders* is used to refer to those people who migrated from the mainland to Taiwan in the aftermath of World War II and the Chinese civil war or who are descended from those immigrants. *Taiwanese* is used to refer to people who trace their heritage on the island to "Han" migrants of earlier eras. The terms, though, are crude. While they may have had greater political significance in the first years after the wave of migration in the 1940s, intermarriage and the presence of other population cohorts on the island mean that neither group is as coherent as the terms suggest and, in any event, neither term describes an ethnic group so much as a subcultural cohort. For more considerations of the distinction between mainlanders and Taiwanese, see Melissa J. Brown, *Is Taiwan Chinese? The Impact of Culture, Power, and Migration on Changing Identities*; Christopher Hughes, *Taiwan and Chinese Nationalism: National Identity and Status in International Society*; Stéphane Corcuff, *Memories of the Future: National Identity Issues and the Search for a New Taiwan*; and Alan M. Wachman, *Taiwan: National Identity and Democratization*.

9. An empirical link has been charted between territorial conflict, the generation of enduring rivalry, and the likelihood that such conflicts lead to war. That "territory is an important component in the development of militarized conflict, increases its severity, and promotes its recurrence" is explored in Paul F. Diehl, *A Road Map to War: Territorial Dimensions of International Conflict*, xvi.

10. Huth identifies international actors that seek to transform the control of contested territory as "challengers" and identifies as "targets" those actors that control contested territory and that are the subject of challenges. Of course, the PRC would not identify itself as challenging the status quo, just as the political leadership of the ROC would not identify itself as defecting from it. The terms *challenger* and *target* are, therefore, subjective. Paul K. Huth, *Standing Your Ground: Territorial Disputes and International Conflict*, 130.

11. John W. Garver, *Protracted Contest: Sino-Indian Rivalry in the Twentieth Century*, 79, 106–109.

12. He Duanduan, Wei Chao, and Hao Tan, *"Taihai guancha: 'Taidu'—xueruo liang'an huyi de zhongguo haifang"* [Taiwan Strait Observation: 'Taiwan Independence'—Weakens Both Sides of China's Coastal Defense]; and Renmin Wang, *" 'Taidu'—xueruo liang'an huyi de Zhongguo haifang—fang Zhongguo junshi kexueyuan de Luo Yuan zhuren"* ['Taiwan Independence': Weakens Both Sides of China's Coastal Defense—Interview with Director Luo Yuan of China's Academy of Military Sciences].

13. Some illustrative examples are Zhang Wenmu, *"Shilun dangdai Zhongguo 'haiquan' wenti"* [On China's contemporary 'sea power']; Yiming, *"Zhong Mei Ri Taihai shengsi jiaoliang"* [Sino-U.S.-Japan Life and Death Struggle for the Taiwan Strait]; Lin Xinhua, *"Shilun Zhongguo fazhan haiquan de zhanlüe"* [The Strategy of China's Development of Sea Power].

14. Zhang Guoxian, *"Lun Taiwan de diyuan zhanlüe jiazhi"* [On Taiwan's Strategic Value], 7. Although this cannot be construed as an influential source, it is indicative of how extreme the argument about Taiwan can be. Regarding Taiwan's total area, the Central Geological Survey of the ROC Ministry of Economic Affairs states that the island is 35,960 square

kilometers, which is 13,880.56 square miles. See http://www.moeacgs.gov.tw/english/twgeol/twgeol_setting.jsp.

15. One exception is Zhang Wei and Zuo Liping, *"Xianggang de diyuan youshi buketidai—yong diyuan zhanlüe fangfa guance Xianggang de lishi yu weilai"* [Hong Kong's Irreplaceable Geographic Superiority—Using Geostrategy to Survey Hong Kong's History and Future]. Regarding the countdown prior to the retrocession of Hong Kong, an electronic device to display days remaining before the event was erected outside the Hong Kong and Macao Affairs Building in Beijing on July 1, 1994. On December 19, 1994, a large digital clock devised to count days, hours, minutes, and seconds prior to July 1, 1997, was erected in front of the Museum of Chinese History and Revolution, on the east side of Tiananmen Square. A clock to count down time remaining until the handover of Macao did not materialize until May 5, 1998. *South China Morning Post*, July 1, 1994, 7; Xinhua News Agency, "Beijing Countdown to H. K.'s Return Clock Starts Countdown to H. K.'s Return"; Xinhua News Agency, "Countdown Clock to be Moved to Great Wall"; Patrick Baert, "China Quietly Marks Two-Year Countdown to Macau's Return"; and *China Daily,* "China Countdown to Macao's Return Starts; Preparatory Body Set Up."

16. For a summary of militarized disputes about territory in which the PRC was involved, see "Table 1. Territorial Disputes, 1950–1990" and "Appendix A: Summary Description of Territorial Dispute Cases, 1950–1990," in Huth, *Standing Your Ground*; and "Table 1.1: China's Territorial Disputes, 1949–2002" in Fravel, "The Long March to Peace," 3.

17. *Salience* is the term employed by students of international relations to identify the degree of importance actors involved in a given conflict attach to the issue or issues in dispute. This is related to the notion that leaders of states are actors motivated more by a "quest for issue satisfaction," than by general imperatives to advance the national interest, maximize state power, or strive for security in an anarchic international system, as realists are characterized as suggesting. Diehl, "What Are They Fighting For?"; Paul R. Hensel, "Contentious Issues and World Politics: The Management of Territorial Claims in the Americas, 1816–1992."

18. Diehl, *A Road Map to War*, x.

19. Tang Shiping, *Suzao Zhongguo de lixiang anquan huanjing* [Model China's Ideal Security Environment], 223.

20. For a period, the political science subdiscipline of comparative politics was dominated by theoretical approaches that ignored or downplayed the role of the state as an autonomous agent of influence on political processes. An influential volume reasserted the significance of "the state" as a variable. See, Peter B. Evans, Dietrich Rueschemeyer, Theda Skocpol, *Bringing the State Back In*.

21. Wang Chunyong and Lu Xue, *Taiwan wenti de diyuanzhanlüe fenxi* [A Geostrategic Analysis of the Taiwan Issue], 113.

22. Amitav Archaya, "International Relations Theory and Cross-Strait Relations"; Tun-jen Cheng, "The Mainland China-Taiwan Dyad as a Research Program"; and Wu Yu-shan, "Theorizing on Relations Across the Taiwan Strait: Nine Contending Approaches."

23. See Gerrit W. Gong, *Taiwan Strait Dilemmas: China-Taiwan-U.S. Policies in the New Century*, esp. chapters 3–6.

24. Everett C. Dolman, "Geostrategy in the Space Age: An Astropolitical Analysis," 83.

25. Wang Weinan and Zhou Jianming, *"Diyuan zhengzhi zhong de Zhong Mei guanxi yu Taiwan wenti"* [The Geopolitics of Sino-U.S. Relations and the Taiwan Issue]; Liu Zhongmin and Zhao Chengguo, *"Guanyu Zhongguo haiquan fazhan zhanlüe wenti de ruogan sikao"*

[Several Considerations Concerning the Strategy for Developing China's Sea Power]; Liu Hong, *"Taiwan wenti de diyuan zhengzhi sikao"* [Geopolitical Considerations of the Taiwan Issue]; Lu Zhenguang, *"Taiwan diyuan zhanlüe diwei de xingcheng yu bianqian"* [The Formation and Change in Taiwan's Geostrategic Status]; Yang Yongbin, *"Lengzhan hou Taiwan zai Meiguo dui Hua guanxi zhong de diyuan zhanlüe zuoyong"* [The Geostrategic Function of Taiwan in the U.S.'s Post-Cold War Relations with China]; Wang Chunyong and Lü Xue, *"Taiwan wenti di diyuan zhanlüe fenxi"* [A Geostrategic Analysis of the Taiwan Issue]; and Colin S. Gray, "Inescapable Geography," 164–165.

26. Assessing the salience assigned by states to issues is difficult. For one thing, as Diehl suggests, in international conflicts it is often hard to know what, exactly, is at issue. Conflicts "may involve more than one issue and/or the issues(s) involved are perceived differently by participants in the dispute." Diehl, "What Are They Fighting For?" 335.

27. William R. Thompson proposes that international politics is a system of interactive forces susceptible to evolutionary change. His paradigm "reverses prevailing tendencies to theorize about equilibrium states. From an evolutionary perspective, equilibrium is never quite attained. We may be moving away from or toward equilibrium, but such a state is never attained. Things are always in motion and rarely at rest." See, William R. Thompson, "Evolving Toward an Evolutionary Perspective," 4.

28. The merits of annexing or purchasing Taiwan was proposed to London by British representatives in China, as it was by American, French, and German officials serving in East Asia during the mid-nineteenth century to their governments. However, the dependence of foreign powers on a "cooperative policy" of mutual access to commercial opportunity served, for a while, to check national ambition. Leonard H. D. Gordon, "Taiwan and the Powers: 1840–1895," 98–99; F. Q. Quo, "British Diplomacy and the Cession of Formosa, 1894–95," 143.

29. Quo, "British Diplomacy and the Cession of Formosa," 144.

30. The historical irony is that Britain was Japan's principal tutor in the establishment of Japan's Imperial Navy, illustrating the Chinese maxim *"qing chu yu lan"* [azure emerges from blue]. See, John Curtis Perry, "Great Britain and the Emergence of Japan as a Naval Power."

31. Gordon, "Taiwan and the Powers," 103–106.

32. Bruce A. Elleman, *Modern Chinese Warfare, 1795–1989,* 88–89.

33. Gordon, "Taiwan and the Powers," 106–107.

34. Kwang-Ching Liu and Richard J. Smith, "The Military Challenge: The North-West and the Coast," 259ff.

35. Barbara W. Tuchman, *Stilwell and the American Experience in China, 1911–1945,* 169.

36. The U.S. Department of State Far Eastern Affairs Division prepared a report entitled "Formosa," February 17, 1942, reproduced in Richard C. Bush, *At Cross Purposes: U.S.–Taiwan Relations Since 1942,* 14.

37. The bombing began at the end of November 1943, but was much intensified beginning in November 1944, after which "Formosa's skies were seldom free of hostile planes" that carpet-bombed portions of Taipei, and destroyed Jilong [Keelung] and Gaoxiong [Kaohsiung] harbors. "Rail centers were heavily damaged. Hangars, runways and airfield maintenance areas were mauled." George H. Kerr, *Formosa Betrayed,* 33–35.

38. John W. Garver, *The Sino-American Alliance.*

39. Jon W. Huebner, "The Abortive Liberation of Taiwan," 256–275.

40. Peter Howarth, *China's Rising Sea Power: The PLA Navy's Submarine Challenge,* 174.

41. Ye Zicheng, *"Lun dangdai Zhongguo de diyuan taishi he san xian diyuan zhanlüe tixi"* [On the Geopolitical Situation and the Contemporary Chinese Geostrategic Three Line System].

42. Zhao Junyao, *"Cong 'Zhi Tai bi gao lu' kan Qing dai Taiwan haiyang wenhua diyu xing-tai"* [The Geographical Dimension of the Qing Dynasty's Taiwan Maritime Culture From the 'Record of the Governance of Taiwan'], 61–62; the link between security and the geographic features associated with China's boundaries is explored in Michael D. Swaine and Ashely J. Tellis, *Interpreting China's Grand Strategy: Past, Present, and Future,* esp. chapter 3.

43. Shen Weilie and Lu Junyuan, *Zhongguo guojia anquan dili* [The Geography of China's National Security], 343.

44. Zhu Tingchang, *"Lun Taiwan de diyuan zhanlüe diwei"* [On Taiwan's Geostrategic Position], 66.

45. On the reasons why territory may be salient, see Gary Goertz and Paul F. Diehl, *Territorial Changes and International Conflict.* There is an extensive literature that gives voice to the notion that states go to war over territory because of the perceived value of that territory. See Diehl, "Territory and International Conflict: An Overview"; Hensel, "Contentious Issues and World Politics: The Management of Territorial Claims in the Americas."

46. Hensel, "Contentious Issues and World Politics: The Management of Territorial Claims in the Americas"; John Vasquez, "Why Do Neighbors Fight? Proximity, Interaction, or Territoriality," 277–293; John Vasquez and Christopher Leskiw, "The Origins and War Proneness of Interstate Rivalries," 295–316.

47. Monica Duffy Toft observes that in analyses of violence arising from disputes about territory between ethnic groups "material-based explanations tend to overlook the frequent conjunction between material and nonmaterial factors. They thus oversimplify the motives of the actors." Monica Duffy Toft, *The Geography of Ethnic Violence,* 6.

48. Newman, "Real Spaces, Symbolic Spaces," 13.

49. Writing of the Chinese nation, I use the word to mean the Chinese people, not as a synonym for China. Naturally, as with most communal identities, the term *Chinese* implies greater coherence within the group to which it is applied than may actually be the case. "Chinese-ness" is not an identity corresponding to a population that has unambiguous racial, social, ethnic, religious, linguistic, dietary, or other identifying boundaries, even though it is commonly used in the PRC to imply that such a group exists.

50. These categorical assertions ought also to apply to what students of territorial disputes label "latent" controversies—those that have not yet emerged, but which share characteristics of existing territorial disputes. In the case of the PRC, one might consider Mongolia and the tracts of territory ceded to Russia in the nineteenth century, formerly the northern reaches of Manchuria, to be latent disputes. Beijing has not pressed a claim to either tract in any concerted way since 1949, but the claims made by the PRC to Taiwan and Tibet might be seen to apply just as well to Mongolia and the Russian Far Eastern provinces.

51. For reasons why territory can move people to violence, consider Toft, *The Geography of Ethnic Violence,* esp. chapter 1.

52. One possible exception is that Premier Wen Jiabao reportedly is wont to cite verses by the poet Yu You-jen, who wrote about his grief concerning national division. Yu's poem is: "Bury me on the highest mountain top, So that I can get a sight of my mainland. Mainland, I see none, Tears of sorrow cascade. Bury me on the highest mountaintop, So that I can get a glimpse of my hometown. Hometown, I see none, But lives forever in my mind The lofty sky is deeply blue, The vast wilderness not seen through. All boundless universe, will you hear me, And this elegy of the nation." *People's Daily,* "Premier Wen Makes His Media Debut."

53. There is, of course, a growing community of people from Taiwan who have taken up residence or are sojourners on the mainland, but their motives—to the extent that they can be plumbed—are largely, though not exclusively, commercial.

54. Wang Cunli and Hu Wenqing, *Taiwan de gu ditu* [Taiwan's Ancient Maps], 188 ff.

55. Newman, "Real Spaces, Symbolic Spaces," 4.

56. Ibid., 5.

57. Michael McDevitt, "Geographic Ruminations," 1–6.

58. For an overview of the decline and renaissance of geography as a variable in international relations, see Jakub Joachim Grygiel, "The Case for Geopolitics: Venice, Ottoman Empire, and Ming China," 6–41.

59. Colin S. Gray and Geoffrey Sloan, *Geopolitics, Geography and Strategy*, 2.

60. Zhang Tiejun, "Chinese Strategic Culture: Traditional and Present Features," 73–90 passim; Mark C. Elliott, *The Manchu Way: The Eight Banners and Ethnic Identity in Late Imperial China*, 376, n. 12.

61. Tu Wei-ming, "Cultural China: The Periphery as the Center."

62. Bernard Cole, "The Modernization of the PLAN and Taiwan's Security," 52.

63. Paul Dodge, "Circumventing Sea Power: Chinese Strategies to Deter U.S. Intervention in Taiwan," 394ff.

64. John M. Collins, *Military Geography*, 11.

65. Ibid., 59; Charles A. Meconis and Michael D. Wallace, *East Asian Naval Weapons Acquisitions in the 1990s*, esp. 141–149.

66. For an overview of geopolitical and geostrategic studies in the PRC, see Wen Yunchao, *"Guanyu diyuan yanjiu de lilun tantao"* [A Theoretical Study of Geopolitical Research]; Lin Limin, *"21 Shiji Zhongguo diyuan zhanlüe huajing qianyi"* [An Overview of China's 21st Century Geostrategic Environment]; Liu Miaolong, Kong Aili, and Zhang Wei, *"Diyuan zhengzhi lishi, xianzhuang yu Zhongguo de diyuan zhanlüe"* [The History and Status of Geopolitics and the Geopolitical Strategies of China]; for evidence of interest in applying these concepts see Cheng Yawen, *"Cong shijie tixi shijiao sikao Zhongguo diyuan zhanlüe wenti"* [Reflections on China's Geostrategy from the Perspective of the World System]; Chen Guangzhong, *"Lun diyuan huanjing yu diyuan zhanlüe dui junshi zhanlüe de yingxiang"* [On the Influence of the Geopolitical Environment and Geostrategy on Military Strategy]; and Lang Danyang and Chen Zuhua, *"Shidai biange yu diyuan zhanlüe siwei de fanshi zhuanhuan"* [Changing Times and the Transformation of Geostrategic Thought].

67. Gray and Sloan, *Geopolitics, Geography and Strategy*, 2.

68. Grygiel, "The Case for Geopolitics," 2.

69. Ibid., chapter 2.

70. *"Diyuan zhanlüe zhong de Taiwan jiqi dui daguo anquan de zuoyong"* [The Geostrategic Role of Taiwan and the Security of the Great Powers].

71. Teng, *Taiwan's Imagined Geography*, 15–17.

CHAPTER 3

1. The Chinese phrase *bu lun, bu lei* is analogous to the English phrase "neither fish nor fowl."

2. Steven Phillips, *Between Assimilation and Independence: The Taiwanese Encounter Nationalist China, 1945–1950*, 3.

3. Central News Agency, "Taipei to Recognize Communist China as a 'Political Entity'"; Huang Fu-san, *A Brief History of Taiwan*, chapter 9.

4. Republic of China, "Act Governing Relations between Peoples of the Taiwan Area and the Mainland Area."

5. Article four of the Constitution of the ROC states "The territory of the Republic of China according to its existing national boundaries shall not be altered except by resolution of the National Assembly." The territory to which it refers is all of what was China when the Constitution was promulgated in 1947, not just Taiwan and appertaining islands. President Chen Shui-bian has asserted repeatedly his intention to refrain from proposing constitutional amendments that would affect the issue of sovereignty over territory. In his second inaugural address, he stated: "I am fully aware that consensus has yet to be reached on issues related to national sovereignty, territory and the subject of unification/independence; therefore, let me explicitly propose that these particular issues be excluded from the present constitutional re-engineering project." See Republic of China, "Constitution of the Republic of China"; and Chen Shui-bian, "President Chen Shui-bian's Inaugural Speech, 'Paving the Way for a Sustainable Taiwan.'"

6. I am indebted to Steven Goldstein for articulating the implications of this point.

7. As subsequent chapters will make clear, Taiwan is not so much the subject of this work as an object of consideration, where China is the subject and its attitude toward Taiwan the principal theme.

8. Teng, *Taiwan's Imagined Geography*, esp. chapter 1.

9. Ernest May, *"Lessons" of the Past: The Use and Misuse of History in American Foreign Policy*; Yuen Foong Khong, *Analogies at War: Korea, Munich, Dien Bien Phu, and the Vietnam Decisions of 1965*.

10. James Millward, *Beyond the Pass: Economy, Ethnicity, and Empire in Qing Central Asia, 1759–1864*, 13.

11. Peter Perdue, *China Marches West: The Qing Conquest of Central Eurasia*, 565.

12. Michael Hunt, *Genesis of Chinese Communist Foreign Policy*, 116–117; cf. Prasenjit Duara, *Rescuing History from the Nation: Questioning Narratives of Modern China*, 58; Laura Hostetler, *Qing Colonial Enterprise: Ethnography and Cartography in Early Modern China*, 33; Ross Terrill, *The New Chinese Empire: And What it Means for the United States*, 3, 185.

13. Hostetler, *Qing Colonial Enterprise*, 75–76.

14. Pamela Kyle Crossley, *A Translucent Mirror: History and Identity in Qing Imperial Ideology*, 341.

15. Nicola di Cosmo, "Qing Colonial Administration in Inner Asia"; Edward Rhoads, *Manchus and Han: Ethnic Relations and Political Power in Late Qing and Early Republican China, 1861–1928*, 293.

16. Hostetler, *Qing Colonial Enterprise*, 76.

17. Peter Perdue writes that Qing historian Wei Yuan, whose *Record of Sacred Military Campaigns* [*Shengwuji*] was the basis for twentieth-century Chinese nationalist accounts of Qing expansion, was criticized by PRC historians for characterizing as "wasteland" much of the territory delimited by the Treaty of Nerchinsk (1689) and for writing that Taiwan "from ancient times was not part of China." Perdue, *China Marches West*, 509.

18. Perdue, "Comparing Empires: Manchu Colonialism," 255.

19. Ibid.; Hostetler, *Qing Colonial Enterprise*, 75–76; Liu Xiaoyuan, *Frontier Passages*, esp. prologue.

20. Paine, *Imperial Rivals*, 351.

21. Hunt, *Genesis of Chinese Communist Foreign Policy*, 10.

22. Perdue, *China Marches West*, 520.

23. Ibid., 544.

24. Liu Xiaoyuan, *Frontier Passages*, 17.

25. Ibid.

26. The axiomatic nature of this trade-off was understood in China as early as the first century, B.C., when a policy debate about how, or whether, to underwrite expenses associated with garrisoning troops in distant posts to defend against the Xiongnu was recorded by Huan Kuan as the *Discourse on Salt and Iron*. A grand secretary representing the court claimed that far-flung outposts were justified because "When the frontier is strengthened, the central domain will know peace." Rejecting this view, a panel of literati pointed out that there would be no need to find ways for the state to finance the stationing of troops far from home if it had not been for the expansionist policy of the state that led to the conquest of distant lands. They said "In the old days, the empire was smaller and everyone was secure. Now, we have pushed out the frontier and are overextended, that is why there is suffering." Summarizing their view, the literati are quoted as saying, "Do not try to cultivate the field too large, the weeds will only grow luxuriantly." Esson Gale, *Discourses on Salt and Iron*, 99–105.

27. Perdue, *China Marches West*, 507. Liu Xiaoyuan characterizes the Qing's "buffer strategy" as the restoration of a Chinese alternative to the strategy of linear defense. Liu, *Frontier Passages*, 16.

28. Ibid.

29. Teng, *Taiwan's Imagined Geography*, 3–5, 26–27, 34–59; Ronald Knapp, "The Shaping of Taiwan's Landscapes."

30. See, for instance, Hsieh Chiao-min, *Taiwan—Ilha Formosa: A Geography in Perspective*, 123–139; and Michael Stainton, "The Politics of Taiwan Aboriginal Origins."

31. Eduard Vermeer, "Up to the Mountains and Out to the Sea: The Expansion of the Fukienese in the Late Ming Period."

32. John Wills, "The Seventeenth-Century Transformation: Taiwan Under the Dutch and Cheng Regimes," 85.

33. In 1557, Portugal was granted a leasehold on the territory in exchange for payment of tribute to the Ming court. In 1582, a formal lease was signed that required the payment of annual rent, but China retained sovereignty over the Portuguese administered territory until 1685, at which point Macao became a foreign trade port. In 1974, Portugal renounced sovereignty over Macao, although it continued to administer it until December 20, 1999, when the People's Republic of China formally "resumed sovereignty" over the territory, designating it a special administrative region. See Federal Research Division. Library of Congress, Country Studies: Macao.

34. See Armando Cortesão and Avelino Teixeira da Mota, *Portugaliae monumenta cartographica*; Macabe Keliher, *Out of China, or Yu Yonghe's Tales of Formosa: A History of Seventeenth-Century Taiwan*, 191; Hsu Wen-hsiung, "From Aboriginal Island to Chinese Frontier: The Development of Taiwan before 1683," 11.

35. James Davidson writes, "A Dutch navigating officer named Linschotten, employed by the Portuguese, so recorded the islands in his charts, and eventually the name of Formosa, so euphonious and yet appropriate, replaced all others in European literature." This was, apparently, Jan Huygen van Linschotten (or Johan Huighens van Lynschotten) who served as secretary to the Portuguese Archbishop of Goa. His 1583 *Navigatio ac Itinerarium* was a compilation of impressions gathered from Portuguese ship captains he interviewed, and in it was recorded the name Formosa, associated with Taiwan. James Davidson, *The Island of Formosa: Past and Present*, 10; and Keliher, *Out of China*, 190–191.

36. In 1519, thirty-five years before the completion of the map on which Taiwan was identified as *J. Fermosa*, an atlas was produced by Lopo Homem, Pedro and Jorge Reinel,

and António de Holanda that is known, now, as the Atlas Miller. On it, a number of features are labeled with some variation of the term *fermosa*. For instance, there is a river running north/south at about the place where Singapore is now located that is labeled *R. Fermoso*. On the plate displaying the South American continent, in the region that is now Brazil, there is a *C. Fremoso*, *G. Fremoso*, and a *G. Fromosa*. On the plate displaying the northern hemisphere, labeled *Terra Corte regalis*, an island that appears at a location that might make it Greenland or Iceland features two places marked *C. fremoso* and one *R. fermoso*. L'Atlas Miller, Bibliothèque nationale de France.

37. Readers accustomed to associating the name Formosa with Taiwan may be amused to know that Formosa (or sometimes Formoso) is the name of a province in Argentina, and its capital, as well as a number of cities in Brazil, Colombia, Peru, Portugal, and South Africa. There is an island called Formosa on the Atlantic Ocean coast of Guinea-Bissau, a Formosa Bay on the Indian Ocean coast of Kenya, and, in Brazil, a mountain range and several rivers called Formosa. In the Maida Vale section of London, near "Little Venice," there is a Formosa Street. Some distance down the Thames River toward Windsor Castle, near the village of Cookham, is the largest island on the Thames, Formosa Island. In the United States, there is a Formosa in Arkansas and Virginia, a Formosa Junction in Illinois, and a town called Formoso, Kansas, just a few miles from the geographic center of the United States. The Portuguese were also responsible for dubbing the Penghu islands, a small archipelago southwest of Taiwan that had attracted communities of fishermen and traders at least as early as the fourteenth century, as the Pescadores. *Times Atlas of the World*; Lambert van der Aalsvoort, *Feng zhong zhi she* [A Leaf in the Wind], 18; and Wills, "Taiwan Under the Dutch and Cheng Regimes," 86.

38. Wills, "Taiwan Under the Dutch and Cheng Regimes," 86–87.

39. Ibid., 88.

40. Daniel Defoe wrote that the Dutch "*buy* to *sell* again, *take* in to *send* out, and the greatest Part of their vast Commerce consists in being supply'd from All parts of the World, that they may supply All the World again." In that way, they commanded the market for "African slaves, Brazilian sugar, Russian caviar, Italian marble, Hungarian copper, fish from the North Sea, and furs from the Baltic." The Dutch foray in search of trading opportunities in the Pacific was dominated by the *Vereenigde Oost-Indische Compagnie* [the United East India Company] that had been established in 1602. As Van Warwijk plied the waters of the western Pacific and Indian Ocean, the company commissioned the English mariner, Henry Hudson, to seek out what Verrazzano and Gomez did not find: a northeast passage from the Atlantic, through the Arctic, to the East Indies. Davidson, *The Island of Formosa*, 10; Edwin Burrows and Mike Wallace, *Gotham: A History of New York City to 1898*, 14–20.

41. Davidson, *The Island of Formosa*, 12.

42. Ibid., 12.

43. Wills, "Taiwan Under the Dutch and Cheng Regimes," 88.

44. The assertion that Ming officials *ceded* Taiwan to the Dutch—implying that the island was the Ming's to cede—is noted in the historical accounts offered by Chinese nationalists and communists in justification of their claims to the island. Describing the sources for his work, Davidson states, "I had also at my disposal the original works of Valentyn, Coyett, and other Dutch writers, the archives of the Spanish Mission, and many ancient Japanese and Chinese writings." Davidson, *The Island of Formosa*, ii, 12.

45. Davidson states that in addition to the aboriginal population of the island, notably the Sakkam tribe that inhabited the region around what is now Tainan, the Dutch found

settlements amounting to 25,000 Chinese and a few Japanese merchants of considerable means. Ibid., 13.

46. As an indication of what a ferocious Dutch enterprise the Ming encountered, it is worth observing that at roughly the same moment when the Dutch took Taiwan, the *Geoctroyerde West-Indische Compagnie* [West India Company] was engaged in a massive drive to supplant Spanish domination of trade in Africa and the Americas and to establish its own. Consequently, in 1622, agents of the company began to arrive on the northeast shores of North America. The colony of *Nieu Nederlandt* [New Netherland] was founded in the summer of 1624 by company agents who began to build settlements on the banks of the Hudson, Delaware, and Connecticut Rivers, as well as on Governor's Island in New York Harbor, and on Manhattan's southern tip. There, a blockhouse dubbed Fort Amsterdam was erected as the base for the West India Company's operations in North America. In 1626, the director of the New Netherland colony, Peter Minuit, purchased the island of Manhattan from the Lenape people who had dwelled there, and the whole settlement was then named New Amsterdam. Burrows and Wallace, *Gotham*, 17–24.

47. Evidence of Chinese collaboration in the Dutch colonization of Taiwan prompts one analyst to view Taiwan after 1624 as a "Sino-Dutch hybrid colony." Tonio Andrade, "Pirates, Pelts, and Promises: The Sino-Dutch Colony of Seventeenth-Century Taiwan and the Aboriginal Village of Favorolang."

48. Davidson, *The Island of Formosa,* 31; Tonio Andrade, "The Company's Chinese Pirates: How the Dutch East India Company Tried to Lead a Coalition of Pirates to War against China, 1621–1662."

49. Andrade, "The Company's Chinese Pirates," 19–30.

50. Wills, "Taiwan Under the Dutch and Cheng Regimes"; see, also, William Campbell, *Formosa Under the Dutch*; Davidson, *The Island of Formosa*, 9–48.

51. Zheng was then in control of Taiwan, the Penghu islands, and Xiamen, to which he assigned an errant son as commander. He sent an emissary to the Philippines to urge the Spanish colonizers to pay tribute to his kingdom, thereby inciting a campaign to exterminate Chinese who lived in the Spanish colony. This led Zheng to plan an invasion of the Philippines with the intention of displacing the Spanish and enlarging his domain. Davidson, *The Island of Formosa*, 51–52.

52. Ibid., 55–56.

53. The Dutch were able to recapture a fortress in the northern city of Jilong [Keelung], but held it with only 200 men and remained for five years. Ibid., 56–57.

54. Wills, "Taiwan Under the Dutch and Cheng Regimes," 96.

55. Ibid., 97.

56. Davidson, *The Island of Formosa*, 59.

57. The Qing banner forces organized by the Manchus had only limited ability to extend a military presence throughout China's territories when they dislodged the Ming regime in 1644. Three Ming generals who had been entrusted with governorships over the southern provinces of Yunnan, Guizhou, Guangdong, and Fujian battled with the Qing for eight years, ultimately stretching their control as far north as the Yangzi River before being driven back and defeated by the Qing. Ibid., 60.

58. Wills, "Taiwan Under the Dutch and Cheng Regimes," 100–101.

59. Davidson, *The Island of Formosa*, 60.

60. Wills, "Taiwan Under the Dutch and Cheng Regimes," 101–102.

61. In an opinion piece published in the *Taipei Times*, Lai Fu-shun claims that a reading of Qing sources reveals, also, that the Kangxi Emperor said, "Taiwan is a foreign land that is not so much related to China . . . Taiwan is just an island that is not included on the map of China's Fukien Province." Teng, *Taiwan's Imagined Geography*, 34; Lai Fu-shun, "A Rewriting of History, Beijing Style."

62. Teng, *Taiwan's Imagined Geography*, 35.

63. John Shepherd, "The Island Frontier of the Ch'ing, 1684–1780," 108–109; Teng, *Taiwan's Imagined Geography*, 35, n. 3.

64. This is not a strategy the logic of which is exclusive to the case of China and Taiwan. The Tokugawa Shogunate had long viewed the Bonin islands as lying outside the realm of their own empire, but when Commodore Perry "vigorously advocated annexation" of the islands by the United States, the Japanese began to fear that they would be used as a naval base "by a western power on the very doorstep of Japan." This prompted Japan's effort to colonize and then annex the Bonin islands. See Hyman Kublin, "The Discovery of the Bonin Islands: A Reexamination," 36–37.

65. The Qing then designated the entire island as Taiwan. Theretofore, "Taiwan" referred only to a small island in the harbor of what is now Tainan, where the Dutch first established their fortifications. In the early seventeenth century, the area that is now known as Tainan was called Sakkam, after the aboriginal tribe that then inhabited it. When the Qing made Taiwan the name of the island, the town of Sakkam [Tainan] was designated as the capital and called Taiwanfu. Davidson, *The Island of Formosa*, 63–64.

66. I am obliged to Edward Friedman for urging that nothing more be read into what scarce evidence there is of the debate at court. Just as it is impossible to know why the Kangxi Emperor was persuaded, it is also not possible to know why Shi Lang proposed that Taiwan be subsumed by the Qing empire. Lai Fu-shun writes, "there has been inadequate discussion of Shi's motive for asking Emperor Kangxi to annex Taiwan. Chinese scholars have only scratched the surface of the matter, concentrating on Shi's suggestion that Taiwan be absorbed by China as a southeastern outpost and defensive bulwark, but they are unaware of his other intentions. In fact, it is all too clear that he was motivated by the pursuit of personal wealth and fame. In fact, he accumulated his fortune by forcibly occupying territory and charging illegal fees at local ports, committing the largest-known instance of corruption in Taiwan's history." Lai, "A Rewriting of History, Beijing Style."

67. It appears that Shi Lang may have overestimated the Qing capacity to subdue the residents of the island, who rose in rebellion frequently. Indeed, one commentator reports of the early eighteenth century, "no part of the Chinese empire was so frequently disturbed by rebellion as Formosa." So perilous did it appear that the Qing's official representative in Fujian, obliged to visit Taiwan each year, rarely went. In 1721, one local figure even succeeded in amassing a force of rebels eager to oust the Qing officials and establish a new kingdom which, for about two months, they did. They captured Taiwanfu and the Qing civil and military forces retreated to Amoy [Xiamen], only to return in force some time after to suppress the rebellion. Davidson, *The Island of Formosa*, 70, 71–73; Shepherd, "The Island Frontier of the Late Ch'ing, 1684–1780," 109, 113–115.

68. The prohibition against Han migration to Taiwan was akin to policies the Qing adopted toward other frontier territories where the dominant population was not Han, namely Manchuria and Mongolia. Shepherd, "The Island Frontier of the Ch'ing, 1684–1780," 108, 112.

69. Teng, *Taiwan's Imagined Geography*, chapter 1.

70. Ibid., 38.

71. Ibid., 39–41.

72. Teng writes, "The term *huangfu* evokes images of barrenness, starkness, untamed growth, and waste, for the word *huang* (meaning wild or uncultivated), when used in various combinations, refers to fallow fields, desert, jungle, or wild forest. These images shaped the traditional disdain for the borderlands of China—the steppe to the north beyond the Great Wall, the desert to the northwest, and the jungle to the south—as untamed expanses." The "Tribute of Yu," or "Yugong," is a chapter in the *Shujing* [Classic of Historical Documents] of the fourth century, B.C. which itself is one of the five Confucian canonical classics. Ibid., 43.

73. Ibid., 41; cf. Richard Smith, "Mapping China's World: Cultural Cartography in Late Imperial Times."

74. Teng, *Taiwan's Imagined Geography*, 42.

75. Ibid.

76. Teng explains that the Chinese term for hedge, *fanli*, is associated with the term *fan*, which refers to barbarians living on the edge of civilization. "Shi's metaphor of Taiwan as a hedgerow furthermore implicitly suggested a new paradigm of the Chinese empire—one that extended beyond the seas." Ibid., 43–44.

77. Ibid., 44; James Millward, "'Coming onto the Map': 'Western Regions' Geography and Cartographic Nomenclature in the Making of Chinese Empire in Xinjiang."

78. Teng, *Taiwan's Imagined Geography*, 45.

79. Ibid., 44.

80. "Hence, the offering of maps to the ruler was conventionally known as the 'presentation of rivers and mountains' (*xian jiangshan*). This trope expresses both the strategic importance of maps in war and conquest and the role of the map as a simulacrum of the terrain it represents. In keeping with this practice, Shi Lang, too, had submitted a map of Taiwan to the emperor after his conquest of the island." Ibid., 44–45.

81. Kwang-Ching Liu and Richard Smith, "The Military Challenge: The North-West and the Coast," 260.

82. Shepherd, *Statecraft and Political Economy on the Taiwan Frontier*; Teng, *Taiwan's Imagined Geography*; illustrative maps are found in Keliher, *Out of China*, 162–163; Wang Cunli and Hu Wenqing, *Taiwan de gu ditu—Ming qing shiqi* [Taiwan's Ancient Maps from the Ming and Qing Periods], 168, 169, 190.

83. Teng, *Taiwan's Imagined Geography*, 58.

84. Ibid., 59.

85. For an overview of this phenomenon, see Steven Phillips, "Confronting Colonization and National Identity: The Nationalists and Taiwan, 1941–45."

86. Perdue, *China Marches West*, 547–565.

87. Hsu, "From Aboriginal Island to Chinese Frontier: The Development of Taiwan Before 1683," 11.

88. The Chinese reading of the characters used in Japanese and Chinese to designate the Ryukyu archipelago is Liuqiu. The archipelago, which extends in a gentle crescent from just beyond the northeastern coast of Taiwan northeastwards to Japan's southernmost main island, Kyushu, is now known in Japan as Okinawa Prefecture, with Okinawa the name of the largest island in the chain.

89. Komei Isozaki, "Foreign Relations of the Kingdom of Ryukyu and the East Asian Diplomatic Order of the Modern Era," 33.

90. Isozaki, "Foreign Relations of the Kingdom of Ryukyu," 37; Robert Sakai, "The Satsuma-Ryukyu Trade and the Tokugawa Seclusion Policy," 392.

91. Ibid., 392–393.

92. Miyako is the largest in a cluster of eight islands, the Miyako islands, that is located southwest of Okinawa, due east of Taiwan, in the midst of the arc formed by the Ryukyu chain.

93. The mariners were reportedly beheaded in circumstances that were represented at the time as acts of wanton savagery by the aborigines. Popular political empowerment that came with democratization on Taiwan has led, among other things, to efforts by Aboriginal and Taiwanese historians to rectify what they perceive as inaccuracies in the narratives imposed by Chinese and others about their past. The incident of 1871, known as the *Mudanshe* [Mudan Village] incident, has been the subject of a revisionist effort that aims to contextualize the killings. See, for instance, Kyodo News Service, "Taiwan Natives Seek to Regain Respect Lost via Japanese Expedition."

94. Ch'en Ta-tuan, "Sino-Ryukyuan Relations in the 19th Century," 104, as cited by Edwin Pak-Wah Leung, "The Quasi-War in East Asia: Japan's Expedition to Taiwan and the Ryukyu Controversy," 263–264.

95. Ibid., 266.

96. Ibid., 258.

97. Ibid., 259.

98. Wayne McWilliams, "East Meets East: The Soejima Mission to China, 1873," 240.

99. On July 11, 1854, Perry concluded a pact referred to as the "Treaty with Lew Chew," which was ratified by the U.S. Senate on May 3, 1855, and signed by President Filmore on May 9. The texts were in Chinese and English. France and the Netherlands followed suit in 1855. See, George Kerr, "Sovereignty of the Liuchiu Islands," 97.

100. The punitive expedition itself of June 18, 1867, accomplished little, as the American force was repulsed by aboriginal fighters. No agreement was secured by the aboriginal population to desist from molesting stranded mariners until 1,000 Qing forces were sent to the island by the governor of Fujian province in the fall of 1867, which was sufficiently distasteful that the chief of the tribe responsible for the deaths of the *Rover* sailors agreed to negotiate with U.S. Consul Charles LeGendre. Ron Hall, "Henry Bell and Alexander Mackenzie Died Almost Unnoticed on the Faraway Asiatic Station," 22.

101. For more on the *Rover* Incident, the shipwreck of 1871, and the role of LeGendre, see Robert Eskildsen, "Leading the Natives to Civilization: The Colonial Dimension of the Taiwan Expedition."

102. Ernst Presseisen, "Roots of Japanese Imperialism: A Memorandum of General LeGendre," 108–111.

103. "Soejima to Okuma, 17 February 1873," MS B-26 in the Okuma Collection, Waseda University Library, as reproduced in McWilliams, "East Meets East," 243.

104. Ibid.

105. Ibid., 244.

106. Ibid., 264, esp. n.91.

107. This passage from the diary of the Soejima mission is reproduced as *Shi Shin Nikki*, Japanese Foreign Ministry, ed. *Nihon Gaiko Bunsho*, VI, Tokyo: 1936, 178; McWilliams, "East Meets East," 265.

108. Ibid.

109. Ibid. On the distinction between "cooked" and "raw" aborigines, see Teng, *Taiwan's Imagined Geography*, chapter 5.

110. McWilliams, "East Meets East," 266.

111. This passage is drawn from *Nihon Gaiko Bunsho*, VI, 160–161; Ibid.

112. Ibid.

113. Leung, "Japan's Expedition to Taiwan and the Ryukyu Controversy," 272–274.

114. Ibid., 274–275.

115. Ibid., 276–278.

116. *Complete Works of Li Hung-chang, Peng-tiao han-kao*, 19, 1b–2b, as cited, Ibid., 278.

117. Kerr, "Sovereignty of the Liuchiu Islands," 96.

118. Li made the following points: the Ryukyu islands were a semi-independent kingdom, China had not exercised sovereignty over the Ryukyu kingdom, the kingdom had paid tribute to China, the population of the islands was not Chinese, no Chinese officials were stationed on the islands, China levied no taxes nor offered aid in the event of war, China made available trading privileges and educational opportunities to the population, and the Ryukyu kingdom preferred association with China to association with Japan. Ibid., 99–100. On the various renderings of the term Ryukyu, see Kerr, *Okinawa: The History of an Island People*, xvii (1).

119. Kerr, *Okinawa*, 90.

120. The Sino-Japanese War and especially the negotiations at Shimonoseki are masterfully presented in S. C. M. Paine, *The Sino-Japanese War of 1884–1885: Perceptions, Power and Primacy*.

121. Edward I-te Chen, "Japan's Decision to Annex Taiwan: A Study of Ito-Mutsu Diplomacy, 1894–1895," 65; Mutsu Munemitsu, *Kenkenroku: A Diplomatic Record of the Sino-Japanese War, 1894–1895*, 144–145.

122. Japan was represented by Prime Minister Count Ito Hirobumi and Foreign Minister Viscount Mutsu Munemitsu. The Qing court was represented by Li Hongzhang and his son, Li Jingfeng.

123. The Treaty comprised eleven articles, and the most onerous obligations were Art. I: recognize the independence of Korea; Art. II: cede Fengtian province [the Qing name for the province that has been, since 1929, Liaoning], Taiwan, and the Penghu islands; Art. IV: pay an indemnity of 200,000,000 Kuping taels of silver; Art. VI: provide Japan with a host of commercial privileges including "most favored nation status," access to four treaty-port cities, steam passage on inland rivers; Art. VIII: allow Japanese military forces to occupy Weihaiwei in Shandong as a guarantee that the indemnity will be paid in full. The *Peking and Tientsin Times, History of the Peace Negotiations, Documentary and Verbal, Between China and Japan, March–April, 1895*, 26–28; and Paine, *The Sino-Japanese War of 1894–1895*, 247–293.

124. Paine, *The Sino-Japanese War*, 274.

125. Edward I-te Chen, "Four Chinese Leaders and the Reunification of Taiwan: 1900–1943," 1–2.

126. On April 23, 1895, six days after the Treaty had been signed in Shimonoseki, ministers of the three states visited the Japanese Foreign Minister to see Vice Foreign Minister Hayashi for the purpose of firmly stating their objection to the cession of the Liaodong peninsula. Mutsu, *Kenkenroku*, 203–253; Paine, *The Sino-Japanese War*, 287.

127. Letter from Customs House, Tamsui, 27 May 1895, typescript copy, Collection # C0031, Folder 4, Letter 1298, Department of Rare Books and Special Collections, Firestone Library, Princeton University; see also, John King Fairbank, Martha Henderson Coolidge, and Richard Smith, *H. B. Morse: Customs Commissioner and Historian of China*, 129–133; and John Foster, *Diplomatic Memoirs, vol. II*, 153.

128. Fairbank, Coolidge, and Smith, *H. B. Morse*, 129; Gordon, "Taiwan and the Powers," 108, n. 42.

129. Zhoushan, sometimes rendered as Chushan, Choushan, or Chusan, is an archipel-ago at the mouth of Hangzhou Bay on the coast of Zhejiang province, comprising about 100 islands.

130. While the British government saw no threat in Japan's imminent conquest of Tai-wan, merchants in northern China evidently did. The *North China Daily News* published an article stating succinctly the reason why Taiwan had then and continues to have geo-strategic significance: "The island of Formosa commands the great water road between northern and southern ports: between Hong Kong and Shanghai. Its occupation by a weak and unaggressive power like China is a matter so insignificant that it attracts no attention. But the ownership is probably about to change. It will most likely pass into the hands of a rising and resolute naval power whose avowed intention is the undermining, if possible, of the British Empire! Japan might, and to carry out her programme most certainly would, make Formosa a naval station, and with inimical intention towards England could thereby inconvenience British trade very considerably." Two days later, the paper reinforced the message writing, in part, "The occupation of Formosa has … been decided with the idea … some day of becoming the basis of operations against England." Quo, "British Diplomacy and the Cession of Formosa," 144, 148–150.

131. Fairbank, Coolidge, and Smith, *H. B. Morse*, 129; Harry Lamley, "The 1895 Taiwan Republic: A Significant Episode in Modern Chinese History," 739–762.

132. Quo cites evidence that the British soon recognized that they had erred in failing to take Taiwan when it was offered and in encouraging the Qing court to proceed, accord-ing to the terms of the Treaty of Shimonoseki, to cede Taiwan to Japan. The Qing, for its part, was desperate to avoid ceding Taiwan to Japan and approached France for assistance, but to no avail. Quo, "British Diplomacy and the Cession of Formosa," 151; and Fairbank, Coolidge, and Smith, *H. B. Morse*, 129.

133. Foster took it upon himself to send telegrams to the *Zongli Yamen* "urging that early measures be taken to carry out the treaty stipulation as to Formosa [Taiwan]." Why Foster was so eager to press for the cession of Taiwan is not indicated in his various notes, diary, or published memoirs. Foster, *Diplomatic Memoirs, vol. II*, 153–154.

134. John W. Foster, *Diary Written by John Watson Foster, Shimonoseki—1895*.

135. So fearful was Li Jingfeng of being targeted by insurrectionists on the island, he ac-cepted Foster's counsel that his duty could be served by signing an instrument of transfer from the security of the Japanese man-of-war commanded by Japan's Admiral Kabayama, and anchored off Sandiao Jiao [Samtiao] on the northeast coast of Taiwan, twelve miles southeast of the port of Jilong. This was done in the early evening, and Li's delegation then returned immediately to Shanghai. Foster writes, "We had been in the waters of Formosa [Taiwan] just thirty-six hours, and never did a public official turn his face homeward from a successful mission with greater delight than did Li Ching-fong." Foster, *Diplomatic Mem-oirs, vol. II*, 159–160.

136. Teng, *Taiwan's Imagined Geography*, 35, n. 3.

CHAPTER 4

1. Harry Lamley argues that the Qing was willing to let Taiwan go so long as it was ensured that the Liaodong peninsula remained part of China. There is also a myth, con-cocted perhaps by Li Hongzhang's detractors, that Li had all along aimed to rid the Qing of Taiwan because it was a difficult place to administer. This theme is highlighted in the recol-lections of the man who, in 1895, had been Japan's Vice-Foreign Minister, Hayashi Tadasu. Hiyashi wrote that Li had shrewdly "surrendered nothing which he was not prepared and

glad to get rid of, except the indemnity. He always considered Formosa [Taiwan] a curse to China. . . . In this he proved himself a true prophet, for even to-day (1915) the Japanese have not succeeded in pacifying Formosa, and insurrections are frequent in spite of the drastic methods used by the Japanese *gendarmarie.*" In 1913, two years before Hayashi published his recollections, a volume purporting to be the memoirs of Li Hongzhang was published. In it, a full chapter is devoted to his long-standing disregard for Taiwan and his effort, dating to 1873, to persuade the court that it should be rid of Taiwan, even if that meant *giving* it to Great Britain. Li is cited as writing, among other vividly disparaging remarks, that "Taiwan was a black ulcer spot upon the beautiful and sacred body of the empire, and that to cause its removal, by whatever means, would be a blessing to the country." Harry Lamley, "The 1895 Taiwan War of Resistance: Local Chinese Efforts Against a Foreign Power," 24, 61; on observations by Hayashi Tadasu, see Paine, *The Sino-Japanese War,* 292, n. 201; on Li Hongzhang's apparent contempt for Taiwan, see William Mannix, *Memoirs of Li Hung Chang,* 260–270; on suspicions that the foregoing publication is fraudulent, see J. O. P. Bland, *Li Hung-chang,* 32–33; Ian Nish, "An Overview of Relations between China and Japan, 1895–1945," 602.

2. Despite their outrage against the Treaty of Shimonoseki, neither Kang Youwei nor Liang Qichao were inhibited from taking refuge in Japan after the 100-Day Reform they devised was crushed in 1898 by conservatives at court. Moreover, Liang was less than encouraging of the efforts by Taiwanese nationalists to combat Japanese colonialism. In Japan, Liang was sought out by a leading Taiwanese activist who hoped to receive advice about a strategy for resisting Japanese colonialism. Rather than to offer encouragement that resistance would be supported by the Chinese government, Liang preached moderation and made clear his view that Taiwan should not expect support from China. He advised Taiwanese nationalists to seek ways of mitigating the sting of colonial status by working within the Japanese legal and political systems to cultivate support for their independence from sympathetic Japanese figures and to seek representation in Japan's Diet. Chen, "Four Chinese Leaders and the Reunification of Taiwan," 2–6; and Nish, "An Overview of Relations Between China and Japan, 1895–1945," 602.

3. Liu Xiaoyuan, *A Partnership for Disorder,* 65.

4. Steven Phillips, "Confronting Colonization and National Identity: The Nationalists and Taiwan, 1941–45," 2.

5. Phillips notes "while China could agree to regain territory, it could not consent to losing territory." Ibid.

6. Ibid.

7. Ibid., 3.

8. Ibid.

9. Chen, "Four Chinese Leaders and the Reunification of Taiwan," 7–8.

10. Sun Yat-sen. *The Vital Problem of China,* 13.

11. Ibid., 13–14.

12. Ibid., 48.

13. Ibid., 145.

14. Fletcher Brockman, "Foreign Control at Peking Means War, Says Sun Yat-sen," *New York Times* (July 22, 1923), xx5 (page 1).

15. Sun, *San Min Chu I: Three Principles of the People,* Lecture one, 2.

16. Ibid., Lecture one, 3.

17. Ibid., Lecture one, 5.

18. Ibid., Lecture two, 9. Sun subsequently writes that Korea was "formerly a tributary of China in name, but an independent nation in reality." Ibid., Lecture six, 41.

19. Ibid., Lecture two, 9.

20. Ibid., Lecture two, 9–10.

21. Chen, "Four Chinese Leaders and the Reunification of Taiwan," 13, citing Dai Jiato, *"Nihon no toyo seisaku ni tsuite"* [Regarding Japan's East Asian Policy], *Kaizo*, March 1925, 117–124, as presented in Fuji Shozo, *Son Bun no Kenkyu* [A Study of Sun Yat-sen], Tokyo, 1966, 229–230.

22. Chiang Kai-shek, *Resistance and Reconstruction: Messages During China's Six Years of War*, and Chiang Kai-shek, *All We Are and All We Have: Speeches and Messages Since Pearl Harbor.*

23. Chinese Ministry of Information, *The Collected Wartime Messages of Generalissimo Chiang Kai-shek, 1937–1945, vol. 1.*

24. Ibid., 54–55.

25. Ibid., 80.

26. "Japan: Enemy of Humanity: A message to friendly nations on the first anniversary of China's War of Resistance, July 7, 1938," Ibid., 83–88.

27. "An Appeal to Japan: A revised press report summarizing Generalissimo Chiang's Message to the people of Japan, on the first anniversary of the Sino-Japanese War, July 7, 1938," Ibid., 89.

28. "To the People of Manchuria: A message to the Chinese people in the Northeast (Manchuria) on the seventh anniversary of the Mukden Incident (September 18, 1931)," Ibid., 110.

29. Liu Xiaoyuan, *A Partnership for Disorder*, 65.

30. Beginning in 1940, the Guomindang initiated efforts to foster revolutionary movements on Taiwan, support Taiwanese political opposition to Japan, and establish an agency that was intended to lay the groundwork for a Guomindang office in Taiwan. Ibid.

31. Chiang Kai-shek, *"Gaoli Taiwan shi Zhongguo de shengmingxian"* [Korea and Taiwan are China's Lifelines], *Taiwan wenti yanlun ji*, Chongqing, 1943, 1–2, as cited in Phillips, "Confronting Colonization and National Identity," 6, n. 16, 17.

32. Chiang Kai-shek, "To the People of Japan: A Message to the people of Japan, on July 7, 1939, on the second anniversary of the Sino-Japanese War," in *The Collected Wartime Messages of Generalissimo Chiang Kai-shek*, 275.

33. Phillips, "Confronting Colonization and National Identity."

34. Keith Sainsbury, *The Turning Point: Roosevelt, Stalin, Churchill, and Chiang Kai-shek, 1943—The Moscow, Cairo, and Tehran Conferences*, 139.

35. Robert Madsen, "The Struggle for Sovereignty Between China and Taiwan," 147.

36. Sainsbury, *The Turning Point*, 188.

37. Ibid.

38. Robert Dallek, *Franklin D. Roosevelt and American Foreign Policy, 1932–1945*, 428.

39. Madsen, "The Struggle for Sovereignty Between China and Taiwan," 148.

40. Richard Bush argues that the four factors affecting the outcome were "U.S. government 40; Washington's desire to keep China in the war; Roosevelt's vision for post-war security; and the impact of personal diplomacy." For a detailed analysis of the international interplay leading to the U.S. decision to endorse the Chinese request to have Taiwan returned to China, see Bush, *At Cross Purposes*, esp. chapter 2.

41. For a summary of the atmospherics of the conference, see Ron Cyneful Robbins, "Sixty Years On: The Atlantic Charter, 1941–2001."

42. The Atlantic Charter was endorsed by more than twenty nations in the "Declaration of the United Nations" signed in Washington, D.C., on January 1, 1942. The signatories, China included, pledged to subscribe to the aims of the Atlantic Charter.

43. The Atlantic Charter.

44. I am grateful to Niu Jun, in whose debt I remain for sharing thoughts about the role of the Atlantic Charter in the transition in Chinese attitudes toward Taiwan. See also, *Zhonghua mingguo zhongyao shiliao chu bian* [ROC Important Historical Materials], Section 3, volume 3. Taipei: Academic Sinica, 1981, 796–797, cited in Christopher Hughes, *Taiwan and Chinese Nationalism: National Identity and Status in International Society*, 6.

45. Liu Xiaoyuan, *A Partnership for Disorder*, 37.

46. The Alliance was an amalgam of political movements comprising activists on Taiwan and Taiwanese activists on the mainland. This community was divided as to the wisdom of becoming part of China again or establishing its independence. They were not divided in their determination to end Japan's colonization. Bush, *At Cross Purposes*, 11; Phillips, "Confronting Colonialism and National Identity," 8ff.

47. *Foreign Relations of the United States, 1942* (China), 731; George Kerr, *Formosa Betrayed*, 52.

48. U.S. Department of State, *Foreign Relations of the United States, 1942* (China) 730.

49. Ibid., 730–731.

50. "China Seeks Formosa Rendition," *New York Times*, April 6, 1942, 4.

51. Service's statement on the Ryukyu islands reads, "Regarding the Liu Chius, he said that it was unfortunately inevitable during wartime that there should be exaggerated statements by private individuals concerning war aims; that the truth of the matter was that the people of the Liu Chius were not Chinese and the number of Chinese residents there probably were not more than a few tens, that the islands, which had only been tributary to China, had been entirely separated from it for almost eighty years; that they were unimportant economically and strategically, and that they were now in effect an integral part of Japan, to which they were geographically closely related." *Foreign Relations of the United States, 1942* (China), 732–733.

52. Ibid., 102–103.

53. Cited in Bush, *At Cross Purposes*, 12.

54. *Foreign Relations of the United States, 1942* (China), 174.

55. The first version was published by Chung Cheng Publishing House, the official publisher of the Guomindang, in Chongqing, on March 10, 1943, two days before the thirty-first anniversary of Sun Yat-sen's death. According to Philip Jaffe, the authorship of the book is a matter of contention. While its writing was undertaken in November 1942, a question pertains to how much was actually written by Chiang and how much by Dao Xisheng, a Japanese-educated scholar formerly of Peking University and, earlier, a secretary to Chiang Kai-shek. Dao had a checkered political career, having broken with the Guomindang and fled to Japan with Wang Jingwei. Dao returned to China in 1940 bearing evidence of Wang's effort, considered traitorous, to reach a peace accord with Japan. Ultimately, Dao was appointed Chairman of the Cultural Branch of the Second Department of the Generalissimo's Personal Headquarters and was a prominent editorialist and propagandist on behalf of the Guomindang. See Chiang Kai-shek, *China's Destiny and Chinese Economic Theory, with Notes and Commentary by Philip Jaffe*, 20–21.

56. Chiang Kai-shek, *China's Destiny*, (Macmillan edition), x. This is the authorized English translation by Wang Chung-hui [Wang Zhonghui]. Unless otherwise noted, all references to Chiang's text are drawn from this authorized translation.

57. Ibid., 3.

58. Ibid., 8.

59. Ibid., 9.

60. Ibid.

61. The original version excluded the Ryukyu islands. Ibid., 9–10.

62. Invoking Sun Yat-sen's Will, Chiang writes that abrogating the unequal treaties by which the Qing ceded territory to foreign powers was Sun's dying wish. However, it appears that Chiang, not Sun, extended this wish to Taiwan (which was ceded by an unequal treaty) and to the Ryukyu islands (which were not). It is also noteworthy that Chiang does not identify the land ceded to Russia in the Treaties of Aigun (1858) and Peking (1860)—formerly a portion of the Qing empire's northeastern reaches—among the strategic regions that contribute to China's defense.

63. Ibid., 12.

Chapter 5

1. The evolution of the CCP's attitude toward distinctions between Han and non-Han peoples is taken up in Liu Xiaoyuan, *Frontier Passages*; see also, Frank Hsiao and Lawrence Sullivan, "The Chinese Communist Party and the Status of Taiwan, 1928–1943"; Jörg-Meinhard Rudolph, *Die Kommunistische Partei Chinas und Taiwan (1921–1981)*; Liu Xiaoyuan, *A Partnership for Disorder: China, the United States, and Their Policies for the Postwar Disposition of the Japanese*; and Michael Hunt, *Genesis of Chinese Communist Foreign Policy*, 223.

2. The Communist International, or Comintern—also known as the Third International—was established by Lenin to ensure the survival of the Russian revolution by spreading communist ideology to the capitalist West. It was formally inaugurated in March 1919, to encourage a world revolution that would overthrow the bourgeoisie and found an international Soviet republic that would lead to the abolition of the state. The Comintern sent agents to advise fledgling communist movements in other states, including China, and through them sought to foster a worldwide revolutionary alliance that was guided by the leadership of the Communist Party of the Soviet Union. While its stated purpose was revolution, it responded to the foreign policy imperatives of the Soviet Union even when these seemed contrary to the ideological objectives of the communists in other states. Ultimately, it served Moscow as a conduit for funds and oversight so that the Kremlin could covertly manipulate and constrain the activities of communist parties in other states. See, Dan Jacobs, "Comintern."

3. Hunt, *Genesis of Chinese Communist Foreign Policy*, 85.

4. The CCP's stance on peripheral territories and their peoples may reflect the posture of the Comintern on the "national question." Accordingly, the CCP endorsed the Leninist line concerning "colonies and oppressed peoples" that Moscow imposed. The CCP was instructed that it was expected to "support the liberation movements in such colonies not only in word but also in deed, demanding the expulsion of the imperialists from the colonies." Liu Xiaoyuan, *Frontier Passages*, 33.

5. "*Zhongguo gongchandang dierci quanguo dahui xuanyan*" [Manifesto of the Second Party Congress], July 1922, as reproduced in Saich, *The Rise to Power of the Chinese Communist Party*, 42.

6. Holding the Congress in Moscow was intended by Stalin as a means of enforcing compliance by the CCP to his ideological preferences. Consequently, "There can be little doubt that the policies adopted by the Sixth Congress of the CCP were, in fact, the Comintern's."

Richard Thornton, *The Comintern and the Chinese Communists*, xvi; Hunt, *Genesis of Chinese Communist Foreign Policy*, 111–112.

7. This formulation in which Taiwanese are identified in the same category as other "national minorities" was reiterated later that year by the Fifth National Congress of the Chinese Communist Youth League. Hsiao and Sullivan, "The Chinese Communist Party and the Status of Taiwan," 447; Liu Xiaoyuan, *Frontier Passages*, chapter 3, esp. 67–75.

8. *"Zhonghua suweiai gongheguo xianfa dagang"* [Outline of the Constitution of the Chinese Soviet Republic], November 7, 1931, as reproduced in Saich, *The Rise to Power of the Chinese Communist Party*, 553.

9. A Central Committee notice of that era calls for the reassertion of Chinese sovereignty over Shandong and Manchuria, both then held by Japan. However, Taiwan—also a Japanese colony at that time—was not even mentioned. Hsiao and Sullivan, "The Chinese Communist Party and the Status of Taiwan," 448.

10. *"Wei kang-Ri jiuguo gao quanti tongbao shu"* [Message to Compatriots on Resistance to Japan to Save the Nation], August 1, 1935, as reproduced in Saich, *The Rise to Power of the Chinese Communist Party*, 694.

11. Ibid., 696.

12. Ibid., 696–697.

13. This same formulation, equating the people of Taiwan with those of Korea and anti-imperialists in Japan, is evident in the "Resolution of the CC [Central Committee] on the Current Political Situation and the Party's Tasks" of December 25, 1935, in which the CCP called for a broadening of the party's base and an accommodation with all anti-Japanese forces in a "united front" to prevent the "Japanese imperialists [from] turning China into a colony" and to fight for China's "freedom, independence, and unification." This widespread effort to rally forces against Japan focused on a program of ten specific tasks, the ninth of which is "To unite the workers and peasants of Korea, Taiwan, and Japan itself and all anti-Japanese forces to form a consolidated alliance." *"Zhongyang wei muqian fan-Ri tao-Jiang de mimi zhishi shu"* [The Party Center's Secret Letter of Instruction on Opposing Japan and Condemning Chiang at the Present Time], October 1935; *"Zhongyang guanyu muqian zhengzhi xingshi yu dang de renwu jueyi"* [Resolution of the CC on the Current Political Situation and the Party's Tasks], December 25, 1935; Zhang Guotao, *"Guanyu minzu geming de gaochao yu dang de celüe luxian de baogao"* [Report on the High Tide of the National Revolution and the Party's Tactical Line], January 28, 1936, all in Ibid., 700–701, 714, 723.

14. Hsiao and Sullivan, "The Chinese Communist Party and the Status of Taiwan," 449.

15. "Report of the Central Executive Committee and the People's Committee of the Chinese Soviet Republic to the Second All-Soviet Congress, January 25, 1934," in Mao Zedong, *Collected Works*, vol. iv, pt. iv, 193.

16. Snow was assisted in his interviews by Wu Liangping, who served as the interpreter. Snow recorded what he heard from Wu in English, Wu translated the comments back into Chinese for Mao to read and correct, and then Wu retranslated the corrected answers back into English. Snow adds "because of such precautions I believe these pages to contain few errors of reporting."

Snow's work was originally published in 1938 by Random House and was subsequently reissued in 1944. Edgar Snow, *Red Star Over China*, 106.

17. Ibid., 110.

18. One must recall that in 1931 the Mukden Incident led to the annexation by Japan of Manchuria and the establishment of the separate state of Manchukuo. The League of Na-

tions called for the withdrawal of Japanese troops and empaneled the Lytton Commission to investigate competing claims by both Japan and China related to Manchuria and their conflict. The Commission's Report in 1932 rejected many of Japan's key assertions and recommended the establishment of a regime in Manchuria that would be consistent with China's sovereignty over the region. Unsuccessful efforts by the League to encourage conciliation by both disputants were followed by further deliberations. These resulted in recommendations that the full Assembly call on Japan to withdraw its troops and League member states to refrain from recognizing the independence of Manchukuo. At that stage, on February 24, 1933, the Japanese delegation walked out of the League Assembly. Subsequently, Japan withdrew from the League and persisted in consolidating control over the northeast. Dorothy Borg, *The United States and the Far Eastern Crisis of 1933–1938*, 1–22; and Louise Young, *Japan's Total Empire: Manchuria and the Culture of Wartime Imperialism*, 427–428.

19. Snow, *Red Star Over China*, 110.

20. In one footnote, Snow observes that Mao erroneously labeled Korea as a former colony. Snow writes, "Not really a 'Chinese colony' but a neighbor over whom China claimed suzerainty before her defeat by Japan in 1895." Ibid., 110, 421.

21. Ibid., 136.

22. For another comprehensive interpretation of this problem, see Liu, *A Partnership for Disorder*, 158–163.

23. Zhang Guotao, "*Guanyu minzu geming de gaochao yu dang de celüe luxian de baogao*" [Report on the High Tide of the National Revolution and the Party's Tactical Line], January 28, 1936, as reproduced in Saich, *The Rise to Power of the Chinese Communist Party*, 731.

24. Liu Shaoqi, "*Guanyu guoqu baiqu gongzuo gei zhongyang de yifengxin*" [Letter to the Party Center Concerning Past Work in the White Areas], March 4, 1937, Ibid., 777.

25. Hungdah Chiu, "Comparison of the Nationalist and Communist Chinese Views of Unequal Treaties," in Edmund S. K. Fung, "The Chinese Nationalists and the Unequal Treaties, 1924–1931," 239–267; Dong Wang, "The Discourse of Unequal Treaties in Modern China."

26. Carlson describes "Tun" as "Chu Teh's assistant political director" and writes "Tun had been a worker before joining the Eighth Route Army. He had spent some time in France and had studied the labor movement there. He was short, chunky and physically tough, and his mind was as keen as mustard." Evans Fordyce Carlson, *Twin Stars of China: A Behind-the-Scenes Story of China's Valiant Struggle for Existence by a U.S. Marine who Lived and Moved with the People*, 250, 252.

27. Ibid., 251.

28. "*Zhonggong kuangda de liuzhong quanhui zhengzhi jueyian*" [Political Resolution Adopted by the Enlarged Sixth Plenum of the CCP], November 6, 1938, as reproduced in Saich, *The Rise to Power of the Chinese Communist Party*, 822. For more evidence that this attitude prevailed during the Sixth National Congress, see Hsiao and Sullivan, "The Chinese Communist Party and the Status of Taiwan," 450–451.

29. Mao Zedong, "*Fan touxiang tigang*" [Outline for Opposing Capitulation], June 10 and 13, 1939, as reproduced in Saich, *The Rise to Power of the Chinese Communist Party*, 867.

30. Ibid., 868.

31. Ibid.

32. "*Zhongguo gongchandang guanyu Su-Ri zhongli tiaoyue fabiao yijian*" [Statement of the CCP on the Publication of the Soviet-Japanese Neutrality Pact], April 16, 1941, Ibid., 964.

33. *Xinhua Ribao* of June 16, 22, 1941, as cited in Hsiao and Sullivan, "The Chinese Communist Party and the Status of Taiwan," 453.

34. Hunt, *Genesis of Chinese Communist Foreign Policy,* 220; *Jiefang Ribao,* September 29, 1941, as cited in Rudolph, *Die Kommunistische Partei Chinas und Taiwan,* 32.

35. *Jiefang Ribao,* November 23–26, 1941; Rudolph notes that neither this speech nor the references by Zhou Enlai and Liu Shaoqi were published in their collected works. Rudolph, *Die Kommunistische Partei Chinas und Taiwan,* 33.

36. *"Zhongguo gongchandang wei Taipingyang zhanzheng de xuanyan"* [CCP Declaration on the War in the Pacific], December 9, 1941, as reproduced in Saich, *The Rise to Power of the Chinese Communist Party,* 966.

37. Liu, *A Partnership for Disorder,* 159.

38. With apologies to Ray Huang, who wrote *1587, A Year of No Significance: The Ming Dynasty in Decline.* New Haven: Yale University Press, 1981.

39. This is a central point in Liu, *Frontier Passages.*

40. For an exploration of how the Comintern may have inspired the CCP to see itself as the model for revolution in other colonial areas see Steven Goldstein, "The Chinese Revolution and the Colonial Areas: The View form [sic] Yenan, 1937–1941."

41. Hunt, *Genesis of Chinese Communist Foreign Policy,* 117.

42. Ibid., 118–119.

43. Ibid., 105–106.

44. Sino-Soviet relations soured after Sun's death in 1925, but initially even Chiang saw value in cooperative relations with the Soviet Union, if only for instrumental reasons. Ibid., 103.

45. Liu, *A Partnership for Disorder,* 161; Rudolph, *Die Kommunistische Partei Chinas und Taiwan,* 17.

46. Hsiao and Sullivan, "The Chinese Communist Party and the Status of Taiwan," 455, esp. n. 28; 458, n. 39; Liu, *A Partnership for Disorder,* 161; Rudolph, *Die Kommunistische Partei Chinas und Taiwan,* 16ff; Jane Degras, *The Communist International, 1919–1943,* 91.

47. Degras, *The Communist International,* 26.

48. Ibid., 396, 400.

49. At the conclusion of the Russo-Japanese War, the Treaty of Portsmouth, signed on September 5, 1905, secured for Japan a sphere of influence in Manchuria and possession of the southern portion of Sakhalin Island. Japan had already taken the Kuril islands in 1875 and annexed the Ryukyu islands in 1879.

50. Ibid., 440–442.

51. Hunt, *Genesis of Chinese Communist Foreign Policy,* 120.

52. Ibid., 108–109.

53. Ibid., 110–113.

54. Mao contrasts subjectivism, which he says is characterized by enthusiasm for the abstract and conclusions drawn from impressions, with objectivity, which he says requires that one begin with "objectively existing reality, to extract the regulating laws therefrom, and to make them a basis for our actions." He criticizes those who "fail to seek truth from facts." Mao Zedong, *"Gaizao women de xuexi"* [Reform Our Studies], May 5, 1941 (reworked and published in February, 1942), as reproduced in Saich, *The Rise to Power of the Chinese Communist Party,* 1001 ff., esp. 1003–1004.

55. Mao Zedong, *"Fandui zhuguan zhuyi he zongpai zhuyi"* [Oppose Subjectivism and Sectarianism], September 10, 1941, Ibid., 1009.

56. Ibid., 1008 ff.

57. Hunt, *Genesis of Chinese Communist Foreign Policy,* 213.

58. Ibid., 214; Steven Goldstein contends that the Sinification of Marxism was not exclusively a reflection of "Mao's distrust of Soviet intentions and the need to bolster his own positions against the challenge of his Moscow trained opponents," in the CCP, but actually drew from Comintern injunctions against a doctrinaire approach to the application of revolutionary tactics. See Goldstein, "The Chinese Revolution and the Colonial Areas," 599–600.

59. For details about Taiwanese political organizations operating on the mainland during the war against Japan, see J. Bruce Jacobs, "Taiwanese and Chinese Nationalists, 1937–1945"; Steven Phillips, "Confronting Colonization and National Identity, 1941–1945," 8, n. 21, 22.

60. According to Jacobs, in the Hokkien dialect spoken by many Taiwanese and other people originating south of the Min River in Fujian, "Taiwanese colloquially refer to the Chinese mainland as the 'Tang Mountains.' . . . Thus, the term 'Half-Mountain Person' means 'Half-Mainlander.'" Jacobs, "Taiwanese and Chinese Nationalists, 1937–1945," 86.

61. George Kerr, *Formosa Betrayed*, 45; Jacobs, "Taiwanese and Chinese Nationalists, 1937–1945," 85.

62. According to Kerr, one of the oldest of these Taiwanese organizations was established in 1925 as the Formosa Comrades Society. Though he gives no Chinese equivalent, one wonders whether this was a communist organization. Kerr, *Formosa Betrayed*, 45; Jacobs, "Taiwanese and Chinese Nationalists, 1937–1945," 88.

63. Liu, *A Partnership for Disorder*, 162.

64. Ibid.

65. Jacobs, "Taiwanese and Chinese Nationalists, 1937–1945," 89–90.

66. Liu, *A Partnership for Disorder*, 162.

67. Jacobs, "Taiwanese and Chinese Nationalists, 1937–1945," 91.

68. Liu, *A Partnership for Disorder*, 162.

69. Evidently, the abrupt shift to this new posture was not made flawlessly by all. In April 1942, an editorial in *Xinhua Ribao* criticized the Guomindang for failing to respond with sufficient speed to the demands of the Taiwanese and observed that "the destiny of Taiwan will finally have to be decided by the Taiwanese people themselves." To this suggestion of independence, the TRA objected, reiterating the view of the TRA that Taiwan should become a province of China. Ibid., 163.

70. Kerr, *Formosa Betrayed*, 46.

71. Goldstein, "The Chinese Revolution and the Colonial Areas," 607.

72. Ibid.

73. Hunt, *Genesis of Chinese Communist Foreign Policy*, 212–225.

74. Hsiao and Sullivan, "The Chinese Communist Party and the Status of Taiwan," 465.

CHAPTER 6

1. Steven Phillips, *Between Assimilation and Independence: The Taiwanese Encounter Nationalist China, 1945–1950*, 53.

2. There was, however, a vicious crackdown on suspected communists on Taiwan, an effort to curtail subversion. See Phillips, *Between Assimilation and Independence*, 98–99.

3. The February 28 incident has come to symbolize the political suppression of Taiwanese by the Guomindang regime and, thus, may be seen as a prominent turning point in relations between Taiwanese and refugees from the mainland. See Lai Tse-han, Ramon Myers, and Wei Wou, *A Tragic Beginning: The Taiwan Uprising of February 28, 1947*.

4. Phillips, *Between Assimilation and Independence,* 94–98.

5. Jon Huebner, "The Abortive Liberation of Taiwan," 259.

6. United States, National Security Council, "The Strategic Importance of Formosa," NSC 37, 1.

7. Ibid.

8. The JCS added that "unfriendly control of Taiwan makes it even more essential that strategic control of the Ryukyus, as previously recommended by the Joint Chiefs of Staff, remain in United States hands." See United States. Department of State, "The Strategic Importance of Formosa."

9. United States, National Security Council, "The Position of the United States With Respect to Formosa," NSC 37/1, 6.

10. United States, National Security Council, "The Current Position of the United States With Respect to Formosa," NSC37/2, 1.

11. United States, National Security Council, "The Strategic Importance of Formosa," NSC37/3, 3.

12. United States, National Security Council, "Supplementary Measures With Respect to Formosa," NSC 37/5, 2.

13. June Grasso, *Truman's Two-China Policy,* esp. 108–113.

14. Phillips, *Between Assimilation and Independence,* 193, n. 69.

15. It was about this juncture, in May 1949, that a plan emerged to ensure that Taiwan did not fall into Soviet hands for use as a base for "offensive operations." That plan, "Joint Outline Emergency War Plan OFFTACKLE," was ultimately approved on December 8, 1949. John Lewis Gaddis, "The Strategic Perspective: The Rise and Fall of the 'Defensive Perimeter' Concept, 1947–1951," 80–81, esp. n. 51, 54.

16. United States, National Security Council, "The Position of the United States with Respect to Formosa," NSC 37/7, 1-2.

17. Ibid., 2.

18. "President Truman's Statement on the U.S. Policy Respecting the Status of Formosa [Taiwan], January 5, 1950," *American Foreign Policy, 1950–1955, Basic Documents, II.* Washington, D.C.: U.S. Government Printing Office, 1957, 2448–2449, as reproduced in Winberg Chai, ed., *Chinese Mainland and Taiwan: A Study of Historical, Cultural, Economic and Political Relations,* 159–160.

19. Gaddis, "The Strategic Perspective," 85-86, esp. n. 66, 68.

20. Ibid., 87–89.

21. To be sure, some Americans—Douglas MacArthur no less than others—had long advocated that the United States do more to defend Chiang Kai-shek's anticommunist regime on Taiwan and were jubilant that Washington was firmly opposing communist expansion.

22. "Report, CCP Southern Bureau, 'Opinions on Diplomatic Affairs and Suggestions to the Central Committee,' 16 August 1944," as reproduced in Zhang Shuguang and Chen Jian, *Chinese Communist Foreign Policy and the Cold War in Asia,* 7.

23. Ibid., 2.

24. "Instructions, CCP Central Committee, 'On the Strategies in the Struggle Against the United States and Chiang [Jieshi],' 28 November 1945," Ibid., 52–53.

25. Hurley, who had been sent to China by President Roosevelt to mediate between the CCP and the Guomindang, was ultimately judged by the leadership of the CCP to be untrustworthy and partial. See, Chen Jian, *Mao's China and the Cold War,* 23–24.

26. "Instruction, CCP Central Committee, 'How to Deal with the Changing U.S. Policy toward China,' 19 December 1945," Zhang and Chen, *Chinese Communist Foreign Policy and the Cold War in Asia,* 57–58.

27. "Instruction, CCP Central Committee, 'Force American Troops to Withdraw from China,' 29 September 1946," Ibid., 76–77.

28. "Instruction, CCP Central Committee, 'On the Termination of American Mediation in China,' 30 January 1947," Ibid., 78–79.

29. "Symposium: Rethinking the Lost Chance in China," *Diplomatic History,* 21:1, 71–116; Steven Goldstein, "Sino-American Relations, 1948–1950: Lost Chance or No Chance?" 119–142; Nancy Bernkopf Tucker, *Patterns in the Dust: Chinese American Relations and the Recognition Controversy, 1949–1950;* Yuan Ming, "The Failure of Perception: America's China Policy, 1949–1950," 143–152; Thomas Christensen, *Useful Adversaries,* 77–137; and Chen Jian, *Mao's China and the Cold War,* 38–48.

30. Zhang and Chen, *Chinese Communist Foreign Policy and the Cold War in Asia,* 81–83.

31. He Di, "The Last Campaign to Unify China," 75.

32. Huebner, "The Abortive Liberation of Taiwan," 259–260, n. 17, 18, 19.

33. On the very day that the *Renmin Ribao* article warned readers that the United States planned to hold Taiwan for the purpose of launching aggressive acts against China, the U.S. Secretary of State Dean Acheson wrote a letter to supporters of the ROC in Congress who urged that the United States do more to underwrite the survival of the Guomindang-led government. Acheson wrote, in part, that offering military "material and advice" to the ROC would by no means assure its capacity to prevail, but would "prolong hostilities and the suffering of the Chinese people and would arouse in them deep resentment against the United States." For Washington to provide what the ROC would need to sustain itself and resist the CCP would demand an "unpredictably large American armed force in actual combat, a course of action which would represent direct United States involvement in China's fratricidal warfare and would be contrary to our traditional policy toward China and the interests of this country." See "Secretary Acheson to Senator Tom Connally, Chairman of the Senate Committee on Foreign Relations, March 15, 1949," the final document in the last annex to the U.S. government's "white paper" on China. United States, Department of State. *United States Relations with China, with Special Reference to the Period 1944–1949,* 1053–1054.

34. Huebner, "The Abortive Liberation of Taiwan," 260.

35. Ibid., 256.

36. Phillips, *Between Assimilation and Independence,* 135, n. 101, 102.

37. See, for instance, John Garver, *The Sino-American Alliance: Nationalist China and American Cold War Strategy in Asia,* esp. chapter 6.

38. This, at least, is what Mikoyan stated in 1960, in a report cited by Odd Arne Westad, *Decisive Encounters: The Chinese Civil War, 1946–1950,* 233.

39. Ibid., 249.

40. "Memorandum, Liu Shaoqi to Stalin (Based on Shi Zhe's memoirs), 4 July 1949," in Zhang and Chen, *Chinese Communist Foreign Policy and the Cold War in Asia,* 119.

41. "Letter, Mao Zedong to Zhou Enlai, 10 July 1949," Ibid., 123.

42. "Telegram, CCP Central Committee to Liu Shaoqi, 26 July 1949 (Extract)," Ibid.

43. Westad, *Decisive Encounters,* 255.

44. He Di, "The Last Campaign to Unify China," 74.

45. Ibid.

46. "Telegram, CCP Central Military Commission to Su Yu and Others, 14 June 1949," in Zhang and Chen, *Chinese Communist Foreign Policy and the Cold War in Asia*, 117; He Di, "The Last Campaign to Unify China."

47. Mao Zedong's cable to Su Yu, Zhang Zheng, Zhou Jingming, and the CCP Eastern Chinese Bureau, June 21, 1949, as cited in He Di, "The Last Campaign to Unify China," 74.

48. Ibid., 74–75.

49. "Record of Conversation Between Comrade I.V. Stalin and Chairman of the People's Government of the People's Republic of China Mao Zedong on 16 December 1949."

50. Ibid.

51. For a description of the PRC's air and naval forces in 1949 and efforts to build and buy better equipment, see He Di, "The Last Campaign to Unify China," 77, 81.

52. "Telegram, Mao Zedong to Su Yu, 28 March 1950," in Zhang and Chen, *Chinese Communist Foreign Policy and the Cold War in Asia*, 147; and Chen Jian, *China's Road to the Korean War*, chapter 4.

53. He Di, "The Last Campaign to Unify China," 82–83.

54. Ibid., 83.

55. Thinking about the nationalistic narrative used by the PRC to justify its wish for unification, it is striking that Mao decided to refrain from taking either Hong Kong or Macao at that juncture. For more on the PLA's campaigns to take territory held by the Guomindang forces after October 1, 1949, see Westad, *Decisive Encounters*, 282–289.

56. He departed the mainland for the last time on December 10, 1949. Ibid., 288.

57. James Millward and Nabijan Tursun, "Political History and Strategies of Control, 1884–1978," 85–87; and Linda Benson, *The Ili Rebellion: The Moslem Challenge to Chinese Authority in Xinjiang, 1944–1949*.

58. Alexander Huang, "The PLA Navy at War, 1949–1999: From Coastal Defense to Distant Operations," 252–254.

59. Warren Smith, *Tibetan Nation: A History of Tibetan Nationalism and Sino-Tibetan Relations*, 277–322.

60. Westad, *Decisive Encounters*, 297, 299–310.

61. "Instruction, General Information Agency, 'On the Propaganda about U.S. Imperialists' Open Intervention in the International Affairs of China, Korea, and Vietnam,' 29 June 1950," in Zhang and Chen, *Chinese Communist Foreign Policy and the Cold War in Asia*, 153–154.

62. "Recollection, Xiao Jinguang, 'The Taiwan Campaign was Called Off,' 30 June 1950," Ibid., 155.

63. "Telegram, CCP Central Military Commission to Chen Yi, 11 August 1950 [Extract]," Ibid., 157. Mao Zedong must have been concerned that postponing the campaign would tarnish his credibility. He wrote to Hu Qiaomu, director of *Xinhua She* and the General Information Bureau, to ask that Hu "Please check whether or not in our past pronouncements we have ever contemplated attacking Taiwan in 1950. It is said that the New Year proclamation of this year mentioned something about attacking Taiwan within this year. Is this true? Please note that from now on we will only speak about our intentions of attacking Taiwan and Tibet, but say nothing about the timing of the attacks." "Memorandum, Mao Zedong to Hu Qiaomu, 29 September 1950," Ibid., 160.

64. "Speech, Zhou Enlai, at the 18th Meeting of the Standing Committee of the Chinese People's Political Consultative Conference, 24 October 1950," Ibid., 186–191.

65. "Instruction, CCP Central Committee, 'On the Propaganda About Current Affairs,' 25 October 1950," Ibid., 192–197.

66. Ibid.

67. Only days before Wu made his impassioned plea, the PRC launched a massive counteroffensive aimed at blunting the campaign that Douglas MacArthur expected would end the Korean War—enabling him to make good on his boast to "have the boys home by Christmas," 1950—by establishing UN control of the entire Korean peninsula, up to the Yalu River at China's border. "Speech at the United Nations Security Council by Wu Hsiu-chuan [Wu Xiuquan], Special Representative of the People's Republic of China to the U.N., Condemning U.S. Armed Aggression Against Taiwan," in Foreign Languages Press, *Important Documents Concerning the Question of Taiwan*, 26.

68. Ibid., 66. Tanaka Giichi was reputedly the author of a memorial to the Japanese emperor in which the strategic view Wu cites was laid out as a policy for Japan's expansion. See Bunsho Hashikawa, "Japanese Perspectives on Asia: From Dissociation to Coprosperity," 346. It is worth observing that from the time of its first appearance in a Chinese publication, the authenticity of this memorial has been challenged. See John Stephan, "The Tanaka Memorial (1927): Authentic or Spurious?"

69. "Speech at the United Nations Security Council by Wu Hsiu-chuan," *Important Documents Concerning the Question of Taiwan*, 67.

70. "Statement by Chou En-lai, Foreign Minister of the People's Republic of China, Refuting Truman's Statement of June 27, 1950—June 28, 1950," Ibid., 13.

71. "Statement by Chou En-lai, Foreign Minister of the People's Republic of China, Refuting Truman's Statement of June 27, 1950—June 28, 1950," Ibid., 14.

72. "Chairman Mao Tse-tung's Address at the Eighth Meeting of the Central People's Government Council—June 28, 1950," Ibid., 11.

73. Wang Xiaodong, "The West in the Eyes of a Chinese Nationalist," 18.

74. John Garver, *The Sino-American Alliance: Nationalist China and American Cold War Strategy in Asia*.

75. Steven Goldstein, "The United States and the Republic of China, 1949–1978: Suspicious Allies."

76. Considering that islands cannot be "onshore," and that the term "offshore" offers no clue about how near or far from shore an island is, this apparently meaningful descriptive is actually rather meaningless.

77. For an account of the conflicts that highlight Mao Zedong's preoccupation with the United States, see Gong Li, "Tension Across the Taiwan Strait in the 1950s: Chinese Strategy and Tactics," 141–172.

78. *Current Digest of the Soviet Press*, 16:25 (July 15, 1964), 5–6, reproduced as "Document 18: From a 1959 Mao Interview," in Hung-dah Chiu, *China and the Taiwan Issue*, 243.

79. There is much evidence that Khrushchev, too, was sensitive to the geostrategic consequences of Taiwan. In 1959, Mao tried to reassure Khrushchev that the PRC did not want war with the United States. Both he and Zhou Enlai made several statements bearing on the issue of how China planned to "liberate" Taiwan. Mao claimed that by shelling Jinmen, "we did not intend to undertake any large-scale military actions in the area of Taiwan, and only wanted to create complications for the United States." Khrushchev responded, "It is not worth shelling the islands in order to tease cats." He elaborated, "As for the firing at the off-shore islands, if you shoot, then you ought to capture these islands, and if you do not consider necessary capturing these islands, then there is no use in firing. I do not understand this policy of yours. Frankly speaking, I thought you would take the islands and was upset when I learned that you did not take them." Mao, however, drew a distinction between Beijing's approach to the United States and its approach to Taiwan. He said, "We say that we

will definitely liberate Taiwan. But the roads to liberation may be different—peaceful and military. . . . There were military actions in this region but they did not constitute war. In our opinion, let Taiwan and other islands stay in the hands of the Jiang Jieshi-ists [Chiang Kai-shekists] for ten, twenty and even thirty years. We would tolerate it." "Discussion between N. S. Khrushchev and Mao Zedong."

80. Zhang Baijia and Jia Qingguo, "Steering Wheel, Shock Absorber, and Diplomatic Probe in Confrontation: Sino-American Ambassadorial Talks Seen from the Chinese Perspective," 181.

81. James Mann, *About Face*, 3–78; William Burr, *The Kissinger Transcripts: The Top Secret Talks with Beijing and Moscow*, 27–68; Romberg, *Rein In at the Brink of the Precipice*.

82. People's Republic of China, "The Taiwan Question and Reunification of China."

83. That the PRC sees the problem as one of foreign interference is highlighted by the white paper's continued return to that theme. For instance, in a passage concerning Beijing's refusal to renounce the use of force, the white paper states the PRC's preference is to unify by peaceful means, however, "The Chinese Government is under no obligation to undertake any commitment to any foreign power or people intending to split China as to what means it might use to handle its own domestic affairs." In another passage, the white paper differentiates "Taiwan compatriots" who wish "to run the affairs of the island as masters of their own house," an ambition that Beijing deems to be "reasonable and justified," from others who advocate "Taiwan independence." The white paper distinguishes the former group as "radically distinct from those handful of 'Taiwan independence' protagonists who trumpet 'independence' but vilely rely on foreign patronage in a vain attempt to detach Taiwan from China, which runs against the fundamental interests of the entire Chinese people including Taiwan compatriots."

84. Ibid.

85. Wang Jisi, "From Paper Tiger to Real Leviathan: China's Images of the United States Since 1949," Ibid., 17.

86. According to Gong Li, "Only a very small minority believes that U.S. policy toward Taiwan is designed to protect U.S. interests in the Asia-Pacific and live up to its international commitments, as the U.S. claims." Gong Li, "The Official Perspective: What Chinese Government Officials Think of America," 30.

87. People's Republic of China, Ministry of Foreign Affairs, "What Is the Political Intention of the U.S. Congress in Passing the So-Called 'Taiwan Relations Act'?"

88. Wang, "From Paper Tiger to Real Leviathan," 13.

89. Wang Jisi claims that since 2000, "a more balanced and stable view" of the United States has emerged in China, although in terms of the "global power equation, the United States seems to loom even larger in Chinese over-all strategic thinking," because of the muscular foreign policy of the George W. Bush administration. Still, Wang sees in official characterizations, a diminution of emphasis on fostering "multi-polarity" as a way of "opposing hegemony." Ibid.; Wang Jisi, "China's Changing Role in Asia," 12.

90. Ibid., 13.

CHAPTER 7

1. "China's Worries At Sea," *Jiefangjun Bao* [Liberation Army Daily], January 2, 2004.

2. *Taipei Times*, "Editorial: China's Dangerous Leap Backwards," December 20, 2004, 8.

3. China FBIS Report, "PRC Highlights: PLA Deputies on Anti-Secession Law, Military Reshuffles, More," *Ta Kung Pao*, March 19, 2005.

4. The notion of "imagined geography" emerges from works by Edward Said, Derek Gregory, and Gearóid Ó Tuathail, among others, and is a geographic analogue to the "imagined community" articulated in Benedict Anderson, *Imagined Communities: Reflections on the Origin and Spread of Nationalism*. See also, Edward W. Said, *Orientalism*; Teng, *Taiwan's Imagined Geography*, 15–17; Gearóid Ó Tuathail, *Critical Geopolitics: The Politics of Writing Global Space*.

5. A. Z. Hilali, "China: Geo-political Environment and Security Perceptions."

6. Colin Gray, "Inescapable Geography," 162.

7. Lu Junyuan, *Diyuan zhengzhi de benzhi yu guilu* [On the Essence and Laws of Geopolitics].

8. Dai Xu, *"Kongjun zhongjiang Liu Yazhou tan Ilake zhanzheng fenxi wo jun fazhan fangxiang"* [Air Force Lieutenant General Liu Yazhou Discusses the Iraq War and Analyzes the Development of the Air Force]; "Interview with Lieutenant General Liu Yazhou of the Air Force of the People's Liberation Army," 6–7. Lieutenant General Liu Yazhou is the son-in-law of former PRC president Li Xiannian. Since the late 1990s, he has published a sequence of provocative essays about strategic matters that have been widely publicized, along with commentary and criticism they have generated on Chinese language Web sites. See Alfred Chan, "A Young Turk in China's Establishment: The Military Writings of Liu Yazhou."

9. Presumably, "cold weaponry" is that array of weapons used before the advent of gunpowder and explosives. Dai, *"Liu Yazhou tan Ilake zhanzheng"*; "Interview with Lieutenant General Liu Yazhou," 29.

10. It is no coincidence that the Great Wall was built in the north of China where, Liu Yazhou states, there was no natural barrier to adversaries. Liu notes about the wall "generation after generation repaired it, generation after generation defended it, and generation after generation lost" to hostile foes who breached it. He implies that the human-made barrier could not overcome the liabilities of geography. However, Liu says that in the present era of airpower "all of our geographic superiority has lost efficacy." So, although the Great Wall did not accomplish the objectives Liu claims it was intended to serve, technology can affect the salience of geography. Ibid.

11. Teng, *Taiwan's Imagined Geography*, 15.

12. Sallie Yea, "Maps of Resistance and Geographies of Dissent in the Cholla Region of South Korea," 70.

13. Christopher B. Krebs, "Imaginary Geography in Caesar's *Bellum Gallicum*," 119.

14. Ibid.

15. Yea, "Maps of Resistance and Geographies of Dissent," 88.

16. Brian S. Osborne, "Landscapes, Memory, Monuments, and Commemoration: Putting Identity in Its Place."

17. Yea, "Maps of Resistance and Geographies of Dissent," 90.

18. For a consideration of how shame figures in China's nationalist narrative, see William A. Callahan, "National Insecurities: Humiliation, Salvation, and Chinese Nationalism," esp. 201–204.

19. Osborne, "Landscapes, Memory, Monuments, and Commemoration," 39.

20. An illustrative sampling might include Nicholas D. Kristof, "The Rise of China"; Samuel S. Kim, "China as a Great Power"; Larry M. Wortzel, "China Pursues Traditional Great-Power Status"; Ted C. Fishman, *China, Inc.: How the Rise of the Next Superpower Challenges America and the World*; Roger Des Forges and Xu Luo, "China as a Non-Hegemonic Superpower? The Uses of History among the *China Can Say No* Writers and Their Critics";

Michael E. Brown, Owen R. Coté, Jr., Sean M. Lynn-Jones, and Steven E. Miller, eds., *The Rise of China: An International Security Reader*; Geoffrey Murray, *China: The Next Superpower: Dilemmas in Change and Continuity*; Francis A. Lees, *China Superpower: Requisites for High Growth*; Laurence J. Brahm, *China as No. 1: The New Superpower Takes Centre Stage*; David L. Shambaugh, *Greater China: The Next Superpower?*; William H. Overholt, *China: The Next Economic Superpower.*

21. Martin Edmonds and Michael M. Tsai, eds., *Taiwan's Maritime Security*, part I; David L. Shambaugh, *Modernizing China's Military: Progress, Problems, and Prospects*; Bernard D. Cole, *The Great Wall at Sea: China's Navy Enters the Twenty-first Century*; Srikanth Kondapalli, *China's Naval Power*; Charles A. Meconis and Michael D. Wallace, *East Asian Naval Weapons Acquisitions in the 1990s: Causes, Consequences, and Responses,* chapters 7, 8.

22. For an explication of the doctrinal shift that has occurred since the 1980s, see James C. Mulvenon and David M. Finkelstein, eds., *China's Revolution in Doctrinal Affairs: Emerging Trends in the Operational Art of the Chinese People's Liberation Army*; see also, Li Nan, "The PLA's Evolving Warfighting Doctrine, Strategy and Tactics, 1985–1995: A Chinese Perspective."

23. David M. Finkelstein, "China's National Military Strategy," 117.

24. Ibid.

25. Ibid.

26. This is a central argument in Alastair Iain Johnston, "Realism(s) and Chinese Security Policy in the Post-Cold War Period."

27. A comprehensive study of the PRC's maritime ambitions is offered in Alexander Chieh-Cheng Huang, "Chinese Maritime Modernization and Its Security Implications: The Deng Xiaoping Era and Beyond"; see also, Alexander Huang, "The Chinese Navy's Offshore Active Defense Strategy: Conceptualization and Implications."

28. The "first island chain" is ordinarily considered to include the Kuril islands, Japan and the Ryukyu islands, Taiwan, the Philippines, and Indonesia (Borneo to Natuna Besar). Bernard D. Cole, "The PLA Navy and 'Active Defense,'" 129ff; Huang, "The Chinese Navy's Offshore Active Defense Strategy," 16ff.

29. Shambaugh, *Modernizing China's Military*, 67. For a description and illustrations of the concept of "strategic depth," consider Robert Harkavy, "Strategic Geography and the Greater Middle East," 47–50.

30. That would entail projecting naval power out to the Bonin islands, the Mariana islands, Guam, and the Palau islands.

31. This line of reasoning has caught the attention of the U.S. Department of Defense, as reflected in its 2006 version of *The Military Power of the People's Republic of China*, esp. 15.

32. For the transportation of petroleum resources to the PRC and the rest of East Asia, the two principal chokepoints through which most oil passes are the Straits of Hormuz and the Malacca Strait. See, for instance, Jean-Paul Rodrigue, "Straits, Passages and Chokepoints: A Maritime Geostrategy of Petroleum Distribution."

33. See, e.g., You Ji, "The Evolution of China's Maritime Combat Doctrine and Models, 1949–2001," 1–2.

34. On the constituents of sea power, see Geoffrey Till, *Seapower: A Guide for the Twenty-First Century*, 78–112.

35. The heading of this subsection recalls, with apologies, the work of Kenneth Waltz, who wrote *Man, the State, and War; a Theoretical Analysis.* People's Republic of China, *China's National Defense in 2004.*

36. James R. Holmes and Toshi Yoshihara, "The Influence of Mahan on China's Maritime Strategy"; James R. Holmes, "Mahan Is Alive in China"; Ian Storey and You Ji, "China's Aircraft Carrier Ambitions: Seeking Truth from Rumors," 86.

37. Holmes and Yoshihara, "The Influence of Mahan on China's Maritime Strategy," 25.

38. Ibid., 26.

39. One must tread carefully through evidence of a pervasive interest in Mahan and maritime expansion to avoid drawing the erroneous conclusion that it is a reading of Mahan that gave birth to the politicization of geography in PRC strategic thought. The inclination to think in geostrategic terms, which may well be universal, was certainly well entrenched in China before Mahan.

40. See Bernard D. Cole, "The Organization of the People's Liberation Army Navy," in James Mulvenon and Andrew Yang, eds., 466–471; Huang, "Chinese Maritime Modernization and its Security Implications," 9–17, 91–95, 226–230; Elizabeth Speed, "Chinese Naval Power and East Asian Security," 4–5; and You Ji, "The Evolution of China's Maritime Combat Doctrine and Models," 3–6.

41. Jeffrey Goldberg, "China's Mahan."

42. Finkelstein, "China's National Military Strategy," 128–129.

43. You Ji, "The Evolution of China's Maritime Combat Doctrine and Models," 6–9, 19–22. The precise limits of the PRC's naval ambitions have been the subject of debate within the PRC and abroad. Cole, "The PLA Navy and 'Active Defense'"; Cole, "The Organization of the People's Liberation Army Navy," 471; Huang, "Chinese Maritime Modernization and its Security Implications," 193–196, 230–232; Speed, "Chinese Naval Power and East Asian Security," 6–7. See, also United Nations, "United Nations Convention on the Law of the Sea," and People's Republic of China, "Law of the People's Republic of China on the Exclusive Economic Zone and the Continental Shelf."

44. Cole, "The PLA Navy and 'Active Defense'"; and Huang, "Chinese Maritime Modernization and its Security Implications," 230. You Ji suggests that setting the target at the "second island chain" was done not by Liu, but by more "zealous commanders." You Ji, "The Evolution of China's Maritime Combat Doctrine and Models," 9.

45. Huang, "Chinese Maritime Modernization and its Security Implications," 192–193, 196–201, 239.

46. Speed, "Chinese Naval Power and East Asian Security," 14–20.

47. Robert S. Ross, "Geography of the Peace: East Asia in the Twenty-first Century."

48. Ibid., 170.

49. Ibid., 192.

50. Ibid., 193.

51. You Ji, "The Evolution of China's Maritime Combat Doctrine and Models," 2–3.

52. Ross, "Geography of the Peace," 193. Paul Dodge argues that as the PRC expands its military, it can, at best, develop "pockets of excellence" that may "challenge the U.S. in an asymmetric fashion." See Paul Dodge, "Circumventing Sea Power: Chinese Strategies to Deter U.S. Intervention in Taiwan," 392.

53. Holmes and Yoshihara, "The Influence of Mahan," 35.

54. Bullock, "China's Bluewater Ambitions," 62.

55. Cole, Great Wall at Sea, 167.

56. People's Republic of China, China's National Defense in 2004.

57. Till, Seapower, 50–51.

58. Ibid., 155–157.

59. Ibid., 157–158.

60. Alexander Huang, "The PLA Navy at War, 1949–1999," 243-244, esp. n. 6; Ronald O'Rourke, *China Naval Modernization: Implications for U.S. Navy Capabilities—Background and Issues for Congress*, 24; You Ji, "The Evolution of China's Maritime Combat Doctrine and Models," 2ff.

61. You Ji, "The Evolution of Chinese Maritime Combat Doctrine," 21–22.

62. Ibid.

63. People's Republic of China, *China's National Defense in 2006*.

64. Ibid., sec. II, "National Defense Policy."

65. Ibid., sec. IV, "The People's Liberation Army."

66. For the Chinese language text, see *"2006 nian Zhongguo de guofang"* at http://www.chinamil.com.cn/site1/2006ztpd/2006zggfbps/index.htm.

67. Ross, "Geography of the Peace," 192–193.

68. He also reiterated that the PLA(N)'s expanding capacities notwithstanding, he did not consider it a threat to the United States. Reuters, "U.S. Eyes China's Naval Power on High-Level Visit."

69. Cao Zhi and Chen Wanjun, "Hu Jintao Emphasizes When Meeting Deputies to 10th Navy CPC Congress, Follow the Principle of Integrating Revolutionization, Modernization, and Regularization, and Forge a Powerful People's Navy That Meets the Demands of our Army's Historic Mission; Guo Boxiong, Cao Gangchuan, and Xu Caihou Attend."

70. *Xinhua She, "Zhongguo renmin yiding yao jiefang Taiwan"* [The Chinese People Certainly Will Liberate Taiwan].

71. Zhang Wankun, "China's Foreign Relations Strategies Under Mao and Deng: A Systematic Comparative Analysis."

72. Mao Zedong, "On the People's Democratic Dictatorship," June 30, 1949, in Saich, *The Rise to Power of the Chinese Communist Party*, 1368.

73. Avery Goldstein, *Rising to the Challenge: China's Grand Strategy and International Security*, 29–30.

74. Ibid., 133.

75. Charles Krauthammer, "The Unipolar Moment."

76. Deng Xiaoping's foreign policy injunctions were summarized in twenty-eight Chinese characters as *lengjing guancha, wenzhu zhenjiao, chenzhuo yingfu, taoguang yanghui, shanyu shouzhuo, juebu dangtou, yousuo zuowei* [observe and analyze developments calmly, secure our own position, deal with changes patiently and confidently, conceal our capabilities and avoid the limelight, be good at keeping a low profile, never become a leader, and strive to make achievements]. See, Zhang, "China's Foreign Relations Strategies Under Mao and Deng," 14; John Garver renders them as "observe the situation calmly, stand firm in our position, respond cautiously, conceal our capabilities and await an opportune moment to make a comeback, be good at guarding our weaknesses, never claim leadership." John W. Garver, "China's U.S. Policies," 204; H. Lyman Miller and Liu Xiaohong, "The Foreign Policy Outlook of China's 'Third Generation' Elite," 140–141. Late in 2006, there were hints that the PRC might begin to moderate its adherence to Deng's injunction. See Joseph Kahn, "China, Shy Giant, Shows Signs of Shedding Its False Modesty."

77. For instance, the PRC's "foreign policy of peace" includes a paragraph that declares, "China opposes hegemonism and preserves world peace. China believes that all countries, big or small, strong or weak, rich or poor, are equal members of the international commu-

nity. Countries should resolve their disputes and conflicts peacefully through consultations and not resort to the use or threat of force. Nor should they interfere in others' internal affairs under any pretext. China never imposes its social system and ideology on others, nor allows other countries to impose theirs on it." People's Republic of China, Ministry of Foreign Affairs, "China's Independent Foreign Policy of Peace."

78. Ibid.

79. It implies, but does not specify, that the United States is among those countries that has "stirred up a racket about a 'China threat,' and intensified their preventive strategy against China and strove to hold its progress in check." People's Republic of China, *China's National Defense in 2006,* sec. I: The Security Environment.

80. People's Republic of China, *China's National Defense in 2004.*

81. People's Republic of China, *China's National Defense in 2006.*

82. Julia Rosenfield, "Assessing China's 2004 Defense White Paper: A Workshop Report."

83. Ma Dazheng, "Definition of Borderland."

84. The Taiwan Strait is between 90–105 nautical miles wide, or 103–120 statute miles wide, where one nautical mile equals 1.15 statute miles. See, for instance, Cole, "Command of the Sea," 123.

85. Xu Zhuangzhi and Cao Zhi, "China: Army, Armed Police Forces Comment on 'Letter of Apology' from USA." The comments came in the wake of the collision, on April 1, 2001, of a U.S. EP-3 surveillance aircraft and PRC fighter jet that resulted in the death of the PRC pilot and the loss of his plane.

86. After all, in 1982 Great Britain sent an armada about 8,000 miles away to fight in defense of its sovereignty over the Falkland islands.

87. Alan K. Henrikson, "Distance and Foreign Policy: A Political Geography Approach," 454–455.

88. Liu Yazhou, *"Da guo ce"* [Grand Strategy].

89. Wang Weinan and Zhou Jianming, *"Diyuan zhengzhi zhong de Zhong Mei guanxi yu Taiwan wenti"* [The Geopolitics of Sino-U.S. Relations and the Taiwan Issue], 50; Wang Xiaocai, *"Meiguo dui Hua diyuan zhengzhi guanyu Taiwan wenti"* [The American Geopolitical View on China and the Taiwan Issue], 32.

90. General Douglas MacArthur referred to Taiwan as an "unsinkable aircraft carrier" in the text of a speech that was scheduled for delivery before a convention of the Veterans of Foreign Wars in Chicago, and that appellation has come to be associated, ever after, both with him and Taiwan. He wrote, "As a result of its geographic location and base potential, utilization of Formosa [Taiwan] by a military power hostile to the United States may either counter-balance or overshadow the strategic importance of the central and southern flank of the United States front line position. Formosa in the hands of such a hostile power could be compared to an unsinkable aircraft carrier and submarine tender ideally located to accomplish offensive strategy and at the same time checkmate defensive or counter-offensive operations by friendly forces on Okinawa and the Philippines." At the time, his use of this phrase was controversial because it was not consistent with the policy of the Truman administration and, consequently, the speech was ultimately withdrawn and its reading at the convention cancelled after a radio broadcast highlighted MacArthur's invocation of Taiwan's strategic importance. Despite the notoriety of MacArthur's characterization of Taiwan, he was neither the first to use "unsinkable aircraft carrier" nor the first to apply it to Taiwan. For instance, in a report published in spring 1940, one British military commentator referred to Norway as "an unsinkable airplane carrier." In 1941, it

was reported that Italian analysts had dubbed Malta an "unsinkable aircraft carrier," an epithet that evidently stuck—even appearing as a clue in one of Louis Baron's storied crossword puzzles. The sobriquet was also applied to Ceylon, which was initially compared with Malta, and to many other islands, including those in the Pacific. For example, "unsinkable carrier" was used in reference to Japanese-held islands in the Gilbert and Marshall archipelagos as well as to Nauru. In *The New York Times*, the first reference to Taiwan as an "unsinkable aircraft carrier" was in 1945, five years before MacArthur's V. F. W. speech. See, "V. F. W. Announce Cancellation"; "Texts of Controversial MacArthur Message and Truman's Formosa Statement; After MacArthur Withdrew his Message on Formosa"; "Big Transport Set Afire in Raid, Men Ashore Bombed, Berlin Says"; "Naples Raided Five Hours"; "The Fronts" (April 5, 1942); Louis Baron, "Crossword Puzzles"; H. G. Quaritch Wales, "Huge India Looms Up as Key to War in East"; "The Fronts" (November 21, 1943); and "Chinese Capture Three Coast Cities."

91. While the United States may not, in fact, depend on the strategic opportunities that Taiwan's spot on the globe provides, it is certainly likely that the U.S. Pacific fleet worries less about operations in the Western Pacific than it would if the PRC could exploit Taiwan to its own advantage. That the United States does not "need" Taiwan because of where Taiwan is located does not necessarily mean that U.S. strategic interests are better served if Taiwan and the PRC unify. Nancy Bernkopf Tucker suggests that the United States may benefit from the continuation of the cross-Strait dispute because so long as it does not trigger military conflict, the enormous resources that Beijing has tied up in preparing for conflict cannot be devoted to challenging U.S. interests elsewhere in Asia or the Pacific. She writes that if unification were to occur, "The People's Liberation Army (PLA) would be free to change its priorities, redeploy its forces, and reconceptualize its strategic objectives. For Washington, this change means a less predictable, more flexible, and potentially less-burdened opponent, though one still noted for its lack of transparency." Secondarily, if the PRC did succeed in subordinating Taiwan, Tucker writes that the PRC would then have the option for "more significant projection of Chinese naval and air power beyond coastal waters." Nancy Bernkopf Tucker, "If Taiwan Chooses Unification, Should the United States Care?" 21–22.

92. If one questions which state it was that Zhu intended by his reference to "a certain country," consider the unexpurgated version of the same remarks in an earlier report, "It is because that in (CCTV version reads: "the United [probable STC: *mei* 5019; pause to correct his statement]) a certain country, there are some people who have always been against China. They have always considered China a potential enemy. They have always wanted to use Taiwan, which is an unsinkable aircraft carrier, to oppose China." See *Xinhua* General Overseas New Service, "More on Zhu Rongji Warning Against Taiwan Independence"; and *Beijing Xinhua Domestic Service,* "Comparison: Live News Conference by Zhu Rongji."

93. Jin Yinan, *"Foreign Weapons" Cannot Save Taiwan Independence.*

94. *People's Daily,* "U.S. Arms Sales to Taiwan Escalate Cross-Straits Tension."

95. The inclination to see the United States as using Taiwan for nefarious purposes associated with the encirclement or containment of China did not originate in that period, but seems to have flourished since the late 1990s. See Cole, *Great Wall at Sea,* 12–13, n. 40.

96. Lin Zhibo, "New Academic Analysis: Will There Be an All-out U.S. Intervention in a Taiwan Strait War?"

97. Hai Dun, *"Sanchong daolian zuo changying wangxiang fuzhu Zhongguo long—Zhongguo zhoubian de Meiguo hangmu jidi"* [The Triple Island Chain as a Long Tassel Vainly Hoping to Bind the Chinese Dragon—U.S. Aircraft Carrier Bases on China's Periphery], 44–45.

98. In the summer of 2005, U.S. Army Colonel Al Wilner took up a post at the American Institute in Taiwan [AIT] in Taipei as the first active-duty military officer to serve in Taiwan since 1979. Prior to Colonel Wilner's arrival, retired military officers were engaged by AIT as contractors to help manage Washington's defense-related activities on Taiwan. *China Daily,* "U.S. Should Keep Its Hands Off Taiwan"; and Agence France-Presse, "U.S. Confirms It Is Posting Military Officers to Taiwan Mission."

99. You Ziping was the associate dean of the Ship Research and Development Academy (the Seventh Academy of the Ministry of National Defense). He is currently associated with the Academy and is an adviser to the General Equipment Division of the PRC's Commission of Science, Technology and Industry for National Defense [COSTIND].

100. See Wu Yung-chiang, "United States Attempts to Use Japan and Taiwan to Contain China"; Shen Weilie and Lu Junyuan, eds., *Zhongguo guojia anquan dili* [The Geography of China's National Security], 162–163; Hou Songling and Chi Diantang, *"Zhongguo zhoubian haiyu de zhanlüe diwei he diyuan zhanlüe jiazhi chutan"* [Preliminary Exploration of the Geostrategic Position and Value of China's Peripheral Maritime Space].

101. You Ziping, *"Shenhua haiyang qiangguo zhanlüe de yanjiu yu shijian"* [Deepen the Research and Practice of Strategic Maritime Power], 7.

102. Lin Zhibo, "Will There Be an All-out U.S. Intervention in a Taiwan Strait War?"

103. Yiming [anonymous], *"ZhongMeiRi Taihai shengsi jiaoliang"* [Sino-U.S.-Japan Fight to the Death in the Taiwan Strait].

104. Zhu Feng and Andrew Thompson, "Why Taiwan Really Matters to China."

105. Paragraph ten of the "Joint Statement: U.S.–Japan Security Consultative Committee," jointly issued on February 19, 2005, states, "In the region, common strategic objectives include: . . . Encourage the peaceful resolution of issues concerning the Taiwan Strait through dialogue." Japan, Ministry of Foreign Affairs, "Joint Statement: U.S.–Japan Security Consultative Committee"; Emma Chanlett-Avery, Mark E. Manyin, and William H. Cooper, "Japan-U.S. Relations: Issues for Congress," 6–7; and Wu Xinbo, "Taiwan Strait: Japan and the United States Alike, 'Fight Shoulder to Shoulder.'"

106. Kyodo News Service, "Japan, U.S. to Study Joint Operation Plan for Taiwan Contingency," and "China Expresses 'Grave Concern' Over Japan-U.S. Contingency Plan."

107. Liu Xinhua, *"Shilun Zhongguo fazhan haiquan de zhanlüe"* [On China's Strategy for the Development of Sea Power], 71.

108. Yiming, *"ZhongMeiRi Taihai shengsi jiaoliang."*

109. Hai Dun, *"Sanchong daolian zuo changying wangxiang fuzhu Zhongguo long,"* 45.

110. Operational is used here as a reference to tangible requirements for military operations. This is different from the usage employed by social science theorists who "operationalize" a theory by applying its principles to a body of empirical evidence to determine how well it predicts the outcomes specified.

111. Gray, "Inescapable Geography," 165.

112. China FBIS Report, "PRC Highlights: PLA Deputies on Anti-Secession Law, Military Reshuffles, More."

113. Osborne, "Landscapes, Memory, Monuments, and Commemoration," 39.

114. Lasater anticipates that if the United States should fail to respond effectively, this "would severely weaken U.S. influence, credibility, and power in the Asian Pacific" with "immediate and profound" implications that would be "favorable to the PRC and unfavorable to the United States." Martin L. Lasater, "A U.S. Perception of a PLA Invasion of Taiwan," 264.

115. John J. Mearsheimer, "Better to be Godzilla than Bambi," 47. Officially, the PRC government balks at suggestions that the expansion of its power is a threat to any other state and rejects implications that the "rise of China" is incompatible with the interests of the United States in Asia. Mearsheimer, himself, has been criticized in the PRC as fomenting the "China threat" thesis. See, for instance, Zhou Yihuang, "Will China's Rise Trigger Sino-U.S. Confrontation?"

116. On the PRC's quest for international status, consider Yong Deng, "Better than Power: International Status in Chinese Foreign Policy," 51–72.

117. Zhang Wenmu, *Shijie diyuan zhengzhi zhong de Zhongguo guoji anquan liyi fenxi* [Analyzing China's International Security Interests in World Geopolitics] as cited in Liu Zhongmin, *"Haiquan wenti yu lengzhanhou ZhongMei guanxi: maodun de renzhi yu jiannan de xuanze"* [Sea Power Issues and Post-Cold War Sino-U.S. Relations: Contradictory Perceptions and Difficult Options], 57.

118. This white paper was issued at a moment when the memory of the U.S. display of force (1996) in the region around Taiwan was fresh and while there was talk in Washington of including Taiwan in a theater missile defense system, something that the PRC opposed. Since the 2000 version of this report, the language was modified to make much the same point, but without explicitly invoking the image of Taiwan being incorporated into the security sphere of another state. See People's Republic of China, Information Office of the State Council, *China's National Defense.*

119. The "one country, two systems" model by which the PRC had long proposed to incorporate Taiwan into China was devised, in part, to reassure Taiwan that after peaceful reunification, it would be allowed to conduct its own commercial and foreign relations and maintain its own military. Even in the most generous of articulations by PRC officials, this arrangement was never described with sufficient specificity as to make evident what degree of control the PRC would reserve the right to impose on Taiwan if it chose to do so. For instance, there has been no public explication of what relationship Taiwan's military would have to the PLA under the "one country, two systems" model, in what domain Taiwan's armed forces could then operate autonomously, how much leeway the PRC would permit Taiwan to purchase arms from abroad, whether Taiwan would be permitted to determine for itself the extent of military-to-military relations it had with other states, or indications of Beijing's posture on other potentially thorny details in which, it is said, the devil resides.

120. However, unlike the suzerain relationships maintained by the Chinese court with peripheral states, an accession by Taiwan to the PRC's demand that Taipei recognize the "one China principle" might provide a foundation for the legitimate exercise of sovereign power on the island by Beijing on an occasion when doing so was judged to be expedient.

121. Hou Songling and Chi Diantang, *"Zhongguo zhoubian haiyu de zhanlüe diwei he diyuan zhanlüe jiazhi chutan"* [A Preliminary Exploration of the Geographic Position and Geostrategic Value of China's Peripheral Maritime Space], 51, citing Zhu Tingzhang, ed., *Zhongguo zhoubian anquan huanjing yu anquan zhanlüe* [China's Peripheral Security Environment and Security Strategy], 203; Shen Weilie and Lu Junyuan, eds., *Zhongguo guojia anquan dili* [The Geography of China's National Security], 343.

122. Shen Weilie and Lu Junyuan, eds., *Zhongguo guojia anquan dili*, 342.

123. Ibid., 343.

124. Ibid.; Liu Xinhua, *"Shilun Zhongguo fazhan haiquan de zhanlüe,"* 71.

125. Passages cited in this paragraph are all from Shen Weilie and Lu Junyuan, eds., *Zhongguo guojia anquan dili*, 344.

126. Ibid., 344–345.

127. Zhang Wenmu, "Sino-American Relations and the Question of Taiwan," 44.

128. *Ta Kung Pao*, "PRC Expert Gives Five Reasons China Should Not Allow Taiwan Independence."

129. Ibid.

130. Lou Douzi, "Looking at Navy and Air Force Dispositions Following Establishment Restructuring (1)." This article was contributed to an on-line forum provided by *Jiefangjun Bao* [Liberation Army Daily] by its author under what appears to be a pseudonym, making difficult an identification of the individual who wrote it or an assessment of the authority with which it was written.

131. *Jiefangjun Bao*, "China's Worries at Sea"; see also, Allen T. Cheng, "Taiwan Issue Hinders Mainland Security, Says Naval Strategist; The Comments Reflect Fear of an Enemy Launching an Invasion."

132. Cheng, "Taiwan Issue Hinders Mainland Security."

133. Ibid.

134. Ibid.

135. Li Nan, "The PLA's Evolving Warfighting Doctrine, Strategy and Tactics," 450, n. 43.

136. Ji Guoxing, "Rough Waters in the South China Sea"; Li Jinming and Li Dexia, "The Dotted Line on the Chinese Map of the South China Sea: A Note"; Peter Kien-Hong Yu, "The Chinese (broken) U-shaped Line in the South China Sea: Points, Lines, and Zones."

137. For more on the PRC's interests in and disputes about the islands of the South China Sea see Andrew Scobell, "China's Strategy Toward the South China Sea," 40–51; Stein Tønnesson, "Sino-Vietnamese Rapprochement and the South China Sea Irritant"; Chien-peng Chung, *Domestic Politics, International Bargaining and China's Territorial Disputes*, chapter 6.

138. Tang Ming and Shen Yaoshan, "An Ocean Dream Based on 6,000 Uninhabited Islands." For more on the establishment of territorial waters, see United Nations, "United Nations Convention on the Law of the Sea"; People's Republic of China, "Law of the People's Republic of China on the Territorial Sea and the Contiguous Zone," and "Statement of the Chinese Government on the Baseline of the Territorial Sea of the People's Republic of China."

139. See, for instance, *Zhongguo xiandai guoji guanxi yanjiusuo haishang tongdao anquan ketizu* [China Institute for Contemporary International Relations (CICIR) Maritime Security Taskforce], *Haishang tongdao anquan yu guoji hezuo* [Sea Lane Security and International Cooperation], esp. chapters 3, 5, 15, and 16.

140. Peter Howarth, *China's Rising Sea Power: The PLA Navy's Submarine Challenge*, 35. For a full description of the strategic nuclear objectives the PRC is assumed to have and impediments it faces in realizing those ambitions, see 28–40.

141. Ibid.

142. Ibid., 36–37.

143. Ibid., 37.

144. Ibid., 38.

145. Ibid., 38.

146. See the Web site of the Central Geological Survey (CGS), under the ROC's Ministry of Economic Affairs (MOEA), at http://www.moeacgs.gov.tw/english/twgeol/twgeol_setting.jsp.

147. Howarth, *China's Rising Sea Power*, 40.

148. According to the CGS, "The Central Range trends northerly for a length of 350 kilometers, with more than 25 summits exceeding 3,000 meters above sea level. The highest peak in the Hsuehshan range is Hsuehshan (Mt. Sylvia), which is 3,885 meters above sea level and the highest peak in the Central Range is Yushan (Mt. Morrison), 3,952 meters above sea level. Yushan is "the highest mountain in the island group on the western side of the Pacific Ocean." http://www.moeacgs.gov.tw/english/twgeol/twgeol_setting.jsp. The development of space-based detection capabilities would overcome the impediment.

149. Norman Friedman, *Seapower as Strategy: Navies and National Interests*, 40; and Till, *Seapower*, 155–157.

150. Although the rationale Howarth advances about Taiwan's significance to Beijing's nuclear strategy is consistent with the geostrategic rationales advanced in PRC publications and statements cited in this chapter, his work makes scant direct reference to contemporary PRC sources.

151. *Zhongguo Tongxun She*, "Article on Modernization of China's Navy."

152. Michael Pillsbury has described the manner in which debates about security issues have unfolded in the 1990s and commented on the nature of such debates. See, Michael Pillsbury, *China Debates the Future Security Environment*, xix–xxii, 17–25.

153. Tang Shiping and Cao Xiaoyang, "Land in the Middle, Part 3: The False Triangle."

154. The journal, which was shut down by the government in September, 2004, after publishing an article critical of North Korea's economy, had published six articles by Zhang Wenmu and four by Tang Shiping in the period 2001–2003. On the PRC's censorship of the journal, see the Web site of the Committee to Protect Journalists at http://www.cpj.org/cases04/asia_cases04/china.html.

155. Tang Shiping, *"Zailun Zhongguo de da zhanlüe"* [Once Again on China's Grand Strategy]. Tang also argues that to avoid igniting a security dilemma with the United States and other Asian states, the PRC should not build or acquire an aircraft carrier or vainly attempt to develop a "blue water navy," an ambition that Zhang Wenmu very much supported.

156. In one respect, Zhang Nianzhi is reflecting a pessimism about the likelihood of peaceful unification, or unification on any terms. He sees a difference in popular will on the mainland and in Taiwan as the source of the difficulties, thus acknowledging but moving well beyond the standard rhetorical focus on the leadership of Taiwan and the "separatists" who are ordinarily characterized as a small portion of the population. Zhang's essay accepts that the election victory of Chen Shui-bian in March, 2004, is an indication that there has been a fundamental shift in attitudes on Taiwan. This is not a view that had great currency in the PRC at the time Zhang wrote it. Chang Nien-chih [Zhang Nianzhi], "The Taiwan Issue Is a Part of the Peaceful Rise of China."

157. Ibid.

158. Liu Yazhou, *"Da guo ce"* [Grand Strategy].

159. Henrikson, "Distance and Foreign Policy," 448–449.

160. Zhang Zhaozhong and Guo Xiangxing, *Xiandai haijun qishi lu* [A Record of the Inspiring Modernization of the Navy] (Beijing: People's Liberation Army Press, 1993), 26–27, as cited in Johnston, "Chinese Realism(s)," n. 55.

CHAPTER 8

1. See, e.g., Julian J. Kuo, "Cross-Strait Relations: Buying Time Without Strategy," and Zhao Suisheng, "Reunification Strategy: Beijing Versus Lee Teng-hui," 204–240.

2. According to Paul Huth's analysis of 129 territorial disputes between 1950 and 1990, half entailed some form of militarization, but conflict involving 1,000 or more of the challenger's troops occurred in fewer than 20 percent of all cases. Huth, *Standing Your Ground*, 34.

3. Allan Collins points out as an aspiring hegemon the PRC may inadvertently trigger a state-induced security dilemma because other states—Taiwan, the United States, and Japan, for instance—"are unlikely to be able to distinguish this approach from a revisionist state that harbours malign intent. Indeed, given how aggressive the hegemon appears, they are much more likely to interpret its actions as hostile." Allan Collins, "Stated-Induced Security Dilemma," 34, 35.

4. Unfortunately, the literature on territorial disputes is dominated by studies that do not assess conflicts, such as the Taiwan issue, flowing from overlapping rivalries. Even a work that invites one to consider "A Unified Explanation of Territorial Conflict" is structured around the examination of data drawn from dyadic conflicts. Paul D. Senese and John A. Vasquez, "A Unified Explanation of Territorial Conflict: Testing the Impact of Sampling Bias, 1919–1992," 275–298.

5. The historical analogy is imperfect, as any historical analogy is. When Monroe was addressing Congress on December 2, 1823, his message was that the United States would not tolerate further colonial encroachments by European states on the independent states of the Western hemisphere. About the colonization of such states, Monroe said "we could not view any interposition for the purpose of oppressing them, or controlling in any other manner their destiny, by any European power in any other light than as the manifestation of an unfriendly disposition toward the United States." See, for instance, "The Monroe Doctrine," as reproduced by the Avalon Project, Yale Law School, at http://www.yale.edu/lawweb/avalon/monroe.htm and Ernest R. May, *The Making of the Monroe Doctrine*. In a *China Daily* commentary, Pang Zhongying, a professor at Tsinghua University Institute of International Studies, refutes the contention that the PRC has a Monroe Doctrine, as Jane Perlez suggests in her *New York Times* article of October 9, 2003, "The Charm From Beijing." Reflecting the prevailing view that the PRC eschews hegemonism, Pang asserts that "An Asian 'Monroe Doctrine' does not suit China given that China is not a hegemonic country." See Pang Zhongying, "Comment: Developing an Asian Partnership."

6. Grygiel, "The Case for Geopolitics," 7–9.

7. Goldstein, *Rising to the Challenge.*

8. Norimitsu Onishi and Howard W. French, "Ill Will Rising Between China and Japan As Old Grievances Fuel New Era of Rivalry," A1.

9. The concern about strategic realignment—with a focus on the United States and Japan—emerges in the PRC's 2006 white paper on national defense, which states, in part "There are growing complexities in the Asia-Pacific security environment. There is a new adjustment going on in the strategic alignment and relations among major countries in the region, and new changes have occurred in the hotspots in the region. The United States is accelerating its realignment of military deployment to enhance its military capability in the Asia-Pacific region. The United States and Japan are strengthening their military alliance in pursuit of operational integration. Japan seeks to revise its constitution and exercise collective self-defense. Its military posture is becoming more external-oriented." People's Republic of China, *China's National Defense in 2006*, sec. 1: The Security Environment.

10. According to the PRC's white paper on national defense of 2006, "China's national defense and military modernization, conducted on the basis of steady economic development, is the requirement of keeping up with new trends in the global revolution and

development in military affairs, and of maintaining China's national security and development." Ibid., Preface.

11. The extent of the PRC commitment to naval and maritime development is suggested in Christopher J. Pehrson, *String of Pearls: Meeting the Challenge of China's Rising Power Across the Asian Littoral.*

12. Gregory Kulacki, "Lost in Translation: A Tabloid Newspaper? An Amateur Space Enthusiast? U.S. Government Assessments of China's Military Prowess Are Sometimes Based upon Shaky Sources."

13. The possibility that the PLA uses the Taiwan issue as a lever to secure funding for expansion is taken up in Mel Gurtov and Byong-Moo Hwang, *China's Security: The New Roles of the Military,* 278.

14. Cole, "The PLA Navy and 'Active Defense.'"

15. Ian Nish, "An Overview of Relations Between China and Japan, 1895–1945," 613.

16. Herbert Butterfield, *History and Human Relations,* 21, as cited in Alan Collins, "State-induced Security Dilemma: Maintaining the Tragedy," 29.

17. In the absence of any universal metric of what constitutes a "status quo" power and what constitutes a "revisionist" or "expansionist" power, labeling the aims of the PRC to develop greater sea power and to assert sovereignty over Taiwan by reference to these terms will introduce in these final pages concepts that demand a fuller account than this work can offer.

18. For analysis of the cross-Strait dispute and its international implications from the vantage of the security dilemma, see Collins, "State-induced Security Dilemma."

19. The Sirens are creatures that feature in Greek mythology. From the island of Sirenum scopuli, they were said to have the head of a woman and the body of a bird and with the "irresistible charm of their song they lured mariners to their destruction on the rocks surrounding their island." Orpheus managed to save the Argonauts from the Sirens by taking out his lyre and singing "a song so clear and ringing that it drowned the sound of those lovely fatal voices." Odysseus, when he sailed by the Sirens, had his "sailors stuff their ears with wax. He had himself tied to the mast for he wanted to hear their beautiful voices." As the Sirens sang, "Odysseus' heart ran with longing but the ropes held him and the ship quickly sailed to safer waters" (Odyssey XII, 39). See, Micha F. Lindemans, "Sirens," *Encyclopedia Mythica,* from *Encyclopedia Mythica Online* at http://www.pantheon.org/articles/s/sirens.html.

Glossary

active defense (*jiji fangyu*) 积极防御
active offshore defense (*jijide jinhai fangyu*) 积极的近海防御
adopt a low profile (*taoguang yanghui*) 韬光养晦
Anti-Secession Law (*fan fenlie guojia fa*) 反分裂国家法
Association for Relations Across the Taiwan Strait (ARATS) (*Haixia liang'an guanxi xuehui*) 海峡两岸关系协会
beyond the seas (*haiwai*) 海外
border, boundary (*bianjie*) 边界
border area, frontier (*bianjiang*) 边疆
break through (*chongchu*) 冲出
break through this chain (*dapo zheigen suolian*) 打破这根锁链
bridgehead and springboard (*qiaoliang he tiaoban*) 桥梁和跳板
candidates' memorial (*gongche shangshu*) 公车上书
China proper (*neidi*) 内地
chip (*chouma*) 筹码
chokepoint (*zusedian*) 阻塞点
coastal/littoral defense (*yanhai fangyu*) 沿海防御
coastal waters/area (*jinhai haiyu*) 近海海域
command of the sea (*zhihaiquan*) 制海权
communist bandits (*gongfei*) 共匪
consensus (*gongshi*) 共识
contain (*ezhi*) 遏制
continental shelf (*dalujia*) 大陆架
Court of Colonial Affairs (*Lifanyuan*) 理藩院
defensive depth (*fangyu zongshen*) 防御纵深
de-Sinify (*fei Zhongguohua*) 非中国化
elastic/flexible diplomacy (*tanxing waijiao*) 弹性外交
entering the map (*ru bantu*) 入版图
Exclusive Economic Zone (EEZ) (*zhuanshu jingjiqu*) 专属经济区

first island chain (*diyi daolian*) 第一岛链

foreign affairs office (Qing Dynasty) (*Zongli yamen*) 总理衙门

forward strategic chain (*qianyan zhanlüe lianhuan*) 前沿战略连环

frontier, border (*bianjie*) 边界

guards (*e*) 扼

gateway to the sea (*tongwang dahai de menhu*) 通往大海的门户

geopolitics (*diyuan zhengzhi*) 地缘政治

geostrategic (*diyuan zhanlüe*) 地缘战略

gradual extension of strategic depth for offshore defensive operations (*zhubu zengda jinhai fangyu de zhanlüe zongshen*) 逐步增大近海防御的战略纵深

hedge (*fanli*) 藩篱

high degree of autonomy (*gaodu de zizhiquan*) 高度的自治权

international living space (*guoji shengcun kongjian*) 国际生存空间

Jiang's eight points (*Jiang badian*) 江八点

listen to his words, watch his actions [judge by deeds, not just words] (*ting qi yan, guan qi xing*) 听其言观其行

local wars under modern, high-tech conditions (*gao jishu tiaojianxia jubu zhanzheng*) 高技术条件下局部战争

look down and control East Asia (*kanzhi DongYa*) 瞰制东亚

lost territory (*shi di*) 失地

lure the enemy in deep (*youdi shenru*) 诱敌深入

maritime hegemony (*haishang baquan*) 海上霸权

maritime space (*haiyu*) 海域

military strategy (*junshi zhanlüe*) 军事战略

National Security Law (*anquanfa*) 安全法

National Unification Council (*Guojia tongyi weiyuanhui*) 国家统一委员会

National Unification Guidelines (*Guojia tongyi gangling*) 国家统一纲领

natural defensive barrier (*tianran pingzhang*) 天然屏障

offshore defense (*jinyang fangyu*) 近洋防御

one China principle (*yige Zhongguo yuanze*) 一个中国原则

one China, different interpretations (*yige Zhongguo gezi biaoshu*) 一个中国各自表述

one country, two systems (*yiguo liangzhi*) 一国两制

peaceful unification (*heping tongyi*) 和平统一

peripheral area (*zhoubian diqu*) 周边地区

periphery (*zhoubian*) 周边

pin 品

pragmatic diplomacy (*wushi waijiao*) 务实外交

protective screen (*pingzhang*) 屏障

protective screen of the interior provinces (*fudi shusheng zhi pingzhang*) 腹地数省之屏障

rat running across the street with everybody shouting 'smack it' (*laoshu guojie, renren handa*) 老鼠过街, 人人喊打

restoration (*guangfu*) 光复

[re]unification (*tongyi*) 统一

sea control (*zhihai*) 制海

sea-lanes of communication (*haishang jiaotongxian*) 海上交通线

sea/maritime hegemony (*haiyang baquan*) 海洋霸权

sea/maritime power (*haishang liliang*) 海上力量

sea/maritime power/rights (*haishang quanli*) 海上权力

second island chain (*dier daolian*) 第二岛链

separatist activities (*fenlie zhuyi de huodong*) 分裂主义的活动

separatists, splittists (*fenliezhuyi fenzi*) 分裂主义分子

special state-to-state relationship (*teshu guo yu guo guanxi*) 特殊国与国关系

stepping stone/springboard (*tiaoban*) 跳板

Straits Exchange Foundation (SEF) (*Haixia jiaoliu jijinhui*) 海峡交流基金会

strategic depth (*zhanlüe zongshen*) 战略纵深

strategic frontier, forward position (*zhanlüe qianyan*) 战略前沿

strategic gateway of the southeast (*dongnan zhi suoyue*) 东南之锁钥

strategic goals (*zhanlüe mudi*) 战略目的

strategy (*zhanlüe*) 战略

tactics (*zhanshu*) 战术

Taiwan issue/question (*Taiwan wenti*) 台湾问题

Temporary Provisions Effective During the Period of Communist Rebellion (*Dongyuan kanluan shiqi linshi*) 动员戡乱时期临时

the hard harder, the soft softer (*ying de geng ying ruan de geng ruan*) 硬的更硬软的更软

throat (*yanhou*) 咽喉

two-state theory (*liangguolun*) 两国论

unsinkable aircraft carrier ([*yong*] *bu chenmo de hangkong mujian*) [永] 不沉没的航空母舰

use Taiwan to control China (*yi Tai zhi Hua*) 以台治华

vacation diplomacy (*dujia waijiao*) 度假外交

wilderness (*huangfu*) 荒服

Works Cited

ABBREVIATIONS IN WORKS CITED

CAJ   China Academic Journals. CAJ is a database in the China
                National Knowledge Infrastructure (CNKI) and is available
                from East View Information Services. http://china.eastview
                .com.
CWIHP   Cold War International History Project. www.CWIHP.org.
LexisNexis   LexisNexis is a division of Reed Elsevier. http://web.
                lexis-nexis.com.
NSA   National Security Archive. http://nsarchive.chadwyck.com.
ProQuest   ProQuest Historical Newspapers. http://proquest.umi.com.
WNC   World News Connection is provided to the National
                Technical Information Service (NTIS) by the Foreign
                Broadcast Information Service (FBIS) and is available from
                Dialog, a Thompson business. http://wnc.dialog.com.

Agence France-Presse. "US Confirms It Is Posting Military Officers to Taiwan Mission."
    December 21, 2004. LexisNexis.
Allen, Kenneth W., and Jeffrey M. Allen. "Controlling the Airspace over the Taiwan Strait."
    In Tsang, ed. If China Attacks Taiwan: Military Strategy, Politics, and Economics, 94–121.
Anderson, Benedict. Imagined Communities: Reflections on the Origin and Spread of National-
    ism. London: Verso, 1983.

Andrade, Tonio. "The Company's Chinese Pirates: How the Dutch East India Company Tried to Lead a Coalition of Pirates to War against China, 1621-1662." *Journal of World History* (December 2004). http://www.historycooperative.org/journals/jwh/15.4/andrade.html.

———. "Pirates, Pelts, and Promises: The Sino-Dutch Colony of Seventeenth-Century Taiwan and the Aboriginal Village of Favorolang." *Journal of Asian Studies* 64, no. 2 (May 2005): 295–321.

Archaya, Amitav. "International Relations Theory and Cross-Strait Relations." A paper presented to the International Forum on Peace and Security in the Taiwan Strait, Taipei, Taiwan, July 26–28, 1999. www.taiwansecurity.org.

The Atlantic Charter. www.yale.edu/lawweb/avalon/wwii/atlantic.htm.

l'Atlas Miller. Bibliothèque nationale de France (Paris). Department Cartes et Plans. Numéro d'entré: DON 0400383, BN, C.Pl., Ge DD 6607, recueil de pl. Ge A 1454.

Baert, Patrick. "China Quietly Marks Two-Year Countdown to Macau's Return." *Agence France-Presse*. December 21, 1997. LexisNexis.

Baron, Louis. "Crossword Puzzles." *New York Times*. November 8, 1942. ProQuest.

BBC Summary of World Broadcasts. "Cross-Strait Relations; Taiwan President's Six Points for Cross-Strait Relations." *Lien Ho Pao* (Taipei) [United Daily News]. April 9, 1995. LexisNexis.

Beijing Xinhua Domestic Service. "Comparison: Live News Conference by Zhu Rongji." March 15, 2000. WNC Document Number: 0FRIOGW00WGIP3.

Benson, Linda. *The Ili Rebellion: The Moslem Challenge to Chinese Authority in Xinjiang, 1944–1949*. Armonk, NY: M. E. Sharpe, 1990.

Bernstein, Richard, and Ross H. Munro. *The Coming Conflict with China*. New York: Knopf, 1997.

Binnendijk, Hans, and Ronald N. Montaperto. *Strategic Trends in China*. Washington, DC: National Defense University Press, 1998.

Bitzinger, Richard A. "Research Report—Just the Facts, Ma'am: The Challenge of Analysing and Assessing Chinese Military Expenditures." *The China Quarterly* 173 (2003): 164–175.

Bland, J. O. P. *Li Hung-chang*. London: Constable and Company, Ltd., 1917.

Borg, Dorothy. *The United States and the Far Eastern Crisis of 1933–1938: From the Manchurian Incident Through the Initial Stage of the Undeclared Sino-Japanese War*. Cambridge: Harvard University Press, 1964.

Borg, Dorothy, and Waldo Heinrichs, eds. *Uncertain Years: Chinese-American Relations, 1947–1950*. New York: Columbia University Press, 1980.

Bradsher, Keith. "Taiwan's Leader Defies Beijing's Warnings." *New York Times*. February 28, 2006, A-9. LexisNexis.

Brahm, Laurence J. *China as No. 1: The New Superpower Takes Centre Stage*. Oxford: Butterworth-Heinemann, 1996.

Brockman, Fletcher S. "Foreign Control at Peking Means War, Says Sun Yat-sen." *New York Times*. July 22, 1923, xx5 (page 1). ProQuest.

Brown, Melissa J. *Is Taiwan Chinese? The Impact of Culture, Power, and Migration on Changing Identities*. Berkeley: University of California Press, 2004.

Brown, Michael E., Owen R. Coté, Jr., Sean M. Lynn-Jones, and Steven E. Miller, eds. *The Rise of China: An International Security Reader*. Cambridge: MIT Press, 2000.

Bullock, Christopher R. "China's Bluewater Ambitions: The Continental Realities of Chinese Naval Strategies." *Georgetown Journal of International Affairs* 105 (Summer/Fall 2002): 57–63.

Burr, William Burr, ed. *The Kissinger Transcripts: The Top Secret Talks with Beijing and Moscow*. New York: The New Press, 1998.

Burrows, Edwin G., and Mike Wallace. *Gotham: A History of New York City to 1898*. New York: Oxford University Press, 1999.

Bush, Richard C. *At Cross Purposes: U.S.–Taiwan Relations Since 1942*. Armonk, NY: M. E. Sharpe, 2004.

———. "Chinese Decisionmaking Under Stress: The Taiwan Strait, 1995–2004." In Scobell and Wortzel, eds. *Chinese National Security Decisionmaking Under Stress*, 135–60.

———. "Lee Teng-hui and Separatism." In Tucker, ed., *Dangerous Strait*, 70–92.

Butterfield, Herbert. *History and Human Relations*. London: Collins, 1951.

Callahan, William A. "National Insecurities: Humiliation, Salvation, and Chinese Nationalism." *Alternatives* 29 (2004): 199–218.

Campbell, Kurt M., and Derek J. Mitchell. "Crisis in the Taiwan Strait." *Foreign Affairs* 80 (July/August 2001): 14–25.

Campbell, William. *Formosa Under the Dutch: Described From Contemporary Records, With Explanatory Notes and a Bibliography of the Island*. London: Kegan Paul, 1903.

Cao Zhi and Chen Wanjun. "Hu Jintao Emphasizes When Meeting Deputies to 10th Navy CPC Congress, Follow the Principle of Integrating Revolutionization, Modernization, and Regularization, and Forge a Powerful People's Navy That Meets the Demands of our Army's Historic Mission; Guo Boxiong, Cao Gangchuan, and Xu Caihou Attend." *Xinhua Domestic Service*. December 27, 2006, reproduced as "Hu Jintao Calls for Building Strong Navy." WNC NewsEdge Document Number: 200612271477.1 _a3c70078befcff23.

Carlson, Evans Fordyce. *Twin Stars of China: A Behind-the-Scenes Story of China's Valiant Struggle for Existence by a U.S. Marine who Lived and Moved with the People*. New York: Dodd, Mead, and Company, 1941.

Central Broadcasting System (Taipei). "Taiwan and China:" First Foreign Policy Report Out; Recognized 'The Truth of National Separation.'" BBC Summary of World Broadcasts. January 21, 1993. LexisNexis.

Central News Agency (Taipei). "Former MAC Head Admits Coining '1992 Consensus' Term." February 21, 2006. www.cna.com.tw/eng.

———. "Taipei to Recognize Communist China as 'Political Entity.'" April 30, 1991. LexisNexis.

———. "Taiwan and China: Taiwan Foreign Minster's End of Year Address." January 7, 1993. BBC Summary of World Broadcasts. LexisNexis.

Central People's Broadcasting Station (Beijing). "Chinese Radio: Taiwan President Will See only a Pig's Reflection." BBC Summary of World Broadcasts. August 21, 1999. LexisNexis.

Chai, Winberg, ed. *Chinese: Mainland and Taiwan: A Study of Historical, Cultural, Economic and Political Relations*. Chicago: Third World Institute of Policy Research, 1994.

Chan, Alfred. "A Young Turk in China's Establishment: The Military Writings of Liu Yazhou." *China Brief: A Journal of Analysis and Information* 5, no. 19 (September 13, 2005): 3–5.

Chang Maubo. "Three Parties United in Opposing Abolition of NUC." *Central News Agency* (Taipei). February 27, 2006. http://english.www.gov.tw/TaiwanHeadlines/index. jsp?recordid=17669&action=CNA.

Chang Nien-chih [Zhang Nianzhi]. "The Taiwan Issue Is a Part of the Peaceful Rise of China." *Ta Kung Pao* (Hong Kong). March 28, 2004. Reproduced as "TKP Article Views Different Popular Will Between Mainland, Taiwan." WNC Document Number: ohve7ttoobripf.

Chang, S. C. "KMT Supports Motion to Recall President." *Central News Agency* (Taipei). February 27, 2006. LexisNexis.

Chanlett-Avery, Emma, Mark E. Manyin, and William H. Cooper. *Japan-U.S. Relations: Issues for Congress*. Washington, DC: The Library of Congress, Congressional Research Service, CRS Issue Brief (IB97004). March 31, 2006.

Chao Chien-min. "The Republic of China's Foreign Relations Under President Lee Teng-hui: A Balance Sheet." In Dickson and Chao, eds. *Assessing the Lee Teng-hui Legacy in Taiwan's Politics: Democratic Consolidation and External Relations*, 177–203.

Chao, Linda, and Ramon H. Myers. *The First Chinese Democracy: Political Life in the Republic of China*. Baltimore: Johns Hopkins University Press, 1998.

Chase, Michael A. "U.S.–Taiwan Security Cooperation: Enhancing an Unofficial Relationship." In Tucker, ed. *Dangerous Strait,* 162–185.

Chen, Edward I-te. "Four Chinese Leaders and the Reunification of Taiwan: 1900–1943." A paper presented at the 38th Annual Conference of the American Association for Chinese Studies, University of Maryland, College Park, November 8–10, 1996.

———. "Japan's Decision to Annex Taiwan: A Study of Ito-Mutsu Diplomacy, 1894–1895." *The Journal of Asian Studies* 37, no. 1 (November 1977): 61–72.

Chen Guangzhong. *"Lun diyuan huanjing yu diyuan zhanlüe dui junshi zhanlüe de yingxiang"* [On the Influence of the Geopolitical Environment and Geostrategy on Military Strategy]. *Junshi lishi yanjiu* (2000, no. 2): 171–184. CAJ.

Chen Jian. *China's Road to the Korean War: The Making of the Sino-American Confrontation*. New York: Columbia University Press, 1994.

———. *Mao's China and the Cold War*. Chapel Hill: University of North Carolina Press, 2001.

Chen Shui-bian. "President Chen Shui-bian's Inaugural Speech, 'Paving the Way for a Sustainable Taiwan.'" May 20, 2004. http://www.president.gov. tw/en/.

Ch'en Ta-tuan. "Sino-Ryukyuan Relations in the 19th Century." Ph.D. diss., University of Indiana, 1963, 104. Cited in Leung, "The Quasi-War in East Asia," 263–264.

Cheng, Allen T. "Taiwan Issue Hinders Mainland Security, Says Naval Strategist; The Comments Reflect Fear of an 'Enemy' Launching an Invasion." *South China Morning Post.* January 2, 2004. LexisNexis.

Cheng, Tun-jen. "The Mainland China-Taiwan Dyad as a Research Program." In Cheng, Huang, and Wu, eds. *Inherited Rivalry: Conflict Across the Taiwan Straits*, 1–22.

Cheng, Tun-jen, Chi Huang, and Samuel S. G. Wu, eds. *Inherited Rivalry: Conflict Across the Taiwan Straits*. Boulder and London: Lynne Rienner, 1995.

Cheng Yawen. *"Cong shijie tixi shijiao sikao Zhongguo diyuan zhanlüe wenti"* [Reflections on China's Geostrategy from the Perspective of the World System]. *Shijie jingji yu zhengzhi* [World Economics and Politics], no. 10 (2004).

Chiang Kai-shek. *All We Are and All We Have: Speeches and Messages Since Pearl Harbor, December 9, 1941–November 17, 1942*. New York: the John Day Company, 1948.

———. *China's Destiny*. New York: Macmillan Company, 1947.

———. *China's Destiny and Chinese Economic Theory, with Notes and Commentary by Philip Jaffe*. New York: Roy Publishers, 1947.

———. *Resistance and Reconstruction: Messages During China's Six Years of War 1937–1943*. New York and London: Harper & Brothers Publishers, 1943.

China Daily (Beijing). "China Countdown to Macao's Return Starts; Preparatory Body Set Up." May 6, 1998. LexisNexis.

———. "U.S. Should Keep Its Hands off Taiwan." July 29, 2005. http://taiwansecurity .org/News/2005/CD-290705.htm.

China FBIS Report. "PRC Highlights: PLA Deputies on Anti-Secession Law, Military Reshuffles, More." *Ta Kung Pao* (Hong Kong). March 19, 2005. WNC NewsEdge Document Number: 200503191477.1_e8ec0e503ba0c785.

Chinese Ministry of Information. *The Collected Wartime Messages of Generalissimo Chiang Kai-shek, 1937–1945, vol. 1*. New York: John Day Company, 1946.

Chiu Hung-dah, ed. *China and the Taiwan Issue*. New York: Praeger, 1979.

———. "Comparison of the Nationalist and Communist Chinese Views of Unequal Treaties." In Cohen, ed. *China's Practice of International Law*, 239–267.

Christensen, Thomas J. "Coercive Contradictions: *Zhanyixue*, PLA Doctrine, and Taiwan Scenarios." In Mulvenon and Finkelstein, eds. *China's Revolution in Doctrinal Affairs*, 307–327.

———. *Useful Adversaries: Grand Strategy, Domestic Mobilization, and Sino-American Conflict, 1947–1958*. Princeton: Princeton University Press, 1996.

Chung Chien-peng. *Domestic Politics, International Bargaining and China's Territorial Disputes*. London: Routledge, 2004.

Cohen, Jerome Alan, ed. *China's Practice of International Law: Some Case Studies*. Cambridge: Harvard University Press, 1972.

Cole, Bernard D. "Command of the Sea." In Tsang, ed. *If China Attacks Taiwan*, 122–158.

———. *The Great Wall at Sea: China's Navy Enters the Twenty-first Century*. Annapolis: Naval Institute Press, 2001.

———. "The Modernization of the PLAN and Taiwan's Security." In Edmonds and Tsai, eds. *Taiwan's Maritime Security*, 52–76.

———. "The Organization of the People's Liberation Army Navy." In Mulvenon and Yang, eds. *The People's Liberation Army as Organization*, 466–471.

———. "The PLA Navy and 'Active Defense.'" In Flanagan and Marti, eds. *The People's Liberation Army and China in Transition*, 129–138.

Collins, Alan. "State-induced Security Dilemma: Maintaining the Tragedy." *Cooperation and Conflict: Journal of the Nordic International Studies Association* 39, no. 1 (2004): 27–44.

Collins, John M. *Military Geography: For Professionals and the Public*. Washington, DC: Brassey's, 1998.

Corcuff, Stéphane, ed. *Memories of the Future: National Identity Issues and the Search for a New Taiwan*. Armonk, NY: M. E. Sharpe, 2002.

Cortesão, Armando, and Avelino Teixeira da Mota. *Portugaliae monumenta cartographica*, vol. 1. Lisbon: n.p., 1960.

Crane, Keith, Roger Cliff, Evan Medeiros, James Mulvenon, and William Overholt. *Modernizing China's Military Opportunities and Constraints*. Santa Monica, CA: RAND Corporation, 2005.

Crossley, Pamela Kyle. *A Translucent Mirror: History and Identity in Qing Imperial Ideology*. Berkeley: University of California Press, 1999.

Culver, John, and Michael Pillsbury. "Defense Policy and Posture II." In Binnendijk and Montaperto, *Strategic Trends in China*, sess. five.

Dai Xu. *"Kongjun zhongjiang Liu Yazhou tan Ilake zhanzheng fenxi wo jun fazhan fangxiang"* [Air Force Lieutenant General Liu Yazhou Discusses the Iraq War and Analyzes the Development of the Air Force]. *Kongjun junshi xueshu* [Military Science of the Air Force] n.d. http://news.sina.com.cn/c/2004-05-31/ba3372448.shtml.

Dallek, Robert. *Franklin D. Roosevelt and American Foreign Policy, 1932–1945*. New York and Oxford: Oxford University Press, 1995.

Davidson, James W. *The Island of Formosa, Past and Present; History, People, Resources, and Commercial Prospects: Tea, Camphor, Sugar, Gold, Coal, Sulphur, Economical Plants, and Other Productions*. Macmillan/Kelley and Walsh, 1903. Reprinted, Taipei: Southern Materials Center/Oxford University Press, 1988.

Degras, Jane, ed. *The Communist International, 1919–1943, Documents, volume II: 1923–1928*. London: Oxford University Press, 1960.

Deng Xiaoping. *"Zhongguo dalu he Taiwan heping tongyi shexiang"* [An Idea for the Peaceful Unification of Mainland China and Taiwan]. *Renmin Ribao* (June 26, 1983). In *Collected Works of Deng Xiaoping*, vol. 3. http://english.people. com.cn/dengxp/contents3.html.

Deng Yong. "Better than Power: International Status in Chinese Foreign Policy." In Deng and Wang, eds. *China Rising*, 51–72.

———. "Diplomatic Consequences." In Tsang, ed. *If China Attacks Taiwan*, 179–192.

Deng Yong and Fei-ling Wang, eds. *China Rising: Power and Motivation in Chinese Foreign Policy*. Lanham, MD: Rowman and Littlefield, 2005.

Des Forges, Roger, and Xu Luo. "China as a Non-Hegemonic Superpower? The Uses of History Among the *China Can Say No* Writers and Their Critics." *Critical Asian Studies* 33, no. 4 (2001): 483–508.

Di Cosmo, Nicola. "Qing Colonial Administration in Inner Asia." *The International History Review* 20, no. 2 (June 1998): 287–309.

Dickson, Bruce J., and Chien-min Chao, eds. *Assessing the Lee Teng-hui Legacy in Taiwan's Politics: Democratic Consolidation and External Relations*. Armonk, NY: M. E. Sharpe, 2002.

Diehl, Paul F. "Territory and International Conflict: An Overview." In Diehl, ed. *A Road Map to War*, viii–xx.

———. "What Are They Fighting For? The Importance of Issues in International Conflict Research." *Journal of Peace Research* 29, no. 3 (August 1992): 333–344.

———, ed. *A Road Map to War: Territorial Dimensions of International Conflict*. Nashville: Vanderbilt University Press, 1999.

———, ed. *The Dynamics of Enduring Rivalries*. Urbana: University of Illinois Press, 1998.

"Discussion between N. S. Khrushchev and Mao Zedong, October 3, 1959." Identifier 5034C225-96B6-175C-904C329159CA3F25. CWIHP.

"Diyuan zhanlüe zhong de Taiwan jiqi dui daguo anquan de zuoyong" [The Geostrategic Role of Taiwan and the Security of the Great Powers]. *Taiwan yanjiu* [Taiwan Research] (1996, no. 1). CAJ.

Dodge, Paul. "Circumventing Sea Power: Chinese Strategies to Deter U.S. Intervention in Taiwan." *Comparative Strategy* 23, no. 4–5 (October/December 2004): 391–409.

Dolman, Everett C. "Geostrategy in the Space Age: An Astropolitical Analysis." In Gray and Sloan, eds. *Geopolitics, Geography, and Strategy*, 83–106.

Duara, Prasenjit. *Rescuing History from the Nation: Questioning Narratives of Modern China*. Chicago: University of Chicago Press, 1995.

Edmonds, Martin, and Michael M. Tsai, eds. *Taiwan's Maritime Security*. London: Routledge, 2003.

Elleman, Bruce A. *Modern Chinese Warfare, 1795–1989*. London: Routledge, 2001.

Elliott, Mark C. *The Manchu Way: The Eight Banners and Ethnic Identity in Late Imperial China*. Stanford: Stanford University Press, 2001.

Enav, Peter. "Taiwan Leader Halts China Unification Panel, Drawing Protest from Beijing." *Associated Press*. February 28, 2006. LexisNexis.

Eskildsen, Robert. "Leading the Natives to Civilization: The Colonial Dimension of the Taiwan Expedition." Harvard University, Edwin O. Reischauer Institute of Japanese Studies. *Occasional Papers in Japanese Studies* (2003, no. 1) (March 2003). http://www.fas.harvard.edu/~rijs/pdfs/eskildsen.pdf.

Evans, Peter B., Dietrich Rueschemeyer, and Theda Skocpol, eds. *Bringing the State Back In.* Cambridge: Cambridge University Press, 1985.

Fairbank, John King, Martha Henderson Coolidge, and Richard J. Smith. *H. B. Morse: Customs Commissioner and Historian of China.* Lexington: University Press of Kentucky, 1995.

Feigenbaum, Evan A. "China's Challenge to *Pax Americana.*" *Washington Quarterly* 24, no. 3 (Summer 2001): 31–43.

Finkelstein, David M. "China's National Military Strategy." In Mulvenon and Yang, eds. *The People's Liberation Army in the Information Age,* 99–145.

Fishman, Ted C. *China, Inc.: How the Rise of the Next Superpower Challenges America and the World.* New York: Scribner, 2005.

Flanagan, Stephen J., and Michael E. Marti, eds. *The People's Liberation Army and China in Transition.* Washington, DC: Center for the Study of Chinese Military Affairs, National Defense University, 2003.

Florcruz, Jaime A. "The View From Beijing: Speaking Loud Enough for a Home Audience to Hear." *TIME Asia.* March 6, 2000. http://www.time.com/time/asia/magazine/2000/0306/taiwan.beijing3.html.

Foster, John W. *Diary Written by John Watson Foster, Shimonoseki–1895.* Typescript copy, 17. Collection no. C0031. Folder 2. Department of Rare Books and Special Collections. Firestone Library, Princeton University.

———. *Diplomatic Memoirs, vol. II, 1891–1909.* Boston: Houghton Mifflin, 1909. Reprinted, Elibron Classics, 2001.

Fravel, M. Taylor. "Regime Insecurity and International Cooperation: Explaining China's Compromises in Territorial Disputes." *International Security* 30, no. 2 (Fall 2005): 46–83.

———. "The Long March to Peace: Explaining China's Settlement of Territorial Disputes." Ph.D. diss., Stanford University, 2003.

Friedman, Edward, ed. "China's Dilemma on Using Military Force." In Friedman, ed. *China's Rise, Taiwan's Dilemmas and International Peace,* 205–226.

———. *China's Rise, Taiwan's Dilemmas and International Peace.* London and New York: Routledge, 2006.

Friedman, Norman. *Seapower as Strategy: Navies and National Interests.* Annapolis, MD: Naval Institute Press, 2001.

Fung, Edmund S. K. "The Chinese Nationalists and the Unequal Treaties, 1924–1931." *Modern Asian Studies* 21, no. 4 (1987): 793–819.

Gaddis, John Lewis. "The Strategic Perspective: The Rise and Fall of the 'Defensive Perimeter' Concept, 1947–1951." In Borg and Heinrichs, eds. *Uncertain Years: Chinese-American Relations, 1947–1950,* 61–118.

Gale, Esson M., trans. *Discourses on Salt and Iron: A Debate on State Control of Commerce and Industry in Ancient China, Chapters I–XXVIII.* Translated from the Chinese of Huan K'uan with introduction and notes. Taipei: Ch'eng-wen Publishing Company, 1967.

Garver, John W. "China's U.S. Policies." In Deng and Wang, eds. *China Rising,* 201–243.

———. *Protracted Contest: Sino-Indian Rivalry in the Twentieth Century.* Seattle: University of Washington Press, 2001.

———. *The Sino-American Alliance: Nationalist China and American Cold War Strategy in Asia.* Armonk, NY: M. E. Sharpe, 1997.

Gill, Bates. "Chinese Military Hardware and Technology Acquisitions of Concern to Taiwan." In Lilley and Downs, eds. *Crisis in the Taiwan Strait*, 105–128.

Goertz, Gary, and Paul F. Diehl. *Territorial Changes and International Conflict*. London: Routledge, 1992.

———. "Enduring Rivalries: Theoretical Constructs and Empirical Patterns." *International Studies Quarterly* 37, no. 2 (June 1993): 147–171.

Goldberg, Jeffrey. "China's Mahan." *United States Naval Institute Proceedings* 122, no. 3 (March 1996): 44–47.

Goldman, Emily, and Tom Mahnken, eds. *The Information Revolution in Asia*. Houndmills, UK: Palgrave Macmillan, 2004.

Goldstein, Avery. *Rising to the Challenge: China's Grand Strategy and International Security*. Stanford: Stanford University Press, 2005.

Goldstein, Lyle, and Bill Murray. "China's Subs Lead the Way." *Naval Institute Proceedings*. (March 2003): 58–61.

Goldstein, Steven M. "The Chinese Revolution and the Colonial Areas: The View form [sic] Yenan, 1937–1941." *The China Quarterly* 75 (September 1978): 594–622.

———. "Sino-American Relations, 1948–1950: Lost Chance or No Chance?" In Harding and Yuan, eds. *Sino-American Relations, 1945–1955*, 119–142.

———. "The United States and the Republic of China, 1949–1978: Suspicious Allies." *Working Paper*. Stanford University, Asia-Pacific Research Center (February 2000). Publication Number 0-9653935-9-3.

Gong, Gerrit W., ed. *Taiwan Strait Dilemmas: China-Taiwan-U.S. Policies in the New Century*. Washington: CSIS Press, 2000.

Gong Li. "Tension Across the Taiwan Strait in the 1950s: Chinese Strategy and Tactics." In Ross and Jiang, eds. *Re-examining the Cold War*, 141–172.

———. "The Official Perspective: What Chinese Government Officials Think of America." In McGiffert, ed. *Chinese Images of the United States*, 25–32.

Gordon, Leonard H. D. "Taiwan and the Powers: 1840–1895." In Gordon, ed. *Taiwan: Studies in Chinese Local History*, 93–116.

———, ed. *Taiwan: Studies in Chinese Local History*. New York: Columbia University Press, 1970.

Gray, Colin S. "Inescapable Geography." In Gray and Sloan, *Geopolitics, Geography and Strategy*, 161–177.

Gray, Colin S., and Geoffrey Sloan. *Geopolitics, Geography and Strategy*. London: Frank Cass, 1999.

Grygiel, Jakub Joachim. "The Case for Geopolitics: Venice, Ottoman Empire, and Ming China." Ph.D. diss., Princeton University, 2002.

Gurtov, Mel, and Byong-Moo Hwang. *China's Security: The New Roles of the Military*. Boulder: Lynne Rienner, 1998.

Hai Dun. *"Sanchong daolian zuo changying wangxiang fuzhu Zhongguo long—Zhongguo zhoubian de Meiguo hangmu jidi"* [The Triple Island Chain as a Long Tassel Vainly Hoping to Bind the Chinese Dragon—U.S. Aircraft Carrier Bases on China's Periphery]. *Jianzai wuqi* [Shipborne Weapons] (October 2004): 44-45. CAJ.

Hall, Ron. "Henry H. Bell and Alexander S. Mackenzie Died Almost Unnoticed on the Faraway Asiatic Station." *Military History* 17, no. 1 (April 2000): 22.

Halloran, Richard. "Taiwan." *Parameters* (Spring 2003): 22–34.

Harding, Harry, and Yuan Ming, eds. *Sino-American Relations, 1945–1955: A Joint Reassessment of a Critical Decade*. Wilmington, DE: SR Books, 1989.

Harkavy, Robert. "Strategic Geography and the Greater Middle East." *Naval War College Review* 54, no. 4 (Autumn 2001): 37–54.

Hashikawa, Bunsho. "Japanese Perspectives on Asia: From Dissociation to Coprosperity." In Iriye, ed. *The Chinese and the Japanese,* 328–355.

He Di. "The Last Campaign to Unify China; The CCP's Unrealized Plan to Liberate Taiwan, 1949–1950." In Ryan, Finkelstein, and McDevitt, eds. *Chinese Warfighting,* 73–90.

He Duanduan, Wei Chao, and Hao Tan. *"Taihai guancha: 'Taidu'—xueruo liang'an huyi de Zhongguo haifang"* [Taiwan Strait Observation: 'Taiwan Independence' —Weakens Both Sides of China's Coastal Defense]. *Chuanjian zhishi* [Naval and Merchant Ships] (March 11, 2002). http://www. futurechina.org.tw/fcn/ideas/fcs20020311.htm.

Henrikson, Alan K. "Distance and Foreign Policy: A Political Geography Approach." *International Political Science Review* 23, no. 4 (2002): 437–466.

Hensel, Paul R. "Contentious Issues and World Politics: The Management of Territorial Claims in the Americas, 1816–1992." *International Studies Quarterly* 45, no. 1 (March 2001): 81–109.

Hilali, A. Z. "China: Geo-political Environment and Security Perceptions." *China Report* 30, no. 3 (July/September 1994): 309–330.

Holmes, James R. "Mahan Is Alive in China." *The National Interest.* July 7, 2004. http:// www.inthenationalinterest.com/Articles/Vol3Issue27/ Vol3Issue27Mahan.html.

Holmes, James R., and Toshi Yoshihara. "The Influence of Mahan on China's Maritime Strategy." *Comparative Strategy* 24, no. 1 (January–March 2005): 23–51.

Hostetler, Laura. *Qing Colonial Enterprise: Ethnography and Cartography in Early Modern China.* Chicago: University of Chicago Press, 2001.

Hou Songling and Chi Diantang. *"Zhongguo zhoubian haiyu de zhanlüe diwei he diyuan zhanlüe jiazhi chutan"* [Preliminary Exploration of the Geostrategic Position and Value of China's Peripheral Maritime Space]. *Dangdai yatai* [Contemporary Pacific] 2003, no. 10: 47–52. CAJ.

Howarth, Peter. *China's Rising Sea Power: The PLA Navy's Submarine Challenge.* London and New York: Routledge, 2006.

Hsiao, Frank S. T., and Lawrence R. Sullivan. "The Chinese Communist Party and the Status of Taiwan, 1928–1943." *Pacific Affairs* 52, no. 3 (Autumn 1979): 446–467.

Hsieh Chiao-min. *Taiwan—Ilha Formosa: A Geography in Perspective.* Washington, DC: Butterworths, 1964.

Hsu Wen-hsiung. "From Aboriginal Island to Chinese Frontier: The Development of Taiwan Before 1683." In Knapp, ed. *China's Island Frontier,* 1–29.

Huang Fu-san. *A Brief History of Taiwan: A Sparrow Transformed into a Phoenix,* chapter 9. Taipei: Government Information Office, 2005. http://www. gio.gov.tw/taiwan-website/ 5-gp/history/tw10.html.

Huang, Alexander C. "The PLA Navy at War, 1949–1999: From Coastal Defense to Distant Operations." In Ryan, Finkelstein, and McDevitt, eds. *Chinese Warfighting,* 241–269.

Huang, Alexander Chieh-Cheng. "Chinese Maritime Modernization and its Security Implications: The Deng Xiaoping Era and Beyond." Ph.D. diss., George Washington University, 1994.

———. "The Chinese Navy's Offshore Active Defense Strategy: Conceptualization and Implications." *Naval War College Review* 47, no. 3 (Summer 1994): 7–32.

———. "Taiwan's View of Military Balance and the Challenges It Presents." In Lilley and Downs, eds. *Crisis in the Taiwan Strait,* 279–300.

Huang Jing. "Economic and Political Costs." In Tsang, ed. *If China Attacks Taiwan*, 193–206.

Huebner, Jon W. "The Abortive Liberation of Taiwan." *The China Quarterly* 110 (June 1987): 256–275.

Hughes, Christopher. *Taiwan and Chinese Nationalism: National Identity and Status in International Society*. London: Routledge, 1997.

Hunt, Michael H. *Genesis of Chinese Communist Foreign Policy*. New York: Columbia University Press, 1996.

Huth, Paul K. *Standing Your Ground: Territorial Disputes and International Conflict*. Ann Arbor: University of Michigan Press, 1996.

Important Documents Concerning the Question of Taiwan. Peking: Foreign Languages Press, 1955.

International Crisis Group. "Taiwan Strait I: What's Left of 'One China'?" *ICG Asia Report* 53 (June 6, 2003).

———. "Taiwan Strait II: The Risk of War." *ICG Asia Report* 54 (June 6, 2003).

"Interview with Lieutenant General Liu Yazhou of the Air Force of the People's Liberation Army." *Heartland: Eurasian Review of Geopolitics* (2005, no. 1): 5–32.

Iriye, Akira, ed. *The Chinese and the Japanese: Essays in Political and Cultural Interactions*. Princeton: Princeton University Press, 1980.

Isozaki, Komei. "Foreign Relations of the Kingdom of Ryukyu and the East Asian Diplomatic Order of the Modern Era." Master's Thesis, The Fletcher School of Law and Diplomacy, Tufts University, 2001.

Jacobs, Dan N. "Comintern." In Wang, ed. *Modern China*, 71–72.

Jacobs, J. Bruce. "Taiwanese and Chinese Nationalists, 1937–1945: The Origins of Taiwan's 'Half-Mountain People' (Banshan Ren)." *Modern China* 16, no. 1 (January 1990): 84–118.

Japan. Ministry of Foreign Affairs. "Joint Statement: U.S.–Japan Security Consultative Committee." February 19, 2005. http://www.mofa.go.jp/region/namerica/us/security/scc/joint0502.html.

Japan Times. "Japan, U.S. Mull Plan for Taiwan Crisis." Thursday, January 4, 2007. http://www.japantimes.co.jp/.

Ji Guoxing. "Rough Waters in the South China Sea: Navigation Issues and Confidence-Building Measures." *Asia Pacific Issues: Analysis from the East-West Center* 53 (August 2001).

Jiang Zemin. "Continue to Promote the Reunification of the Motherland." January 30, 1995. http://www.fmprc.gov.cn/eng/ljzg/3568/t17784.htm.

Jiefangjun Bao [Liberation Army Daily] (Beijing). "China's Worries at Sea." January 2, 2004. http://www.uscc.gov/researchpapers/research_archive.htm.

Jin Yinan. "'Foreign Weapons' Cannot Save 'Taiwan Independence.'" Reproduced as "*Jiefangjun Bao* Signed Article on Taiwan's 'Munitions Purchases.'" *Beijing Xinhua Domestic Service*. Tuesday, April 24, 2001. WNC Document Number: 0GCEH6901PQ0LP.

Job, Brian, André Laliberté, and Michael D. Wallace. "Assessing the Risks of Conflict in the PRC-ROC Enduring Rivalry." *Pacific Affairs* 72, no. 4 (Winter 1999–2000): 513–535.

Johnston, Alastair Iain. "China's International Relations: The Political and Security Dimensions." In Kim, ed. *The International Relations of Northeast Asia*, 65–100.

———. "Realism(s) and Chinese Security Policy in the Post-Cold War Period." In Kapstein and Mastanduno, eds. *Unipolar Politics*, 261–318.

Kahn, Joseph. "China, Shy Giant, Shows Signs of Shedding Its False Modesty." *New York Times*. December 9, 2006, A1.

Kan, Shirley A. *China/Taiwan: Evolution of the 'One China' Policy—Key Statements from Washington, Beijing, and Taipei.* Washington, DC: Library of Congress, Congressional Research Service, CRS Report for Congress (RL30341). March 12, 2001.

Kapstein, Ethan B., and Michael Mastanduno, eds. *Unipolar Politics: Realism and State Strategies After the Cold War.* New York: Columbia University Press, 1999.

Keliher, Macabe. *Out of China, or Yu Yonghe's Tales of Formosa: A History of Seventeenth-Century Taiwan.* Taipei: SMC Publishing, 2003.

Kerr, George H. "Sovereignty of the Liuchiu Islands." *Far Eastern Survey* 14, no. 8 (April 25, 1945): 96–100.

———. *Formosa Betrayed.* London: Eyre and Spottiswoode, 1965.

———. *Okinawa: The History of an Island People.* Rutland, Vermont and Tokyo: Charles E. Tuttle Company, 1958.

Khong, Yuen Foong. *Analogies at War: Korea, Munich, Dien Bien Phu, and the Vietnam Decisions of 1965.* Princeton: Princeton University Press, 1992.

Kim, Samuel S. "China as a Great Power." *Current History* 96, no. 611 (1997): 246–251.

———, ed. *The International Relations of Northeast Asia.* Lanham, MD: Rowman and Littlefield, 2004.

Knapp, Ronald G. "The Shaping of Taiwan's Landscapes." In Rubinstein, ed. *Taiwan: A New History,* 3–26.

———, ed. *China's Island Frontier: Studies in the Historical Geography of Taiwan.* Honolulu: University of Hawaii/Research Corporation of University of Hawaii, 1980.

Ko Shu-ling. "Taiwan President Accuses KMT, China of Lying over Consensus Term." *Taipei Times.* February 23, 2006. LexisNexis.

Kondapalli, Srikanth. *China's Naval Power.* New Delhi: Knowledge World, 2001.

Krasner, Stephen D., ed. *Problematic Sovereignty: Contested Rules and Political Possibilities.* New York: Columbia University Press, 2001.

Krauthammer, Charles. "The Unipolar Moment." America and the World, *Foreign Affairs* 70, no. 1 (1990/91): 23–33.

Krebs, Christopher B. "Imaginary Geography in Caesar's *Bellum Gallicum*." *American Journal of Philology* 127, no. 1 (2006): 111–136.

Kristof, Nicholas D. "The Rise of China." *Foreign Affairs* 72, no. 5 (November/December 1993): 59–74.

Kublin, Hyman. "The Discovery of the Bonin Islands: A Reexamination." *Annals of the Association of American Geographers,* 43, no. 1 (March, 1953).

Kulacki, Gregory. "Lost in Translation: A Tabloid Newspaper? An Amateur Space Enthusiast? U.S. Government Assessments of China's Military Prowess Are Sometimes Based upon Shaky Sources," *Bulletin of the Atomic Scientists* 62, no. 3 (May/June 2006): 34–39. http://www.thebulletin.org/article.php?art_ofn=mjo6kulacki.

Kuo, Julian J. "Cross-Strait Relations: Buying Time Without Strategy." In Dickson and Chao, eds. *Assessing the Lee Teng-Hui Legacy,* Armonk, NY: M. E. Sharpe, 2002, 204–240.

Kyodo News Service, Japan Economic Newswire. "China Expresses 'Grave Concern' over Japan-U.S. Contingency Plan." January 5, 2007. LexisNexis.

———. "Japan, U.S. to Study Joint Operation Plan for Taiwan Contingency." January 3, 2007. LexisNexis.

———. "Taiwan Natives Seek to Regain Respect Lost via Japanese Expedition." January 3, 2005. LexisNexis.

Lai Fu-shun. "A Rewriting of History, Beijing Style." *Taipei Times*. January 19, 2002, 8. http://www.taipeitimes.com/News/archives/2002/01/19/ 0000120594.

Lai Tse-han, Ramon H. Myers, and Wei Wou. *A Tragic Beginning: The Taiwan Uprising of February 28, 1947*. Stanford: Stanford University Press, 1991.

Lamley, Harry J. "The 1895 Taiwan Republic: A Significant Episode in Modern Chinese History," *Journal of Asian Studies* 27, no. 4 (August 1968): 739–762.

———. "The 1895 Taiwan War of Resistance: Local Chinese Efforts Against a Foreign Power." In Gordon, ed. *Taiwan: Studies in Chinese Local History*, 23–77.

Lampton, David M., ed. *The Making of Chinese Foreign and Security Policy in the Era of Reform*. Stanford: Stanford University Press, 2001.

Lang Danyang, and Chen Zuhua. "*Shidai biange yu diyuan zhanlüe siwei de fanshi zhuanhuan*" [Changing Times and the Transformation of Geostrategic Thought]. *Shijie jingji yu zhengzhi* [World Economics and Politics] 1999, no. 11: 23–27. CAJ.

Lasater, Martin L. "A U.S. Perception of a PLA Invasion of Taiwan." In Yu, ed. *The Chinese PLA's Perception of an Invasion of Taiwan*, 229–269.

Lee Teng-hui. "Responses to Questions Submitted by *Deutsche Welle*." In Republic of China, Government Information Office, comp. *Getting Real: International Media Perspectives on the Special State-to-State Relationship Between the ROC and the PRC*. Taipei: Government Information Office, 1999, 26–33.

———. *The Road to Democracy: Taiwan's Pursuit of Identity*. Tokyo: PHP Institute, 1999. Originally published in Japanese as *Taiwan no shochu*.

Lees, Francis A. *China Superpower: Requisites for High Growth*. New York: St. Martin's Press, 1997.

Letter from Customs House, Tamsui, 27 May 1895. Typescript copy. Collection no. C0031. Folder 4, Letter 1298. Department of Rare Books and Special Collections. Firestone Library, Princeton University.

Leung, Edwin Pak-Wah. "The Quasi-War in East Asia: Japan's Expedition to Taiwan and the Ryukyu Controversy." *Modern Asian Studies* 17, no. 2 (1983): 257–281.

Levine, Steven I. "Perception and Ideology in Chinese Foreign Policy." In Robinson and Shambaugh, eds. *Chinese Foreign Policy*, 30–46.

Lewis, John Wilson, and Xue Litai. "China's Search for a Modern Air Force." In Brown, Coté, Jr., Lynn-Jones, and Miller, eds. *The Rise of China*, 74–104.

Li Jinming and Li Dexia. "The Dotted Line on the Chinese Map of the South China Sea: A Note." *Ocean Development and International Law* 34 (2003): 287–295.

Li Nan. "The PLA's Evolving Warfighting Doctrine, Strategy and Tactics, 1985–1995: A Chinese Perspective." *The China Quarterly* 146 (June 1996): 443–463.

Li Xiaobing. "PLA Attacks and Amphibious Operations During the Taiwan Strait Crises of 1954–55 and 1958." In Ryan, Finkelstein, and McDevitt, eds. *Chinese Warfighting*, 143–172.

Li Zhenguang. "Taiwan diyuan zhanlue diwei de xingcheng yu bianqian" [The Formation and Change of Taiwan's Geostrategic Status]. *Guoji zhengzhi yanjiu* [Research on International Politics] 2001, no. 4: 120–124, 136. CAJ.

Lilley, James R., and Chuck Downs, eds. *Crisis in the Taiwan Strait*. Washington, DC: National Defense University, 1997.

Lin Limin. "*21 Shiji Zhongguo diyuan zhanlüe huanjing qianyi*" [An Overview of China's 21st Century Geostrategic Environment]. *Shijie jingji yu zhengzhi* [World Economics and Politics] 1999, no. 12: 55–59. CAJ.

Lin Xinhua. "*Shilun Zhongguo fazhan haiquan de zhanlüe*" [The Strategy of China's Development of Sea Power]. *Fudan xuebao* [Fudan Journal] 2001, no. 6: 68–72. CAJ.

Lin Zhibo. "New Academic Analysis: Will There Be an All-out US Intervention in a Taiwan Strait War?" Reproduced as "Chinese Commentator Discusses Whether US Will Resort to Force to Defend Taiwan." *Beijing Renmin Wang, Renmin Ribao,* Tuesday, July 20, 2004. WNC Document Number: 0i198tf03vxhmc.

Lindemans, Micha F. "Sirens." *Encyclopedia Mythica* from *Encyclopedia Mythica Online* at http://www.pantheon.org/articles/s/sirens.html.

Liu Hong. *"Taiwan wenti de diyuan zhengzhi sikao"* [Geopolitical Considerations of the Taiwan Issue]. *Yangzhou jiaoyu xueyuan xuebao* [Journal of Yangzhou College of Education] 21, no. 4 (December 2003): 47–51, 92. CAJ.

Liu Kwang-ching, and Richard J. Smith. "The Military Challenge: The North-west and the Coast." In Twitchett and Fairbank, eds. *The Cambridge History of China, vol. 11,* 202–73.

Liu Miaolong, Kong Aili, and Zhang Wei. *"Diyuan zhengzhi lishi, xianzhuang yu Zhongguo de diyuan zhanlüe"* [The History and Status of Geopolitics and the Geopolitical Strategies of China]. *Dili yanjiu* [Geographical Research] 13, no. 3 (September 1994): 69–75. Reprinted in English in *The Journal of Chinese Geography* 6, no. 1 (1996): 18–25. CAJ.

Liu Xiaoyuan. *Frontier Passages: Ethnopolitics and the Rise of Chinese Communism, 1921–1945.* Washington, DC: Wilson Center Press/Stanford: Stanford University Press, 2004.

———. *A Partnership for Disorder: China, the United States, and Their Policies for the Postwar Disposition of the Japanese Empire, 1941–1945.* Cambridge: Cambridge University Press, 1996.

Liu Xinhua. *"Shilun Zhongguo fazhan haiquan de zhanlüe"* [On China's Strategy for the Development of Sea Power]. *Fudan xuebao (Shehui kexueban)* [Fudan Journal (Social Science edition] (2006, no. 6): (2001): 68–72. CAJ.

Liu Yazhou. *"Da guo ce"* [Grand Strategy]. Undated Web site posting. http://www.chinaaffairs.org/gb/detail.asp?id=56766.

Liu Zhongmin. *"Haiquan wenti yu lengzhanhou Zhong Mei guanxi: maodun de renzhi yu jiannan de xuanze"* [Sea Power Issues and Post-Cold War Sino-U.S. Relations: Contradictory Perceptions and Difficult Options]. *Waijiao pinglun* [Foreign Affairs Review] 85 (December 2005): 55–60. CAJ.

Liu Zhongmin and Zhao Chengguo. *"Guanyu Zhongguo haiquan fazhan zhanlüe wenti de ruogan sikao"* [Several Considerations Concerning the Strategy for Developing China's Sea Power]. *Zhongguo haiyang daxue xuebao* [Journal of the Ocean University of China] (2004, no. 6): 55–60. CAJ.

Lou Douzi. "Looking at Navy and Air Force Dispositions Following Establishment Restructuring (1)." *Jiefangjun Bao* [Liberation Army Daily], "National Defense Forum." Wednesday, July 14, 2004. WNC Document Number: 0i0y4vu01v7q3a.

Lu Junyuan. *Diyuan zhengzhi de benzhi yu guilu* [On the Essence and Laws of Geopolitics]. Beijing: Shishi chubanshe, 2005.

Lu Ya-li. "Lee Teng-hui's Role in Taiwan's Democratization." In Dickson and Chao, eds. *Assessing the Lee Teng-hui Legacy in Taiwan Politics,* 53–72.

Ma Dazheng. "Definition of Borderland." Web site of China Borderland History Research Center, Chinese Academy of Social Sciences. Posted June 17, 2004. http://www.cass.net.cn/webnew/yanjiusuo/bjzx/show_News. asp?id= '2053'.

Ma Ying-jeou. "Cross-Strait Relations at a Crossroad: Impasse or Breakthrough?" In Zagoria, *Breaking the China-Taiwan Impasse,* 39–65.

Madsen, Robert A. "The Struggle for Sovereignty Between China and Taiwan." In Krasner, ed. *Problematic Sovereignty,* 141–193.

Mann, James. *About Face: A History of America's Curious Relationship with China from Nixon to Clinton.* New York: Alfred Knopf, 1999.

Mannix, William Francis, ed. *Memoirs of Li Hung Chang.* Boston and New York: Houghton Mifflin Company, 1913.

Mao Zedong. *Collected Works (1917–1949).* Joint Publications Research Service, 1978. www. marxists.org/reference/archive/mao/works/collected-works-pdf/index.htm.

May, Ernest R. *"Lessons" of the Past: The Use and Misuse of History in American Foreign Policy.* Oxford: Oxford University Press, 1973.

———. *The Making of the Monroe Doctrine.* Cambridge: Harvard University Press, 1975.

McDevitt, Michael. "Geographic Ruminations." In Wortzel, ed. *The Chinese Armed Forces in the 21st Century,* 1–6.

McGiffert, Carola, ed. *Chinese Images of the United States.* Washington, DC: Center for Strategic and International Studies, 2005.

McWilliams, Wayne C. "East Meets East. The Soejima Mission to China, 1873." *Monumenta Nipponica* 30, no. 3 (Autumn 1975): 237–275.

Mearsheimer, John J. "Better to be Godzilla than Bambi." In Zbigniew Brzezinski and John J. Mearsheimer. "Clash of the Titans." *Foreign Policy* 146 (January–February 2005): 46–50.

Meconis, Charles A., and Michael D. Wallace. *East Asian Naval Weapons Acquisitions in the 1990s: Causes, Consequences, and Responses.* Westport, CT: Praeger, 2000.

"Message to Compatriots in Taiwan, January 1, 1979." http://www.china. org.cn/english/taiwan/7943.htm.

Miller, H. Lyman, and Liu Xiaohong. "The Foreign Policy Outlook of China's 'Third Generation' Elite." In Lampton, ed. *The Making of Chinese Foreign and Security Policy in the Era of Reform,* 123–150.

Millward, James A. "'Coming onto the Map': 'Western Regions' Geography and Cartographic Nomenclature in the Making of Chinese Empire in Xinjiang." *Late Imperial China* 20, no. 2 (December 1999) 61–98.

———. *Beyond the Pass: Economy, Ethnicity, and Empire in Qing Central Asia, 1759–1864.* Stanford: Stanford University Press, 1998.

Millward, James A., and Nabijan Tursun. "Political History and Strategies of Control, 1884–1978." In Starr, ed. *Xinjiang,* 63–98.

"The Monroe Doctrine." Avalon Project. http://www.yale.edu/lawweb/avalon/monroe.htm.

Moody, Peter R., Jr. "Some Problems in Taiwan's Democratic Consolidation." In Dickson and Chao, eds. *Assessing the Lee Teng-hui Legacy in Taiwan Politics,* 27–50.

Mulvenon, James, and David M. Finkelstein, eds. *China's Revolution in Doctrinal Affairs: Emerging Trends in the Operational Art of the Chinese People's Liberation Army.* Alexandria, VA: The CNA Corporation (November 2005). http://www.cna.org/nationalsecurity/css/asia/news.aspx.

Mulvenon, James C., and Andrew Yang, eds. *The People's Liberation Army as Organization: Reference Volume v1.0.* Santa Monica, CA: RAND Corporation, 2002.

Mulvenon, James C., and Richard H. Yang, eds. *The People's Liberation Army in the Information Age.* Santa Monica, CA: RAND Corporation, 1999.

Murray, Geoffrey. *China: The Next Superpower: Dilemmas in Change and Continuity.* New York: St. Martin's Press, 1998.

Mutsu, Munemitsu. *Kenkenroku: A Diplomatic Record of the Sino-Japanese War, 1894–1895.* Princeton: Princeton University Press, 1982.

Nathan, Andrew J., and Robert S. Ross. *The Great Wall and the Empty Fortress: China's Search for Security*. New York and London: W. W. Norton & Co., 1997.

Newman, David. "Real Spaces, Symbolic Spaces: Interrelated Notions of Territory in the Arab-Israeli Conflict." In Diehl, ed. *A Road Map to War*, 3–34.

New York Times. "Big Transport Set Afire in Raid, Men Ashore Bombed, Berlin Says." April 21, 1940, 1. ProQuest.

———. "China Seeks Formosa Rendition." April 6, 1942. ProQuest.

———. "Chinese Capture Three Coast Cities." January 10, 1945. ProQuest.

———. "The Fronts." April 5, 1942, E1. ProQuest.

———. "The Fronts." November 21, 1943, E1. ProQuest.

———. "Naples Raided Five Hours." October 23, 1941, 10. ProQuest.

———. "Texts of Controversial MacArthur Message and Truman's Formosa Statement; After MacArthur Withdrew His Message on Formosa." August 29, 1950, 16. ProQuest.

———. "V. F. W. Announce Cancellation." August 28, 1950. ProQuest.

Nish, Ian. "An Overview of Relations Between China and Japan, 1895–1945." *The China Quarterly* 124 (December 1990): 601–623.

O'Hanlon, Michael E. "The Risk of War Over Taiwan Is Real." *Financial Times*, May 1, 2005. http://www.brookings.edu/views/op-ed/ohanlon/20050501.htm.

———. "Why China Cannot Conquer Taiwan." *International Security* 25, no. 2 (Fall 2000): 51–86.

Okazaki, Hisahiko. "The Strategic Value of Taiwan." A paper prepared for The US-Japan-Taiwan Trilateral Strategic Dialogue, Tokyo Round, March 2, 2003. http://www.okazaki-inst.jp/okazaki-eng.html.

Onishi, Norimitsu, and Howard W. French. "Ill Will Rising Between China and Japan as Old Grievances Fuel New Era of Rivalry." *New York Times*. August 3, 2005, A1.

O'Rourke, Ronald. *China Naval Modernization: Implications for U.S. Navy Capabilities—Background Issues for Congress*. Washington, DC: Library of Congress, Congressional Research Service, CRS Report for Congress (RL33153). November 18, 2005.

Osborne, Brian S. "Landscapes, Memory, Monuments, and Commemoration: Putting Identity in its Place. *The Canadian Ethnic Studies Journal* 33, no. 3 (Fall 2001): 39–79.

Overholt, William H. *China: The Next Economic Superpower*. London: Weidenfeld and Nicolson, 1993.

Paine, S. C. M. *Imperial Rivals: China, Russia, and Their Disputed Frontier*. Armonk, NY: M. E. Sharpe, 1996.

———. *The Sino-Japanese War of 1894–1895: Perceptions, Power and Primacy*. Cambridge: Cambridge University Press, 2003.

Pang Zhongying. "Comment: Developing an Asian Partnership." *China Daily* (Beijing). November 4, 2003. http://www1.chinadaily.com.cn/en/doc/ 2003-11/04/content_278069.htm.

Pehrson, Christopher J. *String of Pearls: Meeting the Challenge of China's Rising Power Across the Asian Littoral*. Carlisle Barracks, PA: Strategic Studies Institute, U.S. Army War College, 2006.

Peking and Tientsin Times. *History of the Peace Negotiations, Documentary and Verbal, Between China and Japan, March–April, 1895*. Tientsin: The Tientsin Press, 1895.

Peng Dehuai. "PRC Defense Minister P'eng Teh-huai's Second Message to Compatriots in Taiwan, October 25, 1958." *Peking Review* 1, no. 35 (October 28, 1959), 5.

People's Daily. "U.S. Arms Sales to Taiwan Escalate Cross-Straits Tension: Experts." April 27, 2001. http://english.people.com.cn/ english/200104/27/eng20010427_68709.html.

———. "Premier Wen Makes His Media Debut: Full Text." March 19, 2003. http://english.peopledaily.com.cn/200303/19/eng20030319_113558.shtml.

People's Republic of China. *"2006 nian Zhongguo de guofang"* [China's National Defense in 2006]. http://www.chinamil.com.cn/site1/2006ztpd/2006zggfbps/index.htm.

———. *China's National Defense in 2006.* Beijing: Information Office of the State Council of the People's Republic of China, December 2006. http://www.daily.com.cn/china/2006-12-29/content_771191_2htm.

———. *China's National Defense in 2004.* Beijing: State Council Information Office, December 27, 2004. http://english.gov.cn/ official/2005-07/28/content_18078.htm.

———. *Constitution of the People's Republic of China,* adopted December 4, 1982. http://english.people.com.cn/constitution/constitution.html.

———. Information Office of the State Council. *China's National Defense.* July 1998. http://www.fas.org/nuke/guide/china/doctrine/cnd9807/index. html.

———. "Law of the People's Republic of China on the Exclusive Economic Zone and the Continental Shelf" (Adopted at the 3rd Meeting of the Standing Committee of the Ninth National People's Congress and promulgated by Order No. 6 of the President of the People's Republic of China on June 26, 1998) http://www.chinalaw.gov.cn/jsp/jalor_en/disptext.jsp?recno=5&&ttlrec=12.

_____. "Law of the People's Republic of China on the Territorial Sea and the Contiguous Zone" (Adopted at the 24th Meeting of the Standing Committee of the Seventh National People's Congress on February 25, 1992, promulgated by Order No. 55 of the President of the People's Republic of China on February 25, 1992, and effective as of the date of promulgation.) http://www.chinalaw.gov.cn/jsp/jalor_en/disptext.jsp?recno=9&&ttlrec=12.

———. Ministry of Foreign Affairs. "China's Independent Foreign Policy of Peace." August 18, 2003. http://www.fmprc.gov.cn/eng/wjdt/wjzc/t24881.htm.

———. Ministry of Foreign Affairs. "What Is the Political Intention of the U.S. Congress in Passing the So-called 'Taiwan Relations Act'?" November 15, 2000. http://www.fmprc.gov.cn/eng/ljzg/3568/t17797.htm.

———. National People's Congress Standing Committee. *"Quanguo renda chang wei gao Taiwan Tongbao shu"* [National People's Congress Standing Committee Appeals to Taiwan Compatriots]. January 1, 1979. http://www.gwytb.gov.cn:8088/detail.asp?table=OneCP&title=One%2DChina+Principle&m_id=6.

———. State Council. "Statement of the Chinese Government on the Baseline of the Territorial Sea of the People's Republic of China." May 15, 1996. http://www.chinalaw.gov.cn/jsp/jalor_en/disptext.jsp?recno=3&&ttlrec=12.

———. Taiwan Affairs Office and the Information Office of the State Council. "The Taiwan Question and Reunification of China." Beijing, 1993. http://www.china.org.cn/english/taiwan/7953.htm.

Perdue, Peter C. "Comparing Empires: Manchu Colonialism." *The International History Review* 20, no. 2 (June 1998): 255–262.

———. *China Marches West: The Qing Conquest of Central Eurasia.* Cambridge: Harvard University Press, 2005.

Perry, John Curtis. "Great Britain and the Emergence of Japan as a Naval Power." *Monumenta Nipponica* 21, no. 3/4 (1966): 305–321.

Phillips, Steven E. "Confronting Colonization and National Identity: The Nationalists and Taiwan, 1941–45." *Journal of Colonialism and Colonial History* 2, no. 3 (2001). http://muse.jhu.edu.

———. *Between Assimilation and Independence: The Taiwanese Encounter Nationalist China, 1945–1950*. Stanford: Stanford University Press, 2003.

Pillsbury, Michael, ed. *Chinese Views of Future Warfare*. Washington, DC: National Defense University Press, 1998.

———. *China Debates the Future Security Environment*. Washington, DC: National Defense University, 2000.

Pollack, Jonathan D. "Short-range Ballistic Missile Capabilities." In Tsang, ed. *If China Attacks Taiwan*, 57–71.

"President Chen's Concluding Remarks at National Security Conference." February 27, 2006. http://www.gio.gov.tw/taiwan-website/4-oa/20060227/2006022703.html.

Presseisen, Ernst L. "Roots of Japanese Imperialism: A Memorandum of General LeGendre." *The Journal of Modern History* 29, no. 2 (June 1957): 108–111.

Quo, F. Q. "British Diplomacy and the Cession of Formosa, 1894–95." *Modern Asian Studies* 2, no. 2 (1968): 141–154.

"Record of Conversation Between Comrade I. V. Stalin and Chairman of the People's Government of the People's Republic of China Mao Zedong on 16 December 1949." *Cold War International History Project Bulletin* 6–7 (Winter 1995/96). CWIHP.

Renmin Wang [People's Network]. *"'Taidu'—xueruo liang'an huyi de Zhongguo haifang—fang Zhongguo junshi kexueyuan de Luo Yuan zhuren"* ['Taiwan Independence': Weakens Both Sides of China's Coastal Defense—Interview with Director Luo Yuan of China's Academy of Military Sciences]. March 11, 2002. http://www1.chinataiwan.org/web/webportal/W2001021/Uadmin/A4460975.html.

———. *"'Yiding yao jiefang Taiwan,' Zhonggong dangshide 80 ju kouhao (30)"* ["We Certainly will Liberate Taiwan," 80 Slogans from CCP Party History, number 30]. http://www.people.com.cn/GB/shizheng/252/5303/5304/20010608/484737.html.

Republic of China. "Constitution of the Republic of China." http://www.gio.gov.tw/info/news/constitution.htm.

———. Executive Yuan. Mainland Affairs Council. "Act Governing Relations Between Peoples of the Taiwan Area and the Mainland Area." http://www.mac.gov.tw/english/index1-e.htm.

———. Government Information Office, comp. *Getting Real: International Media Perspectives on the Special State-to-State Relationship Between the ROC and the PRC*. Taipei: Government Information Office, 1999.

Reuters. "Taiwan President a Rat: China." *The Tribune* (Chandigarh, India). August 23, 1999. http://www.tribuneindia.com/1999/99aug23/world.htm.

———. "U.S. Eyes China's Naval Power on High-Level Visit." *Epoch Times* November 13, 2006. http://en.epochtimes.com/news/6-11-13/48081.html.

Rhoads, Edward J. M. *Manchus and Han: Ethnic Relations and Political Power in Late Qing and Early Republican China, 1861–1928*. Seattle: University of Washington Press, 2000.

Rigger, Shelley. *Politics in Taiwan: Voting for Democracy*. London: Routledge, 1999.

Robbins, Ron Cyneful. "Sixty Years On: The Atlantic Charter, 1941–2001." *Finest Hour* no. 112 (Autumn 2001). http://www.winstonchurchill.org/i4a/pages/index.cfm?pageid=281.

Robinson, Thomas W., and David Shambaugh, eds. *Chinese Foreign Policy: Theory and Practice*. Oxford: Clarendon Press, 1994.

Rodrigue, Jean-Paul. "Straits, Passages and Chokepoints: A Maritime Geostrategy of Petroleum Distribution." *Les Cahiers de Geographie du Quebec* 48, no. 135 (2004): 357–374. Special issue on maritime strategic passages.

Romberg, Alan D. *Rein In at the Brink of the Precipice: American Policy Toward Taiwan and U.S.–PRC Relations.* Washington, DC: The Henry L. Stimson Center, 2003.

Rosenfield, Julia. "Assessing China's 2004 Defense White Paper: A Workshop Report." Alexandria, VA: The CNA Corporation, n.d. www.cna.org/nationalsecurity/css/asia/2004%20Final%20Workshop%20Report.pdf.

Ross, Robert S. "China II: Beijing as a Conservative Power." *Foreign Affairs* 76 (March/April 1997): 33–44.

———. "Geography of the Peace: East Asia in the Twenty-first Century." In Brown, Coté, Jr., Lynn-Jones, and Miller, eds. *The Rise of China,* 167–204. Previously published in *International Security* 23, no. 4 (Spring 1999): 81–118.

Ross, Robert S., and Jiang Changbin, eds. *Re-examining the Cold War: U.S.–China Diplomacy, 1954–1973.* Cambridge: Harvard University Asia Center, 2001.

Rubinstein, Murray A., ed. *Taiwan: A New History.* Armonk, NY: M. E. Sharpe, 1999.

Rudolph, Jörg-Meinhard. *Die Kommunistische Partei Chinas und Taiwan (1921-1981).* Munchen: Minerva Publication, 1986.

Ryan, Mark A., David M. Finkelstein, and Michael A. McDevitt, eds. *Chinese Warfighting: The PLA Experience Since 1949.* Armonk, NY: M. E. Sharpe, 2003.

Saich, Tony, ed. *The Rise to Power of the Chinese Communist Party.* Armonk, NY: M. E. Sharpe, 1996.

Said, Edward W. *Orientalism.* New York: Pantheon, 1978.

Sainsbury, Keith. *The Turning Point: Roosevelt, Stalin, Churchill, and Chiang Kai-shek, 1943— The Moscow, Cairo, and Tehran Conferences.* Oxford: Oxford University Press, 1986.

Sakai, Robert K. "The Satsuma-Ryukyu Trade and the Tokugawa Seclusion Policy." *The Journal of Asian Studies* 23, no. 3 (May 1964): 391–403.

Sawyer, Ralph D., trans. *The Seven Military Classics of Ancient China.* Boulder: Westview Press, 1993.

Scobell, Andrew. "China's Strategy Toward the South China Sea." In Edmonds and Tsai, eds. *Taiwan's Maritime Security,* 40–51.

———. *Chinese Army Building in the Era of Jiang Zemin.* Carlisle, PA: U.S. Army War College, Strategic Studies Institute, 2000.

Scobell, Andrew, and Larry Wortzel, eds. *Chinese National Security Decisionmaking Under Stress.* Carlisle, PA: U.S. Army War College, Strategic Studies Institute, 2005.

———, eds. *Civil-Military Change in China: Elites, Institutes, and Ideas After the 16th Party Congress.* Carlisle, PA: U.S. Army War College, Strategic Studies Institute, September 2004.

Senese, Paul D., and John A. Vasquez. "A Unified Explanation of Territorial Conflict: Testing the Impact of Sampling Bias, 1919–1992." *International Studies Quarterly* 47 (2003): 275–298.

Shambaugh, David L. *Greater China: The Next Superpower?* Oxford: Oxford University Press, 1995.

———. *Modernizing China's Military: Progress, Problems, and Prospects.* Berkeley: University of California Press, 2002.

Shen Weilie and Lu Junyuan, eds. *Zhongguo guojia anquan dili* [The Geography of China's National Security]. Beijing: Shishi chubanshe, 2001.

Shepherd, John R. "The Island Frontier of the Ch'ing, 1684–1780." In Rubinstein, ed. *Taiwan: A New History,* 107–132.

———. *Statecraft and Political Economy on the Taiwan Frontier, 1600–1800.* Stanford: Stanford University Press, 1993.

Shih Hsiu-chuan. "Su Chi Admits the '1992 Consensus' Was Made Up." *Taipei Times.* February 22, 2006, 3. www.taipeitimes.com.

Smith, Richard J. "Mapping China's World: Cultural Cartography in Late Imperial Times." In Yeh, ed. *Landscape, Culture and Power in Chinese Society*, 53–109.

Smith, Warren W., Jr. *Tibetan Nation: A History of Tibetan Nationalism and Sino-Tibetan Relations.* Boulder: Westview Press, 1996.

Snow, Edgar. *Red Star Over China: First Revised and Enlarged Edition.* New York: Grove Press, 1981.

Speed, Elizabeth. "Chinese Naval Power and East Asian Security." Institute of International Relations, University of British Columbia. Working Paper 11 (August 1995). www.iir.ubc.ca/pdffiles/webwp11.pdf.

Stainton, Michael. "The Politics of Taiwan Aboriginal Origins." In Rubinstein, ed. *Taiwan: A New History*, 27–44.

Starr, S. Frederick, ed. *Xinjiang: China's Muslim Borderland.* Armonk, NY: M. E. Sharpe, 2004.

Stephan, John J. "The Tanaka Memorial (1927): Authentic or Spurious?" *Modern Asian Studies* 7, no. 4 (1973): 733–745.

Stokes, Mark A. "Chinese Ballistic Missile Forces in the Age of Global Missile Defense: Challenges and Responses." In Scobell and Wortzel, eds. *China's Growing Military Power*, 107–167.

Storey, Ian, and You Ji. "China's Aircraft Carrier Ambitions: Seeking Truth from Rumors." *Naval War College Review* 57, no. 1 (Winter 2004): 77–93.

Su Chi. *Wei xian bian yuan: cong liang guo lun dao yi bian yi guo* [Brinksmanship: From Two State Theory to One Country on Each Side]. Taipei: Tianxia wenhua chuban gufen youxian gongsi, 2003.

Sun Yat-sen. *San Min Chu I: Three Principles of the People, with two supplementary chapters by Chiang Kai-shek.* Taipei: China Publishing, n.d.

———. *The Vital Problem of China.* Taipei: China Cultural Service, 1953.

Swaine, Michael D. "Chinese Decision-Making Regarding Taiwan, 1979–2000." In Lampton, ed. *The Making of Chinese Foreign and Security Policy in the Era of Reform, 1978–2000*, 287–336.

Swaine, Michael D., and James C. Mulvenon. *Taiwan's Foreign and Defense Policies: Features and Determinants.* Santa Monica, CA: RAND Corporation, 2001.

Swaine, Michael D., and Ashely J. Tellis. *Interpreting China's Grand Strategy: Past, Present, and Future.* Santa Monica, CA: RAND Corporation, 2000.

"Symposium: Rethinking the Lost Chance in China." *Diplomatic History* 21, no. 1 (Winter 1997): 71-116.

Ta Kung Pao (Hong Kong). "PRC Expert Gives Five Reasons China Should Not Allow Taiwan Independence." March 24, 2004. WNC Document Number: ohvhx4ho2igjx2.

Taipei Times. "Editorial: China's Dangerous Leap Backwards." December 20, 2004. http://www.taipeitimes.com/News/edit/archives/2004/12/20/2003215973.

Tang Ming and Shen Yaoshan. "An Ocean Dream Based on 6,000 Uninhabited Islands." Reproduced as "JFJB Article on Protection, Use of China's Uninhabited Islands." *Jiefangjun Bao.* Friday, November 7, 2003. WNC Document Number: ohpzwoeo4e36kz.

Tang Shiping. "Zailun Zhongguo de da zhanlüe" [Once Again on China's Grand Strategy]. *Zhanlüe yu guanli* [Strategy and Management] (2001, no. 4): 29–37. CAJ.

———. *Suzao Zhongguo de lixiang anquan huanjing* [Model China's Ideal Security Environment]. Beijing: Zhongguo shehui kexue chubanshe, 2003.

Tang Shiping and Cao Xiaoyang. "Land in the Middle, Part 3: The False Triangle." *Asia Times Online*, November 7, 2002. http://www.atimes.com/ atimes/China/DK07Ad03.html.

Taylor, Jay. *The Generalissimo's Son: Chiang Ching-kuo and the Revolutions in China and Taiwan*. Cambridge: Harvard University Press, 2000.

Teng, Emma Jinhua. *Taiwan's Imagined Geography: Chinese Colonial Travel Writing and Pictures, 1683–1895*. Cambridge: Harvard University Asia Center, 2004.

Terrill, Ross. *The New Chinese Empire: And What it Means for the United States*. New York: Basic Books, 2003.

Thompson, William R. "Evolving Toward an Evolutionary Perspective on World Politics and International Political Economy." In Thompson, ed. *Evolutionary Interpretations of World Politics*, 1–15.

———, ed. *Evolutionary Interpretations of World Politics*. New York and London: Routledge, 2001.

Thornton, Richard. *The Comintern and the Chinese Communists, 1928–1931*. Seattle: University of Washington Press, 1969.

Till, Geoffrey. *Seapower: A Guide for the Twenty-first Century*. London: Frank Cass, 2004.

Times Atlas of the World. Edinburgh: John Bartholemew and Sons, 1981.

Tkacik, John. "Premier Wen and Vice President Zeng: The 'Two Centers' of China's 'Fourth Generation.'" In Scobell and Wortzel, eds. *Civil-Military Change in China*, 95–178.

Toft, Monica Duffy. *The Geography of Ethnic Violence*. Princeton: Princeton University Press, 2003.

Tønnesson, Stein. "Sino-Vietnamese Rapprochement and the South China Sea Irritant." *Security Dialogue* 34, no. 1 (March 2003): 55–70.

Tsang, Steve, ed. *If China Attacks Taiwan: Military Strategy, Politics, and Economics*. London: Routledge, 2006.

Tu Wei-ming. "Cultural China: The Periphery as the Center." *Daedalus* 134, no. 4 (2005): 145–167. Originally published in *Daedalus* 120, no. 2 (1991): 1–32.

Tuathail, Gearóid Ó. *Critical Geopolitics: The Politics of Writing Global Space*. Minneapolis: University of Minnesota Press, 1996.

Tuchman, Barbara W. *Stilwell and the American Experience in China, 1911–1945*. New York: Macmillan, 1970.

Tucker, Nancy Bernkopf. "Dangerous Strait: An Introduction." In Tucker, ed. *Dangerous Strait*, 1–15.

———. "If Taiwan Chooses Unification, Should the United States Care?" *Washington Quarterly* 25, no. 3 (Summer 2002): 15–28.

———, ed. *Dangerous Strait: The U.S.–Taiwan–China Crisis*. New York: Columbia University Press, 2005.

———. *Patterns in the Dust: Chinese American Relations and the Recognition Controversy, 1949–1950*. New York: Columbia University Press, 1983.

Twitchett, Denis, and John K. Fairbank, eds. *The Cambridge History of China, vol. 11, Late Ch'ing, 1800–1911, Part 2*. Cambridge: Cambridge University Press, 1980.

"'2004 nian Zhongguo de guofang' baipishu" [China's National Defense in 2004 White Paper]. http://news.xinhuanet.com/mil/2004-12/27/content_2384731_3.htm.

United Nations. "United Nations Convention on the Law of the Sea of 10 December 1982." http://www.un.org/Depts/los/convention_agreements/convention_overview_convention.htm.

United States Congress. *Congressional Record.* Senate. 103d Cong., 2d. sess., 1994. Vol. 140. No. 96: S9337. "The Grief of Being Born a Taiwanese: Dialogue between President Lee Teng-hui and Writer Ryotaro Shiba." *Asahi Weekly.* May 6–13, 1994.

United States. Department of Defense. *Annual Report to Congress: The Military Power of the People's Republic of China, 2005.* Arlington, VA: Office of the Secretary of Defense, July 2005.

———. *Annual Report to Congress: The Military Power of the People's Republic of China, 2006.* Arlington, VA: Office of the Secretary of Defense, 2006.

———. *Quadrennial Defense Review Report.* Arlington, VA: Office of the Secretary of Defense, February 2006. http://www.defenselink.mil/qdr/.

United States. Department of State. *Foreign Relations of the United States, 1942 (China).* Washington, DC: Government Printing Office, 1956.

———. National Security Council. "The Current Position of the United States with Respect to Formosa." Top Secret, National Security Council Report, NSC 37/2. February 3, 1949. Item Number: PD00104. NSA.

———. National Security Council. "The Position of the United States with Respect to Formosa." Top Secret, National Security Council Report, NSC 37/1. January 19, 1949. Item Number: PD00103. NSA.

———. National Security Council. "The Position of the United States with Respect to Formosa." Top Secret, National Security Council Report, NSC 37/7. August 22, 1949. Item Number: PD00109. NSA.

———. National Security Council. "The Strategic Importance of Formosa," Secret, National Security Council Report, NSC 37, December 1, 1948. Item Number: PD00102. NSA.

———. National Security Council. "The Strategic Importance of Formosa." Top Secret, National Security Council Report, NSC 37/3, February 11, 1949. Item Number: PD00105. NSA.

———. National Security Council. "Supplementary Measures with Respect to Formosa." Top Secret, National Security Council Report, NSC 37/5. March 1, 1949. Item number: PD00107. NSA.

———. *United States Relations with China, with Special Reference to the Period 1944–1949.* Washington, DC: United States Department of State, August 1949.

van der Aalsvoort, Lambert. *Feng zhong zhi ye: Fu er mo sha jianwen lu* [A Leaf in the Wind: Seen and Heard in Formosa]. Taipei: Jingdian zazhi, 2000.

Vasquez, John A. "Why Do Neighbors Fight? Proximity, Interaction, or Territoriality." *Journal of Peace Research* 32, no. 3 (August 1995): 277–293.

Vasquez, John, and Christopher Leskiw. "The Origins and War Proneness of Interstate Rivalries." *Annual Review of Political Science* 4 (2001): 295–316.

Vermeer, Eduard B. "Up to the Mountains and Out to the Sea: The Expansion of the Fukienese in the Late Ming Period." In Rubinstein, ed. *Taiwan: A New History,* 45–83.

Wachman, Alan M. *Taiwan: National Identity and Democratization.* Armonk, NY: M. E. Sharpe, 1994.

Wales, H. G. Quaritch. "Huge India Looms Up as Key to War in East." *New York Times.* April 19, 1942, E5. ProQuest.

Waltz, Kenneth. *Man, the State, and War: A Theoretical Analysis.* New York: Columbia University Press, 1959.

Wang Chunyong, and Lu Xue. *"Taiwan wenti de diyuan zhanlüe fenxi"* [A Geostrategic Analysis of the Taiwan Issue]. *Jiefangjun waiguo yu xue yuan xuebao* [Journal of the PLA Institute of Foreign Languages] 23, no. 3 (May 2000): 113–116. CAJ.

Wang Cunli and Hu Wenqing. *Taiwan de gu ditu—Ming Qing shiqi* [Taiwan's Ancient Maps from the Ming and Qing Periods]. Taipei: Yuanzu wenhua, 2002.

Wang Dong. "The Discourse of Unequal Treaties in Modern China." *Pacific Affairs* 76, no. 3 (2003): 399–426.

Wang Jisi. "China's Changing Role in Asia." Occasional Paper of the Atlantic Council of the United States, Asia Programs. January 2004. http://www. acus.org/docs/ 0401-China_Changing_Role_Asia.pdf.

———. "From Paper Tiger to Real Leviathan: China's Images of the United States Since 1949." In McGiffert, ed. *Chinese Images of the United States*, 9–22.

Wang Ke-wen, ed. *Modern China: An Encyclopedia of History, Culture, and Nationalism*. New York and London: Garland Publishing, Inc., 1998.

Wang Weinan and Zhou Jianming. *"Diyuan zhengzhi zhong de Zhong Mei guanxi yu Taiwan wenti"* [The Geopolitics of Sino-U.S. Relations and the Taiwan Issue]. *Taiwan yanjiu jikan* [Taiwan Research Quarterly] (2005, no. 4): 45–51, 57. CAJ.

Wang Xiaocai. *"Meiguo dui Hua diyuan zhengzhi guanyu Taiwan wenti"* [The American Geopolitical View on China and the Taiwan Issue]. *Yunyang shifan gaodeng zhuanke xuexiao xuebao* [Journal of Yunyang Teachers College] 20, no. 5 (October 2000): 29–33. CAJ.

Wang Xiaodong. "The West in the Eyes of a Chinese Nationalist." *Heartland: Eurasian Review of Geopolitics* 1 (2000): 17–31.

Wen Yunchao. *"Guanyu diyuan yanjiu de lilun tantao"* [A Theoretical Study of Geopolitical Research]. *Dili kexue jinzhan* [Progress in Geography] 18, no. 2 (June 1999): 172–175. CAJ.

Westad, Odd Arne. *Decisive Encounters: The Chinese Civil War, 1946–1950*. Stanford: Stanford University Press, 2003.

Wills, John E., Jr. "The Seventeenth-Century Transformation: Taiwan Under the Dutch and Cheng Regimes." In Rubinstein, ed. *Taiwan: A New History*, 84–106.

Worden, Robert L. *Macau: A Country Study*. Washington, DC: Federal Research Division, Library of Congress, 2000. http://lcweb2.locgov/frd/cs/motoc.html.

Wortzel, Larry M. "China Pursues Traditional Great-Power Status." *Orbis* 38, no. 2 (1994): 157–175.

———, ed. *The Chinese Armed Forces in the 21st Century*. Carlisle, PA: U.S. Army War College, Strategic Studies Institute, 1999.

Wu Xinbo. "Taiwan Strait: Japan and the United States Alike, 'Fight Shoulder to Shoulder.'" *Global Times* (June 20, 2005).

Wu Yu-shan. "Theorizing on Relations Across the Taiwan Strait: Nine Contending Approaches." *Journal of Contemporary China* 9, no. 25 (2000): 407–428.

Wu Yung-chiang. "United States Attempts to Use Japan and Taiwan to Contain China." *Ta Kung Pao* (Hong Kong) (August 2, 2005). Reproduced as "CASS Researcher on U.S. Use of Japan, Taiwan to Contain China, Current Talks." WNC.

Xiao Yang. *"Jiandingbuyide weihu yige Zhongguo de yuanze"* [Resolutely Safeguard the One China Principle]. *Renmin Ribao* [People's Daily], fourth edition. August 11, 1999. Reproduced by the People's Republic of China, Taiwan Affairs Office of the State Council at http://www.gwytb.gov.cn: 82/hxlt/hxlto.asp?offset=350&hxlt_m_id=246.

Xinhua Domestic Service. "Chinese Paper Says 'Two-State Theory' Part of Long-term Plot." *BBC Summary of World Broadcasts*. August 20, 1999. LexisNexis.

———. *Jiefangjun Bao* commentator's article: " 'Dependence on Foreigners' Cannot Save Li Teng-hui—Second Commentary on the 'Four Cards' Behind the 'Two-State Theory.' " Reproduced as "*Jiefangjun Bao* Raps 'Two-State Theory.' " *Xinhua.* August 19, 1999. WNC.

Xinhua General Overseas News Service. "Jiang Zemin on Reunification of China." October 12, 1992. LexisNexis.

———. "Ye Jianying Explains Policy Concerning Return of Taiwan to Motherland and Peaceful Reunification." September 30, 1981. LexisNexis.

Xinhua News Agency. "Beijing Countdown to H. K.'s Return Clock Starts Countdown to H. K.'s Return." December 19, 1994, item no.: 1219152. LexisNexis.

———. "China Calls Taiwan President 'Sinner Condemned by History.' " July 16, 1999. LexisNexis.

———. "Countdown Clock to Be Moved to Great Wall." July, 9, 1997. item no.: 0709025. LexisNexis.

———. "Hu Jintao Cites Four Points of Opinion on Taiwan Work When Addressing Taiwan Deputies." Tuesday, March 11, 2003. FBIS-CHI-2003-0311. WNC.

———. "Military Expert: Splitting of Motherland Is Invitation of Destruction." August 12, 1999. LexisNexis.

———. "More on Zhu Rongji Warning Against Taiwan Independence." March 15, 2000. WNC Document Number: 0FRIOGR01JZVRO.

———. "Xinhua: Hu Jintao Slashes 'Taiwan Independence' Attempt." February 28, 2006. WNC.

Xinhua She [New China News Agency]. *"Ye Jianying xiang Xinhuashe jizhe fabiao de tanhua"* [Ye Jianying's Talk with Xinhua News Agency Journalists]. September 30, 1981. http://news.xinhuanet.com/ziliao/2003-01/23/content_704801.htm.

———. Editorial. *"Zhongguo renmin yiding yao jiefang Taiwan"* [The Chinese People Certainly Will Liberate Taiwan]. March 15,1949. http://www.people.com.cn/GB/33831/33 836/34138/34259/2569298.html.

Xu Shiquan. "The 1992 Consensus: A Review and Assessment of Consultations Between the Association for Relations Across the Taiwan Strait and the Straits Exchange Foundation." In Zagoria, ed. *Breaking the China-Taiwan Impasse,* 81–102.

Xu Zhuangzhi and Cao Zhi. "China: Army, Armed Police Forces Comment on 'Letter of Apology' From USA." *Xinhua* (April 12, 2001). LexisNexis.

Yang Yongbin. *"Lengzhan hou Taiwan zai Meiguo dui Hua guanxi zhong de diyuan zhanlüe zuoyong"* [The Geostrategic Function of Taiwan in the U.S.'s Post-Cold War Relations with China]. *Haerbin xueyuan xuebao* [Journal of Harbin Institute] 22, no. 2 (April 2001): 18–20. CAJ.

Ye Zicheng. *"Lun dangdai Zhongguo de diyuan taishi he san xian diyuan zhanlüe tixi"* [On the Geopolitical Situation and the Contemporary Chinese Geostrategic Three Line System]. *Taipingyang xuebao* [Pacific Journal] (1997, no. 4): 7–11. CAJ.

Yea, Sallie. "Maps of Resistance and Geographies of Dissent in the Cholla Region of South Korea." *Korean Studies* 24 (2000): 69–93.

Yeh Wen-hsin, ed. *Landscape, Culture and Power in Chinese Society.* Berkeley: University of California,Center for East Asian Studies, 1998.

Yiming [anonymous]. *"Zhong Mei Ri Taihai shengsi jiaoliang"* [Sino-U.S.-Japan Fight to the Death in the Taiwan Strait]. *Lianzheng liaowang* (2005, no. 10): 48–50.

You Ji. "The Evolution of China's Maritime Combat Doctrine and Models, 1949–2001." Institute of Defense and Strategic Studies Working Paper 22, May 2002.

————. "Learning and Catching Up: China's RMA Initiative." In Goldman and Mahnken, eds. *The Information Revolution in Asia*, 97–124.

————. "A New Era for Chinese Naval Expansion." *ChinaBrief* 4, no. 5 (March 1, 2006): 4–6.

You Ziping. *"Shenhua haiyang qianggo zhanlüe de yanjiu yu shijian"* [Deepen the Research and Practice of Strategic Maritime Power]. *Jianchuan kexue jishu* [Ship Science and Technology] 27, no. 1 (February 2005): 5–10. CAJ.

Young, Louise. *Japan's Total Empire: Manchuria and the Culture of Wartime Imperialism*. Berkeley: University of California Press, 1998.

Yu Maochun. "Political and Military Factors Determining China's Use of Force." In Tsang, ed. *If China Attacks Taiwan*, 17–34.

Yu, Peter Kien-hong. "The Chinese (broken) U-shaped Line in the South China Sea: Points, Lines, and Zones." *Contemporary Southeast Asia* 25, no. 3 (December 2003): 405–431.

————. *The Chinese PLA's Perception of an Invasion of Taiwan*. New York: Contemporary U.S. Asia Research Institute, 1996.

Yu Xin. "Li Denghui's Secessionist Ambition Is Not Dead Yet." Central People's Radio Station. August 21, 1999. Reproduced as "Beijing Radio Blasts Li's 'Sessionist Ambition.'" WNC Document Number: 0FH3AS300DHBV0.

Yuan Ming. "The Failure of Perception: America's China Policy, 1949–1950." In Harding and Yuan, eds. *Sino-American Relations, 1945–1955*, 143–152.

Zagoria, Donald A., ed. *Breaking the China-Taiwan Impasse*. Westport, CT: Praeger, 2003.

Zhang Baijia and Jia Qingguo. "Steering Wheel, Shock Absorber, and Diplomatic Probe in Confrontation: Sino-American Ambassadorial Talks Seen from the Chinese Perspective." In Ross and Jiang, eds. *Re-examining the Cold War*, 173–199.

Zhang Guoxian. *"Lun Taiwan de diyuan zhanlüe jiazhi"* [On Taiwan's Strategic Value]. *Huabei shuili shuidian xueyuan xuebao (shekeban)* [Journal of North China Institute of Water Conservancy and Hydroelectric Power (Social Science edition)] 18, no. 4 (November 2002): 5–7. CAJ.

Zhang Shuguang and Chen Jian, eds. *Chinese Communist Foreign Policy and the Cold War in Asia: New Documentary Evidence, 1944–1950*. Chicago: Imprint Publications, 1996.

Zhang Tiejun. "Chinese Strategic Culture: Traditional and Present Features." *Comparative Strategy* 21 (2002): 73–90.

Zhang Wankun. "China's Foreign Relations Strategies Under Mao and Deng: A Systematic Comparative Analysis." Public and Social Administration Working Paper Series. City Univeristy of Hong Kong, 1998/2.

Zhang Wei and Zuo Liping. *"Xianggang de diyuan youshi buketidai—yong diyuan zhanlüe fangfa guance Xianggang de lishi yu weilai"* [Hong Kong's Irreplaceable Geographic Superiority—Using Geostrategy to Survey Hong Kong's History and Future]. *21 Shiji* [Twenty-first Century] (1998, no. 2): 21–23. CAJ.

Zhang Wenmu. *"Shilun dangdai Zhongguo 'haiquan' wenti"* [On China's Contemporary 'Sea Power']. *Zhongguo yuanyang hangwu gongbao* [Maritime China] (2005, no. 5): 49–50. CAJ.

————. "Sino-American Relations and the Question of Taiwan." *Heartland: Eurasian Review of Geopolitics* (January 2005), "China-America, The Great Game," 40–46.

————. *"Shijie diyuan zhengzhi zhong de Zhongguo guoji anquan liyi fenxi"* [Analyzing China's International Security Interests in World Geopolitics]. Ji'nan: Shandong renmin chubanshe, 2004, 57. Cited in Liu Zhongmin. *"Haiquan wenti yu lengzhanhou ZhongMei guanxi: maodun de renzhi yu jiannan de xuanze"* [Sea Power Issues and Post-Cold War Sino-U.S. Relations: Contradictory Perceptions and Difficult Options]. *Waijiao pinglun* [Foreign Affairs Review] 85 (December 2005): 55–60. CAJ.

Zhao Junyao. *"Cong 'Zhi Tai bi gao lu' kan Qing dai Taiwan haiyang wenhua diyu xingtai"* [The Geographical Dimension of the Qing Dynasty's Taiwan Maritime Culture from the 'Record of the Governance of Taiwan']. *Zhi da xuebao* [Journal of the Vocational and Technical University of Fujian] (2005, no. 1): 61–62. CAJ.

Zhao Suisheng. "Reunification Strategy: Beijing Versus Lee Teng-hui." In Dickson and Chao, eds. *Assessing the Lee Teng-hui Legacy in Taiwan's Politics,* 204–240.

Zhao Wei. "Two-faced Tactics Cannot Conceal His True Intentions—A Comment on Li Teng-hui's Statements at His News Conference." Reproduced as "Xinhua Commentary on Li Teng-hui's News Conference on His US Visit." BBC Summary of World Broadcasts (June 15, 1995). LexisNexis.

Zhongguo Tongxun She. "Article on Modernization of China's Navy." February 15, 2000. WNC Document Number: 0FQ56TS01YL81J.

Zhongguo xiandai guoji guanxi yanjiusuo haishang tongdao anquan ketizu [China Institute for Contemporary International Relations (CICIR) Maritime Security Taskforce]. *Haishang tongdao anquan yu guoji hezuo* [Sea Lane Security and International Cooperation]. Beijing: Shishi chubanshe, 2005.

Zhongguo Xinwen She [China News Service]. "China: Army Paper on Taiwan President's Dream." July 21, 1999. LexisNexis.

_____. "Chinese Soldiers, Armed Police Condemn Taiwan 'Two-State Theory.'" August 8, 1999. LexisNexis.

Zhou Yihuang. "Will China's Rise Trigger Sino-US Confrontation?" *Zhongguo jingjibao* [China Economic Times] (December 26, 2003). http://english.people.com.cn/200312/26/eng20031226_131270.shtml.

Zhu Feng and Andrew Thompson. "Why Taiwan Really Matters to China." *China Brief* 4, no. 19 (September 30, 2004). http://www.jamestown.org/publications_details.php?volume_id=395&issue_id=3090&article_id=2368616.

Zhu Tingchang. *"Lun Taiwan de diyuan zhanlüe diwei"* [On Taiwan's Geostrategic Position]. *Shijie jingji yu zhengzhi luntan* [World Economics and Politics] (2001, no. 3): 66–69. CAJ.

Zhu Tingchang, ed. *Zhongguo zhoubian anquan huanjing yu anquan zhanlüe* [China's Peripheral Environment and Security Strategy]. Beijing: Shishi chubanshe, 2002.

Zhuang Pinghui. "Net Buzzes with Calls for Beijing to Get Tough." *South China Morning Post* (Hong Kong) (February 28, 2006): 4. LexisNexis.

Index

Studies in Asian Security

A SERIES SPONSORED BY THE EAST-WEST CENTER

Muthiah Alagappa, Chief Editor
Distinguished Senior Fellow, East-West Center